THE LAW IS A WHITE DOG

HOW LEGAL RITUALS

MAKE AND

UNMAKE PERSONS

PRINCETON UNIVERSITY PRESS
Princeton & Oxford

THE LAW

IS A

WHITE

DOG

COLIN DAYAN

Copyright 2011 © by Princeton University Press

Published by Princeton University Press, 41 William Street, Princeton, New Jersey 08540

In the United Kingdom: Princeton University Press, 6 Oxford Street, Woodstock, Oxfordshire OX20 1TW

press.princeton.edu

Library of Congress Cataloging-in-Publication Data

Dayan, Joan
  The law is a white dog : how legal rituals make and unmake persons / Colin Dayan.
    p. cm.
Includes bibliographical references and index.
ISBN 978-0-691-07091-9 (cloth : alk. paper) 1. Persons (Law)—United States. 2. Slavery—Law and legislation—United States. 3. Torture—United States. 4. Civil rights—United States. 5. Law—United States—Social aspects. I. Title.
    KF465.D39 2011
    346.73012—dc22   2010027474

British Library Cataloging-in-Publication Data is available

This book has been composed in Berling

Printed on acid-free paper. ∞

Printed in the United States of America

10 9 8 7 6 5 4 3 2 1

"Legal Slaves and Civil Bodies" appeared in *Materializing Democracy: Toward a Revitalized Cultural Politics*, ed. Russ Castronovo and Dana D. Nelson. Reprinted by permission of Duke University Press. Copyright 2002, Duke University Press. "Due Process and Lethal Confinement" appeared in *Killing States: Lethal Decisions/Final Judgment* (Summer 2008), *South Atlantic Quarterly* 107(3). Reprinted by permission of Duke University Press. Copyright 2008, Duke University Press. "Held in the Body of the State: Prisons and the Law" appeared in *History, Memory, and the Law*, ed. Austin Sarat and Thomas R. Kearns (Ann Arbor: University of Michigan Press, 1999). Reprinted by permission of the University of Michigan Press. Quotations from *The Story of Cruel and Unusual* (2007) reprinted by permission of Colin Dayan, *The Story of Cruel and Unusual*, and the MIT Press. "Legal Terrors" appeared in *Representations* 92 (Fall 2005). Reprinted by permission of the University of California Press.

For David, again

... dogs believe in thieves and ghosts

—Nietzsche, *Thus Spoke Zarathustra*

CONTENTS

PREFACE

THIS IS A BOOK ABOUT EXTRANEOUS PERSONS. SUBORDINATED AND expelled from society, they take on new shapes: humans, things, dogs, and spirits that are brought together under the umbrella of legal history. Their transformations prompt us to think about what it means to be considered in terms of law. I offer some broad perspectives on metamorphosis, invoking only some of the manifold ways that law dwells on, messes with, and consumes persons. It is through law that persons, variously figured, gain or lose definition, become victims of prejudice or inheritors of privilege. And once outside the valuable discriminations of personhood, their claims become inconsequential.

Law is the protagonist of this plot. The social, economic, and even spiritual practices of remote times persist in legal forms and pronouncements. My treatment of ghostly properties and human and nonhuman animal materials appeals for an understanding of legal reality, lively, ever-present, and reimagined by those outside the guild of lawyers. I see my task as uncarthing what Sir Frederick Maitland described as the "dry bones" of law and giving them life in unexpected places. For some readers, it will seem that I make legal effects revel in what is least akin to judicial activities and the operations of law. But the generous reader will, I reckon, follow me on the journey through a series of haunts, sites that recapitulate, if fitfully, the transmutations that are so much a part of legal history.

I seek to know what happens to conventional historical and legal sources when they are pressed to answer unconventional questions. But my main objective is to ask how law encapsulates, sustains, and invigorates philosophies of personhood. What I offer as *idioms of servility* demonstrate, I wish to suggest, that state-sanctioned degradation in America is propelled by a focus on personal identity, the terms by which personality is recognized, threatened, or removed. I treat the legal history of dispossession as a continuum along which bodies and spirits are remade over time. In this narrative I devote special attention to the obscene made lawful: slavery, torture, indefinite solitary confinement, preventive detention. Along the way I show how rituals considered otherworldly, primitive, irrational, and superseded maintain their presence in what we consider our truly civil and modern society.

The irrational haunts the civilizing claims of the reasonable. The shadows of the Furies, buried so that the polis could be born, still pursue the icons of order. So the modern state, its counterfeits and its terrors, betrays a subterranean legacy. Each chapter here explores a different site of incapacitation through what I think of as sinkholes of law where precedents gather, festering as they feed on juridical words, past and present. The animating principle of such an account of law is a challenge to chronology. Entwined and cumulative, these chapters proceed as episodes in making and unmaking persons.

In the long history of what I call "negative personhood," I focus on slaves, animals, criminals, and detainees who are disabled by law. Legal thought relied on a set of fictions that rendered the meaning of persons shifting and tentative: whether in creating slaves as *persons in law* and criminals as *dead in law*, or in the perpetual re-creation of the rightless entity. The medieval fiction of civil death lives on in the present. The felon rendered dead in law is no anachronism but a continuing effect of dehumanizing practices of punishment. What does it mean to exist in a negative relation to law? In my attempt to characterize legal disabilities, I analyze competing genealogies of race prejudice, as well as traditions of penality that transform persons into cadavers. Rituals of old world vengeance like the *deodand*, corruption of blood and civil death jostle with a philosopher of personal identity like John Locke, a critic of the common law like Jeremy Bentham, as well as dogs and ghosts, demons and zombies, judges and poets who bear witness to undying legal effects.

What I aim to do in this book is to question *the spirit of law*. In each chapter I try to lay a foundation for this questioning by bringing together different disciplines and modes of inquiry. Both the organization and the irresolution resulting from it are deliberate. While dramatizing a perplexing legal history too often lost in linearity, I preserve a discontinuous but thematically linked approach to the questions I raise. I want to make readers complicit in a world without demarcations such as those between past and present, primitive and civilized. For the oppressed and outlawed, such distinctions matter but they matter differently. They are more seamless and easily convertible. For those who adhere to a myth of progress or faith in reason, the continuum between past and present must be made to be deeply felt.

I choose not to spare my readers the experience of lingering phantoms that guarantee a politics that is both rigorous and visible, what Peter Geshiere calls "the modernity of witchcraft." The dispossession accomplished by slavery, as I have argued elsewhere, became the model for possession in vodou: turning a person not into a thing but into a spirit, filled with thought, armed with personality. In Creole, *lwa* is the term for both law and god. Those dispossessed by the *loi d'état* when possessed by their *lwa* communicate across species boundaries, breaking down and challenging legal taxonomies. So the white dog of my title is invested with ambiguous power.

Disabilities are made indelible through time in fictions of law, law words that wield the power to transform. I will argue that residues of terror are never really dead and gone but, through the terms of law, survive and always find new bodies to inhabit, new persons to target. I try to show how the ghosts of Enlightenment past become the demons of modernity. I also suggest how what we call *supernatural* or think of as ghostly is really quite natural, corporeal, easily recast as *reasonable*.

The spiritually injured entities I describe as *depersonalized*. Disfigured as persons, they are then judged outside the law's protection or most susceptible to its violence. Practices of law, I argue, become interchangeable with rituals of belief. The will to repeat, the insistence on the already done that must be redone, accounts for the power of ritual, an action both civil and sacred. I have taken seriously the need to give a material history of what might at first seem spiritual concerns.

Spirits experience life and unfold their potential through the business of humans, tightly bound up as they are with the stress and uncertainties of society. As with other rituals of remembrance and reenactment, both spirit possession and the legal idiom transmit traditions in a particularly historical way. But the meaning of civil life must be reconsidered when played out under the eye of the law. The cadavers, ghosts, and spirits that motivate this book originate in the life of chattels that have been passed around, injured, or consumed. This making of perishables, consumed by use, recalls the somber intelligence of ritual and the resistance of those who have suffered.

Much of this book has a contemporary resonance—obviously Guantánamo and the secret prison sites in this country and round the world, where our country has made others complicit in its deprivation of rights and willful disregard of the laws of nations and the international obligations which this country, like others, has taken upon itself. This is a political book, then, but it is not a tract. What I have tried to do is show that the shame that is Guantánamo has a history, in our nation and in its treatment of its own. Which brings me to the origin and real impetus of this book: the uses of incarceration in the United States to criminalize, exclude, and do such violence to persons that they are returned to their communities—when they are— diminished and harmed sometimes beyond repair, or redress.

I spent four years doing what I called "my prison work." Every week from 1995 to 1999 I drove from Tucson north on the Pinal Parkway to the prison units in Florence, Arizona, or on I-10 East to Phoenix. In Phoenix I interviewed Terry Stewart, who became director of the Arizona Department of Corrections in 1995. In May and June of 2003, he and three other corrections professionals from state prisons in the United States restructured and reformed the prisons in Iraq, including Camp Bucca and Abu Ghraib. Major-General Antonio M. Taguba of the U.S. Army later condemned both prisons as sites of "egregious acts and grave breaches of international law." Attorney General John Ashcroft's Justice Department implemented Operation Iraqi Freedom through American-style prison security. At the time, Stewart was head of a security consulting firm in Phoenix called Advanced Correctional Management. Stewart had other experience exporting U.S. prison practices. After the overthrow of President Jean-Bertrand Aristide, Stewart visited Haiti to oversee prison reform there. In a 2004 interview, he summed up his philosophy: "We need some place to put the criminals if we are going to have a civil society."

When I interviewed Stewart in the summer of 1996, he was already known for "death-row chain gangs," cell extractions with dogs, the cover-up of rape by correctional officers, and ever-harsher confinement of prisoners in supermax facilities. During our interviews he wore an elegant suit, gold cuff links, and a perfectly starched shirt with his initials "TLS" monogrammed in blue on the cuffs. We sat in a plush, wood-paneled office with mood music playing. I thought of it as "adult contemporary." Its languid rhythms gave a surreal background to our conversation about executions, "drop dead" dates, rock busting (requiring prisoners to spend hours each day pointlessly breaking rocks), lockdown, and classification codes. His examples relied on "mythical inmates." Instead of real prisoners, he used photographic stills in the series of films he directed about inmate work programs, chain gangs, correctional industries, and enhanced cell extractions. When I asked him why only mute images instead of live men, he answered: "What can inmates say? They're liars, they're thieves, they're cheats. Who would believe an inmate anyway?"

Stewart coolly answered my questions about the unseen anguish of inmates during lethal injection: "What happens is that the person goes to sleep. The most you would see is if the injection happens to be on the inhale and the chest is empty you might see movement in the abdomen, but if it happens to be on an exhale, then there's no movement at all.... We'll probably have executions once a week, like they do in Texas."

After these meetings, I sought relief in pages and pages of legal transcripts, depositions, and newspaper clippings from the late sixties on, all dealing with prisons in Arizona. I found the writings of inmates who had not only read but understood the law. They turned to it in the prisons as I did. In a journey that seemed appropriate to the subject to which I had become rather too devoted, I travelled between the Arizona State Prison Complex and the U.S. District Court in Phoenix, alternating between the prison and the law, two sites that were fast becoming reciprocal —sometime collaborators in a new form of punishment that could evade constitutional claims.

In the course of a project that began in the death house and supermaxes of Arizona and outside on the streets, asking officers about the public display of prisoners in chains, I observed much mistreatment. But, more importantly, I began to consider how institutions depend upon technologies of domination that are sustained by the rhetorically powerful forms of law. In anticipating the reactions of readers who feel as if they are being hit by a juggernaut of oppression, I should explain that I do not think that the calamities of state-sponsored exclusion and dehumanization would be removed by better jurists. Instead, I examine the poor treatment, the entombing of the living, not as historical contingency, but as something culturally inevitable in that the past haunts us.

The Law Is a White Dog contests the Enlightenment attachment to rationalism and limitless progress. Hence I dramatize the confounding nature of the encounter with what we identify as Western modernity, its projects, its violence and oppression. I grew up in the South during the sixties, when bloody sit-ins at Charlie Leb's Restaurant on Lucky Street made me know racial violence. It was a time when folks listened to Nancy Wilson sing

"Sufferin' with the Blues" and gaped at men in zebra stripes working in chain gangs on the Atlanta highways. A southern girl brought up under the reasonableness of law, as well as evidence of the ghostly, I found life in making intelligible what authorities ridiculed as superstition.

Just as reason can abide quite comfortably with the unreasonable, I believe that ghost stories can be set alongside legal narratives. If, as I argue, the law creates persons much as the supernatural creates spirits, then such newly invented entities are not what we assume. A series of metamorphoses, both legal and magical, transform persons into ghosts, into things and into animals. But these terms—person, ghost, thing, animal—which we assume to have definite boundaries, lose these demarcations. Categories lose their distinctiveness. I trace this re-creation through various and conflicting sources: Pauline faith, Lockean epistemology, Haitian vodou. If I have made legal reasoning as blooded and vital as the lives of persons lethally affected by it, then I have succeeded in my aim.

THE LAW IS A WHITE DOG

HOLY DOGS, HECUBA'S BARK

I knew a person in Christ above fourteen years ago,
(whether in the body, I cannot tell; or whether out
of the body, I cannot tell: God knoweth;) such
an one caught up to the third heaven.

—St. Paul, 2 Corinthians 12:2

A MOST UNNATURAL BARGAIN

As regards specters or ghosts, I have hitherto heard
attributed to them no intelligible property: they seem
like phantoms, which no one can understand.

—Spinoza to Hugo Boxel, 1674

IN 1989 HELEN ACKLEY SOLD HER FIVE-THOUSAND-SQUARE-FOOT, eighteen-room Victorian house on the Hudson River in Nyack, New York, to a young couple, Jeffrey and Patrice Stambovsky. After making a down payment of $32,500 for the house, they learned that it was haunted. Although Jeffrey did not believe in ghosts and did not mind knowing that the house was thus occupied, his wife refused to live there. Ackley had enjoyed a good relationship with the ghosts for over twenty years, and had become accustomed to steps on the stairs, doors slamming, beds shaking, and chandeliers moving back and forth. She assured the couple that they had nothing to fear. The spirits were friendly and even gave what Ackley called "gifts" to her children: silver tongs and a gold baby ring. She refused to call off the sale. Stambovsky, a Wall Street bond trader, turned not to exorcism but to the law. He filed suit in New York to cancel the contract, telling the press, "We were the victims of ectoplasmic fraud."

Although the house was widely known to be possessed by numerous ghosts, this was not disclosed by Ackley. A lower court dismissed the case, as the state applies the rule of caveat emptor, or "let the buyer beware." Stambovsky appealed. In *Stambovsky v. Ackley* (1991), Judge Israel Rubin, writing for the appellate division of the New York Supreme Court, declared: "[A]s a matter of law, the house is haunted." Since Helen Ackley not only knew of the spectral inhabitants—allegedly dating from the American Revolution—but had even celebrated them in an article, "Our Haunted House on the Hudson," for *Reader's Digest* in May 1977 and in a couple of local newspapers in 1982 and 1989, she was obliged to tell her potential buyers that the house was not vacant as they assumed. Not everyone, after all, shared her enthusiasm for what she described as "elusive spirits … gracious, thoughtful—only occasionally frightening—and thoroughly entertaining." Although Ackley lost the lawsuit, she was glad that her ghosts were declared "officially alive."[1]

In an unusually droll and quite unprecedented decision, Rubin argued that no house inspection could have revealed the presence of ghosts. "A very practical problem arises with respect to the discovery of a paranormal phenomenon," he wrote, "'Who you gonna call?' as a title song to the movie 'Ghostbusters' asks." Rubin continued:

> Applying the strict rule of caveat emptor to a contract involving a house possessed by poltergeists conjures up visions of a psychic or medium routinely accompanying the structural engineer and Terminix man on an inspection of every home subject to a contract of sale. It portends that the prudent attorney will establish an escrow account lest the subject of the transaction come back to haunt him and his client—or pray that his malpractice insur-

ance coverage extends to supernatural disasters. In the interest of avoiding such untenable consequences, the notion that a haunting is a condition which can and should be ascertained upon reasonable inspection of the premises is a hobgoblin which should be exorcised from the body of legal precedent and laid quietly to rest.

Arguing that enforcing this contract would offend the "spirit of equity," Rubin held that "the unwitting purchaser" should recover his money and be released from "a most unnatural bargain." Ghosts are not like termites, after all, and no reasonable inspection of the premises could have made this infestation known to Stambovsky.[2]

The decision in this case made ghost hunters ecstatic and realtors anxious, but it was its style that gave it legal renown. Rubin's approach and his reliance on ghosts as legal matter suggested that judicial speculation owed a great deal to the dead as well as to the unreal. Besides his explicit uses of cinematic and literary allusions to specters, including both *Hamlet* and *Ghostbusters*, he also raised the ghost of equity before the court. A system of jurisprudence that offered an alternative to common law, "equity" originated in England as the "spirit" of fairness, "a court of conscience."[3] Rubin suggested that though courts of chancery have been replaced in New York by the formalities of the regular courts, he intended to resurrect the spirit of equity, for he would "not be stifled by rigid application of a legal maxim." For him the appeal became a matter of conscience, enabling him to transcend the letter of the law when necessary. Or, he put the spirit back in the letter, announcing at the outset that he was "moved by the spirit of equity to allow the buyer to seek rescission of the contract of sale and recovery of his down payment."[4]

The afterlife of this judicial bewitching not only changed the application of the doctrine of caveat emptor, but made legal rights dependent upon supernatural phenomena. In this way Rubin took the realtor's term "stigmatized property"—a house possessed by ghosts or where a murder or suicide had taken place—and asked that we recall such supposedly extinct legal usages as spectral evidence and ineradicable stigma. He declared: "Common law is not moribund. *Ex facto jus oritur* (law arises out of facts)." But what kinds of facts are these? Are they legal facts or legal fictions? Literal or figurative? Bad logic but good law? In Rubin's view, "fairness and common sense dictate that an exception" must be made to the rules of law. Is this the beginning, perhaps, of a rationale for haunting?[5]

Although Ackley had no strict duty to disclose the stigma on the property, nonetheless Rubin went beyond the claims of civil law to consider a unique and equitable remedy. He gave relief to the buyer and showed how legal rules could be surpassed by the force of an archaism no less powerful for being disavowed.

Rubin also called up another ghost, the antiquated legal fiction of civil death: the loss of civil and proprietary rights by monks, nuns, and felons. For the felon, the ritual of alienation occasioned an unnatural status: banished from the community, shorn of personality, condemned to degradation. This retributive and punitive sanction survived in America. The person convicted of felony is alive in fact but dead in law. In this sense, the ghosts that possessed Stambovsky's new home enforced a new framing of an old problem. The house was haunted in law but not in fact. This was more terrifying for some than if he had declared ghosts real. Instead, Rubin posited a reality independent of any conception of what is real. Some commentators thought that "it was as if some other-worldly force entered the courthouse and took possession of the judges" or that Rubin was "speaking in tongues."[6]

Since the most famous cases of civil death in the nineteenth century were in New York, Rubin is on familiar ground. Considering *Stambovsky* in light of this buried history, we will see how legal reasoning manipulates the fictions that sustain idioms of servility.

Statutory law in 1799 enforced the harsh practices of strict civil death, albeit in a novel way. The effects of this severity will be examined fully in the next chapter, but here let us note what happened when the statute changed the common-law wording, "shall be deemed dead to all intents and purposes in the law" to "thereafter be deemed civilly dead." Dispossessed of all the benefits of law, the convict was doomed *in his person* to perpetual incapacitation. Chancellor James Kent, sitting in the New York Court of Chancery until 1823, lamented that civil death ensured "perpetual imprisonment." In *Platner v. Sherwood* (1822), he agreed with the arguments of Platner's lawyers: "Imprisonment for life was a punishment unknown to the common law." Later cases in the Court of Appeals of New York, such as *Avery v. Everett* (1888), demonstrated the eerie staying power of civil death, even if deprivations were ameliorated to allow the convict to retain his right to property.[7]

The fact of property, possessed or lost, became crucial not only to legal status but also to personal identity and the sacrifice of the self to punishment. A creation of law, civil death is the ghost that continues to torment persons convicted of crime. Assuming different forms from state to state, its embodiment depends on statute and judicial argument, and this disenfranchisement still renders precarious the absolute security of personal property.[8]

Rubin takes the specter of legal dispossession and gives it a new role. Fleshed out in law, the errant haunts of a supposedly old and obsolete era resurface in a home in Nyack, New York. Rubin's invocation of equity brings him to commit to law a surprising and unexpected decision. Not only does he mobilize the impulses of equity, but he gives law the power to make ghosts count. This house is not vacant but occupied. What Rubin called its "ghoulish reputation" cannot be exorcised. Since Ackley had made much of the possession of her house by ghosts, the court demanded that she should have admitted the haunting to her unsuspecting buyers. So she was liable for not disclosing the full facts *as she saw them*. A taint or "impairment" deliberately publicized made the house a magnet for ghost hunters, and such a "phantasmal reputation" would significantly decrease the value of the house. In Rubin's words:

Where, as here, the seller not only takes unfair advantage of the buyer's ignorance but has created and perpetuated a condition about which he is unlikely to even inquire, enforcement of the contract (in whole or in part) is offensive to the court's sense of equity. Application of the remedy of rescission, within the bounds of the narrow exception to the doctrine of caveat emptor set forth herein, is entirely appropriate to relieve the unwitting purchaser from the consequences of a most unnatural bargain.[9]

In *Thinking with Demons*, Stuart Clark asked that historians not only take the risk involved in treating supernatural phenomena as real, but also more importantly consider what counts as real. To take up Clark's argument, we might say that Rubin tried "to make intelligibility and not reality" his aim. If a house has been the scene of a murder or suicide, it is, according to realtors, "stigmatized property" or "psychologically impacted." To buyers, a supernatural stigma may matter more than physical characteristics. We can go further and add that Rubin's argument was a reasonable if not wholly literal construction of facts. On the terrain of the undead, reason gambles with irrationality.[10]

There is a real legal problem here. What does it mean if you engage law in the story of ghosts? Does the interpretation qualify as a legal fiction or not? At issue here, and in the ensuing chapters, is not whether ghosts are real or not, but whether or not in the legal world a new situation is being described as uncontroversial. A house looks vacant, but the law decrees it full of spirits. Some buyers might find this supernaturally added value quite enticing: sudden plenitude in the face of apparent vacancy.

The law has a history of such imagining made real. A resilient acceptance of unreality is a necessary part of legal history. At times, there was no special rule of evidence for psychic phenomena, just as there was no need of proof for seemingly irrational racial beliefs. We can turn to the spectral evidence of dreams and visions famously admitted by the presiding Cotton Mather during the Salem witch trials, as well as to other instances when invisible attributes were granted legal validity. What was legally possible long involved give-and-take between such categories as thing and self, physical and incorporeal, wickedness and virtue. Although haunted houses did not often become the subject of legal proceedings, there are much older accounts of tenants who refused to pay rent because of ghosts or to remain for long with spectral nuisances. In a well-known case before the Parlement of Paris around 1550, rollicking spirits made more noise than barking dogs. Just as ghostly occupation of a house remained in the late twentieth century an impediment to its sale, for the purposes of law if not ordinary life the undue influence of communications from the dead, especially when untimely deaths or disputed wills are at issue, must be taken seriously.[11]

DID ANYONE DIE HERE?

… the phantasm of today is so often
a reality of to-morrow.

—*Burchill v. Hermsmeyer* (1919)

The puzzle faced by Rubin's court has a history. Legal complications arising from specters intruding into marriages, divorces, and the buying and selling of houses were the subject of a thesis for the Doctorate of Laws in Jena on June 25, 1700. In his *Disputatio Juridica de Jure Spectrorum* (Juridical Disputation on the Law of Ghosts), republished forty-five years later, Andreas Becker confronted the question of possession and discussed the rights of tenants, wives, husbands, tutors, servants, and criminals when faced with ghosts. He explains that if spirits haunt one of the betrothed on the eve of nuptials, the other can back out of the match. If such "obsession" occurs after marriage, however, it is not legally recognized as a cause for divorce, no matter how much destruction is brought to the household. Haunted houses, "so infested with specters as to be virtually useless," trigger the

7

most protracted analyses. After considering a house presented as dower or rental property but found to be haunted, Becker turns to the rights of a buyer who inadvertently purchases possessed property:

> If a house is sold and the purchaser finds it haunted, can he demand a rescinding of the contract of sale? Yes, if the specters had infested the house before the sale, and he had not known it. His action would be *de dolo* [about trickery], and he might be aided by an *actio ad redhibendum* [action for recovery]. Proof of guilty knowledge on the part of the owner might be difficult, and the best means would be *per delationem juramenti* [by deposing an oath].

In this time of animal trials, demonic possession, and the interrogation of alleged witches by torture, Becker recognized other dark corners of pain and suffering that he refused to ignore or conceal. Faced with demonic infestations, whether in houses or in the conjugal bed, Becker concluded with an insight into the terrors of solitary confinement, telling us something about juridical demons as much in need of reformation as any infernal mysticism:

> As demoniacal apparitions seek dark places in preference, dark prisons are particularly infested with them. Can a judge then thrust a man accused (guilty?) of capital offence into a dungeon which he knows to be suspected of specters? By no means, for he thus exposes him to the risk of committing suicide, and prisons are places for safe-keeping and not for punishment. Those judges are inconsiderate (*inconsulti*) who send the more atrocious criminals to dungeons which are known by experience to be thus infested, for the purpose of repressing their contumacy.

A belief in ghosts rests perhaps all too easily alongside the practices of law, and leads Becker, like William Blackstone and Jeremy Bentham after him, to recognize the dire effects of silent, sequestered places of incarceration. Bentham came to believe that solitude was "torture in effect": "When the external senses

are restrained from action," in "a state of solitude, infantine su-
perstitions, ghosts, and specters, recur to the imagination. This,
of itself, forms a sufficient reason for not prolonging this species
of punishment."[12]

Ghosts are never proof of vacancy but evidence of plenitude.
They return chock full of memories and longing. For them,
nothing is ever past, and sometimes they appear to test the
limits of death or its meaning in a world of terror. The many
forms of the dead in the twenty-first century ask us to look again
at the way ghosts invade the precincts of the normal. When
they tear off the mask of certainty, we begin to know how such
terms as "prelogical," "irrational," or "primitive" are free-floating
and easily manipulated. Indignities and damages continue under
cover of civilization. "Torture," as Edward Peters wrote, "is one
of those signs of increased social rationalism that praisers of rationalism often neglect."[13] The increased reliance on judicial reason invigorates "systems of terror" more sinister because covert.

"When I am a spooky phantom you want to avoid, when there
is nothing but a shadow of a public civil life," the sociologist
Avery Gordon writes in *Ghostly Matters*, then "deep 'wounds
in civilization' are in haunting evidence."[14] Like ghosts, the law
busies itself with property, giving it preeminence. Property bears
the mark of persons that are lost to the living, and the legal, acting as if spectral, leads us into paths of thought so uncertain that
we should be very afraid of such places. Yet, as the endless pro-
cessions of dead people find their way into legal narratives, they
also present threats to comfort and to the inherited prejudice
that takes root there. So law slides backward into the past.

When ghosts come before the law, as we have seen, they are
sometimes treated as if real insofar as they have legal effect.
What seems supernatural or even extraordinary, once in the presence of judges becomes merely unusual. The law instinct, we
might argue, is permanently *primitive*, to invoke all the bias in
the term. The common-law hoard of precedent in its language
and iteration drags into light the myths of modernity and civilization. In its precincts anything can happen: the residues of

9

human materials, forgotten, are dredged up when necessary. Once the doors are opened into the house of law, we find implausible metamorphoses that have the power to exploit and oppress. Once inside, we encounter historical fragments, legal fictions, and spiritual beliefs. We see humans turned into things, ghosts into persons, and corpses into spirits. The intriguing thing is the thoroughly matter-of-fact way these phenomena are dealt with legally.

For legal purposes, in cases of undue influence, defamation, or fraud, spectral emanations may become proof, just like any facts. On this bewitched ground, the fantastic and the commonplace intermingle. In the case of wills, especially, even when the law does not acknowledge the unique gifts of spiritualists, it sometimes admits as valid the communications of the dead. Some early twentieth-century courts refused to invalidate the wills of believers, distinguishing between belief in communion with departed spirits and outright insanity. When property was to be bequeathed, most appellate courts in America allowed the testator's belief in "witchcraft, clairvoyance, spiritual influences, presentiments of the occurrences of future events, dreams, mindreading, and the like," as the Supreme Court of Illinois determined in *Carnahan v. Hamilton* (1914). Blewett Lee, a New York attorney, wrote in the *Harvard Law Review* (1921):

> Justice and common sense require that the judge or jury should put themselves, as well as they can, for this purpose in the place of the believer. If, for example, a person believed that his dead mother told him to make a certain devise, the communication should be dealt with, so far as the believer is concerned, as if it had in fact been made by his mother.

Presenting themselves either in or out of the flesh, spirit messengers exert real pressures on the testator's mind, and courts must attend to evidence of malfeasance from charlatans or criminals, both living and dead. "The more importance is given to these communications," Lee explained, "the easier it will be to break wills or contracts made under their control." Eccentricity was not insanity, however, and except in cases of insane delusion, wills were not invalidated on account of such peculiarities. In numerous eighteenth- and nineteenth-century appellate cases, especially, courts sustained the wills of those advised by mediums channeling the wishes of deceased loved ones into the minds of believers.[15]

In *McClary v. Stull* (1895), the Nebraska Supreme Court upheld a widow's bequest, denying that her superstitious beliefs incapacitated her from making a will. Instead, it legally validated the evidence of spirit possession, as long as the testator's will was her own:

> Law, it is said, is "of the earth, earthy" and that spirit-wills are too celestial for cognizance by earthly tribunals,—a proposition readily conceded; and yet the courts have not assumed to deny to spirits of the departed the privilege of holding communion with those of their friends who are still in the flesh so long as they do not interfere with vested rights or by the means of undue influence seek to prejudice the interests of persons still within our jurisdiction.

This enchantment, once recognized by law, treads perilously in realms that seem to be outside the precincts of reason. For who is to judge whether or not the testator's free agency has been destroyed? A later case in the Supreme Court of South Dakota, *Irwin v. Lattin* (1912), resorted to magical thinking: "It is sufficient to say that a will brought about by an influence which the testator *could not resist is not his will*." But, we might complain, the testator is dead. What kind of psychic power must the law possess when it makes judgments about capacity or disability? As we shall see, this judicial reasoning has the power to give and to take away, to affirm personality and to deny it.[16]

A cure for all kinds of threats, reasonableness has always been a necessary presupposition for extending enslavement and disability. But this legal rationality is tied to figurative power; and at any moment, its metaphors can become more insistent, literal, operating as Robert Cover famously wrote "on a field of pain and death."[17] What constitutes the real in law when driven by the past, when the traffic between the real and the fantastic becomes unfair to the dead and dangerous to the living? Slave law relied on fictions of invisible taint and property rights in human beings, criminal law on civil death and a host of other apparitional constructs, and property, once judged to be infested with ghosts, was legally stigmatized.

Specters are very much part of the legal domain. Human materials are remade and persons are undone in the sanctity of the courtroom. Whether slaves, dead bodies, criminals, ghost detainees, or any one of the many spectral entities held in limbo in the no-man's-lands sustained by state power, they all remain subject to the undue influences and occult revelations of law's rituals.

BENTHAM'S GHOSTS

> If you think that you can think about a thing inextri-
> cably attached to something else without thinking of
> the thing it is attached to, then you have a legal mind.

—Thomas Reed Powell

To think legally is to be capable of detaching ways of thinking from what is being thought about. Perhaps this is what the judge meant in *Ruffin v. Commonwealth* (1871), when he cautioned that the Bill of Rights, when applied to a civilly dead convict, should be given "a reasonable and not a literal construction." To think in law means to reason in a special kind of way, and, as I seek to show, the application of legal rules could and did create a universe unto itself. Lawyers might find Professor Powell's challenge to think analytically sensible, and they do, quoting Powell's words often and for all kinds of reasons.[18] But to one outside the guild of lawyers, they call up all kinds of possibilities. What happens if one is concerned with precedents but not with the content of precedents? Is that something like thinking about the body without the soul? Arguing against Descartes, Locke asked: "Can the Soul think, and not the Man? Or a Man think, and not be conscious of it?"[19] Or perhaps we might think about the skin of the dog that, as we shall see, is valuable in law while the dog itself counts as nothing. Or the zombie flesh that takes directions from someone else: empty of mind, will, affect but fiercely embodied. Or the body fed, kept warm, and clothed in indefinite solitary confinement while the mind is ignored.

To have a legal mind is to know Bentham's greatest fear: to know that ghosts do not exist yet to recognize the grim effects of that unreality. The "subject of ghosts," Bentham wrote toward the end of his life, "has been among the torments of my life." Though persuaded "of the non-existence of these sources of terror," he wrote, when he went to sleep "in a dark room" they "obtrude themselves," and he remained plagued by visitations of ghosts and specters all through his life. It is perhaps such ambiguous if persistent illusoriness that Melville grasps in the "colorless, all-color" of the whale Moby-Dick, when he writes about the mariner's dread of its whiteness: "the shrouded phantom of the whitened waters is horrible to him as a real ghost."[20]

As early as 1764, while he was still a student at Oxford, Bentham heard William Blackstone's Vinerian lectures on English law. The publication between 1765 and 1769 of the *Commentaries on the Laws of England* based on these lectures roused Bentham to fury against the "gothic tangle" of the common law, the very "fictions and circuities" that Blackstone had praised. Though Blackstone recognized that such "arbitrary fictions and expedients" are "troublesome," he insisted that they are "not dangerous":

> We inherit an old Gothic castle, erected in the days of chivalry, but fitted up for a modern inhabitant. The moated ramparts, the embattled towers, and the trophied halls, are magnificent and venerable, but useless. The inferior apartments, now converted

into rooms of convenience, are cheerful and commodious, though
their approaches are winding and difficult.

Bentham must have found in Blackstone's genial words chimeras more maleficent than his childhood phantasms: manifestations from a world of the dead. Bentham's preoccupation with
ghosts inspired all of his writing on law. Early dread became life-
long obsession, as Bentham fought against the common law—
"a thing merely imaginary ... an assemblage of fictitious regulations feigned after the images of these real ones that compose
the Statute Law." Far from being immaterial, these fictions not
only fed on the realities of statutes but, once so embodied, they
had real effects: the "dominion of the one and the few" instead
of "the greatest happiness of the greatest number."[21]

So whenever Bentham thought about the terrible force of
ghosts in their unreality, he raged against legal fictions and the
obscure language that supports their existence. Here he followed
Locke in condemning the "perpetual abuse of words." Though
unreal, legal fictions work wonders on the ordinary, throwing
into doubt even quotidian matters: "A fiction of law may be
defined a willful falsehood," Bentham explained, "having for its
object the stealing legislative power, by and for hands which
durst not, or could not, openly claim it; and but for the delusion
thus produced, could not exercise it." The "word-magic" of legal
fiction remains "a false assertion of the privileged kind," made
by those in power to wield ambiguous, even spectacular effects.
And "though acknowledged to be false," the fiction is "at the
same time argued from, and acted upon, as if true."[22]

Ghosts terrified Bentham precisely because they do not exist.
The more energy he put into refuting their existence, the more
intense became his fear of them. Following Slavoj Žižek's account of the ghostly "as something radically other," Miran Božovič reminds us of the mode of thinking that led to the feint
of the panopticon: "In Bentham's elaborate ontology, ghosts—
as well as hobgoblins, vampires, the devil, etc.,—are classified as
'fabulous maleficent beings,' or, more precisely, imaginary non-

entities." If they were *really* evil—and Božovič gives the example of "vicious dogs"—if ghosts were as "*maleficent*" as dogs, biting and tearing and grinding, they would not frighten as much as when we know them to be unreal. "We might even say," Božovič adds, "that the most unbearable thing would be to succeed in refuting the existence of ghosts."[23]

In Bentham's critique, the history of the common law was evidence of a world gone spectral, with laws and language obscured by "the pestilential breath of Fiction." Even the idea of a legal right was nothing more than a mystifying ruse. Bentham also criticized the demonic "metaphysics" of the French Declaration of the Rights of Man and the Citizen in 1789 in words that anticipate Arendt's confrontation with its vexing paradoxes, its intransigent abstractions: "Words—words without a meaning—or with a meaning too flatly false to be maintained by any body.... Look to the letter, you find nonsense:—look beyond the letter, you find nothing."[24]

Yet this *nothing*, as Bentham knew, had in its very emptiness power to demoralize people, to work real changes on their lives. What Bentham called this "dark spot" of mendacious vacuity can best be understood by thinking about the terror he experienced as a child: in his room at night, or even outside where servants made "every spot" the habitat of specters. It was always a question of the powerful over the weak: stories told, definitions plied, and language made obscure to rout certainty, create fear, secure obedience. He realized that such inventiveness was very much a part of governance, that making terror was actually a very easy way to keep the multitudes quite literally in the dark.

DOGS AND GHOSTS

Howling through the shadows at Hecate's crossroads, sitting at Pontius Pilate's feet, snarling at Jesus crucified, or accompanying the souls of the dead to the other side, dogs inhabit both divine and demonic realms. Like ghosts, dogs are enigmas. So speaks Nietzsche's Zarathustra, haunted by his own thoughts:

Then, suddenly, I heard a dog *howl* nearby.

Had I ever heard a dog howl like this? My thoughts raced back. Yes! When I was a child, in my most distant childhood:

—then did I hear a dog howl like this. And I saw it too, bristling, its head up, trembling in the stillest midnight when even dogs believe in ghosts.[25]

Ghosts like dogs are drawn to the familiar, the everyday, even as they tend toward the paranormal and supernatural. They appear as if somewhere between the real and supernatural, returning as a nightmare white phantom, a silent shade, or heavy with flesh, overripe and in need. In the meeting of the actual and the imaginary, ghosts and dogs bear down on the world of social relations and morality. Dogs and ghosts constantly cross boundaries, visit what they coveted most in life, counting on the heaviness of things to give them pleasure, to make them grieve. Ultimately, no matter how much they suggest the impalpable or transcendent, ghosts always come in bodies. They never obey the command to be wisps of air, some kind of steam, wet in the night or voices on the wind.

Let us take dogs and ghosts as entry into that place where creatures both human and nonhuman are outside community, on the borders of the known, "beyond the pale of civilization, a space haunted by exiled criminals, the insane, real and mythical beasts."[26] Rituals of banishment are crucial to cleansing and purifying a place of human holiness, or more precisely to disposing of the stigmatized outside the body politic. It is in myth that we find the history of rituals that inflict death and dehumanization —and the means by which the end to life and loss of affiliation become one. Antoinette in Jean Rhys's *Wide Sargasso Sea* warned: "There are always two deaths, the real one and the one people know about."[27] Whether we consider public rituals of physical death or secret practices of psychic elimination, dogs figure ubiquitously. Dogs appear as demons, dead spirits, as persons bewitched or things left behind. In all parts of the world and throughout history, they are cast as spectral packs of white dogs, hell-hounds, heath-hounds, the gabble ratchets or Gabriel hounds, the red-eyed, dog-headed gatekeepers to the realms of the dead, whether understood as the religious or the legal recesses of punishment.

What gives dogs their unique capacity to haunt? The history of the spectral like that of the sacred is found most surely in the trash bins of society. What is most damaged, torn, and rotten becomes the stuff of spiritual life. And the transformation introduces changes in our definition of spirit and body. This apparent opposition—between spirit and body—is confounded in the story of Hecuba, which I take as preamble to the shape-shifting and undoing of status that are the focus of this book. Changed into a dog, at once mystified and historicized, ghostly and corporeal, she brings us to the interstices of human and animal, person and god, living and dead.[28]

Laying bare the irreducible link between ghost stories and the properties of death or dislocation, Hecuba defies the consolations of transcendence. In Ovid's *Metamorphoses*, after being stoned for her vengeance on Polymnestor, who killed her son Polydoros for gold and jewels, Hecuba appears changed into a roaming haunt, howling in the Thracian fields:

> The Thracians, at the sight of [Polymnestor's] distress,
> began—with stones and lances—to attack
> the Trojan women. But she tried to catch
> those stones: with a hoarse howl, she snapped her teeth.
> Her jaws could only bark, though set for speech.
> And one can still find in the Cherronesus
> this place: the She-hound's Mound or *Kynos sema*,
> the name it gained from Hecuba's sad change.
> And then, for long, through all the fields of Thrace,
> remembering her many griefs, she howled.
>
> (13:565–75)

Ovid understands the curse of ever-remembered loss, for not only does his Hecuba bark like a dog, but she howls into eternity. In earlier versions of the story, as in Euripides' *Hecuba*, instead of

17

haunting the living, she dives into the sea and disappears. After her sufferings, her grief and indignities, deprived of her husband Priam, her children, and her city, she learns of her own end. The blinded, bleeding Polymnestor, his eyes gone and the flesh of his eye sockets gouged out by the "luckless" Hecuba, foretells her transformation into a dog with "fiery eyes," her death when she leaps from the ship's mast and vanishes in the sea. All that remains after she dies is her tomb on the Chersonese which bears the words: "Grave of the wretched hound, a mark for mariners."[29]

Though these are both well-known accounts of Hecuba's fate, I turn to the amplest if not the most enigmatic of Hecuba's appearances: Lycophron's *Alexandra*, variously dated sometime in the third or second century BC. Though the author is often assumed to be Lycophron of Chalcis, a poet of the Alexandrian court at the time of Callimachus, the real author remains a mystery: his birthplace, name, and occupation are still debated. What we know is that this Alexandrian poet crafted a remarkable amalgam of Homeric echoes, mythic returns from Troy, and other archaic and classical sources into a compressed, fractured, learned, and allusive lyric. With the ghosts of the dead before him, Lycophron retrieves a history disfigured and obliterated. The poet coins neologisms, sunders word order and syntax in a language as clashing as the human and nonhuman animals, the terrible spirits that crowd into Cassandra's vision on the day of Paris's departure for Greece.[30]

Out of the mouth of the Trojan Cassandra, locked away by Priam in what Robert Graves surmises is "a bee-hive tomb," come the "last notes of her Siren-song." Cassandra's prophecies about Troy's ruin are reported to an unbelieving Priam by the woman guardian who cares for her. With her "mazy riddling utterance" come two portraits of Hecuba that deepen the queen's story as they reveal her unfolding identities as mother, victim, predator, dog, ghost. What these metamorphoses have in common is a secret pact with the nonvisionary. Lycophron gathers the simplest, most forsaken things and works them up into figures as terrible as they are ambiguous. The recurring metamorphoses cast their spell in the very twists and turns of the iambic trimeter lines. In a striking passage the "grief-worn dog" turns into lion, captive, and then into the very stones that shower upon her on the coast of Thrace. The stones become a robe and then in turn the black skin of the spectral Maera, the dog attendant upon Hecate, the goddess of the underworld:

> And thy doom I lament, thou grief-worn dog.
> One that same earth, which bare her, opening wide
> Shall swallow utterly in yawning depths,
> As she sees direful ruin close at hand,
> There by her forebear's grove, where concubine
> Who wed in secret now lies joined in death
> With her own offspring ere it sucked the breast
> And ere her limbs were bathed, her travail past.
> And thee shall lead to cruel bridal-feast
> And wedding-sacrifices Iphis' son,
> Grim lion, using his fierce mother's rites;
> Slitting her throat into a vessel deep
> The snake, dread butcher of the wreath-crowned cow,
> Shall smite her with Candaon's thrice-owned sword,
> And slay for wolves the opening sacrifice.
> While thee, aged captive, on the hollow shore,
> Stoned publicly by the Dolonican folk
> Embittered by thy curses and abuse,
> A robe shall cover wrought of showering stones,
> When Maera's dusky form thou shalt assume.[31]

(315–34)

The thicket of competing embodiments sustains this ritual of pained recovery. The poem works best and perhaps solely in the zones of stress and uncertainty between the weight of memory and the call of imagination. Its cluster of contradictions demonstrates what a mind might look like pushed to the limits of recognition. Lycophron omits the plot-driven details of Polymnestor's murder of Polydoros for gold and Hecuba's subsequent revenge so powerfully rendered by Euripides. Instead, though Hecuba appears only twice, her transformation in character captures the experience of the tombless dead.

Enmeshed in a sequence of losses, each harsher than the last, she suffers a gradual deepening of servility that gnaws at her personal identity until there remains nothing but the image and sound of her grief, the bark and the body of a dog. Is Hecuba's mutation into a dog a degrading transformation, punishment for her bloody revenge on Polymnestor? Certainly not here. The shade and shape of the nonhuman realize the excesses of her grief and the absoluteness of her exile from all she held dear, her banishment from civil and political life: a widow, a slave, with no freedom, no family, no possessions.

There is something worse than enslavement: the haunt of the self made extinct, turned loose to roam outside of society, bereft of intimacy and affiliation. After these mutations a self still lingers, a reminder to those who have damaged her: the haunt of her howls in the night. Lycophron's Cassandra mourns, while prophesying her mother's "fame" as an attendant hound of Hecate, the "Triformed," worshipped in Thrace and honored at Pherae in Thessaly: "Mother, poor mother! Not unknown also / Shall be thy fame; for Brimo, Perses' child, / Triformed, shall make thee an attendant hound / With nightly howls these mortals to affright" (1174–77).

In Lycophron, there are ghosts upon ghosts, not surprising since we are in the realm of the dead, but they are always in league with matter, thickened with physicality. Lycophron's poetic cruces involve conversions between matter and spirit, inglorious brutes and rarified spirits. By forcing proximity on those categories most rigorously separated, he probes the displacement of the human element from these beings. Yet what remains after transfiguration is the self that hangs on to consciousness, the *psyche* that E. R. Dodds describes as "the seat of courage, of passion, of pity, of anxiety, of animal appetite," not primarily "the seat of reason."

As in later spirit or possession religions, such as medieval sorcery or modern practices of vodou, there is no room for the metaphysical or transcendent. Instead, there is a loosening of boundaries, a radical materiality, as Dodds writes: "The 'soul' was no reluctant prisoner of the body; it was the life or spirit of the body, and perfectly at home there." Those who practice what is called "witchcraft" or "superstition" acknowledge such potent divisions as that between rational agents and dumb animals, but they strive to make indistinct the terms of distinction. Hecuba's dog reminds us that this hierarchy is dubious, its status ambiguous. What matters most in her metamorphoses is the form that victimization takes: the banishment, torment, and loss equally shared by all personalities, whether animals, humans, gods, or ghosts.[32]

THINKING WITH ZOMBIES

In the figure of the zombie, a cadaver in appearance only, vodou extends the fiction of civil death. The zombie though dead is alive. The dead-alive zombie in "flesh and bones" survives as the remnant of loss and dispossession. These macabre, depersonalized entities are left to wander alone or forced to work together, shorn of tenderness, comradeship, consciousness. In *Myal* (1988) the Jamaican sociologist, poet, and novelist Erna Brodber regards "spirit thievery" as the dead reanimated by the force of mastery. However this relation of domination is configured, memories of servitude are transposed into a new idiom:

> People are separated from the parts of themselves that make them think and they are left as flesh only. Flesh that takes directions from someone. The thinking part of them is also used as nefariously ... "immorally" might be a better word.... In those societies there are persons trained to do the separation and insertion. The name under which they go would be translated as spirit thieves.[33]

Spirit thievery recalls the debilitation of slavery that makes one forever subject to the direction of another. In the violent exclusion from community and kinfolk, the zombie code takes shape. If socially the zombie represents the self undone, the seriatim diminutions of dignity and life, then we can use the image in order to understand how things legally emptied of personhood can be repossessed or turned into vessels for what Mary Midgley has described as "highly sensitive social beings," intelligent, aware.[34]

Zombies are unnatural persons, or, put more precisely, fearsomely tactile if spectrally real beings. They have been excommunicated and anathematized as retribution for violating the laws of their society. Yet every case of zombification demands that we question the nature of this transgression. The zombie phenomenon only makes sense in terms of the features of a well-defined personality who reaps punishment for ambition, greed, disrespect, or slander. We must anchor this ceremonial of disgrace in culture and legal history rather than nature. Far from supernatural, zombies are experienced as highly contextualized spectacles of alienation intended to inspire horror in the minds of the community.

In our "secular," "progressive" times, comprehensive forms of expiation function as the backdrop to civil community. Rituals of expulsion remain intact to intimidate and control. Who gets banned and expelled so that we can live in reasonable consensus? Let us name them now. Criminals. Security Threats. Terrorists. Enemy Aliens. Illegal Immigrants. Migrant Contaminants. Unlawful Enemy Alien Combatants. Ghost Detainees.[35] These are new orders of life; they hover outside the bounds of the civil, beyond the simple dichotomies of reason and unreason, legal and illegal. The receptacles for these outcasts are in the wilderness, the desert, or islands cut off from sociocultural networks of daily life. The management of rubbish, what we might call fecal motives, draws distinctions between the free and the bound, the familiar and the strange. And this ongoing global cultivation of human waste, brazen in its display, makes our sense of inclusion a rare and precarious privilege.

Is there an afterlife of ostracism? What remains once civil has been replaced with penal life? Legal definitions are instrumental in condemning the unthinkable chimera to circumstances where dogmatic divisions between humans and monsters no longer count. As suggestive in their haunt as were unclean spirits, the objects of oppressive state magic are also racially marked, making what Avery Gordon calls "the disposability of a permanently confined life" count in a blatantly phenomenal and therefore pervasively spectral manner.[36] Though alive, they are incessantly dying in new ways. Situated beyond the terror of mortality, these exiled persons work powerfully on the minds of the as-yet included. We cannot ignore the threat of this malediction. The state brings up to date the once formidable anathema of the church. Ecclesiastical exorcism survives in the burlesque of justice that continues to find ways to eliminate the accused without due process, without trial, without evidence, without even a charge.

A GOAT FOR AZAZEL

"And I will set my face against you." In Leviticus the face of God orders retribution for turning away from the law. Besides burnt offerings of bullocks, sheep, goats, turtledoves, there remains the central sacrifice of the Day of Atonement, the sign of true repentance: the goat set apart for Azazel. In the days of the Temple, the High Priest went before two goats, alike and equal. Two lots made of gold were thrown together into a casket from which he drew one lot as sacrifice on the altar for the "Name Most High, and one for the rocky steep," released into the wilderness to Azazel. Putting both hands on the goat, he cried aloud: "A sin-offering unto the Lord." After confessing the sins of the people of Israel, he sent this goat with a scarlet fillet around its jowls and the congregation's sins on its head out beyond the city's gates and into the desert.

And Aaron shall lay both his hands upon the head of the live
goat, and confess over him all the iniquities of the children of
Israel, and all their transgressions in all their sins, putting them
upon the head of the goat, and shall send him away by the hand
of a fit man into the wilderness. (Leviticus 16:21)

Animals sent defiled either out into the wilderness or over cliffs,
are crucial to cleansing and purifying a place of holiness. Laden
with sins, the goat is a terribly polluting force. Sometimes the
goat tried to return to the camp, the place it had known for so
long. In order to prevent this, the appointed person pushed the
goat into an inaccessible area believed to be the place of evil
spirits or demons. This is not so much a sacrifice as a going away.
Something is being sent away for some kind of death somewhere beyond the borders.

Legal directives join in the solemn enactment of social structure, as moral discrimination cedes to obligatory practice. Let us
turn to another site of contamination, also in Leviticus. Not the
cliff or wilderness for the banished goat, but the fungal house. If
possessed of "the plague of leprosy," it must be emptied and in-
spected by a priest.

And he shall look on the plague, and, behold, if the plague be in
the walls of the house with hollow strakes, greenish or reddish,
which in sight are lower than the wall; Then the priest shall go
out of the house to the door of the house, and shut up the house
seven days: And the priest shall come again the seventh day, and
shall look: and, behold, if the plague be spread in the walls of the
house; Then the priest shall command that they take away the
stones in which the plague is, and they shall cast them into an
unclean place without the city. (Leviticus 14:37–40)

In the process of eliminating impurity, the text portrays infec-
tious property as if personally responsible, grotesquely cursed.
What is most striking in this liturgy of disease, priestly inspection, and removal is the formulaic repetitions. How arduous must
be the ritual of purification, severe in its orders of detection, its

suspicion of recurrent defilement. Whether house or human, the severity is unchanging.

What is the design of the juridical no-man's-land that has been created when law loosens the link between human beings, animals, devils, other noxious creatures, or infernal vexations? I have cast this traffic and transplantation of persons across vast social, temporal, and spatial distances in the drama of rituals that are both penal and religious. The stuff of spiritual life becomes the raw material of legal authority. My understanding of law thus summons persons as essential to its sustenance: "No person itself, the law lives in persons."[37] If I may hazard the comparison, the law also lives off persons as do spirits in search of bodies to inhabit, in much the same way as the Haitian *lwa*, the spirits or gods of vodou, can manifest themselves only in the corporeal envelope. In lineaments both human and nonhuman, spirits experience life and unfold their potential.

The drama of vodou permits human practitioners to take on roles, to find newly malleable identities. In the same way, legal persons have no fixed definition, but instead take on changing capacities variously granted by the state, such as legal rights, freedoms, duties, and obligations. Jurisprudence responds to the "craving for the rational" when confronted with what Alexander Nékám regards as the necessities of "social control and valuation." To be acceptable, communal emotions must be endowed with a "rational form." This incarnation is granted through "the art of the law." Nowhere is the artifice as compelling as in the creation of legal persons, entities that have nothing to do with "human personality." These persons, "whether human being or anything else," prove the absoluteness of law's power: "those to whom the law attributes such a legal personality possess it by force of the law and not by nature." In this preternatural performance, "legal rights and enjoyments" can be given to "spirits and gods, devils, and idols, as well as to the unborn and the dead."[38]

Highly context-specific situations help us to dramatize the limits of human personality, to intimate law's usurpation of nature. They form the background to the donning and relinquishing of masks. So diverse are estimates of what counts for persons that we would do well to compare their changing comportment with that of shape-shifters, shedding and taking on different skins. The *loupgaroux* of medieval France or the *san pwèl* and *san po* (hairless or skinless) in contemporary Haiti, the blood-suckers and vampires of the West Indies and the southern United States, remain fully conscious selves even as they shed skin, take on new skin, and assume nonhuman form. In search of human company, these bloodthirsty spirits take on the appearance of dogs, cows, or goats.

SPIRITUAL LEPERS

"I swear I have never seen such a devilish way of thinking as they seem to have," Shaker Aamer, a legal resident of the United Kingdom captured in Afghanistan in December 2001, wrote in his diary during his July 2005 hunger strike at Guantánamo.[39] The occult sorcery of human cruelty brings us closer to thinking about the meaning of monsters.

Some of those called terrorists in the early days of Guantánamo were labeled as threats and imprisoned without being accused of any offense. Objects of contagion, they had to be sealed off. They were subjected to an extrajudicial exhibition of containment that preceded their detention, abuse, and torture. Transmogrified into the chrysalis of confinement, they were drugged, shackled hand and foot, made to wear ear cuffs and mittens, hooded, and blindfolded by blacked-out goggles. These distancing effects, once fixed on their bodies, shrink the space of isolation into a second skin. The place of incapacitation and the incapacitated person collapse into one.

"I am in my tomb," wrote Abdelli Feghoul, in solitary confinement at Camp 6. In the ostensibly more lenient Camp 5 and Camp Echo, prisoners are confined to steel and concrete isolation cells for at least twenty hours a day, with virtually no human contact.[40] Let us remember that the approximately 200 men who remain imprisoned in this offshore pen are held in defi-

ance of international law. In many cases the victims of acknowledged kidnapping, of illegal transfer across international borders
by the U.S. government, they are not guilty or alleged to be
guilty of any crimes. They have not been charged, accused,
tried, or found guilty of anything at all. Not even, as the records show—at least at the time of their seizure and torture—of
hostility to the United States (which is not, let us remember, a
crime).

Since 2002, in response to collective punishment, the captives have initiated a series of individual and coordinated mass
suicide attempts, classified by the military as "manipulative self-
injurious behavior." The hunger strikes bear witness to images of
incapacitation and the realities of protest. In December 2005,
the number of hunger strikes dropped after mobile restraint
chairs (called "torture chairs" by prisoners) were introduced.
Clive Stafford Smith, a lawyer at Guantánamo, writes that the
device "looked rather like an updated electric chair." As well as
straps for the prisoner's arms and legs, "the Guantánamo chairs
had been modified to add two additional straps for the head and
the chest."[41]

The largest hunger strike, in which 131 prisoners partici-
pated, ended in 2006 with twice-daily force-feeding through
nose tubes, a process that involves excruciating pain, bleeding,
and vomiting. Talking to a group of reporters about the chair
to which prisoners were strapped during the insertion of the
feeding tubes, General John Craddock, the head of the United
States Southern Command, assured them, "It's not like 'The
Chair,' it's a chair. It's pretty comfortable, it's not abusive."
Expanding on his notion of nonabusive comfort, he explained
that his soldiers gave those he called "detainees" a choice of
colors for feeding tubes—yellow, clear, and beige—adding,
"They like the yellow."[42]

Seven years after the first captives arrived at Guantánamo,
President Barack Obama on January 22, 2009, issued a series of
executive orders concerning Guantánamo and U.S. policies on
executive detention. Besides requiring the closure of the prison

within a year, he ordered that conditions of confinement there be reviewed by the secretary of defense, who appointed a team of investigators. The "Review of Department Compliance with President's Executive Order on Detainee Conditions of Confinement," presented to Obama by Admiral Patrick W. Walsh in February 2009, describes the practice of "enteral feeding" in chilling detail. In the section called "Medical Ethics—Medical Treatment of Hunger Strikers," the Department of Defense review team presents coercion as care.

The feeding process, the report argues, comports with Common Article 3 of the Geneva Convention. A surprising conclusion, since that article prohibits, among other things, "outrages upon personal dignity, in particular humiliating and degrading treatment." Systematic debasement takes on the appearance of emergency preservation. A physician is aided by "a feeding nurse and one or more Corpsmen," with "periodic consultations from a nutritionist." When prisoners refuse to come out of their cells, the "Joint Detention Group Commander" authorizes a "Forced Cell Extraction" (FCE). The feeding is then done by FCE teams in "feeding chairs" with "head restraints." A footnote explains that the "nasogastric tube used is size 10 or 12 French, which would be 3.5–4.5 millimeters in diameter (slightly larger in diameter than a piece of cooked spaghetti but less than a pencil eraser)."[43]

Aamer, one of the leaders of the hunger strike that began in July 2005, asked Stafford Smith to take down his words when he was in isolation in the supermax unit Camp Echo:

> I am dying here every day.... Mentally and physically, this is happening to all of us. We have been ignored, locked up in the middle of this ocean for four years. Rather than humiliate myself, having to beg for water here in Camp Echo, I have decided to hurry up a process that is going to happen anyway.[44]

The question is whether captives who have chosen to die, whether as protest or in response to unendurable suffering, should have their decisions respected or should be "saved" by force. In other words, should the deliberate, conscious decision to die by starvation be duly regarded, or should the military guards prevent fully aware and responsible individuals from killing themselves in this way? Do we find our ethics by forcing captives held in defiance of law to live in a dying situation, by refusing them an escape from a situation worse than death, where such a thing as *life* acquires new meaning? In this context, to safeguard health is to make persons accept their passage from subject to object. The transition is involuntary, unlike the willed riposte of suicide. The personhood of the men at Guantánamo remains bound up with their right to decide how they maintain and express their group identity, when they warrant recognition, what they do with their bodies. Not allowing persons to choose death as an escape from a murderous fate depends on the skilled manipulation of grim technologies.

On February 23, 2009, on the same day as the presentation of the Department of Defense review, the Center for Constitutional Rights issued its own report on conditions at Guantánamo, revealing that purportedly humane methods there consisted of sensory and sleep deprivation in the camps, as well as force-feeding, described by the euphemism "intensified assisted feeding." Sabin Willett, an attorney for Guantánamo prisoners, described the experiences of one of his clients: "[Y]ou try talking to a man who only wants to see the sun. You will never forget the experience."[45]

Human in form but dead in spirit, these captive entities live on in our minds, preserved in amber, like the corpse kept in cellophane in that singularly unreal photo from Abu Ghraib. Dependent on spectacle for their force—whether the proliferation of effigies from Abu Ghraib and Guantánamo or the haunt of the unseen in lethal injection rooms or supermax cells in the United States—these hints of something worse than death produce a new sign of the self. These dead are not improved by dying.

What happens to the bodies of the dead already entombed at Guantánamo? Lost to their families when living, they remain abandoned in death, deprived of the quick burial required in

Islamic practice.[46] In the haunt of Guantánamo, the spirits of persons lie dead. This nightmarish dispensation puts us on the cusp of a belief in ghosts. The new ghost story is really a very old one, and as always these ghosts are in league with matter. Describing the fate of "outlaws, convicted felons and excommunicates," who take on the shape of wolves, Frederick Pollock and Frederic William Maitland focus on "outlawry" as "the law's ultimate weapon." The decree of outlawry, they explain, occurred not at a time of no law but "when law was weak, and its weakness was displayed by a ready recourse to outlawry."

> He who breaks the law has gone to war with the community; the community goes to war with him. It is the right and duty of every man to pursue him, to ravage his land, to burn his house, to hunt him down like a wild beast and slay him; for a wild beast he is; not merely is he a "friendless man," he is a wolf. Even in the thirteenth century, when outlawry had lost its exterminating character and had become an engine for compelling the contumacious to abide the judgment of the courts, this old state of things was not forgotten; *Caput gerat lupinum* [Let him bear the head of a wolf]—in these words the courts decreed outlawry.[47]

Has outlawry—or, for that matter, law—lost its exterminating character? Not if we consider the Obama administration's revised plan for trial by military commission. The three men accused of planning 9/11, outlaws who desire the transfiguration of martyrdom, will have their chance. They can be exterminated without a genuine hearing. In a very unusual juridical turn, these prisoners will be allowed to plead guilty, thus eliminating the need for "proof," which might necessarily include acknowledgment of torture. Thus, security secrets will not be divulged, nor brutal interrogation techniques.[48]

Lynn White once wrote: "To know the subliminal mind of a society, one must study the sources of its liturgies of inflicting death."[49] The tensions between archaic and modern are fitful and rapidly evaporating. Once considered legal aberrations, the ruins of an irrational past are reconfigured as acceptable. On May 21,

2009, Obama proposed, as if a novel idea, the protracted incarceration of alleged terrorists. In spite of admirable intentions, his suggested "legitimate legal framework"—what he also described as "an appropriate legal regime" for preventive detention—is virtually unprecedented within the law and wholly unconstitutional. It is not unprecedented in actuality. It remains indistinct from the worst though least-discussed excess of Guantánamo: the use of indefinite isolation as psychological torture. Sensory deprivation is the form of discipline preferred by prison management. Now it is offered as the solution to the Guantánamo disgrace. The "rendering" of prisoners as packaged goods during delivery to be later sealed off and warehoused thus presaged their future.

By legitimizing incapacitation without proven crimes or violations of law—and without trial or even charge—President Obama regularizes the anomalous and rationalizes solitary torture. He reimagines *preventive detention* offshore as *prolonged detention* on the mainland. Not as degraded or mendacious a euphemism perhaps as his predecessor's "enhanced interrogation techniques" for torture, but a euphemism nevertheless. In the wily magic of changing terminologies, "prolonged detention" replaces both "indefinite detention" and "administrative segregation"—the latter already an evasive and legally convenient renaming of "solitary confinement."

The majority of prisoners held in long-term, open-ended, and often permanent supermax confinement in the United States are labeled "Security Threat Groups." These alleged gang members usually have no disciplinary infractions; they are locked down and isolated allegedly for the safety of the rest of the prison population. The incarceration of "dangerous terrorism suspects" on our soil without due (or indeed, any) process of law also trades on the promise of security. The new global logic of punishment offers democracy while dispensing with judge and jury. It also ensures the broader establishment of super–maximum security units.[50]

What the United Nations Convention Against Torture, as well as human rights groups such as Human Rights Watch, Amnesty

International, and others have long singled out as torturous solitary-confinement practices in the United States and what Guantánamo detainees have revealed to be the most horrific part of their detention—its systematic psychic cannibalism—President Obama presents as what every reasonable American should admit as worthy of our heritage: "the power of our most fundamental values." He asks us to bear in mind: "Nobody has ever escaped from one of our federal supermax prisons, which hold hundreds of convicted terrorists." His proposal, he says, resulted from approaching "difficult questions with honesty and care and a dose of common sense." When did common sense become so difficult, honesty so terrifying?[51]

"After two days of solitude," J. M. Coetzee writes in *Waiting for the Barbarians*, "my lips feel slack and useless, my own speech seems strange to me.... I build my day unreasonably around the hours when I am fed. I guzzle my food like a dog. A bestial life is turning me into a beast."[52] But this dog, though reduced to appetite alone, at least has the chance to know, to desire. There are other kinds of metamorphoses: the nefarious production of another kind of person—whether canine or ghostly, human relic or spirit—drained of self-identity, forever anomalous, condemned as extraneous to civil society, excluded from belonging.

The incapacitated, the as yet improperly apprehended legal person is sufficiently unreal to make claims on our habits of thought. If more-or-less tangible objects can be either "property" or "persons" in the eyes of the law, what we consider subjects of legal rights and duties can also be stripped of these attributes. We are obliged to consider the creation of a species of depersonalized persons. Deprived of rights to due process, to bodily integrity, or life, these creatures remain *persons in law*. The reasoning necessary to this terrain of the undead sanctions the irrational: the reasonable extension of unspeakable treatment into an unknowable future.[53]

When law is called upon to ascertain a "rational" basis for sustaining the dominion of the dead and the ghostly, much depends on assumptions that most of us claim to find intolerable. But recent events continue to prove how much we can tolerate. How easy it is for fear, dogma, and terror to allow us to demonize others, to deny them a common humanity, the protection of our laws, to do unspeakable things to them. In a morally disenchanted world, daily cruelty and casual violence accompany the call for order, the need for security.

In an age of scientific advances, when "spare-part" medicine is applied to corpses or living bodies, when the unborn fetus becomes rights-bearing, and genetic and embryonic chimeras are realities, the question of legal personhood corresponds with an inscrutable idiom. It is perhaps because of this cohabitation and the "magicalities" it allows that state power is less open to criticism. If witchcraft is "the use of preternatural power by one person to damage others," then the practitioners who inhabit the dark world of stigma know how to make law the basis of extralegality. This sorcery is not overt, and the illusionists who practice it rely on secrecy to guarantee its malignancy and predations.[54]

Life and death, possession and demonism are, to a surprising extent, buttressed by the normal forms and regular course of law. Cultural expectations of legitimate punishment, necessary pain, and reasonable violence are produced, transmitted, sustained in a legal idiom. One of the judges in *Bailey v. Poindexter* (1858), an antebellum case central to my inquiry, declared that to treat the slave as capable of choice was to create "a legal impossibility." Now, the U.S. government and courts are busy turning living, willful, sentient, believing persons into inanimate, rightless objects. These objects are disfigured, reduced to organs that can fail and legally be put at the threshold of life and death, where pain is torture only if it causes death.[55]

DOGS' BODIES

The dead do not die. They haunt the living. Both free and unfree, the undead still speak in the present landscape of terror and ruin. The dogs of hurricane Katrina, citizens turned refugees in the United States; prisoners warehoused indefinitely; disappeared ghost-detainees tortured and held incommunicado in prolonged detention; sick cows kicked and prodded in slaughter—the rationales and rituals of terror proliferate. But perhaps we need to think more deeply about the dying and the dead.

For a long time, as we shall see, the dog could not be the subject of larceny. Only the taking of skin from the dog's dead body was a felony. Dogs, the most intimate and persistent friends of humans, were legally considered as no different in terms of property from human corpses. In the analogy I make here between the *dead body of a human* and *the living body of a dog*, I propose that we consider not just the metaphysical violence but also the literal dispossession, so much a part of legal reasoning. How far can we take this judgment of negated personality or nullified property? In his *Commentaries*, Blackstone writes "that no larceny can be committed, unless there be some property in the thing taken," and here he gives the example not of the theft of a dog but of an enshrouded corpse: "This is the case of stealing a shrowd out of a grave; which is the property of those, whoever they were, that buried the deceased: but stealing the corpse itself, which has no owner, (though a matter of great indecency) is no felony, unless some of the gravecloths be taken with it." There is property in a winding sheet just as in the hide of a dog. What lies inside has paradoxically less intrinsic value than what is most superficial, just skin-deep. Whether living or dead, there is something that links dogs and humans, damaged, diseased, or dead, in Anglo-American law.[56]

Jerry Cruncher, the "resurrectionist" of Dickens's *The Tale of Two Cities*, exhumed bodies and gave them up for dissection. The court ruled that he had not committed larceny but a misdemeanor, since a corpse was *res nullius*: it belonged to no one, no one had any right in it. The origins of the rule nullifying property in corpses are obscure and confused. A corpse awaiting burial has a status distinct from bodies rotting in the earth or turned into mummies. The natural decay making dust of the corporeal remains is quite unlike the labor expended to preserve them. When the body has been worked on and bettered, possessed or occupied by another's labor and thus owned, it gains legal recognition. In this uncertain tenancy, the play of legal reasoning between living and dead becomes a curious, illogical process. A deliberation both casual and terrible, it marks the abrupt legal transition of a dead body from subject to object. The preservation of dignity vies with the trashing of junk. American courts, unlike English, recognized the sometimes-gruesome consequences of the classic notion of no-property-interest in cadavers, and instead granted human remains the status of quasi-property. Thus recognizing the claims and rights of family members, the courts gave them the right to possess the corpse for burial and determine the manner in which it would be laid to rest.[57]

The unloved, unwanted, and abandoned are not always left alone. Sometimes they are lost, taken, discarded, or made ready for predation. Early and late, pre- and postmodern, some entities get special treatment when subjected to prejudice and irregular vengeance. Possessed physically by devils—however they are construed anew over time—or exploited as zombies, they are turned into new human, animal, or other unspecified shapes. The results are real: injuries, murders, and often dazzling transmutations. In the latter case, society creates the highly effective illusion through deference to legal forms and usages, whether as part of state ritual or as religious practice.

Devils enter physically into corpses, borrow their bodily functions. Recent thought experiments about dying and death, organ transplants or persons dead to cognition—such as Karen Quinlan, described as being in a permanent vegetative state and allowed to die—make us think again about phantasms of personhood, spirit possession, and what it means to be considered in terms of law.

When reflecting on humans assailed, transformed, or disposed of, we turn to catastrophe, to the disorder piled onto animals thought to be conscious of wrongdoing, and possessed of intelligence and passion. If animals were so endowed with the "spiritual principle," they could be blamed and incur retribution in the hereafter. Yet the immortality of their souls was contrary to the dogma of the Christian church, which depended on hierarchical estimation in order to validate the privilege of the faithful. Medieval jurisprudence handily solved the problem by portraying animals as infested with hell power, possessed by demons. Yet such diabolic tenancy did not stop with the Middle Ages. The Jesuit father Guillaume-Hyacinthe Bougeant in his *Amusement philosophique sur le langage des bestes* (1739) brings demonology into the eighteenth century:

> ... so the good Catholic becomes an efficient co-worker with God by maltreating brutes and thus aiding the Almighty in punishing the devils, of which they are the visible and bruisable forms. Whatever pain is inflicted is felt, not by the physical organism but by the animated spirit. It is the embodied demon that really suffers, howling in the beaten dog and squealing in the butchered pig.

Jesus casts out the unclean spirits inhabiting the man who called himself "Legion" in the fifth chapter of the Gospel of Mark. The spirits enter a great herd of swine, and the swine thus possessed rush down the cliffs into the sea.[58]

If there is a remedy for the bad magic, the damages of law, we must try to describe what such a healing metamorphosis would look like. The dread of threat and stigma can be countered by a healing that is not so much segregation as coalescence. Mutual adaptability becomes the way to repossession. The path to this cure involves a dog, a white dog. It is neither the sacrificial "sacred White Dog" of the Iroquois, "spotless" and "faithful," "the purest envoy ... to the Great Spirit," as Melville wrote in *Moby-Dick*, nor the evil dog, that nameless terror whose spectral white skin contains the person lost forever to evil enchantment.[59] Instead, we confront a strangely genial dog who gains wonderful ascendancy. The serene outcome, which we can call redemption, depends on a spiritual state that remains bound to the body.

Apollonius of Tyana, a first-century healer, philosopher, itin-
erant preacher, and spiritual adviser—who avoided food, clothing, or sacrifice that involved killing animals—rivaled Jesus of
Nazareth in his miracles and cures, or so those condemned as
pagans by later Christians believed. In Philostratus's lengthy
biography of Apollonius, dating probably from the early third
century A.D., we read about the healing of a boy bitten by a
rabid dog in Tarsus. The dog matters here as much as the boy.
Canine and human become dependent one on the other, and
in their reciprocity and stunning cross-species collaboration we
find an alternative to the ugly hocus-pocus of Judeo-Christian
dogma in the promise of a law that carries with it the Pauline
covenant written "not on tablets of stone but on tablets of
human hearts" (2 Corinthians 3:3).[60]

For thirty days after being bitten by a mad dog, a young boy
ran around on all fours, barking and howling. When Apollonius
met him he ordered that the "dog responsible for all this" should
be tracked down. No one had ever seen the dog, nor had any
idea how to find it, since the victim "no longer even recognized
himself." Apollonius tells Damis, his Boswell, to seek out "a white
shaggy sheepdog, the size of one from Amphilochia [in Northwestern Greece] ... standing by such-and-such a fountain, trembling because it both desires and fears water." "Bring it to me,"
Apollonius says, "just say I sent for it." Dragged by Damis to
Apollonius, the dog lay down at his feet, "weeping like a suppli-
ant at an altar." Then, remarkably, instead of ordering the demons
to depart, Apollonius enacts a ritual as palpable, as immediate as
an embrace. Invoking the memory of King Telephus of Mysia
wounded by Achilles and healed by the touch of his spear, Apollonius gives us an early version of a "hair of the dog that bit
you": the way out of harm—whether drunkenness or madness—
is through the thing that has caused the harm.

After making it [the dog] even tamer and stroking it with his
hand, he makes the youth stand beside him, while he himself

37

held him. Then, so that the crowd should not miss a great miracle, he said, "The soul of Telephus the Mysian has migrated into this boy, and the Fates are planning the same treatment for him." So saying, he told the dog to lick the bite, so that the boy's wounder should also be his healer.

The boy is healed and comes back to himself, recognizing his parents and friends. As I have noted, Apollonius's attention to the dog is crucial. He prays to the river and tells the dog to swim across the Cydnus. On the other side, not in the underworld as the crossing might suggest, but reborn as if from a fate worse than death, he regains consciousness of himself. In words that are both instructive and moving, Philostratus records the dog's metamorphosis:

> When it had crossed the Cydnus, it stood on the bank and let out a bark, which does not happen at all when dogs are rabid, and it bent back its ears and wagged its tail, realizing that it had been cured, since water is the remedy for rabies if the victim has the courage to drink it.[61]

In the Gospels, Jesus heals the possessed by curing them of cognizance. It is a dispossession as costly as it is beneficial. Though cured of their demons, they lose their singular ability to recognize him. But Apollonius heals by replenishment, a bestowal of bounty for both boy and dog. The boy is healed, but so is the dog that brings the story to a close. The dog is renewed, indeed graced with sentience, gratitude, and recognition: not penalized but personalized, for life not for death. But this is only a promise, a story to hold onto, as I turn my attention to a past defined by the grievous assertion of indignity, a death sentence played out in the spheres of ecclesiastical and secular power.

CIVIL DEATH

The prejudice with respect to specters, therefore,
originates from nature; and such appearances
depend not, as philosophers have supposed,
solely upon the imagination.

—George-Louis Leclerc, Compte de Buffon, *Histoire
naturelle, générale et particulière* (1749–78)

GHOSTS OF LAW

IN PORT-AU-PRINCE, HAITI, I HEARD A STORY ABOUT A WHITE DOG.
Reclaimed by an oungan—a priest who "deals with both hands,"
practicing "bad" magic—a ghost dog comes to life. Starving, its
eyes wild, it appears late at night. A Haitian friend called it "the
dog without skin." To have white skin was to have no skin at all.
But this creature was not really a dog. When a person died, the
spirit, stolen by the oungan, awakened from what had seemed
sure death into a new existence in canine disguise. We all agreed
that no spirit formerly in a human habitation would want to
end up reborn in the skin of a dog. Being turned into a dog was
bad enough, but to end up losing its natural color, to turn white,
was worse. In this metamorphosis, the old skin of the dead person, like the skin discarded by a snake, is left behind. But the
person's spirit remains immured in this coarse envelope, locked
in the form of a dog.

I tell this story, a tale of what some call the "supernatural,"
to extend my discussion of the sorcery of law. What the modern

world condemns as witchcraft or projects onto those deemed "uncivilized" remains at its heart. In its manipulation of categories such as the spirit and the flesh, the law perpetuates its claims to mastery and comprehension, all the while investing the juridical order with the power to redefine persons. Legal culture has carved up human differences into hierarchies capacious enough to accommodate subordination. The law's artificial entities—whether disabled as slaves or degraded as felons—are made "vulnerable," in the scholar and activist Ruthie Gilmore's words, to "premature death."[1] This threat persists in a world where the supernatural serves as the unacknowledged legislator of justice.

In varying sites of struggle, sacrifice, and stigma, legal rituals give flesh to past narratives and new life to the residues of old codes and penal sanctions. My intention in this chapter is to contemplate how law materializes dispossession, and in far more corporeal ways than its abstract precepts might at first suggest. In past centuries, a purely juridical application of legal disabilities aimed at humiliating and excluding the criminal or any individual considered "infamous," a term with a long and complicated history. This legal machinery supported public, highly visible punishments that soon gave way to the reconstruction of persons recognized only in so far as they were degraded.[2]

SACRIFICE

In his *Commentaries on the Laws of England,* William Blackstone characterized the artificial person in law, explaining how civil liberty arises on the ruins of the natural:

> But every man, when he enters into society, gives up a part of his natural liberty, as the price of so valuable a purchase; and, in consideration of receiving the advantages of mutual commerce, obliges himself to conform to those laws, which the community has thought proper to establish. And this species of legal obedience and conformity is infinitely more desirable than that wild and savage liberty which is sacrificed to obtain it.[3]

Unlike the Pauline admonition to relinquish the trappings of the physical and be raised a spiritual body in Christ, Blackstone's version of new life depends on a compact with the civil order. The civil, once codified in the institution of law, demands the dual gestures of submission and repression of the natural.

In these fictions of obeisance, the old nature first takes on the skin of the civil, then compacts itself to fit inside that skin. In this way, by the very terms of Blackstone's contract, the state of society never completely transcends that of nature. The natural person who existed before the social contract, though reduced to a repressed spirit in civil skin, nonetheless haunts the margins of the formal community. Blackstone thus reminds his reader that, in heralding the rituals of renunciation and repression as essential to the promotion of a coherent legal order, he means much more than a one-off exchange for the greater good. For the trade is merely one instance of what must be a permanent quasi-religious process, a ritual of citizenship to be staged again and again in order to keep the façade of the civil intact, the natural residuum in check, and thereby assure the stability of civilization.

The image of the dog body that encases the spirit of a dead person can be related figuratively to the *civil body*, the artificial person who possesses self and property, and to the *legal slave*, the artificial person who exists as both subject and object, who is both self and property. In juxtaposing these two conditions of being, I suggest that the potent image of a servile body can be perpetually reinvented. In this ritual, both legal slave and civil body are sacrificed to the civil order. Though both entities are legally distinguished from natural persons, civil bodies are governed by one set of laws and legal slaves by another. Different in position, in rights and in duties, they cannot be the subjects of a common system of laws. The distinctions between them, however, are fragile and ambiguous, and in a world where status, capacity, and honor are reinforced by exclusionary practices, the two conditions interrelate in crucial ways.

In reconstructing this narrative of human unfreedom, I analyze what happens to persons in two cases: the free person of property who commits a felony and undergoes civil death and the enslaved person, who, as bearer of "negative personhood," has undergone social death. In most instances, though the person declared civilly dead has property to lose, the slave never had property, is property in fact, and can never have any independent relation to property. But both of these characterizations possess juridical significance in so far as they recognize the individual as what the historian Edward Peters describes as "a kind of civil ghost."[4] Even the term *citizen*, defined in the Fourteenth Amendment, does not greatly clarify the distinctions between restraint and freedom, capacity and disability. Considering slaves and felons as two extreme states, I raise the unsettling possibility that these exceptions place the citizen who is both non-slave and non-felon in a fearful zone of legal ambiguity.

Rather than focus on the various and sometimes diffuse consequences of social marginalization, I trace instead a developing logic in modern law. By the eighteenth century, Judeo-Christian antecedents and inchoate traditions of punishment were redrawn and fully articulated as a rationale appropriate to the needs of emerging modernity. The law giveth and the law taketh away. The law kills and the law resurrects. Legal practice conflates symbolic control and the inscription of that control on real bodies. If the natural creature possessed of personal status dies not to be reborn in the spirit but in the body of civil society, what kind of body is this?

LEGAL SLAVES, CIVIL BODIES

In *Slavery and Social Death*, Orlando Patterson makes two crucial points that suggest the troubling power of legal authority. In his section "Property and Slavery," he argues against the habitual definition of the slave as someone without a legal personality: "It is a fiction found only in western societies, and even there it has been taken seriously more by legal philosophers than by practicing lawyers. As a legal fact, there has never existed a slave-holding society, ancient or modern, that did not recognize the slave as a person in law." Patterson proposes a theory of negative capability, but he remains silent about the disabling inherent in the legal action that invents a personality only to enslave, reduce, and exclude it. Subsequently, discussing what he calls "liminal incorporation," he writes: "Religion explains how it is possible to relate to the [socially] dead who still live. It says little about how ordinary people should relate to the living who are dead."[5]

Patterson refers first to the actually dead though alive in spirit, as opposed to the actually alive though dead in law; and, second, to the supernatural relation of the believer to the dead who do not die, as opposed to the forever quotidian if uncanny existence of the living person who is dead, who has undergone what the anthropologist Claude Meillassoux called "social death." This depersonalized individual is "marked by an original, indelible defect which weighs endlessly upon his destiny."[6]

Patterson's insistence that slaves in every legal code are treated as persons in law urges us to ask: When and in what way were slaves allowed to be persons? When resurrected as legal personalities, what can they do, what are their possibilities for recognition? And if, finally, Patterson distinguishes the secular ontology of civil life from the realm of myth or religion, what happens if we insist on bringing myth and legal practice back together? A new edge and urgency must be granted to the use of social death here, what one scholar calls Patterson's "agentless abstraction" and another "an academic artifact." Such a judgment is relevant to the historiography of slavery, but not to the powerful mythology that underlay it. Law's encompassing power depends on the manipulation of this nonrecognition that becomes, at the same time, a vehicle of prosecution.[7] In juxtaposing the "social death" of slaves with the "civil death" of felons, we recognize how statute and case law became more effective than social custom in effecting rituals of exclusion and in maintaining the racial line. These legal engines of dispossession, once systematized and firmly embedded in human affairs, were applicable everywhere and recognized by everyone.

What Patterson called the "violent act of transforming free man into slave" was institutionalized by law. For how could one have slaves without making them so legally? If the law did not deal explicitly with the slave in terms of "personhood," then the natural, inalienable rights of persons would devolve onto the slave. The legal strategy worked first to recognize slaves as persons and only then to deprive them of their inherent dignity, what they would otherwise be due by nature or under God. Slave law thus both created and contained the subject, as it scrutinized and redefined the person in law. For this legal nondescript, who had no civil rights to lose, could be deemed, when it served the needs of the owner, something that engenders affection and esteem.[8]

The racialized idiom of slavery in the American social order depended on the legal fiction of "civil death": the state of a person who though possessing *natural life* has lost all *civil rights*. Unnatural death as punishment for crime entails a logic of alienation. Its paradoxes, its oscillation between tangible and intangible, life and death allowed the law to recognize and legitimize political control. This powerful legal and public denunciation decrees the loss of any right whose exercise or enjoyment depends on a positive provision of law. What had been forfeiture of property and corruption of blood—those few circumstances in which civil death was coextensive with physical death— Blackstone noted as specific to the occupations of monks or members of religious orders. They were overlooked as if no longer in the land of the living. But abjuration or banishment on attainder for treason or felony also helped to create forms of punishment that laid the ground for a specifically colonial legal incapacitation.[9]

In the ancient common law there had been three principal results of attainder for treason or felony: forfeiture of property to the king; corruption of blood, which blocked the descent of property; and the extinction of civil rights, the incapacity to perform any legal function. Of Saxon origin, forfeiture was part of the punishment for crime by which the goods, chattels, lands, and tenements of the attainted felon were forfeited to the ruler. According to the doctrine of corruption of blood, introduced after the Norman Conquest, the blood of the attainted person was held to be corrupt, so that he could not transmit his estate to his heirs, nor could they inherit. According to Blackstone, this inequitable and "peculiar hardship" meant that the "chanel" of "hereditary blood" would not only be "exhausted for the present, but totally dammed up and rendered impervious for the future."[10]

Civil death remained distinct from other legal sanctions, since the concept and its attendant disabilities maintained both a strictly hierarchical order and the blood defilement on which that order depends. Corruption of blood operated practically as a severing of bloodlines, thus cutting off inheritance, but also metaphorically as an extension of the sin or taint of the father visited on his children. If we treat *blood* and *property* as metaphors crucial to defining *persons* in civil society, then it is easy to see how corruption of blood and forfeiture of property could become the operative components of divestment. By a negative kind of birthright, bad blood blocked inheritance. Whether slave or criminal, both are degraded below the rank of human beings, not only physically and morally but also politically.

In my pursuit of a conceptual framework for legal disabilities made indelible through time, I follow the call of *blood*, its meaning and effects, both literal and metaphoric, through three sites of disabling: from the feudal *attainder*, the essence of which was corruption of blood as punishment for crime; to its transport to the British colonies and its incarnation as the black taint that legally inscribed slavery; and finally to the disabilities of the post–Civil War period, when slaves were reborn as criminals and translated into "slaves of the state." I take the persistence of stigmatization as a *historical residue* that turns metaphor into a way of knowing and acknowledging history. This incapacitation continues to threaten the weak and socially oppressed with new, potent forms of discrimination and containment.[11]

In rereading the claims of civil death into the history of slavery and incarceration, we recognize the continuum between being judged a felon, being declared dead in law, and being made a slave. Blackstone referred to natural liberty as a "*residuum*," and he figured this residue of nature as a stain. The imprint of corruption becomes the legitimating metaphor for the sacrifice of the civil person. The metaphor of corruption must be grounded in public, highly visible fact in order for the figurative distinction of civil and natural to function in the realm of action.[12]

Blackstone's language thus connected the figurative nature and the material body: "For when it is now clear beyond all dispute, that the criminal is no longer fit to live upon the earth, but is to be exterminated as a monster and a bane to society, the law sets a note of infamy upon him, puts him out of its protection, and takes no further care of him barely to see him executed. He is then called attaint, *attinctus*, stained or blackened."[13] The image of this blackened person, disabled but not necessarily dead, remained as terrifying an example of punishment as the executed body. Moreover, the hereditary defect of blood and its consequences for the criminal's descendants became an alternative death penalty: they were not actually but civilly dead. Strict civil death, the blood tainted by felony, set the stage for blood "tainted" by natural inferiority. This discrimination would soon produce the nonexistence of the person in both the West Indies and the United States. The racialized fiction of blood also supplemented the metaphoric taint, not only defining slaves as property but fixing them, their progeny, and their descendants in that status.

Medieval legal doctrine held that the blood of the attainted person was, as I said, corrupt, so that he could neither inherit nor transmit his estate to his heirs. Thomas Blount explained in his 1670 *Nomo-lexikon: A Law Dictionary*, "Corruption of Blood" is "an Infection growing to the State of a Man (attainted of Felony or Treason) and to his Issue: For, as he loseth all to the Prince, or other Lord of the Fee, as his case is; so his issue cannot be heirs to him, or to any other Ancestor by him. And if he were Noble, or a Gentleman before, he and his children are thereby ignobled and ungentiled."[14]

How was this degradation enacted? To find out, let us turn to a history both spiritual and temporal: the reciprocal disabling firmly embedded in both legal fictions and religious fantasies. Depersonalization took place in the marketplace as well as on the sacrificial altar, through commercial transactions as well as religious rites.[15] The general concept of corruption of blood harks back to the curse put on David's enemy in Psalm 109:13–15: "Let his posterity be cut off; and in the generation following let their name be blotted out. Let the iniquity of his fathers be remembered with the Lord; and let not the sin of his mother be blotted out. Let them be before the Lord continually, that he may cut off the memory of them from the earth." In this banishing ritual, the enemy, his forebears, and his descendants lie under sentence of corruption of blood, turned base, ignoble, execrable, and thus barred from inheritance into the remotest generation.

The term *corruption* itself must be considered cautiously. Although it meant "vile contamination," "infection," or "pollution" in early English as it does now—to the point of acquiring in Nathan Bailey's *An Universal Etymological English Dictionary* (1770) the immediacy of stench, the visibility of blemish—its fundamental meaning remained in the semantic range of destruction, breaking up, dissolution, and decomposition. That is, corruption of the convicted person's blood meant not just that it was tainted but that it legally ceased to flow in either direction; corruption operated *"upwards and downwards,"* so that an attainted person could neither inherit lands or anything else from his ancestors, nor transmit property to his heirs.[16]

What is crucial about the definition of *attainder* is the way a probable mistake in philology became a convenient means of exclusion. The similarity of "tainted" and "attainted," especially in their past-participial forms, would make their blending almost unavoidable. *The Oxford English Dictionary* focuses on what became the gist of attainder—corruption of blood—through a false derivation of *attainder* in *taint* or *blemish*: "L. *attingere* to touch upon, strike, attack, etc.; subsequently warped in meaning by erroneous association with F. *taindre, teindre*, to dye, stain." Beneath an apparently inadvertent, false, or at least loosely mixed-up terminology in late medieval England lies an anatomy of disabling.[17]

Words, once repeated and recalled, are endowed with a resonance that tells the story of greed and racism operating over a long period of time. When did *taint* become allied with *attainder*? The idea of tainted, tinged blood—that venerable if illogical mechanism for exclusion in the slave laws of the Caribbean and the American South—can be traced back to a metaphysics that turned metaphorical blood into biological destiny. The duplicity in meaning—the blending of hit, touch, or knock with tinge or tincture to make stain, blemish, or contamination—suggests that this terminological history is one of cross-fertilization, and not of sequentiality. Corruption of blood in English law probably never had anything to do with ethnicity or biology, but everything to do with taking an attainted person's property to the exclusion of otherwise rightful heirs. In the late 1450s, the really harsh acts of attainder with the full legal force of corruption of blood came into frequent use. Who cared about the nil property that the poor or unlanded, such as blacks or any other potential slaves, had a century later? Nor would considering them and their progeny goods and chattels in themselves be legally relevant.[18]

But as slavery in the colonies became profitable, color soon functioned as presumption of servitude and proof of denigration. Extensive English participation in the slave trade did not develop until well into the seventeenth century, but alternative experiments in unfreedom—the subjugation of the Gaelic Irish, the Vagrancy Act of 1547, indentured servitude, and the English galleys—had already provided a template for domination. As early as 1562, Sir John Hawkins introduced the practice of buying or kidnapping blacks in Africa and transporting them to sell as slaves in the West Indies. According to Winthrop Jordan, the sight of blackness had a powerful effect on the English as soon as they landed on the shores of Africa. In 1578 George Best decided that the blackness of Africans "proceedeth of some naturall infection of the first inhabitants of that country, and so all the whole progenie of them descended, are still polluted with the same blot of infection."[19]

The phantom language of colonial stigma in the eighteenth century was expressed chiefly in terms of juridical incapacity. Though Blackstone denounced slavery, his description of the consequences of attainder presaged a novel inscription of race that built on an old language of criminality and heredity. If pardoned by the king, the attainted offender becomes "a new man" with renewed "credit and capacity," and can transmit to his son "new inheritable blood." Law can make one dead in life, and it can also determine when and if one is to be resurrected. The restoration in blood, even when not possible for the attainted himself, devolved on the innocent son, who could receive the transmission of new blood, and thus reincarnate the privileges of birth and rank his father had lost.[20]

Such promise of purification would not apply to those who suffered the perpetual obliteration of personhood and property understood as domestic slavery. For what had been forfeiture of property and corruption of blood for the rich and powerful became the terms for a categorical redefinition of legal incapacity for the poor and disempowered. Tainted blood itself, now no longer under legal quarantine, was transmitted through the generations. In this light, colonial legal history reveals how the construction of race (and its partner, racial stigmatization) served as the ideological fulcrum that allowed a penal society to produce a class of citizens who are dead in law: stripped of community, bereft of humanity.

GENEALOGIES

In the context of the eighteenth-century British West Indies and southern colonial America, the significance of blood becomes clear. Blood flows into enslaved bodies and racially marks them,

granting them legal recognition according to degrees of mixture: either advancing toward white or regressing toward black.
Emphasis on blood as conduit for the stain of black ancestry
became more necessary as bodies of color began to merge, losing the visible trait of blackness. The supremacy of whiteness
now depended on a fiction threatened by what one could not
always see but must always fear: through wanton *misalliance,*
black blood would not only pollute progeny but infect the very
heart of the nation.

Slavery in the colonies rendered material the conceptual, giving embodiment to what had been abstraction. The spectral corruption of blood found bodies to inhabit and claim. An idea of
lineage thus evolved and turned the rule of descent into the
transfer of pigmentation, which fleshed out in law the terms
necessary to maintain the curse of color. This brand of servility
had the magical effect of dislocation, moving law out of the civil
realm and into the savage, for colonial slave law was "not the law
of England, but the law of the plantations," according to the
lawyers in the case that abolished slavery in England, *Somerset
v. Stewart* (1772).[21] The argument smacks of the rather hypo-
critical shunting of impurity away from England's "air ... too pure
for a slave" (projecting dirt out from the "English garden" and
onto the "West Indian hell," as Rochester put it to Jane in *Jane
Eyre*). But the fact remains that the local laws of the English
colonies legalized extremes of dehumanization that harked back
to times Englishmen might well have judged barbarous, though
they continued to enjoy the fruits of the labor that such treatment made possible.

In *Democracy in America* (1835–40), Alexis de Tocqueville explained how exclusionary practices underpinned a society that
boasted of equality and consensus. Practices of domination hid
behind judicial virtue, along with an idealized federal Constitution that ensured and abetted "the affections and the prejudices
of the people." "The government of the Union," Tocqueville
wrote, "depends almost entirely upon legal fictions; the Union

is an ideal nation, which exists, so to speak, only in the mind, and whose limits and extent can only be discerned by the understanding."[22] Nowhere were the fictions forged in its name more pronounced than in the law of slavery. He compared the Europeans' legally ordained inequality with what he found in the United States, drawing attention to the difference between "imaginary inequality"—the "abstract and transient fact of slavery" among persons "evidently similar"—and the "inferiority" that is "fatally united with the physical and permanent fact of color." He concluded by asking: "If it be so difficult to root out an inequality that originates solely in the law, how are those distinctions to be destroyed which seem to be based upon the immutable laws of Nature herself?" Moreover, Tocqueville recognized that "[n]othing can be more fictitious than a purely legal inferiority." The degraded essence flows, like blood itself, in and out of bodies either literally or figuratively stigmatized, through the enslaved and the free, the legally dead and the metaphorically incarcerated.[23]

By the 1660s, perpetual and hereditary servitude had been formalized in the British North American colonies. With independence, the new United States maintained permanent, lineal bondage as the system of chattel slavery evolved and expanded. The epistemology of whiteness depended on the detection of blackness. Fantasies about hidden taints were then backed up by explicit legal codes, what Virginia Dominguez in *White By Definition* has called "de facto classification by ancestry." Unlike the Spaniards and French, who counted some 128 gradations of color from absolute black to absolute white, and named combinations such as the French *metis, mamelouque, marabou, griffonne,* and *sacatra,* the British in the West Indies used fewer distinctions, such as *sambo, mulatto, mustee,* and *octoroon,* and employed still less subtlety in law. Describing persons of mixed blood, Bryan Edwards in his *History, Civil and Commercial, of the British Colonies in the West Indies* (1793) warned that though discriminations of color are not easily made, the civil law is clear:

In Jamaica, and I believe in the rest of our Sugar Islands, the descendants of Negroes by White people, entitled by birth to all the
rights and liberties of White subjects in the full extent, are such
as are above three steps removed in lineal digression from the
Negro venter. All below this, whether called in common parlance
Mestizes, Quadrons, or Mulattoes, are deemed by law Mulattoes.

In the *Journals of the Assembly of Jamaica (1663–1826)* the adaptation of blood taint to the colonial experience is recognized:
"'corruption of blood' was visited upon 'not the sins of the fathers but the misfortunes of the mothers' unto the third and
fourth generation of intermixture from the Negro ancestor
exclusive."[24]

In colonial America by the eighteenth century, all persons
presumed tinged with black blood were legally mulatto. Here,
too, the term was never as precisely defined as in the French
colonies, where it meant not merely mixed blood (neither
wholly black nor completely white) but referred specifically to
the descendants of a white man and a *négresse* on a genealogical
scale of minute gradations of blood and nuances of color down
through eight generations. In the British West Indies, an octoroon, someone with one-eighth black blood, was legally white
and therefore automatically free (and if male, permitted to the
franchise and militia). Throughout the *Journals of the Assembly
of Jamaica*, we find motions to present bills that would entitle
free mulatto women and their children "to the rights and privileges of English subjects." Unlike Jamaica, some southern colonies
pushed the taint of Negro ancestry back four generations, from
one-eighth to one-sixteenth part black blood. These degrees of
blood, once distinguished and reinforced through the dubious
means of observation, rumor, and reputation, reinforced the
law's legitimation of whiteness.[25]

Emancipation, far from erasing the ancestral taint, gave it new
life and importance. The concept of blackness ensured racial
subordination and thus effected the continuation of enslavement
in other guises. The turn to blood was crucial to this strategy.

Blood provided a pseudo-rational system for the distribution of a mythical essence: blood = race. Once the connection was made, color could be referred to, but now it meant blood. Like the word *blood*, *color* is fictitious, but the law engineered the stigma that ordained deprivation.

LEGAL PERSONALITIES

Black slaves, regarded as outside the social order, reanimated legal precedent and gave new genetic capital to the principles of tainted blood. The sources of the legal rules and principles of slavery in the American South are much debated. Depending whom you read on the origins of slavery in the United States, Roman civil law and the colonial slave codes of the West Indies, the French Antilles, and the Spanish and Portuguese possessions all contributed to the composite rhetoric of disabling and protection in the statute law of the slaveholding states. Yet strategies of divestment were already present in the rights of property and privilege defined in the common law, which would later be tied to the definition of property in persons.[26]

The suddenness and speed with which the institution of slavery took shape in the former English colonies in continental America and the severity of the laws that guaranteed it are exceptional. In "Free to Enslave: The Foundations of Colonial American Slave Law," Jonathan Bush explains how nothing "remotely like a jurisprudence of slavery" emerged in the English colonial world; instead, "only one body of significant slave law existed in the English colonies: the incomplete and analytically inadequate colonial statutes." Though close to two million Africans had already been brought as slaves to the English colonies in the Caribbean and America, slavery "in legal contemplation" was not created until the second half of the eighteenth century. It had rather "simply evolved in practice, as a custom, and then received statutory recognition."[27]

To give birth to this new *person in law* was no easy matter. There was no legal precedent in Roman law, where the slave remained mere chattel (*res*). The feudal *villein* in England, though unprotected in his property, was not a villein, that is, "unfree" in the eyes of the law, *except* in relation to his master.[28] So, in what would become the southern United States, new forms of debasement were invented that both adapted and refined West Indian slave codes. The ethnography of personhood that emerged in some of the cases might seem to alleviate dispossession: the master had no power over life and limb; slaves were regarded as human beings with moral responsibility for crimes; and the letter of the law seemed to offer itself to the spirit of Christianity. But this civil ritual did not so much lessen the stigma of slavery as deepen it. Regulatory beneficence never acted as a defense against the tyranny of the master.

The slave, once recognized as a person in law, becomes part of the process whereby the newborn person, sprung from the loins of the white man's law—in a birth as monstrous as that of Victor Frankenstein's creature—can then be nullified in the slave body. For Thomas Cobb in *An Inquiry into the Law of Negro Slavery in the United States of America* (1858), the law's recognition depends on the alternately generative and destructive force of legal definition: "When the law, by providing for [the slave's] proper nourishment and clothing, by enacting penalties against the cruel treatment of his master, by providing for his punishment for crimes, and other similar provisions, recognizes his existence as a person, he is as a child just born." By invoking the double condition of the unborn and the undead, legal reasoning can eject certain beings from the circle of citizenry, even while offering the promise of protection. Once "brought ... within the pale of the law's protecting power ... his existence as a person being recognized by the law, that existence is protected by the law."[29]

Yet that existence is rigidly curtailed and qualified. When protection from cruel treatment is given, what are the terms by which such dispensation is defined? In *The State of Mississippi v. Isaac Jones* (1820), slaves are first defined as both "chattels" and "men." What happens to this trial of definition when crime is committed *against* a slave who is under the protection of the state? Can murder be committed on a slave, the court asks; and if not, why not? The court explains, returning to the archaic formulation of Saxon and Norman custom, "Taking away the life of a reasonable creature, under the king's peace, with malice aforethought, express or implied, is murder at common law."[30]

Reason is the crux here, but once attached to the slave, in what spirit is the word *reasonable* used? Justice Joshua G. Clarke's questions undo the personhood of the slave even as they appear to retrieve it: "Is not the slave a reasonable creature, is he not a human being . . ., for the killing a lunatic, an idiot, or even a child unborn, is murder, as much as the killing a philosopher, and has not the slave as much reason as a lunatic, an idiot, or an unborn child?" At the center of this rhetorical question lies the ostensibly uninhabited body, the cipher that waits to be filled by a cluster of beings that do or do not possess reason. Clarke claims that the law recognizes a powerlessness that actually exists, rather than effecting a removal of powers, as if the recognition does not create incapacity but merely confirms it. The apparent elevation of a piece of human property into the place of reason remains conditional. The dead slave gets the protection of positive law, but at great cost. In this ritual, the slave has been not only murdered, but gutted, dispossessed of whatever autonomy existed before the law recognized him. This radical qualification of legal identity is shored up by fictions of disability, which treat the figure of the slave as more or less human, not yet born and already dead.[31]

The ritual of civil death, which came into prominence in the United States as slavery was abolished, resurfaced as a literal and legal *via negativa*. The prisoner condemned to life imprisonment fell outside the boundary of human empathy: no longer recognized as a social, political, or individual entity. If we are to understand this apparition without mind and without will, we must think about the language used to portray such disfigured creation. Only then can we begin to understand how deperson-alization—the gradual dismantling of identity—works in contem-porary cases concerning imprisonment and its effects.

In *Avery v. Everett* (1888), to jump ahead for just a moment, the well-known case of civil death in New York, the negative principle acts as a new covenant. While the court held that the convict was not divested of title to his land as a consequence of his sentence to imprisonment for life, Judge Robert Earl's dis-sent is nothing less than a litany of dispossession. The depiction of the civilly dead prisoner is a rite of conversion. The change can be described as a passage from possession to deprivation, from plenitude to emptiness. The creature portrayed by Judge Earl can only be construed by removing from his grasp the priv-ileges or rights that bring enjoyment or ensure civil capacity.

> As the convict could no longer discharge any of his obligations to society, he was to possess no civil rights whatever. As he could not discharge any of the duties of husband or father, the family ties were severed. As he could have no use for property and no power to manage or possess the same, that was to pass away from him. He became civilly dead in the law, and *the law ceased to know or to take any notice of him.* He no longer possessed any rights growing out of organized society, or depending upon or given by law. As to all such rights he was *in law dead and bur-ied.*[32] (italics added)

At first it seems as if the incapacities listed here—obligations to society, duties of husband or father, use for property—result from imprisonment. After all, as the court in *Avery* recognized, statutory law in New York had "extended the consequences of civil death beyond what was understood at common law." But it soon becomes clear that Earl's diminishing mode has less to do with mere physical incarceration than with something mysteri-ous, suggested but not named. There is more to the procedure of taking, as Earl makes clear: "The life convict was not declared civilly dead in the law simply to deprive him of the right to vote, to sit as a juror, to bear arms, to marry and hold office, because his physical conditions were such that he could do none of these things."

Earl points to something intangible, a residue from a hidden past, something in the convict's nature which goes beyond "physical conditions," such as being locked away in prison. Earl does not say more beyond the physical fact of incarceration, but that unspoken something suggests that the prisoner lacks *the right to himself*. To be civilly dead is to be granted a natural life, while encased in unnatural death. The "person of a convict," once emptied by law, no longer needs to vote or do any of the things that other persons civilly alive need to do.[33]

The logic would go something like this: The convict, though actually a living being, is not only dead but buried by the law. The body is there, but restrained in prison. The external physical conditions are clear. The internal spiritual state is not. The physical person (solely body and appetite) has no personhood (the social and civic components of personal identity). What kind of spectral form remains? Those who actually die—as opposed to the civilly dead, the dead who do not in fact die but live in death—transform what we might mean when we say "supernatural." For the legal fiat is both routine and extraordinary. This highly stylized linkage of the commonplace and the unusual has tremendous staying power. What is more pressing, more spectacular than the realm of the flesh-and-bones ghost, the palpable specter watching over its own perpetual degradation?

SLAVES OF THE STATE

Slavery in the United States brought about a new understanding of the limits of human endurance, so that new, more refined cruelties could be invented. On the ruins of the rack, the thumbscrew, the wheel, and the iron boot, modernity constructed enlightened atrocities. In his *Commentaries*, Blackstone described how execution or confiscation of property without accusation or trial, although a sign of despotism so extreme as to herald "the alarm of tyranny throughout the whole kingdom," is not as serious an attack on personal liberties as "confinement of the person, by secretly hurrying him to gaol, where his sufferings are unknown or forgotten." For imprisonment, being "a less public" and "a less striking" punishment is "therefore a more dangerous engine of arbitrary government."[34] Civil death in the United States, first affixed to the blood of a criminal capitally condemned, later was understood to be a result of life imprisonment, a consequence rare at common law.[35]

Civil death set the terms for a new understanding of punishment. Slavery ended, but incarceration did not. Statutory law ensured that the "badges and incidents of slavery" continued to exist under cover of civil death. This legal fiction and the criminal ethnography it fostered miraculously remade persons.[36] When modern definitions of law responded to the theological split between the spiritual and the natural body by dividing the body into the artificial and the natural, something happened to personal identity. Slaves, though legally not *civil persons*, remained *natural humans*. When committing a crime, however, slaves were recognized as possessing a legal mind, a status for which they paid by being punished as criminals. And later on, criminals were punished with the degradation that had once been the lot of slaves, especially if the criminals were former slaves or descendants of slaves.

In New York the projected abolition of slavery was accompanied, hedged, protected, and evaded by means of laws that maintained and even extended certain aspects of it. According to the statute of March 29, 1799, a person convicted for felony and sentenced to imprisonment for life "shall thereafter be deemed dead to all intents and purposes in the law." A felon, thus condemned for life to the state prison, was placed under greater disability than at common law: his estate descended to his heirs as if he were actually dead. At the same time, the legislature passed the Gradual Abolition Act, devising a system of laws for the termination of slavery in New York. Yet as slaves were freed, the revised statute revived disabilities in a new civil context. On the one hand, the gradual abolition statute provided that children born into slavery, though still liable to be servants of the mother's owner, would henceforth be free. On the other, the civil death statute declared that a sentence of perpetual imprisonment entailed the loss of personal rights, including divesting the felon of property and dissolving his marriage, regardless of the desire of the felon or his wife, so that his wife and children owed him nothing.[37]

Chancellor James Kent, while applauding the end of slavery in New York, lamented the radical incapacities recently attached to life imprisonment. Statutory law, in extending *strict civil death* to prisoners, created incapacity where there had been none. And these radical disabilities, once attached to felons, were not, Kent confirmed in *Platner v. Sherwood* (1822), "declaratory of the common law, but created a new rule." Confessing to a mistake in judgment in the earlier equity case *Troup v. Wood* (1820), he condemned strict civil death, with its deprivation of property and the ban on inheritability that had never before been extended to persons condemned to life in the penitentiary.[38]

How is it that civil disabilities—and civil death, more or less extreme—have played so significant a role in the treatment of criminals in a country whose Constitution prohibits acts of attainder and forfeiture? In his dissent to the *Civil Rights Cases* of 1883, Justice John Marshall Harlan suggested how the "substance and spirit" of constitutional amendments had been "sacrificed by a subtle and ingenious verbal criticism" that connected the past prerogatives of the "white race" and the present presumption of the state.[39] Though Article 3 declares that "no attainder of treason shall work corruption of blood, or forfeiture except during the life of the person attainted," and Article 1 provides that "no bill of attainder or ex post facto law shall be passed," the numerous civil disabilities imposed on a convicted offender by statute perpetuate the spirit if not the letter of stigma. In some states, persons convicted of serious crimes are still declared civilly dead, and even if those words are not used, numerous civil disabilities sustain the convict's infamous status, often even after his or her release.

Human Rights Watch has linked the medieval sanction of "civil death" to contemporary U.S. disenfranchisement laws, which "may be unique in the world." The impact of these laws in the United States is striking: "In fourteen states even ex-offenders who have fully served their sentences remain barred for life from voting ... an estimated 3.9 million U.S. citizens are disenfranchised, including over one million who have fully completed their sentences." In the beginning of the twenty-first century, over 150 years after the end of slavery, 13 percent of African American adult males—1.4 million—are disenfranchised. At a rate seven times the national average, this represents "just over one-third (36 percent) of the total disenfranchised population." The prediction for future ex-criminal disenfranchisement rates suggests how black citizens in the United States, once convicted of crime, will be indefinitely excluded from the society in which they live: "Three in ten of the next generation of black men will be disenfranchised at some point in their lifetime. In states with the most restrictive voting laws, 40 percent of African American men are likely to be *permanently* disenfranchised."[40]

During Reconstruction, with the advent of convict-lease and the chain gang, the logic of subordination and disenfranchisement clarified the law of the New South. The felon inherited something like a double debt to society: if he belonged to an intermediate category between slave and citizen, he was also a synthetic or unnatural slave. An entity held between life and death, this body would then resurface in late nineteenth-century case law as the *human* who is no longer granted the moral sensibility and conscience necessary for *personhood*. From this perspective, it is possible to see how the shifting identity of the slave was reborn in the body of the prisoner.

In 1870, Woody Ruffin, an incarcerated felon, committed murder while working in chains on the Chesapeake and Ohio Railroad. Though the crime occurred in Bath County, Virginia, Ruffin was tried in the circuit court of the city of Richmond. Found guilty of murder in the first degree, he was sentenced to be hanged on May 25, 1871. On appeal, his counsel claimed that he had not been tried by an impartial jury "of his vicinage," as laid down by the Virginia Declaration of Rights, and subsequently taken up, in simpler, more detailed language in the Sixth Amendment of the Bill of Rights: "the accused shall enjoy the right to a speedy and public trial, by an impartial jury of the State and district wherein the crime shall have been committed." Justice J. Christian, delivering the opinion of the court in *Ruffin v. Commonwealth* (1871), portrayed the convict, no matter where he might be—whether in the county of Bath or the city of Richmond, whether working in the penitentiary or for an outside contractor—as "civilly dead," ever trapped in the "restraints" and "regulations" of the "eye of the law." A criminal punished with civil death became the "slave of the state," so that once incarcerated, the prisoner endured the substance and visible form of disability: the stigma of chain, the extinction of civil rights and relations.

Called on to define the condition of the convict and to consider the implications of civil death for the applicability of the Bill of Rights, Justice Christian decided:

> The bill of rights is a declaration of general principles to govern a society of freemen, and not of convicted felons and men civilly dead. Such men have some rights it is true, such as the law in its benignity accords to them, but not the rights of freemen. They are the slaves of the State undergoing punishment for heinous crimes committed against the laws of the land.

The prison walls circumscribe the prisoner in a fiction that, in extending the bounds of servitude, became the basis for the negation of rights, thus reconciling constitutional strictures with slavery.[41]

The power of competing analogies to redefine liberty permitted the conversion of slave into prisoner and prisoner into slave. *Ruffin* was decided in November 1871. Ratification of the Thirteenth Amendment to the Constitution had been announced in December 1865. Section 1 of the Thirteenth Amendment outlawed slavery and involuntary servitude "except as punishment for crime whereof the party shall have been duly convicted." This legal exception opened the door to terminological slippage: those who were once slaves were now criminals, and forced labor in the form of the convict-lease system ensured continued degradation. Such an amendment amounted to an escape clause, a corrective loophole that left a form of slavery intact.

During the second session of the Thirty-ninth Congress (December 3, 1866–March 3, 1867), debates centered on the meaning of the exemption in the antislavery amendment. In the very sentence abolishing slavery, provision had been made for its revival under another form and through the action of the U.S. courts. Senator Charles Sumner presented to Congress a notice posted by William Bryan, the sheriff of Anne Arundel County in Maryland:

> Public Sale.—The undersigned will sell at the court-house door, in the city Annapolis, at twelve o'clock, on Saturday, 8th December, 1866, a negro man named Richard Harris, for six months, convicted at the October term, 1866, of the Anne Arundel county circuit court for larceny, and sentenced by the court to be sold as a slave. Terms of sale, cash.

During the same session of Congress, other cases were presented to demonstrate that these sales were lingering relics of the black codes. In Georgia, an "old negro man, between seventy and eighty years old, a much-respected preacher of the Gospel," was arrested for vagrancy and put to work in chains for twelve months. In Maryland, twenty-five-year-old Harriet Purdy was to be sold for a term of one year in the state, and Dilby Harris, aged thirty, was to be sold for a term of two years in the state. No crime was mentioned in either of these advertisements for sale.[42]

Sumner objected to "the phraseology of the amendment," as "an unhappy deference ... to an original legislative precedent at an earlier period of our history." Fearing what he saw as the congressional sanction of servitude, he had still hoped that the phrase "involuntary servitude, except as a punishment for crime" applied only to "ordinary imprisonment." In other words, Sumner was trying to preserve the distinction between a felon—even a felon sentenced to hard labor—and a slave. He was also aware that this distinction was being eroded. Noting that what had seemed "exclusively applicable" had been "extended so as to cover some form of slavery," he asked that Congress "go farther and expurgate that phraseology from the text of the Constitution itself." Throughout the recently disbanded Confederacy, leased prisoners maintained plantations and rebuilt public places. Slave codes shaped the language of contracts for labor, and plantations turned into prisons. The new narratives of servitude and punishment were articulated by prison architecture, criminal dress codes, and the revival of the trappings of slavery—chains, dogs, whips, and other forms of corrective torture—in the New South.[43]

PREMATURE BURIALS

Confinement of prisoners in the United States became an alternative to slavery, another kind of receptacle for imperfect creatures whose civil disease justified containment. I do not mean that slaves can be equated with criminals, as if slavery were a form of punishment. Rather, I am interested in how, once convicted of crime, the criminal can be reduced—not by a master, but by the state—to a condition that is sustained under the sign of death. In the sixth century, the Emperor Justinian declared in his *Institutes*: "Slavery is death." He knew that death takes many forms, including loss of status so extreme that life ceases to be politically relevant. How, then—and this is the crucial question—can corpses be legally fabricated?[44]

Imprisonment allows us to apprehend how the condition of being *civiliter mortuus*, or "dead in law," marks the *disabled citizen* as both a symptom and a symbol of afflictive punishment. Unlike slaves, felons remain citizens: citizens who are restrained in their liberty. The character of prisoners, the alleged danger they pose to prison order, and the need for them to be transformed, all became part of the argument for the restriction of rights, for the negation of the social and spiritual self. This legal curtailment resonates with the ways ex-slaves were effectively deprived of civil rights and reduced to the status of incomplete citizens after emancipation. As far as those imprisoned for life were concerned, the idea was to emulate the results produced by natural death. Numerous nineteenth-century cases demonstrated the staying power of civil death, crucial not only to legal status but to personal identity, and to the sacrifice of that identity to punishment. Instead of explicitly abolishing the status of the person, civil death rendered the prisoner unable to exercise the rights attached to a person.

This resurrection of slavery is often discussed in the turn to convict labor and the criminalization of blacks in the postbellum South. But the penitentiary, zealously discussed and instituted in the North—termed "solitary," as well as "the discipline" or "the separate system"—offered an unsettling counter to servitude, an invention of criminality and prescriptions for treatment that turned humans into the living dead.

Before the abolition of slavery, William Crawford, in his *Report on the Penitentiaries of the United States* to the House of Commons in 1834, urged his audience to consider the criminalization of blacks in the North. He noted that a far greater proportion of blacks than whites were criminals, and concluded that these "oppressed people" were even more "degraded" in the free than in the slave states: "A law has been recently passed, even in Connecticut, discouraging the instruction of coloured children introduced from other States; and in the course of the last year a lady, who had with this view established a school for such children, was prosecuted and committed to prison."[45]

The Thirteenth Amendment marked the discursive link between the civilly dead felon and the slave or social nonperson. Criminality was racialized and race criminalized. The chiasmus that had once made racial kinship a criminal affiliation, once adjusted to the demands of incarceration resulted in a novel banishment and exile. This amendment, too often obscured by attention to the Fourteenth Amendment, is essential to understanding how the burdens and disabilities that constituted the badges of slavery took powerful hold on the language of penal compulsion. Once the connection between prisons and slaves had been made, slavery could resurface under other names not only in the South but also in the North.

How are prisoners turned into something other than civil persons? In this highly controlled practice of transmutation, both prisons and case law, in constant dialogue, not only turn prisoners into "slaves of the state" but recast them anew as civil nonentities. Solitary confinement as a means of reforming criminals is a peculiarly American invention.

Beaumont and Tocqueville, in *On the Penitentiary System in the United States* (1833), contrasted corporal punishment with "absolute isolation," a unique and severe punishment, warning that "this absolute solitude, if nothing interrupt it, is beyond the strength of man; it destroys the criminal without intermission and without pity; it does not reform, it kills." The depression, insanity, and suicide they observed led Beaumont and Tocqueville to contrast the "[p]unishment of death and stripes" for slaves with the separate system for criminals, implying that the unique deprivation fixed in the mind was crueler than corporal discipline. Although civil death might seem a more "decent" alternative to execution, this legal fiction molds the prisoner *as if dead* into the symbolically executed, proving in the words of Elisha Bates that the penitentiary "where no light enters, where no sound is heard, where there is as little as possible to support nature that will vary the tediousness of life, by change" might come to "be regarded with more horror than the gallows."[46]

The great and awesome symbol of solitary confinement was Eastern State Penitentiary in Philadelphia. Popularly known as Cherry Hill, it was completed in 1829 and immortalized by Charles Dickens in his *American Notes* (1842). In describing instances of radical depersonalization that amounted to a second death, Dickens suggested that the prison had become the materialization, the shape and container, of what had been the language of civil death. "The system here, is rigid, strict and hopeless solitary confinement. I believe it in its effects to be cruel and wrong.... I hold this slow and daily tampering with the mysteries of the brain, to be immeasurably worse than any torture of the body." Once the black hood literally covered the face of the criminal condemned to Cherry Hill, the long process of executing the soul began: "In this dark shroud, an emblem of the curtain dropped between him and the living world.... He is a man buried alive; to be dug out in the slow round of years; and in the meantime dead to everything but torturing anxieties and despair."[47]

The benevolent reformers of inhumane punishment co-opted the language of spirit in order to cover the undoing of mind. The practice of solitary confinement, with its spur to turn inward and redeem the old self in the new, actually put the mind in peril. In other words, once the prisoner was characterized as an entity in need of spiritual renewal, no disciplinary rigor seemed too harsh. Even the mental costs of solitary confinement could be forgotten in speculations about religious transfiguration. Fatal to consciousness, such a system of correction reduced the person to something on the fringes of this human world, excluded from recognition and significance.

Critics of the Pennsylvania "separate system" never hesitated to call it inhuman and unnatural. William Roscoe, the noted English historian, penal reformer, and ardent abolitionist, considered the system "destined to contain the epitome and concentration of human misery, of which the Bastille of France, and the Inquisition of Spain, were only prototypes and humble models." But Roberts Vaux, chief spokesman for the Philadelphia Prison Society and later a member of the Board of Commissioners appointed by the governor to erect Eastern State Penitentiary, responded to Roscoe in his "Letter on the Penitentiary System" (1827) by insisting on separation and silence as the only cures for the polluting threat of those whose "unrestrained licentiousness renders them unfit for the enjoyment of liberty."[48]

The language of contagion sustained the common-law definition of "corruption of blood" for the attainted felon, just as civil death maintained forfeiture of property and the degradation attached to that loss. As I noted earlier, though formally abolished in the Constitution, rituals of stigmatization never stopped; and following the abolition of slavery, more devious means of exclusion and containment came on the scene. Once systematized, the residue of past methods of punishment and the suggestive aura of taint ensured continued degradation, but under cover of civil necessity.

Francis Lieber, the abolitionist and lawyer, in the preface and introduction to his translation of Beaumont and Tocqueville's *On the Penitentiary System in the United States*, defended the penitentiary as a fit container for the "poisonous infection of aggravated and confirmed crime," "contracted" bad habits, and "moral contagion." The diseased body had to be rooted out from civil society, and, once expelled, the convict became the visible record of the sacrifice on which civilization maintained itself. Not only did the gradual annihilation of the person, disabled but not dead, dramatize a punishment arguably more harrowing than execution, but solitary confinement became the unique site for the drama of law.[49]

Ever since "the discipline" or "separate system" practiced in Eastern State Penitentiary in Philadelphia, the restraints of extended solitude have proved a more effective means of correction than corporal punishment. As early as 1787, Benjamin Rush, revolutionary America's leading physician, understood solitary confinement as a "benevolent and salutary" advance over public execution and the indiscriminate mingling of prisoners. In "An Enquiry into the Effects of Public Punishments Upon Criminals, and Upon Society," Rush argued against the "reformation of a criminal" through "public punishment." Rather than abolishing punishments, he chose to "change the place and manner of inflicting them." Whereas Blackstone, as we saw, warned against private punishment as a sinister accomplice to arbitrary government, Rush urged that society replace "certain and definite evil" with incarceration that was of "unknown" and indefinite duration in a remote "house of repentance." The unknowability of punishment's limits, as well as the loss of personal liberty, would, by increasing "terror," cure "diseases of the mind."[50]

In another essay, "An Enquiry into the Consistency of the Punishment of Murder by Death, With Reason and Revelation" (1797), Rush unwittingly revealed the questionable nature of what he deemed "the duties of universal beneficence." He argued that if "the horrors of a guilty conscience proclaim the justice and necessity of death," and if God inflicted these "horrors of conscience" as "punishment," then the most effective punishment humans could inflict would be to extend these torments through time, not curtail them by execution:

> Why, then, should we shorten or destroy them by death, especially as we are taught to direct the most atrocious murderers to expect pardon in the future world? No, let us not counteract the government of God in the human breast: let the murderer live— but let it be to suffer the reproaches of a guilty conscience.

He presumed that without any human contact the prisoner, in a kind of premature burial, ultimately might be reborn.[51]

Beaumont and Tocqueville wondered about the nature of this rebirth. They described it in terms that resonate not with Quaker renewal as receiving "light" in the "inward parts" or the possession of "inner light," but with the despair, fear, and personal effacement of Puritan conversion. First "agitated and tormented by a thousand fears," then succumbing to "the terrors" and uncertainty which nearly drive him insane, the inmate experiences "a dejection of mind" that promises not only "a relief from his griefs," but also a submission to the rules of the prison. The remaking of persons through solitary confinement appropriated the detailed, clinical analyses of the stages on the way to personal regeneration: the morphology of conversion that would become prescriptive in the evangelical churches.[52]

Instead of merely an abstract conviction of sin, these visible forms of conversion mandated what Jonathan Edwards, following the Puritan sequence, long before, had seen as the first stage in the alterations in one's mind that would ultimately lead to saving repentance, "evangelical humiliation," and a new identity. These "legal terrors," "legal distresses," or "legal strivings"—as Edwards recounts them in *A Faithful Narrative* (1736), his testimony of the Northampton, Massachusetts, awakening of 1734–35—bring persons, once "debilitated, broken, and subdued with legal humblings," to "a sense of their exceeding wickedness and guiltiness," as well as "the pollution and insufficiency of their own righteousness."[53]

DEATH IN LIFE

Nine years before his death in 1704, John Locke published *The Reasonableness of Christianity, As Delivered in the Scriptures*. In this radical, subversive encounter with the history of law and belief, he made an analogy between the torment of hell and the torture of secular punishment: "Could any one be supposed, by a law that says, 'For felony thou shalt die,' not that he should lose his life; but be kept alive in perpetual, exquisite torments? And would any one think himself fairly dealt with, that was so used?" We must find a way to understand how such a state of extremity as solitary confinement could have been devised as a humane answer to state-sponsored execution, how this misery worse than death was made legally sustainable by a religious subtext. Indefinite containment demanded a submission of *mind* that had been seduced by the carnal and its temptations. In returning to the Puritan understanding of the recognition of God's justice in the sinners' convictions, this lawful incapacitation brought divine dispensation into the prisons of the United States.[54]

When the state decided to punish criminals psychically without executing them, a bold reimagining occurred. Hell came into this world. The criminal was circumscribed by the walls of a cell, condemned to solitude, locked in torment. This second death, psychic and in a sense unnatural—for now, let us call it "soul death"—is brought about without the death of the body. The inversion of spiritual and material replaces the law of heaven with the law of earth. In the fiction of civil death, broadly understood, the state reinvents what happens after literal death. In a secular world, the enthusiastic embrace of something vague like the *soul's salvation* allowed reformers to point to an abstraction, thus masking the concrete object of punishment: the *mind's unraveling.*

Civil death triggered a magic that depends on the dubious exchange between natural and supernatural. Instead of dying in the body to be reborn in Christ, the felon dies in the spirit. The soul is killed before the body dies.

In the realm of the law's authority, the change from what must be done to the body to what is thrust upon the mind lays bare the ruins of personhood. The juridical now concerns itself most with the inmate's body (whether beaten to a pulp or kept intact). Legal action attends to what is bodily but ignores the diminishing of personal dignity, the loss of mental capacity. Like the sorcery that chains the spirit to dog flesh, juridical reason defines a new legal body that buries the mind, recognizing only the corporeal husk emptied of thought.

PUNISHING THE RESIDUE

But he remains in life to whom the mind
and intelligence remains. He may be a mutilated
trunk dismembered all about, the spirit removed
all around and separated from the limbs,
yet he lives and breathes the vital air.

—Lucretius, *De Rerum Natura*

STRAY DOGS

THE EXTREMITY OF CONTEMPORARY PUNISHMENT IN THE UNITED
States—practices (anomalous in the so-called civilized world)
of state-sponsored execution, prolonged and indefinite solitary
confinement, excessive force, and other kinds of psychological
torture—can be traced back to the country's colonial history of
legal stigma and civil incapacity. This terrain of disfigured personhood is everywhere. The "global war on terror" has facili-
tated the export of prison practices from the United States,
where over 2.3 million persons are now incarcerated, to other
locales of containment. In accounting for the continuity of these
landscapes of unfreedom, let us engage with the legal forces that
hover ghostlike on the ever-permeable limits between human
and animal. There is something far worse than being turned into
an animal. Naming that thing requires a great deal of thought,
since the persons redefined in law remain persons—even slaves,
as we have seen, though sometimes called "things," were always
"persons in law."

In *The Origins of Totalitarianism* (1950), Hannah Arendt, writing about refugees displaced after World War II, described the plight of the "rightless," forced to "live outside the scope of all tangible law," "out of legality altogether." She puts her discussion of what it means *to lose the right to have rights* in the context of the French Revolution's Declaration of the Rights of Man, which, "supposedly inalienable, proved to be unenforceable—even in countries whose constitutions were based upon them." Arendt then considers the plight of displaced persons, excluded from the most significant forms of community life. They lack recognition, intent, or responsibility. "Innocence, in the sense of complete lack of responsibility, was the mark of their rightlessness as it was the seal of their loss of political status."[1]

But can these rightless objects ever be *outside of law?* Even in the tortures of Guantánamo Bay, Abu Ghraib, or countless U.S. prisons here and abroad, secret and known, there is no such thing as a "legal black hole," as being "beyond the law." It all depends on *what kind of law* we are talking about. To the extent that probable cause and due process protections of the Constitution were ignored and abolished in service to the war on terror, the directive achieving such ends is illegal by any post–Magna Carta standard. Yet today legal boundaries are equated with the legitimacy of the government's goals. The ends are used to justify the means. Current practices of punishment in the United States derive not only from a colonial legal history that disabled the slave while inventing the legal person, but also from the thoroughly legalistic nature of the American system in general. It is not an absence of law but an abundance of it that allows government to engage in seemingly illegal practices. We need to explore this hyperlegal negation of civil existence.[2]

The negation of civil existence requires that a person be made "superfluous." To be made superfluous is to be outside the pale of human empathy. In Arendt's catalog of the deprived—the refugee, the stateless, Jews made rightless before being exterminated, and a Negro "in a white community"—what matters is that the legal status of these lost entities is *distinct* from that of the criminal. For unlike criminals, they exist without being allowed intentionality, responsibility, or liability. As part of exigent public concern, they seem to exist nowhere, in Arendt's inimitable words—"a stray dog who is just a dog in general." They "begin to belong to the human race in much the same way as animals belong to a specific animal species." The paradox involved in the loss of human rights is that such loss coincides with the instant when a person becomes "a human being in general—without a profession, without a citizenship, without an opinion."[3]

The negation also depends on rituals of knowledge. Before the state can punish, it must appear to know *what* is being judged. The rules of law and the leeway within them enact and enable a philosophy of personhood and create the legal subject. They also recognize forms of punishment that are activated for people of a certain "nature" or "character"—those labeled unfit, barbaric, subhuman, or "the worst of the worst."[4] Once categorized as such, and stigmatized as criminals or security threats, they can be restrained in their liberty, deprived of rights, and ultimately undone as persons.[5]

It is in the mind-destroying setting of the supermax penitentiary that the state attempts to take away awareness, will, and responsibility and thereby institute the superfluousness sanctioned by law. The legally binding incrimination of persons, not always linked to specific actions and offenses, recycles human materials as the anomalies of our new world order.[6]

THE LAWFUL PRISON

In 1996 I first walked through Special Management Units 1 and 2 (referred to as SMU 1 and 2) in the Arizona State Prison Complex–Eyman, just down the road from the Arizona State Prison Complex–Florence. Escorted by deputy wardens, I completed a series of interviews in an attempt to understand how the meaning of punishment changed once addressed specifically in terms of supermax confinement.[7] By examining these extreme forms of incapacitation, I hoped to learn how the bounds of human endurance had been tested, the limits of cruel and unusual punishment extended, and human treatment redefined.[8]

I visited the special security unit, popularly known as SSU, in SMU 1, the first supermax built in Arizona and the model for California's "Pelican Bay." Introduced to the SSU sergeant there, I immediately felt uneasy. He looked like a skinhead. I got confused. I never wrote down his name. I think he was as disconcerted by me. "Did they put any restrictions on you for taking photographs?" he asked. I answered that the only restriction regarded taking pictures of inmates. After that, another officer pressed further: "Who are you? Why are you allowed here with a camera? It's contraband in this unit. Are you writing a thesis?" My original escort, the officer who had taken me there, explained that I had "special permission." "She's somebody special." The overuse of the word *special* made me pause. I stood there thinking about the force of euphemism, the sinister if evasive language that imbued the place: "Special Operations Team" for those who carried out executions. "Special management units," "special treatment units," and "special housing units" for those with "special needs." And here I am, I thought, a "special" person with "special permission."[9]

Nowhere does the power of legality to ensure the extinction of civil rights and legal capacities become more evident than in the restricted settings of special isolation units. Prisons in the United States have always contained harsh solitary punishment cells where prisoners are sent for breaking rules. But what distinguishes the new generation of supermax facilities are the increasingly long terms that prisoners spend in them, their use as a management tool rather than as a means of discipline, and their sophisticated technology for enforcing social isolation.[10]

Conditions of confinement, not overtly as bad as the dank and filthy penitentiaries of old, are now accommodated to the neutralization of individuality. Punishment has been gradually reinvented as an alteration of mind. This change is as profound as it is legally illegible. It is as if with each court case, with each decision to make the prison more legal or to tailor its confines to constitutional expectations in the face of proliferating claims of cruel and unusual treatment, punishment became more refined and hidden, less vulgar and obvious.

What used to be called "solitary confinement" has now become the penal philosophy behind entire prison facilities, built to detain "incorrigibles" for indefinite periods of time. In *Hutto v. Finney* (1978), after hearing about all kinds of barbaric physical abuses and hellish conditions of confinement, the Supreme Court upheld a lower court's order limiting the length of stay in the punitive-segregation unit of the Arkansas prison system to thirty days.[11] But as long as confinement in isolation is identified as an "administrative" precaution, not as a "disciplinary" or "punitive" exercise, there is no agreed-upon time limit beyond which it can be judged cruel and unusual punishment. Expertise and professionalism mask the harsh effects of idleness and deprivation, the preferred "treatment" in these supermaxes.

When it opened in October 1987, SMU 1, a 768-bed structure, was considered the model of efficiency and security. The unit is a cement building of unremitting monotony. Skylights in the hall provide only indirect access to natural light. Each windowless cell is eighty square feet and is equipped with a built-in bunk and a toilet-sink unit. The doors of the cells are heavy-gauge metal. The cement walls and ceilings in the halls are unpainted. The computer system monitors each inmate's movement and opens and closes cell doors. Human contact is reserved for what is known as "cell extraction." When an inmate refuses a transfer to another cell or fails to return his food tray, four or five guards in riot gear immobilize him. Tasers and gas guns are used as "nonlethal weapons." Sometimes attack dogs are "sicced" on stubborn inmates who refuse to "cuff up" or pass their trays through the food slots. A prisoner in SMU 1, with whom I corresponded for a year in 1999, described how dogs are used "as punishment or psychological torture." "The dogs do attack us," he wrote, they are "sicced on us by COs [correctional officers] for minute things that could be handled by talking, or spray, but now more and more inmates become victim to unreasonable dog attacks." Inmates are then removed from their cells with restraints that include at a minimum handcuffs or belly chains (chains fastened at the back with cuffs for the hands). A small place for exercise, called the "dog pen," with cement floors and walls twenty feet high, virtually another cell, provides the only access to fresh air.[12]

SMU 1 was surpassed by SMU 2. Completed in 1996, it was renamed Browning Unit on June 2, 2008, in honor of Army Staff Sergeant Charles R. Browning, previously a correctional officer in SMU 2, who died leading a convoy in Afghanistan. Also a 768-bed unit, it cost taxpayers $40 million. Given the cost of building supermaxes, an official in Arizona joked, "Why don't we just freeze-dry 'em?"[13] The two-page leaflet introducing the public to SMU 2, "the most advanced maximum-security prison design in the nation," provides voluminous "Project Data," as if to emphasize its exhaustive security and massive restriction: the mechanical details and prodigious numbers lend an air of grandeur to this monument to incarceration.

> 390,690 cubic feet of concrete; 2,295,000 cubic feet of earth moved; 22,000,000 pounds of gravel; 11,000,000 pounds of asphalt; 2,363,138 pounds of reinforcing steel used in foundation and walls; 1,408,000 pounds of security steel used in cell door bars security systems; 254,000 masonry blocks placed on site; 1,100 security keys; 183,000 lineal feet of security caulking "no-pick" placed throughout the facility.

Situated on forty acres of desert, SMU 2 is surrounded by two rings of twenty-foot-high fence topped with razor wire, like a hazardous or nuclear waste storage facility. Held between the monotony of sand and concrete, the desert and the walls, I understood what the officers meant when they described the "no-frills" policy of the Arizona Department of Corrections (ADOC).

On one of my first visits, a correctional officer explained, "We razed the desert, bulldozed it, tore up anything that looked green." The extruded-steel cell doors are punched through with holes, making them look "like irregular-shaped Swiss cheese," in the words of an ADOC architect. The stainless steel mirror, sink, and toilet are fastened with adhesives that cannot be chipped. Nothing inside the cells can be moved or removed. Inmates sleep on a poured concrete bed. The water supply to the toilet and sink can be shut off from a nearby control booth. Some officers find that turning off the water after just a few seconds in the morning is a good way to discipline inmates.

The cell doors have traps through which food trays can be passed, when, as one deputy warden put it, "they feed." Second-floor hallways have steel mesh floors so that the hallway below is visible. Skylights intensify the spectacle of light and immaculateness. Cell doors are reflected in the ultra-shined floors, which the deputy warden praised as we walked through the halls during my first tour of SMU 2: "Looking good. Smooth as glass. From now on I'll have to wear sunglasses." Not only is the inmate isolated in his cell, but each cell is further isolated in a separate, steel-door-enclosed enclave of five or six similar cells. Officers and prisoners talk via intercom rather than face-to-face, giving new meaning to the policy of detention, incapacitation, and control.[14]

The room that controls all of SMU 2 is called "Count and Movement." On one wall is a list of inmates, matched with color codes. Making taxonomies for those incarcerated assumes the rightness of labels, the categorical certainty of description. SMU 2's mission statement explains what it means by "the state's most serious offenders": "extreme management cases, prison gang members, and violence oriented maximum custody inmates." The six categories are high risk, death row, protective segregation, security threat group, special needs (mental health), and the violence control unit (also called "special cautionary unit" in SMU 1).[15]

The more the law got involved in prisoners' rights, the more prison officials wielded the power to redefine these rights. A building that takes confinement, trauma, and suffering to their extreme is rationalized as a "general population" unit: the general population of those judged to be threats to security—known as "security threat groups"—and the worst inmates who either repeatedly offend or seem the types who might offend. Supermaxes depend on the typology of a particular kind of prisoner, one who has attained the status of "worst of the worst." Because of that status and the collective anonymity associated with it, an ever-broader population can be put in solitary confinement. In other words, those who have not violated prison rules—often jailhouse lawyers or political activists—find themselves placed apart from other prisoners, sometimes for what is claimed their own protection, sometimes for what is alleged to be the administrative convenience of prison officials, sometimes for baseless, unproven, and generally unprovable, claims of gang membership. The self-sustaining, self-extending character of these supermax structures underpins the obvious financial incentives that encourage their proliferation.[16]

Since the judicial involvement in the treatment and discipline of prisoners in the 1960s, both federal district courts and the Supreme Court have alternately extended and circumscribed the conditions deemed humanly tolerable. How did the Supreme Court change over time, ultimately deciding that the anguish of solitary confinement, its slow but relentless assault on the minds of inmates, was no longer a torment too cruel to be allowed? When did solitary-confinement advocates' belief that minds are, to paraphrase Jeremy Bentham, *subservient to reformation*, get recast as faith in locales for *incapacitation* and *retribution?*

With the William Rehnquist court (1986–2005), a number of cases began to systematically erode the scope of prisoners' rights claims advanced under the Eighth and Fourteenth amendments. Since then, a conception of prisoners' rights—the right to some minimal dignity—has lost out to the characterization of inmates as creatures dispossessed of any claims to personhood except what specific laws or regulations deign to confer upon them. These legal opinions construct a legal person who thus stands in a negative relation to law, with a status so degraded that psychic violence and sensory deprivation continue to pass constitutional muster. The judicial logic relies on the "subjective" expertise of prison administrators and "deference" to their special knowledge.

The Court has also redefined the limits of pain through a language of fastidious distinctions and equivocal formulae. The turn away from prisoners' enforceable rights and the language of rehabilitation was first signaled legally by Justice Rehnquist's opinion in *Bell v. Wolfish* (1979). In this case, the Supreme Court ruled that detainees who had been arrested and jailed, even without being tried or convicted, were subject to the same oppressive practices—such as intrusive body searches—as convicted offenders. The winnowing away of the substance of incarceration (what actually happens to the inmate) in favor of a vague if insistent pragmatics of forms, rules, and labels allowed increasingly abnormal circumstances to be normalized for the incarcerated.[17]

When prison officials renamed punitive or disciplinary segregation as *administrative segregation*, they were in conversation with judges who had been only too willing to blur the distinction between administrative custody and punitive isolation. The courts demanded due process procedures for disciplinary action, so prison officials called the segregation by another name. By this linguistic sleight of hand, they made the illegal legal. Administrative segregation meant that inmates were isolated just as harshly as before, with just as great a loss of privileges and threat of psychological harm, but with its new label their confinement escaped judicial censure. Rules in the Arizona State Prison Complex claim that "special management" is not disciplinary, since inmates in close management are not being "punished." Instead, they are sequestered in order to promote order and security. In thus dismissing the obvious connection between classification and disciplinary procedures, William Bailey, classifications specialist at ADOC, told me: "Classification is nonpunitive in every way. We only deal with the relative risk the inmate represents." In response to my continued questioning about due process claims, he explained: "They're not detention units, they're not punishment units, contrary to what inmates would like you to believe. They are general population units for the highest-risk inmates. In a lot of respects, they're just regular places."[18]

Contemporary terms and rules of judgment concerning punishment and victimization, as well as assumptions about what constitutes the entity called "prisoner," mobilize this drama of redefinition, where what is harsh, brutal, or excessive turns into what is constitutional, customary, or just bearable. Moreover, the language constructs a person whose status—and more precisely, whose very flesh and blood—must be distinct from the status of those outside the prison walls. The raucous public punishments of an earlier time have been transformed and intensified by legally permitted practices that isolate and dehumanize. An inmate in SMU 2 wrote to me, confessing to a shame made palpable and real: "If they only touch you when you're at the end of a chain, then they can't see you as anything but a dog. Now I can't see my face in the mirror. I've lost my skin. I can't feel my mind."[19]

THE CULT OF THE REMNANT

When I entered the special security unit of SMU 1—known as the SSU—my escort showed me a display of makeshift weapons made by prisoners. The deputy warden had asked officers to commemorate the damage done by lethal shanks made from bed frames or typewriter bars, darts made from paper clips wrapped in paper rockets, razors melted onto toothbrushes, and sharpened pencils. "An amazing assortment of weaponry, isn't it?" the young officer asked me. He then showed me a series of photographs of prisoners who had mutilated themselves—row after row of slit wrists, first-degree burns, punctured faces, bodies smeared with feces, eyes pouring blood. A sign above the photo exhibit read, "Idle Minds Make for Busy Hands."[20]

How do we read this display? The room is filled with the concrete reminders of the effects of legal incapacitation. The inmates have made their bodies the collective scene of disability, making visible what the law masks. Once the incarcerated are locked in vacancy, baffled and oppressed by control, expelled from the rudiments of life in society, they have entered the purgatory of civil death. If the fiction of civil death has been deemed *a creature of law*, what remains of the convict? Recall how in *Ruffin v. Commonwealth* (1871), Judge Christian created the "slave of the state," bereft of everything except what "the law in its benignity accords." [21] Once the prisoner is declared legally dead, all that the law allows is the unrecognizable person: the inexact and inelegant but nonetheless effective embodiment of brute matter. Now the savage effects of solitary confinement are offered to visitors as the material fragments, the leavings of the doomed.

In the SSU, we have the doubled figure of state and captive: the state that collects, photographs, and records the emblems of coercion, and the inmates who speak out of their disfigurement, giving utterance to the inhuman face of the law. These captives thus give an alternative history to the argument for "evolving standards of human decency" that ordained the journey out of darkness and into enlightenment. Instead, in their radical embodiment of civil death, inmates make the wounding of their bodies acknowledge and resist the mind's disabling. They have returned to the drawing and quartering, disemboweling, and bloodletting of old in order to testify to the continuation of these tortures in less visible forms.

The image of persons locked down in cells, where the senses are deprived (nothing to see, no one to touch, nothing to do), sets the stage for a peculiarly Cartesian drama. With his "Second Meditation," Descartes supposed: "I have no senses. Body, shape, extension, movement and place are chimeras.... I have no senses and no body. So what remains true?"[22] In the solitude of the special cell, inmates are left alone with their minds. But these thinking things do not have the luxury of ruminating on doubt, experimenting with the limits of thought thinking itself through. Incapacitation does not prove personal identity but validates insignificance. Yet in the inventiveness of self-mutilation, these captives externalize thought, inventing themselves anew, as they make mind matter.

IN THE DESERT

I had been helmeted and vested. When officers helped me to fasten the vest, its Velcro fasteners made me think of camping, and I blushed at the thought of adventure. Those who were locked down could only make themselves heard by screaming or banging on doors. What other choice did they have? The place itself determined the contours of the spectacle: a scene of the subnormal, where crime, guilt, or innocence no longer mattered. These profiles of indignity turned prisoners into objects of terror.

The correctional officers, so young and bright-eyed, seemed to delight in their jobs as escorts. The noise would be deafening, they warned. "When they see a woman, they'll scream obscenities. You'll think you're in the jungle. They'll bellow like beasts." I didn't hear a sound. The officer explained, "They're quiet now. They're wondering what's going on. It's not usual for a visitor to come through here. They're waiting, trying to see who you are." Another officer whispered: "This place is not like any other unit you've seen. You won't be able to see the inmates, but you'll hear them. Sometimes they scream." [23] I looked at the doors. I could not see through them. I thought only in clichés: "the silence is deafening," "the quiet of the dead."

The concrete settings for punishment reveal the inevitable connection between rites of degradation and legal incapacity. When I began research for this book in Arizona in the summer of 1995, rehabilitation had long since been supplanted by incapacitation. The old times of farming, good-time credits, and trusteeship were gone. Cell Block 2 in Florence had become a lockdown unit, and cases were being brought against conditions of confinement there. In court transcripts, I read about pigeon droppings, sparrows roosting, cracked and broken concrete, the lack of cooling and heating, the filth and bad plumbing, but also the indefinite isolation of inmates. "Hard time for hard men," a warden told me. Mike Arra, the department spokesperson who initially arranged my visits suggested that I forget about Cell Block 2, since it had been superseded by the "really impressive" super-maxes—SMUs 1 and 2. No more "garbage in the cells, dirty water, or leaks; everything just real empty and clean," he assured me.[24]

That same summer, then governor Fife Symington announced that chain gangs had *returned* to Arizona. Chain gangs had never existed there, but that did not matter, since chain was easily exploited by the "get tough on crime" politician. The trappings of post-Emancipation convict labor shifted from the New South to the contemporary Southwest.

A group of about twenty male inmates stand shackled. They carry hoes, sickles, and rakes. Eight correctional officers survey the scene. In what seems like a choreographed movement through dust, brush, and stones, I hear an officer shout, "Hard labor, get into it." They appear to be clearing brush and debris from the shoulder of the road between the interstate and the prison. But nothing that they remove or pile up makes any difference. The ground, as far as the eye can see, is nothing but dirt and gravel. They are ordered to clear one section of rocks, weeds, and waste, and then move on. After two hours, there is still no difference in the landscape, no matter how far they have walked, no matter how diligently they work.[25]

"Chain gang technology" was to be a means of instilling a "work ethic" in the inmates not inside the supermaxes, but it was an ethic that had no connection to personal growth or even the possibility of rehabilitation. Instead, officials celebrated the effects of "the public display of chain," described as "attitude adjustment" for those judged "incorrigible."[26] Instead of experiencing meaningful work, and gaining pride and personal satisfaction, chain crews experienced the inconsequence of labor. Hard labor had always been part of prison programs. According to an Arizona statute passed in 1983, inmates must work forty hours per week. Depending on custody level and classification, the kind of work and the amount of hourly pay vary. The chain crews, however, were a different kind of labor. Those on chain did not produce goods—for example, clothing, drivers' licenses, bedding, furniture, or crops—nor did they participate in prison construction, maintenance, or renovation.

Nowhere was the futility of pointless work so well demonstrated as in the internal hard-labor program. Inside the razor-wired exterior fences of the complex detention unit at the Arizona State Prison at Tucson, prisoners broke rocks with sledgehammers. Those who refused to work were chained to a rail as a disciplinary corrective. When I first saw the inmates at their labor, they were breaking small rocks spelling out the letters "CDU." Two months later, the men were still working, the words spelling out in even, smaller, broken rocks: "Complex Detention Unit." Some officers joked about the senseless exercise: "How many did they do today? Are they just busting on the same rock?" Then one officer admitted:

> They do a rock a week. Big rock to little rocks. And where do these rocks come from? We have literally to go to Fort Grant, load up a semi, and drag rocks here. You don't see any rocks in the desert, do you? They were to be used for rip-rapping the washes, for erosion control. But Pima County says they don't want them. These rocks are too little to do any good. We don't know what to do with these little rocks. What are we going to do with these rocks, now that we've got a whole lot of them?[27]

Earning self-discipline through "meaningful work" instills "an improved work ethic" in inmates, Arra assured me.[28]

This official narrative of rehabilitation through meaningful work bore no resemblance to the actual drudgery of nonproductive labor, nor did it reflect the smug pragmatism of prison administrators. There is no significance to chain other than its ability to stigmatize. But chain is not my subject. For, as I would soon recognize, the reinnovation of chain gangs occurred at the same time as the refinements of mind-killing solitude. But the penitentiary's practice of isolation had long added spiritual destruction to bodily degradation.

The Supreme Court has never judged that solitary confinement itself is an unconstitutional punishment. But in 1890, in *In Re Medley*, the Court described its effects:

> A considerable number of the prisoners fell, after even a short confinement, into a semi-fatuous condition, from which it was next to impossible to arouse them, and others became violently insane; others still, committed suicide; while those who stood the ordeal better were not generally reformed, and in most cases did not recover sufficient mental activity to be of any subsequent service to the community.

The judges' opinion not only admitted the terror of isolation but also considered how the removal to "a place where imprisonment always implies disgrace" branded the prisoner with a "peculiar mark of infamy."[29]

After years of analyzing the effects of supermax confinement on inmates' mental health, Harvard psychiatrist Stuart Grassian defined the environment as "strikingly toxic." What he has called "a specific psychiatric syndrome" caused by solitary confinement includes such symptoms as hallucinations, paranoia, and delusions. Inmates have difficulty remaining alert, thinking, concentrating, and remembering due to prolonged sensory deprivation.[30] During a *60 Minutes* episode on California's "Pelican Bay" broadcast on January 15, 1995, Grassian complained, "In some ways it feels to me ludicrous that we have these debates about capital punishment when what happens in Pelican Bay's Special Management Unit is a form of punishment that's far more egregious."[31]

Over a decade later, on March 18, 2009, Governor Bill Richardson repealed the death penalty in New Mexico. He told the story behind the "most difficult decision" of his political life. After going to the state penitentiary where he saw the death chamber, he visited the maximum security unit where offenders sentenced to life without parole (LWOP) would be held. "My conclusion was those cells are something that may be worse than death," he said. "I believe this is a just punishment." Though his words recall the spiritually inclined prison reformers who subjected prisoners to the living death of absolute isolation in early nineteenth-century Philadelphia, Richardson's sense of justice sounds more like vengeance without any hint of redemptive promise. The condemned live without hope of ever attaining freedom.[32]

CULTIVATED DEBILITATION

What is left of persons, once the law has finished with them? In choosing to focus on the mind's entombing in supermax confinement, my polemic is not against judgment per se but against the tendency in contemporary cases to reduce constitutional claims to the most basic terms: bodies emptied of minds, and hence of the defining qualities of personhood. Perhaps nowhere is the pressure to reclaim and return to an earlier kind of law more evident than in supermax confinement. To be turned into ghosts before actual death necessitated the redefinition of punishment. If one assumes that the criminal is civilly dead, with nothing intrinsic worth saving for posterity, without those intangible qualities that constitute what we know to be human, then punishment had to be retooled. A tormenting afterlife that makes no claims on the self is a limbo without end. No fear of mutilation or abuse, but the horrifying reality that there is nothing to fear. In this emptiness, terror is a welcome diversion and death an unrealizable desire.

The legal history of civil death provides a crucial ground for understanding how ostracism is materialized. But only the supermax in its evasion of constitutional claims has created the perfect crucible for transformation. Designed for basic necessities and nothing more, the structure itself dramatizes the minimal requirements of the courts. Awash in unnatural light, everything in the building—what can be seen and how, its location and design—promotes the control of deviance, the assurance of sameness. Its physical space marks the limits of social coercion, as it singles out those to be controlled. If mere physical survival is what matters, if "basic human needs" or the "minimal civilized measure of life's necessities" remains the bottom line for humane—indeed constitutional—treatment, then these immaculate cages embody this new penology of lack. They are locales for perpetual incapacitation, where obligations to society, the duties of husband, father, or lover, and the traits of and criteria for personal identity are no longer recognized, necessary, or validated.

In the new prison management practices, we confront a difficult metamorphosis. To incapacitate is to render incapable, to disable body and mind. Out of this death and dispossession, a new status of being is promoted and legitimated for inmates. The special management units in Arizona and supermaxes more generally entail a substantial modification in inmates' spatial and temporal framework of personal identity and memory. Since the body remains circumscribed in a passivity that has no analogy in normal daily life, the objects of understanding necessary to thinking can only be held onto in memory.

The residue of the past matters. But how long can the mind hold onto these fast-fading remains? In *An Essay Concerning Human Understanding*, published first in 1690, Locke described memory as a "tomb of dead ideas." But he knew that in time they erode into nothing. Once deprived of things to think about, of new impressions or sensations, what can one remember? Memory, preserving a continuous thought through time, is crucial to personal identity, as Locke defined it. If we take this definition as key to our reflection, then we see how this attention to mind and memory shaped the development of radical isolation in prisons. In *A Question of Torture* (2006), Alfred McCoy explains how "sensory disorientation" and the "control over human consciousness for its own sake" became crucial to the CIA's secret efforts to develop new forms of torture: "a hammer-blow to the fundamentals of personal identity."[33]

What lies beyond the blackened eye, the crushed skull, the scalded flesh? If the mind is attacked without relief, while the body is held in a cage, what can the law do about it? The relevant legal categories change upon imprisonment, when a person becomes human material no longer the subject of rights and duties. With refined, legally permitted methods imposing helplessness and persistent deprivation, the prison becomes the site for unheralded metamorphoses. Inmates have described their experience in solitary as *being shot into space*, or, as one inmate wrote me, "I get to watch as my mind gets disfigured beyond anything I can recognize."[34]

PROFANE METAMORPHOSES

The U.S. Constitution nowhere defines what a prisoner is, just as it never mentioned slaves. Slaves were instead called "persons" or "fugitives from labor." What does the word "person" stand for? Locke's *Essay* remains central to my exploration of how modern prison practices, like the dehumanization of slavery, depended on the construction of persons in law. By this I mean not the body or the soul, but the mind and reflection of those incarcerated: persons who think, remember, and can be held accountable. Personal identity thus lies in responsibility: "punishment is annexed to personality, and personality to consciousness."[35] If his *Second Treatise* remains the foundational text for the civil government of the United States—the understanding of the citizen, his rights and liberties, as well as the ideal of property—the *Essay* remains the foundational text for theories of mind, personal identity, and memory.

In the most controversial section, "Identity and Diversity," which he added only in the second edition of his *Essay* (1694), Locke defines a person as a "thinking thing," which can think the same in different places, even hypothetically in different bodies, even in "the little Finger." If it has the same thoughts, then it is the same person. As far as this consciousness can be extended backward to past actions, so far "that consciousness reaches, and no farther." Moreover, this *"Person"* is subject to law. "It is a Forensick Term appropriating Actions and their Merit; and so belongs only to intelligent Agents capable of a Law, and Happiness and Misery." What makes you a person then is the capacity to know the merit or demerit of your actions. Without accountability for past actions of good and evil, one can still be a "rational creature"—man, horse, or dog. All of these are identifiable by the shapes of their bodies, and by greater or lesser degrees of rationality. But what makes a person—and Locke implies that a dog with awareness might also be a person—is responsibility: the capacity to *appropriate* these past actions "to that present *self* by consciousness."[36]

If we turn for a moment to the definition of the slave as a *person in law*, we realize just how strange legal logic had to be in order to birth this being. For this piece of property became a person only in committing a crime. The crime proved consciousness, mind, and will. No longer disabled in law, the slave could be recognized as a thinking thing. He was treated as a person, capable of committing acts for which he might be punished as a criminal. It is quite possible, if we push this reasoning further, that all definitions of personhood, whether applying to a free citizen or a slave, rest ultimately on the ability to blame oneself.

Locke's isolation of the mind prompted penal reform and underwrote solitary confinement in the United States in the nineteenth century. Once the materials of thought are removed, memory alone is left, and nothing comes through the portals of the senses.

Discussing what the mind needs in order to grow into reflectiveness and maturity—gain *"Perception, Remembring, Consideration, Reasoning"*—Locke connects mental incapacitation, the loss of an inward life, with the lack of external sensations. He asks us to imagine a fetus in the womb as nothing more than a vegetable. But as time passes, perception and thought come together to animate the senses. With that movement out from a place "where the Eyes have no Light, and the Ears, so shut up, are not very susceptible of Sounds," the mind awakens and "thinks more, the more it has matter to think on." As long as there are no outward objects, and "little or no variety" to impinge on the senses, the mind has nothing to perceive, and hence nothing to think about. Within the bounds of vacancy, the mind empties itself of thought, or in Locke's superb compound, where there is no sensation, there are no ideas.

Locke's words, though certainly not his intent, were taken up by Benjamin Rush when he promoted solitary confinement in the 1780s. When Rush argued against capital punishment, the old practices of drawing and quartering and other physical mutilations had already ended. But no matter, any extinction of life was inhumane, according to Rush, for it ended the possibilities of recovery. The new system of penal death and rebirth that he encouraged, however, threatened the very personality of the incarcerated.[37]

Rush's claims of curative isolation and rebirth miscarried, given actual accounts of psychic disintegration and insanity. In the battle between the evil of the flesh and the grace of the soul, between the outer and the inner man, a gruesome splitting occurred. Rush's secular punishment mimed but misunderstood the Pauline tension—one that Locke depended on—between the fleshly body and spiritual body, caught up between the material and the immaterial. The penitentiary, in thus splitting the man into two parts, initiated a new kind of death. Locke's analysis of the mind's operations thus became the unwitting template for perfect sensory deprivation. The soul drops out of the equation, and as in Locke's considerations, what is left is body and consciousness: the shape of a man and the identity of the person.

In conditions of radical isolation, only the external shape remains, while personal identity—what makes you recognize yourself as yourself—is annihilated. You are then something other, watching over the death of what you once knew, the gradual decay of all that made you part of the world: "For, it being the same consciousness that makes a Man be himself to himself," Locke wrote, "*personal Identity* depends on that only."[38] As we will see, contemporary alterations of consciousness called "behavior modification" or "mind control," though still disingenuously cast as rehabilitation, are experiments in deprivation that cause what William James described as "the shrinkage of our personality, a partial conversion of ourselves to nothingness." No longer to be able to think of oneself as thinking—or to recast this dilemma slightly, no longer to be thought about at all—is, as James described it, to inhabit a status of the hypothetical: *as if* dead, these selves *know* something worse than natural death, the continual aftershocks of a death both legal and social: "If every person we met 'cut us dead,' and acted as if we were nonexisting things, a kind of rage and impotent despair would ere long well up in us, from which the cruelest bodily tortures would be a relief."[39]

The policy of transforming persons into cadavers has a long legal history and depends on the terms of the dialogue between prison regulations and the law. As elsewhere in this book, we are about to find that legal decisions bring about unlooked-for consequences.

However, before we encounter these consequences, it is worth considering what might have been. For all its apparent dependence on the past, the legitimating potential of the law sometimes relies on radical disregard. Useful precedent may be ignored. I turn to what I consider a phantom decision that in fact was never given life by the Supreme Court. By focusing on its ghostly promise, its lost potential, we can begin to think about what has not yet been actualized, what has instead been forgotten in current juridical models of accountability.

In *Laaman v. Helgemoe* (1977), Judge Hugh H. Bownes of the United States District Court for the District of New Hampshire held that confinement at New Hampshire State Prison constituted cruel and unusual punishment in violation of the Eighth Amendment. The far-reaching relief order articulated the broadest application ever of the Eighth Amendment to prison conditions. Following this decision, which focused on conditions of incarceration that made "degeneration probable and reform unlikely," the Supreme Court changed its own policy of considering prisoners' intrinsic worth and enforceable rights. The stage was set for the strangely malleable *allowable suffering paradigm*, announced in Justice Rehnquist's opinion in *Bell v. Wolfish* (1979), discussed earlier.[40]

Though much attention in *Laaman* was paid to the physical characteristics of the cell, such as inadequate lighting, poor ventilation, and lack of sanitation, this inhabitability had its extension and analogue in the argument against debilitating methods of incarceration itself. Judge Bownes condemned "enforced idleness" as a "'numbing violence against the spirit.'" Warning against the practice of placing inmates in "cages with nothing to do," Bownes emphasized the loss of self-worth "inherent in such a degrading experience":

> The experts confirmed the old saying that idleness is the handmaiden of the devil.... Enforced idleness is a "numbing violence against the spirit," and causes good work habits to atrophy. It leads to degeneration because it severely undermines self-confidence, and the natural reactions to lowered self-esteem are either mental illness or antisocial behavior.[41]

Bownes perceived in the law what many of his contemporaries ignored: protective power. When does this protective power yield to rites of vengeance, practices that target the offender's self-respect? It is this damage that concerns me. American legal culture, especially Supreme Court jurisprudence, casts a cold eye on the mental suffering of prisoners.[42]

SHRINKING THE SPIRIT

In June 2000 the *New Yorker* ran an ad that I tore out and carried with me as I moved from Tucson to Philadelphia and then to Nashville. Toyota advertised its new Avalon—"The most spacious, luxurious sedan we've ever created"—picturing the interior, seats in opulent leather and a man sitting comfortably behind the wheel. Along the top of the two-page spread were the words "Confine the Body and You *Shrink the Spirit*." When the ad appeared, I had been visiting SMUs 1 and 2 in Florence, Arizona—just about an hour's drive from Tucson—for four years.

What the ad described as the "elegantly appointed cure for claustrophobia" seemed timely, if obscene. It appeared at a moment when prison administrators and politicians were urging the public to support these very expensive and cramped high-tech units. I kept thinking that "shrinking the spirit" seemed an appropriate euphemism, since everyone knew how extended isolation could drive prisoners crazy. Not only because of the stressful environment of solitary confinement but also because of excessive harassment and abuse by officers wound as tightly as those they confined.

I corresponded with inmates whose experience in SMU 1 and SMU 2 made me understand what it meant to live with minimal physical requirements—food, clothing, warmth—but without much else. This lack included other personal, perhaps more devastating forms of dispossession. One inmate lamented the loss of his own paintings and the photos he had never received from family and friends. I still have his letters. "This system is all about taking away and not giving," he wrote. "They do what they want, take what they like, destroy what they want, and hurt who they want, and they face nothing for it." On the wall I looked at charcoal drawings, watercolors of fiery women, delicate etchings of flowers or forests. The officer boasted: "They beg to send this art home to their families. Maybe they spent a month or two doing it. But we take it and hang it on this wall. Once they're in SMU, it's not their property. These guys are suspected gang members. There's gang symbolism in these pictures."[43]

How much, I wondered, can you take from a person without running afoul of the law? This game got very depressing. As long as prisoners are deemed threats and too dangerous for the general population—in other words, as long as officials classify them as such—the courts do not judge indefinite isolation as cruel and unusual punishment, nor do they find this confinement "atypical and significant" enough to satisfy the need for due process protections. Once officers substitute the word *administrative* for *disciplinary*, they invent a way of life: a tough regimen of enforced idleness and monotony that supposedly answers the needs of security. "Security," a deputy warden remarked, "is not convenient."[44]

What does it mean to be stripped of life-giving illusions? How much can be taken from prisoners without destroying what Justice Thurgood Marshall once called their "human quality"? Or to put it more precisely: How far can the courts of the United States go in curtailing the constitutional rights of prisoners? What is the residue of rights for those convicted of crime and restrained in their liberty? Does the Constitution even apply to prisoners? We would like to think that it does, but case law has eaten away the requirements of due process and the applicability of the First and Eighth amendments to prisoners.

Though the language of rights is perilously abstract, the practice of taking them away is very concrete. And the effects of that removal are visited not merely on the bodies, but especially on the minds of prisoners. It is perhaps too easy to think of criminals as "brutes," or in the words of one prison director as "lazy bums," or in those of an attorney general, as "Hannibal Lecters." But the texture of society is diminished if not brutally undermined when our prisons begin to make exaggerations literal. Politicians from Barack Obama to the lowliest candidate for local office still gain popularity from "get tough on crime" attitudes. They justify their cowboy toughness by labeling inmates, by calling them names and qualifying them for a new legal status. A warden I once interviewed in Florence, Arizona, was only too eager to typecast inmates while addressing what he considered my "liberal" bias: "Now, you coin this as a 'get tough' posture. I don't think that's real tough, to say: 'Murderer, you're illiterate, you're a dummy; you opted to be a criminal because it was easy for you.'"[45]

What happens when a society gives substance to its own rhetoric, being to a metaphor? Dehumanization is not easy to accomplish. And not all those incarcerated in supermax units are dangerous and violent to themselves or others. Many of the inmates I have known who live in extraordinarily brutal conditions continue to resist the images others have of them. They want to read. They think of ways to get books. "I am an inmate of the Arizona Department of Corrections," began a letter I received in 1999, sent to the Department of English at the University of Arizona. "I am starting a program to help other inmates who want to better themselves to learn to read and write."

On June 28, 2006, in the case of *Beard v. Banks*, the Supreme Court decided that denying newspapers, magazines, and personal photographs to prisoners in level 2 of the long-term segregation unit (LTSU 2) at the State Correctional Institution of Pittsburgh—the prison's highest security unit—did not violate the First Amendment of the Constitution. The next day in *Hamdan v. Rumsfeld*, the same Court granted prisoners at Guantánamo Bay the right to habeas corpus protection. It ruled that the military commissions created by the Bush administration failed to conform to Common Article 3 of the Geneva Conventions, which required a "regularly constituted court affording all the judicial guarantees which are recognized as indispensable by civilized peoples."[46]

The proximity of the two cases, despite their differences, is notable, and forces us to reconsider our assumptions about human rights and the extent of their applicability in domestic and international law. Domestic prison cases are remarkable in their prophetic potential. They prepared the ground locally for the United States' treatment of prisoners at Abu Ghraib, Guantánamo, and other as-yet-unnamed detention sites. Seven Supreme Court cases, decided from 1976 to 1994, about which punishments count as cruel and unusual—and which do not—

were cited in the torture memos of the Bush administration. Yet they continue to be ignored, although their legal reasoning shapes policies critical to the current radical substitution of penal for civil life, not only in the United States but in other countries which are either willing or unwilling recipients of our attention.[47]

WORDS BEHIND BARS

The events that produced *Beard v. Banks* were initiated in April 2000. The Pennsylvania Department of Corrections decided to increase its control over prisoners held in LTSU 2 by placing extreme restrictions on reading, as well as on possession of personal photographs. Prison officials had decided that newspapers could be dangerous. While LTSU 1 is reserved for the "most incorrigible" and "recalcitrant" inmates, LTSU 2 housed the worst of these intractable prisoners, who were categorized as threatening to inmates and correctional officers or belonging to a "Security Threat Group" or other unauthorized organization.[48]

Prisoners in LTSU 2 were isolated twenty-three hours per day in their cells, denied radio and television broadcasts, and prevented from earning a General Education Diploma (GED) or taking special education classes. They ate alone and could not make telephone calls except in emergencies or in regard to legal representation. Unable to speak to or socialize directly with other inmates, they stared at the unpainted, concrete, windowless walls onto which nothing could be posted. Except for the occasional touch of an officer's hand as they were handcuffed and chained to leave their cells, they had no contact with other human beings. Although prisoners could "graduate" out of LTSU 2, the duration of their stay—beyond the minimum requirement of ninety days—was at the discretion of prison administrators, and most did not graduate. In this already severely restricted environment, the new Pennsylvania DOC policy categorically prohibited access to magazines, newspapers, or books, except paperbacks from the prison library—called "leisure books" in

"LTSU Rules and Regulations"—and books of a legal or religious nature.[49]

Prison officials offered two reasons for this sweeping restriction of prisoners' First Amendment rights. Newspapers, they said, could be wound up, turned into projectiles, used as nightsticks, or used to make fires and hide contraband. Moreover, these officials argued, the deprivation of personal photographs and secular periodicals rehabilitates prisoners. Since they like to read about current events and look at photographs of their loved ones, the reasoning goes, if you take these things away, recalcitrant prisoners, those "who have few other privileges to lose," will behave.[50]

In October 2001, Ronald Banks, serving a life term for murder, filed a civil rights complaint in the U.S. District Court in Pittsburgh, on behalf of himself and other prisoners in LTSU 2. He questioned the policy's constitutionality after correctional officers refused to deliver his *Christian Science Monitor.* The suit he brought hinged on some deeply important questions. Do prisoners have a free-speech right under the First Amendment to read secular newspapers and magazines? Or should access to such reading material be a privilege granted at the discretion of prison officials?

The history of First Amendment jurisprudence concerning the incarcerated is a protracted contest between reasonableness and irrationality, between the necessary and the arbitrary. What we trace in these opinions are the changing conceptions of the aims of incarceration, the rights of prisoners, and most fundamentally, the extent to which prisoners are regarded as *persons* in the law. The rules of law carry with them philosophies of personhood. How far rights of expression, or other capacities deemed necessary to civil life, are granted to prisoners necessarily affects and reflects how society sees their status.

What are the legitimate rights of the state concerning the interests of the incarcerated? The Supreme Court's effort to navigate this territory—to define the rights of prisoners and the limits of legitimate regulations—began more than thirty years ago, with a case involving personal correspondence. In *Procunier v. Martinez* (1974), the Court held that the First Amendment did not allow administrators to censor prisoners' personal mail. The majority opinion took prison officials to task for failing to show how the regulations furthered "an important or substantial governmental interest" in security or rehabilitation: how, they wondered, could certain kinds of expression used in letters —notably complaints and grievances—lead to riots, and how might this "suppression of complaints" lead to rehabilitation?[51]

In a concurring opinion joined by Justice William Brennan, Justice Thurgood Marshall argued that "prisoners are ... entitled to use the mails as a medium of free expression not as a privilege, but rather as a constitutionally guaranteed right." Censorship amounted to nothing less than what he called an "artificial increase of alienation from society." He concluded that the First Amendment protected the needs of "the human spirit—a spirit that demands self-expression." Such an affront to dignity could not be tolerated. "When the prison gates slam behind an inmate, he does not lose his human quality; his mind does not become closed to ideas; his intellect does not cease to feed on a free and open interchange of opinions; his yearning for self-respect does not end." Justice William Douglas concurred with Marshall here, arguing that "prisoners are still 'persons.'"[52]

There are certain things about personhood, about what it means to be a person, that are not lost after a conviction. But how far is the reach of personal identity, if criminals are legally degraded—placed under disabilities very like those suffered by slaves? Not only do they lack the civil capacities of free citizens while in prison, but given the nature of the deprivations enacted in recent First Amendment cases (prohibition of reading materials, educational programs, religious practice, and family association), they may face a degraded status even when free. As we have seen, many states have disenfranchisement laws for ex-felons, and some authorities argue that these incapacities follow explicitly from the forfeiture of rights for convicted criminals declared in the Thirteenth Amendment. But I am concerned with the less obvious effects of the series of legal decisions considered here. Taken together, they are lessons in how supposedly lawful prisons become gulags of the unfit and expendable.

In *Turner v. Safley* (1987), the Court determined that prisoners had a right to get married. But the Court went further, setting forth a general standard for rules that restrict inmates' constitutional rights: "[W]hen a prison regulation impinges on inmates' constitutional rights," the *Turner* opinion read, "the regulation is valid if it is *reasonably related to legitimate penological interests*" (emphasis added). In order to establish the reasonableness of prison officials' actions, the Court asked whether there is "a 'valid rational connection' between the prison regulation and the legitimate governmental interest put forward to justify it." Three other factors may be considered in determining the reasonableness of a particular regulation: whether there are alternative means of exercising the right open to inmates; the effect on guards and other inmates of accommodating an asserted constitutional right; and the absence of ready alternatives to the regulation. In the case of inmate-to-inmate mail regulations, the majority decided that, to the extent that prison administrators thought it necessary, these restrictions were valid.[53]

One week after *Turner*, Chief Justice Rehnquist, writing for the majority in *O'Lone v. Shabazz* (1987), applying *Turner's* reasonableness standard, decided that Jumu'ah, the Friday assembly for communal prayer, though central to Muslim practice, was not important enough "to sacrifice legitimate penological objectives to that end." According to Rehnquist, Muslim inmates had other ways to express their faith. Ignoring the particularity and indispensable nature of Jumu'ah, he presented a list of alternatives, such as early breakfast and late dinner during the month of Ramadan and observance of Muslim dietary restrictions. For a Muslim, however, these are not optional substitutes. All are required. But, unlike other rituals that can be performed individually, Jumu'ah is not only obligatory, it must be performed in congregation.[54]

Justice Brennan, joined by Justices Marshall, Harry Blackmun, and John Paul Stevens, dissented. They complained that officials had not demonstrated how observance of Jumu'ah threatened prison security. They were especially troubled by the use of "reasonableness" as a standard for adjudicating constitutional challenges by inmates: surely a rule that, for example, prevents prisoners from reading at all should be subject to a more demanding standard than a rule restricting the times when prisoners can go to the library. As Brennan explained:

> The Constitution was not adopted as a means of enhancing the efficiency with which government officials conduct their affairs, nor as a blueprint for ensuring sufficient reliance on administrative expertise. Rather, it was meant to provide a bulwark against infringements that might otherwise be justified as necessary expedients of governing.[55]

For Brennan, rights matter even for those whom he admits "most of us would rather not think about." Though prisoners exist "in a shadow world," they come into the light when they make a constitutional claim. And when they do, Brennan observes, "they invoke no alien set of principles drawn from a distant culture." Their world is our own, and Brennan concludes, "They ask us to acknowledge that power exercised in the shadows must be restrained at least as diligently as power that acts in the sunlight." The Bill of Rights, and especially the First Amendment, as applied to the states through the Fourteenth Amendment, replenishes to some degree the personal identity that prison takes away. Justice Sandra Day O'Connor, in the majority opinion in *Turner*, even warned that prisoners' rights must be considered: "Prison walls do not form a barrier separating prison inmates from the protections of the Constitution."[56]

In 1996 the Court decided in *Lewis v. Casey* that law libraries and legal assistance were not necessary for the constitutional right of access to the courts. Seven years later, the Court in *Overton v. Bazetta* (2003) unanimously upheld broad restrictions of inmate visitation rights. Here, the justices shifted the emphasis away from prisoners' rights—whether in support or contempt of them—and toward theories of suitable punishment. In a concurring opinion, Justice Clarence Thomas, joined by Scalia, was particularly forceful on this issue. For the condemned, he argued, the general principles of the Constitution must be narrowly interpreted. The force of Thomas's opinion lies in how it dismantles, step-by-step, earlier cases that had preserved some rights for the incarcerated. For Thomas, a person found guilty loses nearly all rights upon imprisonment. Whatever happens after the sentence, no matter how harsh the confinement, does not violate the Constitution.[57]

Criminality is the bane. Deprivation is due. "Rather than asking in the abstract whether a certain right 'survives' incarceration, the Court should ask whether a particular prisoner's lawful sentence took away a right enjoyed by free persons." Thomas then focuses on the history of the American penitentiary. Nineteenth-century practices of what he calls "imposed isolation," though recognized as harmful, humiliating, and cruel settings "for the 'deviant' (i.e., criminal)," he reclaims as models for the Court. More than a hundred years after the Supreme Court in *In re Medley* (1890) argued that solitary confinement was so damaging to prisoners that it not only drove them mad but did not reform, Thomas offered it as a model for correction.[58]

In the majority opinion, Justice Anthony Kennedy granted "substantial deference" to the prison officials' professional judgment and held that a regulation that barred prisoners who had twice committed drug infractions from *any* family visits, including noncontact visits, for at least two years did not violate "the First Amendment right to freedom of association or the Eighth Amendment prohibition against cruel and unusual punishment."[59]

What alternatives to visits from loved ones are available to inmates? They could write letters. Or if that did not work, since many inmates are illiterate (approximately 40 percent of the national prison population is functionally illiterate), they could make phone calls. But those are limited to a few minutes and are costly: the exorbitant rates resulting from bribes paid by telephone companies to correctional facilities can force family members to pay up to a 630 percent markup over consumer rates for collect calls.[60] "Alternatives to visitation need not be ideal, however; they need only be available," the Court declared in *Overton*. In concurring with Justice Kennedy's opinion, Justice Stevens with Justices David Souter, Ruth Bader Ginsburg, and Stephen Breyer reminded the Court that the decision, in spite of its triumph for prison officials, did not break with the warning in *Turner*. They repeated O'Connor's words: "'Prison walls do not form a barrier separating prison inmates from the protections of the Constitution.'"[61]

Since both Justices Antonin Scalia and Thomas had been instrumental in gutting the substance of the Eighth Amendment when applied to prisoners, their reliance on it in *Overton* is especially sinister: "States are free to define and redefine all types of punishment, including imprisonment, to encompass various types of deprivations—*provided only that those deprivations are consistent with the Eighth Amendment.*" In his concurrence with Kennedy, Stevens warned that making First Amendment claims inapplicable for prisoners—the thrust of Thomas's concurrence—resurrected the idiom that could again make the prisoner "a mere slave."[62]

TO READ, PERCHANCE TO THINK

On October 22, 2003, the Philadelphia-based Third Circuit Court of Appeals heard oral arguments in *Banks v. Beard*. Jere Krakoff, a well-known civil liberties lawyer, represented Ronald Banks and the other prisoners; Senior Deputy Attorney General Kemal Mericli represented Pennsylvania. They appeared before Judges Julio M. Fuentes, Max Rosenn (a Nixon appointee who died while still in office, on February 7, 2006, at ninety-six), and Samuel A. Alito Jr. In a lengthy telephone interview with me in 2007, Mericli clarified the question that mattered most to him at the time: "Could we satisfy one burden of proof by calling on a deputy warden and relying on his claims that the regulation is reasonable?"[63]

Judges Fuentes and Rosenn were shocked by such an amorphous and apparently ill-defined test. They pushed Mericli hard to clarify the Pennsylvania Department of Corrections' draconian policy depriving inmates of access to newspapers, magazines, and personal photographs. Mericli sent me tapes of the oral arguments, even though he was the target of Fuentes's and Rosenn's dissatisfaction, not to say exasperation. The judges clearly shared Krakoff's concern about the dangers implicit in such a sweeping restriction of prisoners' First Amendment rights. Didn't Pennsylvania have other ways of achieving its aims? How did prison officials define "religious" as opposed to "secular"? Why permit the *Christian Science Monitor Magazine* but not the *Christian Science Monitor?* "But if religious material is also a part of First Amendment rights," the judges asked, "why deprive them of regular reading material?" Mericli answered: "We think they are not so depraved as to fling human waste with the Koran or set fire to the Bible." Krakoff intervened, "But I'm Jewish, and we used the *Jewish Daily Forward* to wrap up and throw out garbage." More damning, however, was Rosenn's pressing question to Mericli: "Do you have any evidence that ratcheting up the deprivation corrects behavior?" Mericli replied: "We don't, but we have an expert opinion by a recognized authority. That's all we need, according to *Overton v. Bazetta.*"

Siding with the prisoners in its decision in 2005, the court found no reasonable relationship between the ban on newspapers and photographs and any "legitimate penological interests of institutional security and prisoner rehabilitation." In the judges' opinion, the policy did not meet *Turner's* reasonableness test. As they wrote, "inmates are not requesting unlimited access to innumerable periodicals but for the ability to have one newspaper or magazine and some small number of photographs in their cells at one time." They also found that the only deposition in the case, the testimony of Joel Dickson—supervisor of the restricted housing unit, which included LTSU 2—did not support this "deprivation theory" of rehabilitation. The very idea, they argued, was "illogical." Nor, they continued, was there "evidence in the record of the misuse of periodicals or photographs in any of the ways described by the DOC. There was no testimony as to the frequency of fires in the LTSU, nor testimony about any particular fires, in or out of LTSU segregation, and how and with what materials they were set and fueled." The same was true for the materials' potential use as weapons.[64]

Judge Alito dissented. The majority, he argued, "misapplied *Turner.*" Sanctions for prison misconduct could be justified without empirical evidence as long as the regulation provided "some incremental deterrent." *Turner*, he wrote, required only a "*logical connection* between the regulation and the asserted goal," not "empirical evidence that the regulation in fact serves that goal." According to Alito, the majority did not grant enough deference to prison officials' judgment. Their best-guess theories are enough, when pushed "as a last resort," for "the most disruptive and dangerous" prisoners. Nominated by President Bush for the Supreme Court eight months after this dissent, Alito recused himself when *Banks* reached the Supreme Court.[65]

How could a newspaper shaped into a "blow gun," "spear," or "catapult" for human waste be such a threat when used by a man in a cage, a prisoner confronted by uniformed officers? There must be some reason beyond bald claims of security and rehabilitation. Why would inmates be less likely to use religious newspapers for "nefarious purposes" than secular ones? Why couldn't an inmate use writing paper, a prison handbook, blankets, bedsheets, or legal periodicals for fires? As the majority noted in its opinion: "We fail to see ... how an inmate's hour-long possession of *Graterfriends* would require further monitoring when at any time that inmate may be in possession of 10 sheets of writing paper, and as many copies of the *Watchtower*, the *Jewish Daily Forward*, and the *Christian Science Monitor Magazine* as can fit in a records center box."[66]

But perhaps there is method in the apparent madness. Level 2 inmates can read leisure books or romances but are prohibited from reading anything that refers to current political or social events, anything that would allow them to remain informed citizens. The district court had claimed that the ban was "not a blanket prohibition" because if the inmate behaved appropriately, he could be promoted to LTSU 1. But the onus on the prisoner to behave well is misplaced or futile, since, as the appeals court noted, this "promotion" is not really under the prisoner's control. Isolation in LTSU 2, after all, "is not linked to a particular infraction, and is of potentially unlimited duration."[67]

Something horrific occurs in this kind of punishment, something more perhaps than what Mericli described as "getting them to obey the rules." The court's central concern was the ominous leeway prison officials had to decide the *kind of thought* possible or necessary for those categorized as the "worst of the worst." How do prison officials understand cognition when it refers to prisoners? As this case remarkably demonstrates, the mental capacities and intellectual desires of those labeled as "incorrigible" remain below the threshold of concern.[68]

On March 27, 2006, a little more than a year after the Third Circuit decision, Pennsylvania went before the Supreme Court to defend its policy. The crucial question was how far a prison can go in removing the right to receive publications, to read, to be free to inquire and think, if its officials believe such deprivation enhances prison security and encourages inmate rehabilitation. During oral argument, the reasonableness of the restriction —and the seriousness of the issue—was lost in mockery. Justice Scalia sarcastically asked how one might use a "newspaper as a weapon: I mean, you know, maybe disciplining a dog or something." Or, as he quipped during Krakoff's argument: "Do you know what kind of a fire you can make with the Sunday *New York Times*?"[69]

Early in the oral argument, the justices were concerned about what limits should be placed on states that set up supermax units for inmates deemed "incorrigible." But by the end of the argument, several justices were willing to give Pennsylvania credit for trying to change its worst-behaved inmates. Louis J. Rovelli, who appeared for the state of Pennsylvania in Mericli's place, told the justices that the policy is reasonable because inmates can "earn back" the privilege of receiving newspapers and magazines, as well as personal photographs. The state, he insisted, wants to "turn these inmates around."[70]

What kind of conversion does he intend? So complete an annulment of choice, masked by claims of self-improvement, bewildered Justices Stevens, Kennedy, Ginsburg, Breyer, and Souter, who seemed unsympathetic to this line of argument. Asked by Stevens how long inmates could remain in LTSU 2, Rovelli responded that they are there until "their behavior improves." Ginsburg asked about the "rationality" of allowing "paperbacks from the library and not current events." And Breyer found it difficult to understand the security problem if "he's there in leg irons looking at the books."[71]

The Bush administration, represented by the solicitor general's office, supported Pennsylvania, arguing that in matters of prison order and security the Court should defer to official expertise. In his questions for Jonathan L. Marcus, assistant to the solicitor general of the U.S. Department of Justice, Justice Souter worried that the withdrawal of a First Amendment right was not really reasonable but instead an "exaggerated response": "I don't see where the logical stopping point is if we accept the—the behavior modification theory." He pursued his query: "It seems to me that whether we admit it or not, we're making some kind of a judgment as to whether they're carrying the deprivation for behavior modification purposes in these extreme cases too far."[72]

Justice Scalia then asked whether "just because a right is enumerated, it means it cannot be entirely taken away in prison." Marcus argued that only two rights cannot "be limited or even totally prohibited within prison": access to the courts and cruel and unusual punishment. And Justice Ginsburg pressed: "Apart from these two . . . then anything goes for this set of incorrigible prisoners. They can take away—the First Amendment, in other words, is out the window. They have no First Amendment rights that the State needs to respect?" Marcus turned again to behavior: "Pennsylvania does give prisoners the opportunity to regain those privileges if they behave well." For First Amendment rights to be legitimately abridged, he argued, "the connection between the regulation and the goals need merely be logical."[73]

The justices' initial skepticism dissipated completely when Chief Justice John Roberts began questioning Krakoff. Appearing before the Supreme Court for the first time, Krakoff stumbled as he tried to convince the justices that the policy should be struck down. In his respondent's brief, he had argued that the deprivation brought before the Court was nothing less than a "comprehensive suppression of knowledge." "The practical implication of the Department's ban," he had written, "is to literally wall these inmates off from the contemporary world."[74]

Now before the Court, Krakoff could not sustain his argument. Roberts pushed him to identify options for prison officials, to clarify the difference, for example, between depriving inmates of television rights and taking away newspapers and magazines. In response, Krakoff seemed to suggest that prison officials should simply give up the fruitless effort to control inmate conduct. He began to list the things whose removal had not worked as incentives for improvement in less restrictive long-term segregation units—telephone calls, weekly family visits, group activities, and so on. To which Roberts replied, "So your response is they should just grin and bear it." Krakoff agreed. "There comes a time when you take away so many things from these prisoners that you basically—yes, you may have to give up and you may have to keep them in segregation." Kennedy thought there must be some option other than "forgetting about him altogether." And Breyer, initially sympathetic, became impatient, pressing Krakoff, "So far your argument is they're so bad that you might as well give them whatever they want because it won't matter."[75]

Though prison officials made an exception in the reading prohibition for religious and legal materials, Krakoff returned once again to the definition of "religious." The *Christian Science Monitor* is forbidden, the *Jewish Daily Forward* is not: "I suppose ... that the *Jewish Forward* can burn as quickly as the *New York*

Times, that the *Christian Science Monitor*—." At that point Roberts snapped, "Now you're making their situation worse because they tried to make your client's situation better." The hostility was palpable and reflected a willful avoidance of Krakoff's attempt—even if faltering—to expose the apparent gratuitousness of what prison officials claimed as reasonable. Prisoners, Krakoff opined, "could read about the—an ancient war in the Bible, but they couldn't read about Iraq." By the end of the argument, Kennedy also turned on Krakoff: "You're depriving the State of the—of the option to avoid the most extreme circumstances of forgetting about him altogether forever. And it seems to me that—that your—argument is—is at cross ends with its own purpose."[76]

Despite the concerns raised in oral argument, the Court's decision approved indefinite confinement in LTSU, without even requiring a lower court to examine the facts. Justice Breyer wrote the opinion, which Chief Justice Roberts, Justice Kennedy, and Justice Souter joined. Though Justice Alito took no part in the decision, the Court validated his dissent in the Third Circuit Court of Appeals. Breyer's decision focused on the "professional judgment" of prison officials and argued that, using the *Turner* framework, the policies reasonably furthered "legitimate penological objectives." The Court argued that the Pennsylvania Department of Corrections had shown not just a "logical" connection but a "*reasonable* relation" that put its policy "within *Turner*'s legitimating scope." Citing *Overton*, the Court concluded that there was simply no other way to "induce compliance with the rules of inmate behavior, especially for high-security prisoners who have few other privileges to lose."[77]

Justice Thomas, concurring in the judgment and joined by Justice Scalia, dismissed *Turner* as useless and returned to the approach he had laid out in *Overton*. The Constitution does not contain "an implicit definition of incarceration"; and, except for minimal Eighth Amendment claims, it does not apply in prisons. He then returned to his exemplary history of "incarceration as punishment," calling it "traditional" and finding much to praise in the radical disciplinary regimes of the Eastern State Penitentiary (Pennsylvania) and Auburn (New York State) prison models. Though both experiments were condemned for driving prisoners mad, Thomas concluded that they were proof that isolation, denial of reading materials, and deprivation of family contact are appropriate methods of punishment.[78]

Conditions of confinement understood as belonging to a heinous past and with no purpose beyond the retributive became, in Thomas's approach, a new foundation for prison practice. Freedom of speech and the press are central to the First Amendment, and the deprivations permitted in *Beard v. Banks* are far-reaching in their effects. The amicus brief of the ACLU had argued: "To deny prisoners all traditional outlets for learning about political affairs and other news is to deny their very citizenship—i.e., to say that because they are deemed 'recalcitrant,' their knowledge and understanding on matters of public affairs no longer matter." With such a possibly boundless rationale as deterrence, what would prevent officials from depriving inmates of all First Amendment rights, especially if that deprivation allegedly served the purpose of behavior modification?[79]

David Fathi—former senior staff counsel for the ACLU National Prison Project, current director of the U.S. program at Human Rights Watch, and principal attorney in numerous prison cases over recent decades—was outraged by the decision. He later told me,

> The prison policy at issue here is unique and unprecedented: a long-term and indefinite deprivation of virtually all news from the outside world. It is a deliberate attempt to strip prisoners of the most fundamental attribute of citizenship, and even of personhood—the right to know, to learn, and to think about what is happening in the community, the country, the world.[80]

One person's reasonableness is another's madness. In his dissent, Justice Stevens, joined by Justice Ginsburg, warned the Court that the prison regulation "comes perilously close to a state-sponsored effort at mind control." Arguing against its rationale—even when applied to prisoners deemed the most "dangerous and recalcitrant"—he emphasized the dangers in the policy's possibly limitless applicability: "It would provide a 'rational basis' for any regulation that deprives a prisoner of a constitutional right so long as there is at least a theoretical possibility that the prisoner can regain the right at some future time by modifying his behavior." As of 2000, three-quarters of LTSU 2 inmates had been held there for more than two years. Justice Ginsburg put the implications of that level of control into stark relief: "Prisoners are allowed to read Harlequin romance novels, but not to learn about the war in Iraq or Hurricane Katrina." Such "indefinite deprivations" force us to ask again whether complete cognitive restructuring is the ultimate aim.[81]

For the Court, talk of private experience and subjective mental states has become irrelevant. We are far from the days of the Warren court, when attention to psychological anguish, dignity, and human worth mattered. But imprisonment is, of course, a highly abnormal condition, and nowhere as much as in supermax units that isolate behavioral expectations from the realities of normal human experience. Thoughts and emotions are wrenched out of any meaningful context. Instead, helplessness, extreme isolation, and other mechanisms of incapacitation are incorporated into incarceration. Tools of mind alteration are now dubbed "rehabilitation." So with the emphasis on "reasonableness" the courts endorse techniques that force inmates outside the precincts of thought and feeling but leave no marks on the body.

Legal interpretation requires that we recognize how new taxonomies of criminality are being created. In the harrowing conditions of indefinite solitary, the treatment fulfills the assumptions of the state. Abandoned to depression and despair, branded as incapable or irresponsible, these inmates are to be fashioned anew: not reformed, but undone. In removing the social and emotional conditions necessary for agency, radical isolation creates the stigma of ineligibility. Craig Haney, who has spent years studying the psychological assault of supermax confinement, describes the "feeling of unreality," the blunting of perception, the threat of noxious transformation, the "extraordinary—I believe often needless and indefensible—risks to take with the human psyche and spirit": "[T]he virtually complete loss of genuine forms of social contact and the absence of any routine and recurring opportunities to ground one's thoughts and feelings in a recognizable human context leads to an undermining of the sense of self and a disconnection of experience from meaning."[82] What seems arbitrary is instead behavioral readjustment, a project to annihilate individual identity through sensory deprivation.

At the end of a conversation with Deputy Attorney General Mericli, I was assured that in spite of the Supreme Court decision in *Beard v. Banks*, things were not so bad for prisoners. What do they need, after all? "These people are not savants, are not intellectuals, they're not at the Brookings Institution, they're not professors. I don't know what their life is about. What they are, to my mind, they're prisoners in a prison.... " But he demurred, "Thank goodness we've decided that a prisoner is a human being and not a slave of the state. You don't take their humanity away from them. You don't deprive them of basic needs."[83]

What kind of human being? This deprivation does not harm the body but seizes upon the mind, as Justice Stevens wrote: these prisoners are "essentially isolated from any meaningful contact with the outside world." He warned: "[T]he rule at issue in this case strikes at the core of the First Amendment rights to receive, to read, and to think." Are there not other ways to control those who, as the Court recognized, have little else left to lose, from whom nothing much remains to be taken away? Before our discussions about *Beard v. Banks*, Mericli had written me, "It helps to keep all 'brief authority' in perspective to note that once the tumult and the shouting died and the captains and the kings departed the DOC proceeded to quietly abolish LTSU 2 last March." As it turned out, the whole affair—from policy formation to litigation in the nation's highest court—was "just one more penal experiment." The experiment did not work.

Prisoners were not rehabilitated, or, in Mericli's words, "It wasn't working as a system that changed behavior."[84]

But even if that particular lockdown unit is gone, the legal precedent remains. *Beard v. Banks* has retooled punishment and status for prisoners in the twenty-first century. Commonsense reasoning is pulled apart from commonsense experience. The obviously deleterious effects of deprivation are reckoned to ensure a safe prison and a rehabilitated prisoner. So the unreasonable becomes reasonable when the worst excesses are rationalized as necessity.

Annulment of personal dignity anticipates the radical qualifications of identity examined in the next chapter. Throughout legal history the trade-offs between persons and property make the grossest violations of personhood not only necessary but acceptable. New entities in law are codified, but the logic in these procedures sometimes borders on the bizarre. Its fictions have the most striking effects in our social and political experience. Penal incapacitation in its many forms is accompanied by fabulous taxonomies that rework the distinctions between human and inhuman, predator and victim, virtue and vice, even flesh and spirit.

TAXONOMIES

When we reflect on the nature of these men, and their
dissimilarity to the rest of mankind, must we not
conclude, that they are a different species of the same
genus? Of other animals, it is well known, there are
many kinds, each kind having its proper species
subordinate thereto; and why shall we insist, that
man alone, of all other animals, is undiversified in
the same manner, when we find so many irresistible
proofs which denote his conformity to the
general system of the world?

—Edward Long, *The History of Jamaica* (1774)

CONSIDER THE CATTLE

NEAR THE END OF MELVILLE'S NOVEL *ISRAEL POTTER* (1855), ISRAEL,
the disabled and dispossessed beggar, wanders through the streets
of London. In these last pages, no longer depending on the biography that had given shape and structure to most of the novel,
Melville envisions another kind of history that combines fantasy
and horror. Ostensibly describing the "mud and mire" of brick-
making, after he has recalled a drowned slave at the bottom of
the Dismal Swamp in tidewater Virginia, he portrays a crowd
streaming "like an endless shoal of herring, over London Bridge,"
laborers trudging over the flagging of London streets as if on
"the vitreous rocks in the cursed Gallipagos, over which the
convict tortoises crawl." Animals play a key role in his depiction.

In order to tell the story of inhumanity, he depends on what is assuredly not human.[1]

In the final chapter, titled simply "Forty-five Years," Melville condenses Israel's long wandering in the "London deserts" into just a few pages, as if the sufferings he endured were so great that only a few images and scenes could be recounted: the smoke-darkened pits, the earthly dungeons of the brick kilns, the rag-picking and poverty. Then, Israel is granted a reprieve, if only for a moment. He roams into a patch of green, an enclosure in St. James's Park: "a little oval, fenced in with iron palings, between whose bars the imprisoned verdure peered forth, as some wild captive creature of the woods from its cage." This is the scene for what Melville, with impressive understatement, calls "a sort of hallucination."[2]

As with so much of Melville's writing, there is no escape from the torment of confinement, the disgrace of barbarous treatment, whether inflicted on animals or humans. And he invites the connections between animals, slaves, Indians, prisoners, or laborers set off against the self-righteousness and hypocrisy of polite society. How does Melville describe "alien Israel there," looking around him as if in a dream? He seems "like some amazed runaway steer, or trespassing Pequod Indian, impounded on the shores of Narragansett Bay, long ago."[3]

The dream is a lesson in history, not just a nostalgic interlude, with Israel's thoughts of Old Huckleberry the horse, now dead and "long surfeited with clover." Then, picking up on the simile of the fugitive steer, Melville presents another vision. Israel wanders in the fog toward Barbican. In the obscurity, houses turn into shadows on "midnight hills." Suddenly, he hears "a confused pastoral sort of sounds: tramplings, lowings, halloos," and he is called upon to "head off certain cattle, bound to Smithfield, bewildered and unruly in the fog." After the sight of cattle headed for slaughter, he sees a lovely image through the haze, a strange apotheosis: "the white face—white as an orange blossom—of a black-bodied steer in advance of the drove, gleaming ghost-like through the vapors." Both body and spirit, the steer is an icon of matter that is also a ghost. A composite apparition, the white-faced, black-bodied steer looms before Israel and makes us think uneasily of whites in blackface, performing their extravagant mimicries of slaves. Startled into action, Israel starts driving the "riotous cattle" to the right, away from Smithfield Market and into the barnyard of his memories. He dreams himself back home to the Berkshires, "into the mists of the Housatonic mountains; ruddy boy on the upland pastures again." Alone against the horizon, as singular and noteworthy as the not quite white, orange-blossom face of the black-bodied steer, the cattle-boy appears "clear-cut as a balloon against the sky."[4]

This phantom scene would have brought very meaty and not exactly pleasant reminiscences to the minds of Melville's readers. Violations of the natural world were rampant in nineteenth-century London, whether horses starved and worked to exhaustion or cows driven from their rural pastures to Smithfield, to be bound and slaughtered. Some of Melville's audience would have been familiar with Mandeville's invitation in *The Fable of the Bees* to rethink the categorical divide between human and brute, between assumptions of civilization and barbarism: "When a large and gentle Bullock, after having resisted a ten times greater force of Blows than would have kill'd his Murderer, falls stunned at last … what Mortal can without Compassion hear the painful Bellowings intercepted by his Blood, the bitter Sighs that speak the sharpness of his Anguish?"[5]

But Melville also recognized the existence of what he had once called not "ordinarily human": the chattels that gave new meaning to *persons*, the human anomaly constituted by law as *property*.[6] Melville is obsessed with the making and unmaking of human materials, the metamorphoses that straddled the chasm between persons and things, as well as humans and animals. At the end of *Benito Cereno*, Captain Delano prods Don Benito to snap out of his gloom: "But the past is passed; why moralize upon it? Forget it. See, yon bright sun has forgotten it all, and the blue sea, and the blue sky; these have turned over new leaves." Benito answers: "Because they have no memory, because they are not human."[7]

What does it mean in times of torture and dissembling *to be like an animal?* It all began with chattels. Their treatment helps us to understand the limits of cruelty. They are used as examples when humans need most to categorize, to dominate, to justify slavery, genocide, and incarceration. The proximity between humans and animals is sometimes tenuous. Boundaries are permeable, and taxonomies are necessary to ensure the order of things. But when the pressure is on to construct, legally and socially, degradation and inferiority, categories and terminologies get muddled. The hierarchies no longer hold.

THINKING MATTER

In Edward Long's very popular *The History of Jamaica* (1774), the systematic debasement of blacks depended on an imaginary journey to an Africa he had never seen, as well as on comparisons between humans and animals. The pro-slavery apologist and natural historian made recourse to gross analogies in order to prove the natural inferiority of the Negro.

Though Long shared Georges-Louis Leclerc Buffon's passion for classifying "by nearly insensible gradations from the most perfect creature to the most unformed matter, from the best organized animal to the most brute mineral," he took Buffon's "imperceptible nuances" and made them very perceptible. Once they were applied to the results of interbreeding—the successive generations of blacks with the traits and colors of whites—a new typology was necessary. Buffon recognized the arbitrariness of any allegedly "general system" or "perfect method."[8] But Long replaced doubt with certainty, imposing place, position, and rank in a chaos of contradictions.

Long advances in a series of graduated steps from "inanimate to animated matter." "We ascend from mere inert matter into the vegetable and animal kingdoms, by an almost imperceptible deviation." He proceeds through analogy from "inert matter" to "matter endued with thought and reason!" At the crux of his argument is his belief that humans are like other animals that differ from each other in certain qualities, strains, or varieties. Blacks are as different from other humans as are two breeds of dog. Some dogs, he notes, seem akin to the wolf and fox. And there is greater difference, he notes, "between the mastiff and lapdog than between the horse and the ass; and what two animals can be more unlike, than the little black Guinea dog, of a smooth skin, without a single hair upon it, and the rough shock dog [a dog with long, shaggy hair]."[9]

Although he echoes Locke's progression "by gentle degrees" in an ascent "upward from us" toward "infinite Perfection," and descent "from us downwards" toward deformity, Long recasts *An Essay Concerning Human Understanding* (1690–1700). Long's emphasis on palpable and ineradicable differences between the smooth-skinned Guinea dog and the rough shock dog, like so much else in his categorical debasement of blacks, ignores even as it refutes Locke's distrust of essentialized conceptions of sorts and species. The boundaries of animal species are uncertain, Locke insisted, and even the distinction between variety and species is blurred: "I would fain know, why a shock and a hound are not as distinct *Species* as a Spaniel and an Elephant."[10]

When Locke considers the perils of hierarchical thinking, he has in his mind not only the biological classification of things but also the Indies. In uncanny anticipation of Long—soon to be his Jamaican Creole reviser—he mentions "an *English-man* bred in *Jamaica*," and a couple of pages later, challenges histories of monstrous births and dangerous propagation that he has just retold: "[I]f the *Species* of Animals and Plants are to be distinguished only by propagation, must I go to the *Indies* to see the Sire and Dam of the one, and the Plant from which the Seed was gathered that produced the other, to know whether this be a Tiger or that Tea?"[11]

Locke saw that history, purported to be *natural*, could denominate the *unnatural*. He prefaces the stories of forbidden couplings, such as women who "have conceived by Drills [an ape or baboon]," with his skeptical "if History lie not." The attempt to classify and label this species of degenerate mixture was crucial to Long's later story of orangutans that "sometimes endeavor to surprise and carry off Negroe women into their woody retreats," as well as his surmise that "an oran-outang husband" would be no "dishonour to an Hottentot female." Locke was aware of the rage to classify not only such "monstrous Productions" but the racially tinged entities of the Indies, and he subtly casts doubt on the scandalous reports of aberrant mixture and bestial propagation. "There are Creatures, as 'tis said" is followed by a parenthetical clause about the credibility of the very stories he will repeat—"(*sit fides penes Authorem*)"—i.e., let trust be with the author, or trust the writer, even if what is said seems untrustworthy. Creatures might have "language and reason," and even "a shape in other things agreeing with us," but they also possess "hairy tails." On this unthinkable terrain walk bearded ladies and beardless gentlemen, along with "the Issue of a Cat and a Rat." How should we distinguish between an idiot and a baboon? Locke asks. "Shall the difference of Hair only on the Skin be a mark of a different internal specifick Constitution between a Changeling and a Drill, when they agree in Shape, and want of Reason and Speech?"[12]

Since humans lack the knowledge of the real essence of things, our conceptions of species emerge out of a jumble of items like skin, hair, speech, or other visible mutations. We select, define, and name, but such terminological classifications are fictions. What is called the essence of a thing is "*made by the Mind*, and not by Nature." In other words, our belief in the fixity and separateness of species is grounded in convention and prejudice; our truths are nothing more than fictions. Even the nominal essence "man" is a term of vague meaning that does not correspond to the "precise and *unmovable Boundaries of* that *Species*" set by nature.[13]

Long rethinks philosophy as he adapts it to his logic of degradation. Bad logic makes good racism, as his lapses into taxonomic confusion demonstrate. Following gradations of being from mere matter to matter with thought and reason added on, Long converges on the "ape-kind," reflecting that "the oran-outang and some races of black men are very nearly allied, is, I think, more than probable." Long's epistemology of whiteness depends on the systematic debasement of blacks: though they may look like humans, their outer appearance does not mean they possess reason, or what he calls *a superior principle*," since the orangutan also has the form but not the intellect of humans. "The oran-outang's brain," he claims, "is a senseless *icon* of the human ... it is mere matter, unanimated with a thinking principle." It is not only idiots, parrots, and orangutans that utter what might seem to be European words, but God has so diversified His works that sounds resembling Negro utterance can be found in "the gabbling of turkies like that of the Hottentots, or the hissing of serpents."[14]

Long ingeniously adapted Locke's pre-Linnaean elucidation of a clearly divided series of species to an eighteenth-century slave colony. Using biological taxonomies, he argued for an affinity between blacks and animals in order to justify slavery. And in moving from taxonomy to punishment, he sought to demonstrate how the legal status of animals had a great deal to do with the newly implemented rules for the correction of slaves. It was the proximity of the categories of animal and slave in the Jamaican slave codes that prompted the reappraisal of the legal status of the enslaved. A Guinea Negro, "born and trained up in other climates," like "*learned horses, learned* and even *talking dogs* in England," might exhibit through steady application and imitative skills something like a "capacity far exceeding what is ordinarily allowed to be possessed by those animals." But it remains doubtful, he concludes, that they can ever rise far above "their natural baseness of mind" and approach the attainments of rational men.[15]

One might think at first that Long took Locke's obsession with consciousness to its logical conclusion. Again, though blacks might have human organs, such outward embodiment does not necessarily house a rational mind, since the monkey-kind has the form but not the intellect of humans. Yet Locke urged a practice of thought that blurred species boundaries. He subjected the legitimacy of enslavement to sharp and anxious scrutiny. If we look back to Locke from later racialist analogies of blacks to brute matter, we can see how his suggestion that the differences between animal and human consciousness are only a matter of degree unsettled the legal category of *slave*.

There is, he admits, "something in us that has a Power to think," but one can never be sure whether or not that "Substance perpetually thinks or no." Locke dreads the abuse of words, confounding verbal games such as: "*Humanity is Animality, or Rationality, or Whiteness.*" So he sets up a template for understanding what it means to be human by setting up terms for comparison. But the task of definition remains arbitrary; and the assumed oppositions between animals and humans, brutes and men lose definiteness as he considers them.[16]

For Locke, as writer of the *Essay*, there are moments especially perilous for philosophers or divines who would put themselves too far above particulars, wandering in what he once called "that incomprehensible *Inane*." If Descartes proposed that the soul always thinks, then Locke imagined the incredible scene of a movable soul in search of a *place* "to think in." Perhaps "the Soul can, whilst the Body is sleeping, have its Thinking, Enjoyments, and Concerns, its Pleasures or Pain apart, which the Man is not conscious of nor partakes in." In his parable of the double Socrates—waking and sleeping—Locke suggests that supposing "the Soul to think, and the Man not to perceive it" is "to make two Persons in one Man." Out of one Socrates, come two: when the body sleeps, the soul wanders and lives by itself, without the man (who has both body and soul when awake) knowing anything about it. One body, one soul—two entities. For Socrates waking to know or care about the "Happiness or Misery of his Soul, which it enjoys alone by itself whilst he sleeps," is as impossible as his concern "for the Happiness or Misery of a Man in the *Indies*, whom he knows not."[17]

Locke pushes this thought experiment further in his tale of the Dioscuri or "sons of Zeus," Castor and Pollux. Here, two persons become one. If the soul can separate from the body while the body sleeps, then the soul can also find a temporary lodging in another body. Castor's soul, for example, while he is asleep can go and think in the body of his twin Pollux, who is also asleep and thus temporarily without a soul. One soul, two bodies. "For if *Castor*'s Soul can think, whilst *Castor* is asleep, what *Castor* is never conscious of, 'tis no matter what Place it chooses to think in."[18]

When we consider Locke's examples of the double Socrates or Castor and Pollux, we recognize that his most fantastic scenarios for thought and its embodiment are taken from reported wonders of the New World, where, as travel writers noted, anything was possible. A rational parrot competes with "dull irrational *Man*," matter thinks in animals, and limbs continue to think as long as they hold on to the consciousness that the rest of the body has lost. When he focuses on creatures deficient in mind, he asks: "[If] *Changelings* may be supposed something between Man and Beast, 'Pray what are they? … If *Changelings* are something between Man and Beast, what will become of them in the other World? To which I answer, It concerns me not to know or enquire." Then he considers "the dead Body of a Man" and reminds his readers that even if it has the shape of a man, it would be senseless to argue that there is a "living Soul" in the corpse: as idiotic as if one were to say that "there is a rational Soul in a *Changeling*, because he has the outside of a rational Creature, when his Actions carry far less marks of Reason with them … than what are to be found in many a Beast."[19]

But no matter whether puzzling about thoughts that could be limbs, a double Socrates with a single soul, or Castor and Pollux becoming one person, Locke remained serious about the way consciousness, or awareness, made the human a person. In the passage from corpse to changeling to beast, Locke appears to undermine theories of human inequality that depend on turning superficial characteristics—somatic qualities like skin color—into essentializing truths.

Whatever was metaphysical in Locke's thinking had also to be legal. Recall that he describes persons as linked, temporally and spiritually, to accountability, and so personhood belongs only "to intelligent Agents capable of a Law, and Happiness and Misery." His account of personal identity, then, depends only on consciousness, not physical identity. Even if, as he suggests in the *Essay*, the same person could be incarnated in a series of bodies, or in constantly changing particles of matter—for example, "an *Embryo*, one of Years, mad and sober"—then as long as the thread of self-consciousness is maintained, past experience can be revived, if not on earth in heaven. The object of law is not the body or the soul—the substance of each is equally unknowable—but *persons* who think, who remember, who can be held accountable.[20]

At the very least, Locke's argument, in complicating the easy verticality of some great chain of being—what Long defined as the "progression from a lump of dirt to a perfect human being"—kept open and tentative the dominion that his colonial imitator considered absolute. Locke argued in the *Essay* that God can superadd the thinking faculty to matter, giving "created senseless matter … some degrees of sense, perception, and thought." The force of consciousness can adhere to things; and once that happens, distinctions between persons and property are moot. Going so far as to imagine carcasses with thought added on, Locke challenged his readers to imagine new places for thinking in matter. No matter whether you looked like a man or talked like one, the only thing that granted personhood was an awareness of your actions, not only in the present but extended into the past.[21]

How, Locke urged his readers to ask, can one tell the difference between body and spirit or, to press the question further, between barbaric and civilized? He described the *self* as "that conscious thinking thing, (whatever Substance made up of whether Spiritual or Material, Simple or Compounded, it matters not) which is sensible, or conscious of Pleasure and Pain, capable of Happiness or Misery, and so is concern'd for it *self* as far as that consciousness extends." And here, again, is his example: If you allow a piece of the body, e.g., the "little Finger," to depart from the body while carrying consciousness with it, "'tis evident the little Finger would be the *Person*, the *same Person*; and *self* then would have nothing to do with the rest of the Body." Locke's demonstration that *consciousness* could as easily be in our little finger as in our mind presses us to test what we mean when we distinguish *persons* from *things*.[22]

Locke's argument that differences between animal and human consciousness are only differences of degree skewered prejudicial judgments about the mental and physical history of the types of mankind, especially popular in theories of human inequality and pro-slavery ethnographies that saw blacks as akin to brute creation.

Yet while Locke argued that species classification is just a matter of words, or human conventions, his confounding of a hierarchical order nevertheless became crucial to those who believed in clear—so they thought—taxonomic proofs of inferiority. In terms of the legal personality of the slave and the rules regarding mutilation and torture, Locke's analytic of the self served as the unwitting precursor to a new ritual of punishment. Long's taxonomy was, in some respects, parasitic on Locke's view of personal identity that recast materiality in a particularly radical way: the force of consciousness can adhere to things.

Matter and mind were recuperated for the purposes of slavery in the colonies of the Americas, and nowhere as powerfully as in the birth of that legal personality called "slave" through the putting on and taking off of *thought*. Long's elaborate taxonomy placed the reasonable person in the rank of whiteness while relegating the unreasonable—the "senseless *icon* of the human"—to the bottom rung of the hierarchic ladder.[23] Civil and penal law, as practiced in North America and the Caribbean, had the power to give—for the claims of value or the purposes of punishment—a catalog of intangible qualities to chattels: intelligence, volition,

123

morality. Long's *History*, like Thomas Jefferson's *Notes on the State of Virginia*, shows how easy, and instrumental, it was to misuse Locke's arguments about species and species terms to embrace the natural human hierarchy that he so fundamentally questioned. [24]

A COLONIAL SITE

Animals and slaves: forms of unfreedom depend on such inexact but nevertheless effective parallelism. The rules of law, like Long's Creole taxonomies, depend on the strict correlation between human and animal to systematize what might at first appear to us like rampant incongruity. Slaves in the southern United States and the Caribbean occupied the double character of person and property. Their composite nature was further complicated by their division into real and personal property. They were regarded either as affixed to or growing on land, rather like real estate, or as movable goods or chattels.

The creation of a new and hybrid person in law, earmarked for domination, was a weighty matter. Should we approach this novel person—what Thomas Cobb in *Inquiry into the Law of Negro Slavery* (1858) called "a child just born"—by analogy or opposition? That legal personality was not a "child" so much as a combination of "cow" and "jewel," beast and artifact. Both were deemed "perishable" or "fungible," the latter meaning that the creature is like money: any one cow or jewel, snuff box, plate, or slave was as good as any other for the purpose of exchange. Slaves were not simply things, nor were they really human. Instead, they seemed to occupy a curiously nuanced category, where animals, humans, and inanimate things juggled for primacy. As a matter of history, these relationships may well have a common element. As we go backward in time, familiar demarcations become blurred; and what now seem distinct—persons and things, animals and humans, or *personal* versus *real* property (chattels and land)—were intimately blended in some much vaguer notion that was neither exactly the one nor precisely the other.[25]

"Indeed the further we go back, the larger seems the space which the possession of chattels fills in the eye of the law," wrote Frederick Pollock and Frederic William Maitland in *The History of English Law* (1898). The concept of "chattel" or personal property included both animals and slaves. The similarity in the words "cattle" and "chattel" is not accidental. "The typical chattel," Pollock and Maitland continued, "is a beast. The usage which has differentiated *chattel* from *cattle* is not very ancient; when Englishmen began to make their wills in English a gift of one's 'wordly catell' was a gift of all one's movables.... Time was when oxen served as money, and rules native in that time will easily live on into later ages."[26]

In his *History of Jamaica*, Long includes the "Penal Clauses" from the abstract of the "Jamaica *Code Noir*, or Laws affecting Negroe and other Slaves in that Island." Here are the three pertinent clauses of the Black Code which shed light on the complex relationship between chattel and cattle:

> 8. Slaves, destroying fish by poisoning, using nets of meshes less than one inch and a quarter, or destroying turtle eggs, or killing pigeons, in the months of May, June, or July, are punisheable with *thirty-one lashes* on the bare back, on conviction before a justice of the peace.
>
> 9. To put a stop to the wanton slaughter of old breeding cattle and marked young ones, with other abuses of the like sort, no slave to keep any horses, mares, mules, asses, or cattle, on penalty of forfeiting the same. (1711)
>
> 16. Slaves, hunting cattle, horses, mares, etc., with lances, guns, cutlasses, or other instruments of death, unless in company with their master, etc., or other white person by him or them deported, on conviction between 2 justices and three freeholders, to be adjudged guilty of felony, and be transported. (1749)

The 1711 and 1749 entries of the Jamaican *Code noir* on animals set the scene for a drama of exchange and substitution. There are two categories: domestic (*domitae naturae*) and wild (*ferae naturae*). Cows, mares, mules, and other domestic animals are those to which the generic term "cattle" is applied: oxen, cows, horses, sheep, goats, donkeys, mules, and chickens. Relying on taxonomic groups for the rationale of punishment, Long demonstrates how the legal status of animals influenced the newly implemented rules for the correction of slaves. The proximity of the two categories in the Jamaican penal clauses revealed the relative status of animate and inanimate objects, wild animals and domestic species—and, ultimately, rights of possession and service.[27]

The West Indian slave codes were severe. So how do we understand the concern for the fate of animals, especially cows, at the hands of slaves? Both predator and prey, or prospective victimizer and victim, were useful kinds of personal property. Demands for humane treatment make ambiguous the position of slaves in terms of liability. Instead of simply dealing with *slaves* as *animals*—the thorniest of legal fictions—the metonymic relation works on the perceived lack of resemblance between things that are legally qualified as similar.

What establishes the law here is not the appropriateness of the relation between animals and slaves, but a wayward merging that keeps both intact and before us: the body of the cow, horse, or mare and the body of the slave. Those who are treated as property cannot have property, let alone trade it, make judgments about its life and death, or its reproduction. The most salient clauses are #9 and #16: the first concerns ownership of cattle, the second the right to hunt or mistreat domestic animals where not permitted by a white man. In the list of punishments by death or mutilation for offending slaves—those who escape, assault, or steal—we read rules of conduct that remind slaves that they can never be in the position of the master who has the right to mistreat chattels. Not only are they also, like animals, used for breeding, but they bear the marks or brands of slavery, whether literal scars or figurative degradation.

The edict against "wanton slaughter" asserts a higher morality on the part of whites: We look after old breeding cattle, even when they cannot breed. We care for those that are "marked," i.e., which do not have the markings from which we want to breed. So these laws—apparently about noninstrumental care—are intended to reinforce a distinction between those of higher rank and those lower on the hierarchy. But they are also a refusal to allow slaves to make judgments about breeding—which animals are too old to breed, which are nonconforming, and can be killed. Since slaves are deemed to lack judgment, slave owners reserve all judgment, especially judgments about breeding, to themselves.

These laws, ostensibly dealing with the treatment of animals by slaves, suggest more importantly something about the treatment of slaves by their owners, as well as their status as reproductive capital. Once the place of the animal and that of the slave are put into tension, the legal code identifies the approximate nature of chattels, not just as a legal principle but as a metaphysical truth. The legal arrangement keeps the two entities suspended in approximate likeness, making the prohibition of cruel treatment against one the assurance of cruel punishment against the other. These legal commands also posit projected and arbitrary harm or brutality toward animals at the hands of slaves. Why would a slave kill off both "old breeding cattle" and "marked young ones"? Does the slave, in killing a cow that was earmarked or branded, encroach upon an action reserved only for whites? Finally, in prohibiting the slave's hypothetical cruelty to animals, the master's cruelty to slaves is not only displaced but also made invisible to the eyes of the law.

CREATURES OF LAW

Haunting these prohibitive clauses is the deodand in early law. Not only could objects kill, but they could cause death with intent. Whether inanimate (a tree or the wheel of a cart) or animate (a horse or dog), they were believed to possess an evil will and were known as "deodand," meaning "what must be given to God" (*Deo dandum*). Whether beasts, slaves, or things, they had to be surrendered in recompense for blood casually shed.

127

In ancient and biblical sources, for example, Exodus (21:28), the goring ox had to be stoned: "If an ox gore a man or a woman that they die, then the ox shall be surely stoned, and his flesh shall not be eaten; but the owner of the ox shall be quit." In Plato's *Laws*, the law applied to any beast or thing that killed a person, commanding that the accursed "offender" be sent beyond the boundaries of the country, "exterminated" in the literal and original sense of the term. The aim of these measures was to appease the wrathful dead, since the claim of a soul dispatched so unexpectedly from this world outweighed the claim of the dead man's kinsfolk. Vengeance must be wreaked upon the object before the dead could lie in peace.[28]

In English law this peculiar practice centered on forfeiture of the offending object not to the victim or his kin but to the Crown. Any personal chattel that caused the death of any *reasonable* creature was believed to carry homicidal taint and malicious influence. In these deaths by misadventure, the sword, cart, tree, dog, or horse that in legal language *moved to the death* of a person would be surrendered to the king as both expiatory offering and restitution by the owner of the wrongdoing thing.[29]

Imagine the scene. If a man in a stiff drunk tripped over a dog and died, the dog, even if literally motionless, would legally be judged as moving to the death of the deceased. Or if another creature supposed to be "reasonable" is thrown off his horse or falls off his boat and dies, vengeance is taken on the horse or boat. In describing the artificial unreason of the law, Maitland and Pollock quipped that "many horses and boats bore the guilt which should have been ascribed to beer." This early modern ritual remained in practice in England until 1846 when its application to railway engines brought its irrational nature to public notice.[30]

The medieval English belief in "noxal surrender"—whether interpreted as offering the object or animal to God, to the victim's kin, or simply to execution—returned in eighteenth-century America.[31] The historical forms of sacred authority and servile law underwent a continual process of redefinition as they clashed with the demands of domination, the struggles within slavery, and the transatlantic domain of punishment and possession. Ultimately, the artificial unreason of law, shared by pagans and Christians alike, coalesced in a continuum of reinvention in the colonies.

Maitland and Pollock reflect, in relating later mitigations of the deodand: "However firmly we grasp the principle that a slave is a thing, we can not help seeing that the state may with advantage treat slaves as capable of committing crimes and suffering punishments, and when the state has begun to punish the slave it begins to excuse the master." Delivering the slave up to justice in the antebellum South freed the master from his chattel's sin, and often the master would receive restitution from the state for his loss. Lurking in the background of these barters is the sense of the "nonhuman." Penal laws *in terrorem* (for dread or deterrence), the legal terror so much a part of the perpetuation of slavery, depended on keeping intact this fitful valuation of persons and things.[32]

The nearness, the absolute relation between animals and humans becomes imperative whenever civility, with its costly and permanent rituals, is to be guaranteed. Circuits of rectitude, pardon, and retribution depend on an unspoken, secret intimacy with the animals we order, the objects of our discipline and our duplicity. The practice of deodand had another use in the colonies. Ancient forms of terror maintained themselves as they found new content. Old doctrines were ingeniously adapted to new goals. They gave way to new devotions to spirits that were cast sometimes in the form of animals, sometimes as trees. So the haunting continued, preserved most cunningly in legal rules and regulations.

Within this penal logic the rules of law and the exercise of spirit became reciprocal. In this exchange, the meaning of mind and matter reconstituted the logic of punishment as the language of sorcerers. Legally, how much of a body could be dismembered? In the Jamaican Black Code, as in the French *Code noir*, a gradual removal of body parts was allowed: one ear for the first escape, another ear for the second, or sometimes a foot or hand. The judicial code was preliminary to the utterance of guilt and essential to its efficacy. In the French code the soul remained, no matter what tortures were inflicted on the body— castration, flogging, roasting, branding, or loss of ears, nose, hands, and feet. Baptism, however, could, as some Jesuits claimed, allow the slave to shake off the mutilated flesh and rise again incorruptible.

In Jamaica slaves were construed, in varying Acts of Assembly, as things without thought, with no attention paid to their souls. But *duppies*, or the unquiet dead, returned in varying guises. The relics and scraps of bodies bought, bartered, and sold as if cattle, coins, parcels of land, or pieces of furniture returned as ancestor spirits, caught in the evil that had created them. Their metamorphoses record the rudiments of a legal sorcery that converted human animals into things or nonhuman animals. Whether we turn to the English or French Caribbean, or even the American South, these demonic spirits returned, taking vengeance as *lougawou* or vampires, *soucriants* or suckers, shape-shifters known to shed skin and suck blood.[33]

Condemned to wander the earth in the forms of pigs, cows, cats, or dogs, these evil spirits, known in Haiti as *baka* and in Jamaica as *rolling calf* or *roaring calf*, are the surfeit of an institution that turned humans into chattels. Ghosts, too, tell a history. They activate the materiality so critical to the spiritual beliefs of the enslaved, as well as to the harsh practices of the plantocracy. In a reinterpreted and vengeful history, these spectral residues impress their heavy hand. They revive not only the rules and regulations that ordered the dehumanization of slaves in the New World, but also older religious forms of criminal law: blood guilt, revenge, and punishment.

Ostensibly a beneficent protection, a guard against excessive harm, the language of the law, though often counting only as precepts and never enforced in practice, was, in the historian Elsa Goveia's words, the backbone of "police regulations, which lay at the very heart of the slave system." Stressing the way that

English law in the West Indies reduced the possibility that the slave could ever be regarded as "an ordinary man," but must be legally reduced to "mere property," she argues that it was "the absence of laws providing sanctions for the enforcement of slavery" that enabled Somerset to win his freedom in *Somerset v. Stewart* (1772). Goveia claimed that property in slaves "was as firmly accepted in the law of England as it was in that of the colonies," but what did not exist was "the superstructure raised on this basis," the "police laws" that governed slaves as "persons with wills of their own," but "kept in their fixed status as the legal property of their owners."[34]

The law of slavery in the English colonies drew on English precedents. Even the punishment of *attaint* or *attainder*—as I have noted, a word meaning "to strike" or "to hit," but which, through a false derivation in "taint" or "stain," came to mean "corruption of blood"—traveled across the Atlantic. We recall how Blackstone's account of punishment for treason translated the criminal into "a monster" that must be exterminated. "[T]he law sets a note of infamy upon him, puts him out of its protection, and takes no further care of him than barely to see him executed"; and civilly dead, he is henceforth called "attaint, *attinctus*, stained or blackened." The crime of "compassing the death of the king" became in the 1698 penal clauses of the Jamaican *Code noir* "the crime of compassing or imagining the death of a white person, and being attainted thereof by *open deed* (or *overt act*), before two justices and three freeholders, *death.*" Sovereignty is extended to *all* whites, no matter their status, for sacred power derived from the privilege of color and *dominium* over the enslaved.[35]

But the slaves' systemic and inevitable ignorance of the law meant that the punishment for crime guaranteed tyranny, a system of coercion that left no choice of action. Even a pro-slavery apologist like Edward Long recognized that punishing slaves who can have no knowledge or awareness of legal regulations is harsh. His notes to the penal clauses of the Jamaican Black Code complain about punishments, such as death, inflicted on "a poor wretch, for a transgression, committed perhaps through mere ignorance of the law," as "highly tyrannical and cruel." But what about when an all-knowing master, fully aware of his actions and their consequences, partakes in the deliberate and wanton destruction of a slave? Instances of terrible cruelty toward slaves are documented throughout eighteenth-century colonial legislation in the West Indies and, later, in the nineteenth-century southern United States.[36]

The double and complex movement between the extremes of mind and body, what can be removed and what remains, turned the rules of law into tools for unmaking persons throughout the British colonial Americas, whether we turn to the colonies in the West Indies or in North America. In Jamaica, however, as the historian Vincent Brown has shown, slaves were not wholly reckoned in a negative relation to law. Though reduced to and fixed in their status as a special kind of property, slaves were yet to be governed as persons with wills of their own. In a brilliant riposte to Patterson's use of the term "social death" to describe the utter "depersonalization" that signaled an "alienation" both sacrificial and mercantile, Brown distinguishes between metaphor and actuality.[37] Discussing inheritance practices among Jamaican slaves, he clarifies how they often accomplished what they were legally not free to do. But as slavery took shape in the southern United States, the laws that sustained it were exceptional. In his *Inquiry into the Law of Negro Slavery* (1858), Cobb linked the denial of property rights for slaves to what had been corruption of blood in both English and West Indian criminal law: "[A] slave cannot take by descent, there being in him no inheritable blood." What Brown portrays as a reciprocal exchange that thrived on separate but equal possibilities on the eve of emancipation in the West Indies is quite reversed in the southern United States on the eve of the Civil War. While Edmund Burke considered how slaves might become "suitable subjects" in "Sketch of a Negro Code," even abolitionists in the United States—as Frederick Douglass reminded his audience—never quite accepted ex-slaves as equals. Instead, they still bore the "stigma, of the deepest degradation," as Justice Roger Brooke Taney wrote in *Dred Scott v. Sandford* (1857).[38]

Though initially not written into law, the enslavement of these valuable new properties—"chattelized humans and thinking property," as Jonathan Bush puts it—was legitimized through the practices of punishment and effacement necessary to their governance. The law entered the picture to define and codify an already existing tradition, ensuring that it would continue. And this guarantee of paradoxical persons, once made, was widely embraced. There was, quite simply, nothing like it.[39]

In the South, terror and legality went hand in hand. Just as Long's unruly mixtures divided humans into sorts and conditions while daring to defy logic, so the juridical notion of the slave counted on the sometimes-impossible scenarios of racialist ethnography. Once the slave could be shown to have no mind— no legal personality—this terrible negation of thinking in law, itself a kind of magic, was a disfiguration perhaps more terrifying to the enslaved than any corporeal punishment. The reservoir of legal narratives brought to bear on this most problematic form of property reimagined consciousness. It even contributed to another understanding of matter and mind in which property could be both incorporeal and corporeal. Ultimately, a slave was a juridical "thing" that because of its *thinglikeness* always carried the life of the spirit along with it.

THAT CLASS OF PERSONS

One of the most striking moments in the town hall–style debate between Barack Obama and John McCain in Nashville, Tennessee, on October 7, 2008, was McCain's reference to Obama as "*that* one." McCain did not look at Obama as he uttered words that severed his opponent from the recognition that comes with a name. This depersonalization recalled a uniquely American diminishing of personality. The familiar evidence of disdain I take to be part of the enduring history of racial slavery, a story of degraded status as evident in the North as in the South.

Just 150 years ago on March 5, 1857, Chief Justice Roger Brooke Taney judged in *Dred Scott v. Sandford* that no black had been or could be a citizen of the United States. No black, *slave or free*, was a citizen of the United States, and therefore no black could bring suit in a federal court. Even freed blacks are not members of the political community of the United States, Taney argues, since an externally imposed stigma remains integral to an inherent feature of the race: "The unhappy black race were separated from the white by indelible marks, and laws long before established, and were never thought of or spoken of except as property." No matter that the stigma has been read into "this class of persons" after the fact. The husk of skin first becomes an imaginary essence. It stands in for the racial substance of inferiority; and then the imagined quality, the metaphysical state, becomes the unchangeable legal status.[40]

In a repeal of the Missouri Compromise, Taney also ruled that slavery could not be constitutionally prohibited in the Kansas-Nebraska territories. His controversial opinion demonstrates how deeply the law counted on a philosophy of personhood in its delineation of the status or type of the slave. Taney stripped federal courts of jurisdiction over suits brought by blacks whose ancestors were imported into the United States and sold as slaves. Thus, no matter where Scott found himself, he was condemned never to be free of the status that consigned him to degradation in the eyes of the law. No state can have a law making slavery illegal, Taney wrote, since the right to own slaves is substantively protected by the due process clause. Therefore, the Missouri Compromise's ban on slavery in some of the territory northwest of the Ohio River deprived slave owners of their constitutional right to certain types of property without due process of law.[41]

Taney did not know exactly what to call this strange anomaly of slave and free person united in one body. Throughout the opinion, Taney refers to blacks as bought and sold like merchandise, a species of property no different from any other. Yet these chattels and the forever-excluded "free" blacks bear the marks of "degradation" not ultimately as persons and not as property, but, as Taney states in his opinion, as "that class of persons." This classification defines them as not part of the personhood of citizens, absolutely unlike white persons. They are excluded from the social contract, expressed in the Fifth Amendment of the Constitution, that guaranteed all persons against deprivations of "life, liberty, and property." For Taney in 1857, as for McCain in 2008, the anonymity and generality of the word "that" are the source of a lethal distinctiveness: the sign of the other, who must not be referred to by name, touched, or even recognized by a look. *That one* captures the exclusion of the unmentionable one whose name we dare not speak.[42]

On October 16, 1854, Abraham Lincoln confronted Senator Stephen Douglas in his "Speech on the Repeal of the Missouri Compromise" at Peoria, Illinois. Though Lincoln admitted that there remained insoluble problems in schemes for emancipation of slaves—for example, sending them to Liberia or making them "politically and socially, our equals"—he still would not accept that these issues justified allowing slavery in what had been deemed by law free territory. At two points in his speech, Lincoln grappled with the necessary, if ambiguous, interplay of property and personhood. First, he reflected on the absence of the word "slave" or "slavery" in the Constitution, which substituted "other persons" or "such persons" for slaves. In the fugitive-slave clause, which provided for the recovery of fugitives, he explained, "the slave is spoken of as a 'PERSON HELD TO SERVICE OR LABOR.'" Then, he spoke of the abolition of the slave trade: "[T]hat trade is spoken of as 'The migration or importation of such persons as any of the States NOW EXISTING, shall think proper to admit, &c.'"[43]

Lincoln offered a thorny but daring approach to how one might speak about the status of slaves without referring to *persons*. He understood how much labeling and the range of ever-new categories of exclusion mattered in constructing these anomalies of law. Reflecting on the desire to extend slavery into new states such as Nebraska, he challenges his audience to follow a logic based on the law of chattel slavery. If you don't mind my taking a hog to Nebraska, he explained, I can't mind you taking a slave. Satirizing the analogies made between hogs and "negroes," Lincoln ultimately challenges the absurdity of this denial of "the humanity of the negro" while appealing, with only a touch of irony, to the "human sympathies" of those in slave states as well as free.

He recalls how in 1820 the South joined the North in declaring the slave trade piracy and making it punishable with death by hanging. Yet even though the practice was to bring "wild negroes from Africa, to sell to such as would buy them," no one ever imagined "hanging men for catching and selling wild horses, wild buffaloes or wild bears." In the United States and its territories, he explains "433,643 free blacks" are running around without owners. In a Swiftian turn, he jokes about the rationale for treating blacks like animals, asking how this property "worth over two hundred millions of dollars" can be free, if "free horses or free cattle" are not "running at large."

In Lincoln's astonishing answer to the question "How is this?" he admits, as if answering Taney even before *Dred Scott*, that "all these free blacks are the descendants of slaves, or have been slaves themselves, and they would be slaves now, but for SOMETHING which has operated on their white owners, inducing them at vast pecuniary sacrifices, to liberate them." Then comes his second question: "What is that SOMETHING?" The answer is that anyone of "human sympathy" or a sense of "justice" would have to admit "that the poor negro has some natural right to himself." This *right to himself* is a right to self-possession that no one can take away. It is this gist or core or spirit or "I," however we want to define it, that brute "slave-dealers" deny.

Lincoln knew his Blackstone, especially the second book of the *Commentaries* on the *rights of things.*[44] Horses, hogs, and cattle, if left to themselves, might be wild. But once confined, tamed, and nurtured by men, they become property. Hogs, as Blackstone intimated, are considered domestic animals. The rules of ownership are then determined by the distinction I noted earlier between *domitae naturae* and *ferae naturae*: "some being of a *tame*, and others of a *wild* disposition." One can possess horses, sheep, poultry, or any animal that might "continue perpetually in his occupation." But in wild animals, Blackstone wrote, "a man can have no absolute property."[45] Lincoln combines animals wild and tame, savage and domesticated in his examples: first hogs, and then "wild horses, wild buffaloes or wild bears."

I dwell on Lincoln's reasoning here, since the logic of slavery both depended on and tried to evade the consequences of the comparison with animals. Those who would make such a comparison had at once to explain how a slave could be property in the manner of animals, yet have a differential status. Pushed to give slaves some definition within the realm of reason and unreason, human and brute, southern jurists puzzled out how best to relegate a thinking agent to the status of property. Yet Lincoln knew that slaves' personal status depended on bonds of feeling that were not usually applied to animals.

In the next chapter I turn to case law, concentrating on a single, understudied decision made one year after *Dred Scott*. Schemes of disabling here rendered the apparent objectivity of law suspect. Terms such as "will," "choice," and "election" derived their meaning and significance from a set of taxonomies and practices that made it possible to classify the world of slavery and compare it to the legal universe in which free people were allowed to reside. This world is singularly cruel. Its discriminations overturn logic, infect and befoul behavior. And they reside in the rule of law.

A LEGAL ETHNOGRAPHY

Of the legal position of the *servus* Domesday Book tells
us little or nothing; but earlier and later documents
oblige us to think of him as a slave, one who in the
main has no legal rights. He is the *theow* of the Anglo-
Saxon dooms, the *servus* of the ecclesiastical canons.
But though we do right in calling him a slave, still we
might be mistaken were we to think of the line which
divides him from other men as being as sharp as the
line which a mature jurisprudence will draw between
thing and person. We may well doubt whether this
principle—"The slave is a thing, not a person,"—can
be understood by a grossly barbarous age. It implies
the idea of a person, and in the world of sense,
we find not persons but men.

—Frederic William Maitland,
Domesday Book and Beyond (1897)

IDIOMS OF SERVILITY

IN WARNING AGAINST THE ANACHRONISTIC READING OF EARLY ANGLO-
American practices of servitude, Maitland hesitated about thinking of slaves as things. His admonition registered unease with
the sharp divide between person and thing. In exhuming the
history of English common law, he recognized the dangers of
forcing modern ideas onto medieval facts. Neat distinctions mis-
represented the evidence of an untidy, ambiguous past. "As we

go backwards the familiar outlines become blurred; the ideas become fluid, and instead of the simple we find the indefinite."[1] Modern legal conceptions of slaves did not help to clarify whether the *servus* of Domesday Book was considered a person, a thing, or neither. Maitland's understanding of the instability of words and his pursuit of precision help us to appreciate how crucial was the concept of persons to schemes of continued servitude, and the masks of identity such domination required.

But for Maitland to have a concept of *persons* implies an apprehension of *things*, and he questioned whether the status of *servus* was not a great deal more complicated. He doubted that a "grossly barbarous age" could understand the juridical notion of persons, what he called "fictitious persons," and concluded that degrees of servitude were possible: the *servus* thus appeared as the "unfreest of persons rather than as no person but a thing."[2] In the slave codes of the Caribbean and especially the South, the idea of personhood mattered a great deal. Not only were slaves considered unfree, but also, paradoxically, these most legal of entities were at the same time *dead in law*. The law was apparently untroubled by the paradox that the most hyperlegal of inventions remained in a negative relation to law. No degrees of servitude were possible. Instead, there were only two statuses recognized: slavery or freedom, and nothing in between.

The very incommensurability of persons and things was necessary to underpin the institution of slavery. Rather than a "logical inconsistency," Bryan Wagner argues that the paradox was "a precondition for the system's normal operation": "[S]lavery's indignity is not about being turned from a person into a thing but rather about being in a position where it does not matter if you are a person or a thing."[3] These novel identities were the hard-won fruits of colonial slave codes, as we have seen, and later, of the significant appellate cases that ended up in chancery courts. Not simply things and not really human, slaves occupied a curiously nuanced category. Examples ranging from proofs of animality to marks of reason or imbecility—and a great deal in between—became part and parcel of judicial work. The limits of personhood and the extension of thinglikeness became oddly inseparable in this landscape of coercion. New taxonomies had to be created. They formed the conditions for systematic abasement.

But how did judges determine the character of this legal person? In the South the adaptation of Lockean notions of personal identity to slaves was inextricably bound up with the understanding of *person* as a forensic term and the kind of legal incapacity and nonrecognition that signaled negative personhood. Thomas Morris in *Southern Slavery and the Law: 1619–1860* argues that the most crucial legal fiction was that "the slave was an object of property rights, he or she was a 'thing.'"[4] However, what most occupied the thoughts of lawyers and judges in cases about personal rights in the courts of Virginia on the eve of the Civil War was not to affirm the slave as property, but to articulate the personhood of slaves in such a way that it was disfigured, not erased. Slave law depended on this juridical diminution. The peculiar form impairment took and the transformations that ensued gave new meaning to degradation. Body, soul, and mind would be tested. Examples ranging from proofs of animality to marks of reason became part of the courtroom drama. On the newly discovered terrain, that new entity in the double character of person and property became the object of unprecedented study.

POINDEXTER'S WILL

Bailey v. Poindexter's Executor (1858) is one of the most complex, lengthy, and influential cases of testamentary trust. Instead of adhering to the testator's wishes, the Virginia Supreme Court of Appeals held—contrary to precedent—that when a will grants a slave the choice of freedom, the provision giving that choice is void. Slaves have no legal capacity to choose to be free. So harsh is the court's analysis of servile incapacity that I devote this entire chapter to a discussion of the case.[5] Its invention of a new class of legal persons remains as crucial to fathoming the after-lives of racial stigma in the United States as *Dred Scott*, decided a year earlier.

In November 1835, a month before his death at sixty-three, John Lewis Poindexter made his last will and testament. It was admitted to probate in December 1835 in New Kent County, Virginia. The will provided that those of his slaves who had been "loaned" to his wife would have "their choice of being emancipated or sold publicly" after her death. "If they prefer being emancipated," Poindexter declared,

> ... it is my wish that they be hired out until a sufficient sum is raised to defray their expenses to a land where they can enjoy their freedom; and if there should not be enough of the perishable property loaned my wife to pay off the legacies to Ann Lewis Howle and Georgiana Bryan, they are to be hired until a sufficient sum is raised to pay the deficiency. If they prefer being sold and remaining here in slavery, it is my wish they be sold publicly, and the money arising be equally divided between my sister Eliza Marshall, the children or heirs of my brother Carter B. Poindexter, my nephews William C. Howle and Daniel P. Howle, and my niece Nancy Bailey.[6]

Who were these enslaved recipients of the master's gift? We do not know, for he does not name them. They were not Poindexter's personal slaves, whom he did name—"negro woman Louisa and her children, Sarah, Martha, and Barbary and their increase" —on bequeathing them to his nephew Jaquelin L. Poindexter, along with his other chattels, his "Ratler filly, his new saddle and bridle, and his wearing apparel (except his watch)."[7]

But to these unnamed slaves Poindexter left a peculiar legacy. He does not merely present the choice of slavery or liberty, but lays down prior conditions that must be met. In either case, whatever status they choose, money is the determining factor. First, if they choose freedom, they must be hired out to raise enough money to pay for their voyage literally out from slavery. Yet there is another hitch. If his wife lacks enough money to pay the legacies due Ann Lewis Howle and Georgiana Bryan, the slaves' freedom is again deferred until a sufficient sum for that purpose is raised by hiring them out. Lastly, if they choose slavery, the money arising from their sale must be divided equally among the heirs he names.

What kind of choice is this? Freedom or public sale. The condition of slavery in their Virginia home—but *not* with Poindexter's kin—or freedom in exile. Following the Virginia Manumission Act of 1782, manumission of slaves was no longer forbidden. Had Poindexter simply asked that his slaves be emancipated after his death, his wish would have been fulfilled. However, instead of that, he gave them a choice: they could either be free—under certain conditions—or be sold. The one thing that could not happen is that they should remain as slaves in his family's household.

Why did Poindexter decline to make the choice for them himself? Could he have known that by leaving these slaves in this position, he had left them a legacy of choice that left them no choice? Poindexter's gift was an intensely personal expression of ambivalence. It depended on the slaves' capacity to choose. Nevertheless, whichever choice they made put them in the same relation to debt and thus confirmed their status as property. In addition, Poindexter made no provision in his will for the support of these ex-slaves in the land to which they would be transported if they chose freedom.

What kind of option for freedom, then, were they bequeathed? Was it not a manumission that placed them into another state of unfreedom? Perhaps it was not entirely Poindexter's fault. Like many other testators in Virginia who cared for the welfare of their slaves, he was in a bind. New restrictions on the manumission of slaves revised the liberal 1782 act of manumission. "An Act to Amend the Several Laws Concerning Slaves," passed on January 25, 1806, declared that slaves manumitted after May 1 of that year had to either leave their homes in Virginia within the year or be reenslaved. Refusal to accept banishment meant the forfeiture of freedom. This "restriction in disguise upon manumission" accomplished indirectly a ban on the master's power to convert his slave into a free black. Any slave who remained in the state beyond a year was to be sold, the statute decreed, by "the overseers of the poor of any county or corporation in which he or she shall be found, for the benefit of the poor of such county or corporation." The actual operation of the 1806 act was applauded by many who thought manumission dangerous. As the editorial column of the *Richmond Recorder* warned: "There never was a madder method of sinking property, a method more hostile to the safety of society than the freak of emancipating negroes."[8] So Poindexter, not wanting to force emigration on any slave, but wishing to let them choose their future, could only offer the choice of "freedom" or remaining enslaved.

When he wrote his will, Poindexter added a codicil that further complicated the extent of election he intended. After giving his slaves the option of being emancipated or sold publicly, he made the bequests to his heirs dependent on that choice. The predicament that Poindexter introduced in his legacy by giving discretion to slaves was transmitted to his kin.

> I wish it understood that in the event of my negroes loaned to my wife being emancipated at her death, and not sold for the benefit of my sister, &c., &c, that my nephew Jaquelin L. Poindexter shall pay the sum of one thousand dollars, to be equally divided among them; and that I give him my plantation Cedar Lane on that condition.[9]

According to the executor of the estate, when Poindexter died, he left personal and perishable property appraised at $1,146.05, and twenty slaves. By the time his widow died, nothing remained but slaves. Several had died, but thirteen more had been born. With some thirty slaves at issue, it is no wonder that the executor filed a claim in April 1854 in the Circuit Court of New Kent "to obtain a construction of the will of Poindexter." The dispossessed heirs and devisees—including his sister Eliza, the children of his brother Carter Poindexter, his nephews William and Daniel Howle, and his niece Nancy Bailey—were defendants in the suit. Since only the slaves now remained, they became the subject of the case on appeal, heard in November 1855, twenty years after Poindexter's last will and testament. The court decreed that the slaves were made free by the emancipating clause in his will, and since his widow had died, were to be freed immediately. The defendants, confronting their loss of property, challenged the will. They promptly appealed to the court of last resort, the Supreme Court of Appeals in Richmond. The case wound slowly through the system, and over two years later, on February 9, 1858, more than twenty-two years after Poindexter's death, the judgment was reversed. The case was decided in favor of the heirs.

Bailey should be read as a crucible of tensions that coalesced as the Civil War approached. Southern attitudes hardened due to a series of events: violence in the Kansas and Nebraska territories following passage of the Kansas-Nebraska Act in 1854, which allowed the western territories to become slave states; Preston Smith Brooks's caning of Charles Sumner in the Senate chamber for his antislavery speech "The Crime Against Kansas" on May 22, 1856; John Brown's slaughter of pro-slavery farmers in Kansas on May 24, 1856; and, finally, the rejection of the Lecompton Constitution a month before the final decision in *Bailey*. Drafted for the Kansas Territory and written by slavery supporters, the Lecompton Constitution would have permitted slavery, excluded free blacks from living in Kansas, and allowed only male citizens of the United States to vote.

A test case for an archaic ethnography both legal and religious, *Bailey* uses the moral high ground to justify legal facts that translate juridical disabilities into the recognizable terms of public shame. Perpetual incapacity is legitimated by the use of taxonomies: the ordering of the capable and the disabled. The legal exegesis I will analyze hinges on whether the incapacitated can be granted personality, and further, whether the slave can ever be redeemed from chattel status.

REDEMPTION

If we try to measure redemption, we always return to the sound of coins: the payment of a debt, the satisfaction of what is owed, the purchasing back of something that has been lost. Can a slave be redeemed? If we can describe the return of what has been lost or seized, then we begin to understand how legal reasoning defined a newly reclaimed entity: a recipient who could never receive, a gift that could not be given. Self-redemption— whereby the slave, once appraised by a legal authority, could redeem himself by paying his appraised value to his master— though difficult to obtain and scrupulously regulated, was possible in various countries ancient and modern, but not in the West Indies and the American South, which were not governed by English laws.

The strict letter of the Old Testament mattered more to pro-slavery apologists in the South than the presumed spirit of the Gospels. Leviticus recognized the existence of slavery in articulating the rules necessary to keep the slave—when an alien and not an Israelite—incapacitated and forever outside the community. Redemption in Leviticus begins with property (25:23–28), moves on to houses (25:29–33), and then, finally, considers the sets of laws regarding the sale of property and debtor-slaves, the interest on loans to impoverished Israelites (25:35–38) and slavery that has resulted from debt (25:39–45). Israelites cannot buy or sell each other as slaves—they are all "children of Israel" and hence "brothers"—but "the children of the strangers that do sojourn among you, of them shall ye buy, and of their families that are with you, which they begat in your land; and they shall be your possession" (25:45). The Old Testament laws of inheritance regarding those taken from "the nations that are round about you" remain severe. Aliens and heathens, in other words, those who are not Israelites, can be made "an inheritance for your children after you to inherit them for a possession, they shall be your bondmen forever: but over your brethren the children of Israel, ye shall not rule one over another with rigor (25:46)." The master can bequeath these foreign slaves to his children, and that legacy renders these possessions irredeemable.

Mosaic laws were both transformed and reinvigorated in the South's law of slavery, especially that having to do with manumission and inheritance. Sin and redemption took on new and unexpected meanings once pressed upon by idioms of servility necessary to the "peculiar institution." "Redemption" means specifically "the dissolution of slavery by force of a condition previously annexed to it for the benefit of the slave, the performance of which, on his part or behalf, intitles him to his freedom by law, independently of his master's will," James Stephen, the English lawyer and chief architect of the Slave Trade Act (1807), explained in *The Slavery of the British West India Colonies Delineated* (1824). In the South, however, slavery was hereditary and unconditional. Redemption or repayment was not a legal form of release, and slaves could not enjoy redemption by law at any price. Legally, slave status was irremovable and transmitted to the issue, as if a perpetual curse or genetic defect. But manumission by a master's last will and testament, though rare, was possible. "Without the master's will, the terrible relation can never be dissolved," Stephen wrote.[10]

Release through manumission, then, was not simply a gift but an act of creation. Since the slave had no capacity to become free and could never gain it, emancipation meant something new. What was that something? Or, to put it differently, how do you bequeath freedom to enslaved persons who might not be capable of receiving it? And what kind of freedom would individual manumission promise? At mid-century, cases throughout the South struggled to define the limits and extent of manumission, when offered in a last will and testament instead of during the master's life. While manumission by will was prohibited by some courts, others permitted it. Unlike redemption, manumission had nothing to do with any legal right of redemption in the slave but depended on the testator's intention.[11]

146

AN AGREEING MIND

As an experiment in legal metaphysics, the majority argument in *Bailey* offers surreal precision. In it, human reduction is calculated to the minutest degree. The very constitution of the self was transformed through a kind of depersonification: slaves are granted volition yet remain nonentities in relation to civil rights or capacities. Lawyers had to be cautious in ascribing mental incapacity in slaves, since slaves had to be held responsible for crimes. In *An Inquiry into the Law of Negro Slavery in the United States of America*, published six months after *Bailey*, Thomas Cobb explained, "The theory of a complete annihilation of will in the slave is utterly inconsistent with all recognition of him as a person, especially as responsible criminally for his acts."[12] But in articulating this personhood, while still ensuring chattel status, the law demanded a fable that substantially changed the hierarchy of things. *Bailey* added a new wrinkle to the tale, depriving slaves of volition in regard to the choice of freedom or bondage even when, seemingly, the law granted them that choice. Perhaps the best way to comprehend this lack of election is to place the law against the background of religious practice: not only a severe Calvinism but a return to the medieval concept of the deodand, specifically its imputation of guilt to inanimate objects or to animals.

If we recall my earlier definition of the deodand as the soulless object or chattel that must be *given to God*, then we can understand the invention of the slave who has liability but no rights, who remains vulnerable to legal prosecution though deprived of personality. In this rationale, the will to commit crime is different from the will to choose freedom and requires another kind of mind. Implementing such a rationale required that the very constitution of the slave self be transformed, and this metamorphosis focused on the unique personhood of the slave. Can slaves have agency? Since slaves gain a legal personality in committing a crime, we can infer that slave law had to give them awareness and responsibility, the consciousness that Locke insisted on as necessary to the person, in rendering him or her accountable in law. Recall that for Locke the *person* unlike the *human* is a forensic term: a legally binding complex of consciousness, sensation, and memory.

Given the necessities of civil incapacity for sustaining servile status, it should not be surprising that the task of judicial reasoning is double: to pry away consciousness from the slave in civil society, but to reattach it once the slave enters the region of crime.[13] The fiction goes something like this: slaves can commit criminal but not civil acts. Their only possible act, recognized by society and by law, is a negative one. "The civil status," John Howard, the crucial lawyer for the heirs in *Bailey*, reminds the court, "has reference to property and all its relations; the power of holding it, using it, controlling it, acquiring it, and parting with it. The criminal status has reference to the moral relations between man and man."[14]

A series of legal fictions, thought puzzles, and ethnographic conundrums prove that not only do slaves have no *legal mind* but they can own nothing. No act of *self-possession* is legally possible. Everything redounds to the master. Neither the capital produced through chattels, nor even their goodwill or capabilities—no matter how special or loyal—gave slaves any legal rights or privileges as persons. Slaves were naturally closer to what was deemed brute creation. "[L]ike the horse and the cow, the domestication and subjection to service" of the slave, in Cobb's words, "did not impair, but on the contrary improved his physical condition." Sensibility, passion, affection, and appetite are incorporated into this representation of slaves, while the rational faculties such as the intellect, will, and the moral sense—or conscience, which, as in Locke's *Essay*, is closely intertwined with consciousness, and hence personal identity—are excised from this portrayal.[15]

We must grasp the artificiality of this fabrication. What emerges from the judges' verbal exchanges that I examine here is an assemblage of materials—humans, animals, pieces of land, cargo, snuffboxes, plates—that is given legal status. How can we visualize this dissimulation of giving that is actually the most consummate deprivation? Even the extensive comparisons between slaves and goods that abound in the *Bailey* deliberation serve to place the object of legal bounty outside all categories.[16]

Howard's lengthy argument is most fully preserved by the reporter, who, we learn at the beginning of the appellate case record, "found it impossible to combine in one all the arguments on a side; and equally impossible to insert all of them." Howard refers to *Dred Scott* when he says, "By the constitution of the United States, slaves are recognized as property; and though in the apportionment of representation and of direct taxation, they are included under the designation of 'three-fifths of all other persons,' yet their rights as persons are utterly ignored." Then, after a history of chattel slavery that begins with Captain John Smith of Jamestown in 1620, Howard explains the "civil status" of the slave "as purely and absolutely mere property, to be bought and sold, and pass and descend as a tract of land, a horse or an ox."[17]

But what about the mind of this servile and negative person? The attention to mind—specifically what he calls "an 'agreeing mind'"—matters most to Howard. "For the parties to every valid contract must be free agents," he explains, "they must have an 'agreeing mind.'" Since the slave's will is, as he puts it, "under subjection to that of the master, the requisite independence and freedom to make the contract or not, does not exist." No matter what the slave does—whether he picks up a piece of meat for the master's family or plows his own plot of land—he is nothing more than the flesh and blood dramatization of the master's will. "The acts of the slave, indeed, are but the acts of the master, if authorized or ratified by him: otherwise, they are of no legal validity or effect."[18]

To be incapable of consent, to be unable to exercise judgment, to lack an agreeing mind—all these deficiencies were used to fill out in law the special nature of impairment when applied to slaves. Persons who have no mind cannot agree in mind with another, hence they can make no contract. Who are these persons?

Traditionally, idiots and lunatics, drunkards, infants, *femme covert* or married women. Once married, a woman's life was sheltered, literally covered over by her husband, her legal rights merged with his—hence the condition called "coverture." The law of impaired mental capacity, however, expanded in scope as the status of slaves came into judicial purview. By the nineteenth century, "unsoundness of mind" became crucial to the development of American common law, and also in the unfolding of the legal personality of slaves in the southern states. What shocks a late-in-coming reader of *Bailey* is how this elaborate redefinition of slave competence cannily provided the means to invalidate manumission by will. Howard's argument about contractual capacity also introduces the theme of disability and exclusion that becomes proof-text for what *Dred Scott* had only asserted: the permanently disabled status of blacks.[19]

Given the ubiquity of this depersonalization, Howard insists, it would be absurd to attribute legal personality to a chattel slave. In so far as "civil rights and relations are concerned, the slave is not a person but a thing." Howard then concludes this part of his argument by listing the characteristics of civilly alive persons: they possess "legal conscience, legal intellect, legal freedom, or liberty and power of free choice and action, and corresponding legal obligations growing out of such qualities." To grant these characteristics to the slave, however, who is legally a non-self—socially and politically unfit—"implies" in Howard's words, "a palpable contradiction in terms."[20]

These contradictions are fundamental to the arguments of this case, both on the part of the heirs and on the part of the executor who wanted to carry out Poindexter's wishes. What weight is the word "legal" intended to carry in this discussion? Once the word "legal" is attached to words such as conscience, intellect, or choice, they no longer mean what we thought they meant. It is as if whenever "legal" is used, it erodes not just the customary and normal but the very facts of existence. This transforming power gives law a reality that flies in the face of logic, and the most fantastic fictions are put forth as the most natural, the most reasonable thing in the world.

BAD LOGIC, GOOD LAW

Ousted from civil society, slaves have no mind or personality recognized by law. They are legally dead to everything except bodily needs or appetite, legally recognized only as the mediums for their master's will. Although "common observation teaches that our slaves, in some cases, have a very high degree of intellect and moral sense," and even "a strong enough will of their own," none of these considerations affects their legal status. Howard asserts: "The court is not sitting as an ethnological society, to ascertain and determine the peculiar natural or acquired characteristics of the negro race." Nevertheless, without referring explicitly to cranium size or the plural origins of the races to prove inferiority, Howard would have agreed with Oliver Wendell Holmes that often "anthropology comes in to aid the researches of jurisprudence." Not only, according to Howard, must "the legal status of the slave under our laws" be established, but the court must seek to discover the justification for legally incapacitating blacks. For all practical purposes, then, these legal rules had to make intelligible some hardly new, though ever- malleable connections: between humans and non-humans, persons and things, bodies and minds.[21]

Howard turns to legal history in order to demonstrate these connections as he deems legally relevant. In the U.S. Supreme Court case of *Boyce v. Anderson* (1829), Chief Justice John Marshall decided that a carrier cannot have the same control over slaves as over "inanimate matter." The carrier's liability for loss of a slave is not the same as if the loss had been "a common package." Even though the "negligence" of the captain and commandants of a steamboat resulted in the loss of slaves, their owner could not recover their value in damages. Slaves have "volition" and "feelings," and thus, "in the nature of things," Marshall argued, a slave "resembles a passenger, not a package of goods."[22] Yet these attributes, Howard suggests, do not make the character of the slave anything more than an animate "article of transportation." In other words, slaves can be considered property to be transported and, at the same time, not exactly *be* passengers but only *resemble* passengers. This resemblance, as Howard reasons, is tenuous at best:

> [T]herefore the carrier was not held to as high a degree of responsibility in the transportation of slaves, as in the transportation of a common package. The same principle, it is presumed, would apply, *sub modo* to dogs, cattle, wild animals, &c. over which "the carrier has not and cannot have the same absolute control as over a common package." It might be good logic, but it would be bad law, to say that therefore dogs, horses, cattle and animals, *ferae naturae*, were recognized, as something more, in legal contemplation, than mere property. It is alike bad logic and bad law to say that, by this case, slaves are recognized as any thing more.[23]

Though slaves could be recognized as more than just a package of goods, something more valuable than mere merchandise or perishables in the market, they were legally nothing more than chattels. More than mere merchandise, they are nevertheless deemed less than human passengers. Law is not to be mistaken for logic. It is not to be interpreted literally but reasonably. But what kind of reason, we must ask again, defies logic? What is known to the law is unknown to the naked eye, and to common sense. Its fictions are daunting.

PUTTING ON THE PERISHABLE BODY

The meaning of personhood changes when the notion is applied to those who cannot perform a civil act or cannot count in terms of civil rights and relations. What kind of being is created by the law of slavery? What kind of external world can exist for this object of law? In lacking the ability to perform a civil act, to count in terms of civil rights and relations, the slave loses any claims to the capacities necessary for social and political inclusion. In *Bailey*, the rules of law are reclaimed as the last possible bulwark against militant abolitionists, those who threatened to destroy the servile sphere necessary for the order of slavery. But the law is not alone in the task that pro-slavery forces gave it. Scriptural authority was also essential to the judicial diminishing of the slave's legal personality. Legal practice and spiritual belief worked together to redefine matter and spirit, persons and property; and the rules of law thus became inextricable from theological preoccupations.

God mattered to slave owners. What was legally ordained became inextricable from heavenly dispensation. Inheritance promises a kind of immortality, and John Poindexter's will was in legal effect a continuation of his legal personality after death. It transmitted the testator's rights and obligations or duties to others. But his will was blocked. Had Poindexter simply asked that his slaves be emancipated after his death, his wish would have been fulfilled. Instead, he gave them a choice: they could elect freedom or continued servitude. Counsel for his heirs, the appellants in the case, argued that such a choice was tantamount to Poindexter's playing God, as if he could create a new species, as if from beyond the grave he could summon an *anomaly in law*. "No man," Judge William Daniel ultimately concluded, "can create a new species of property unknown to the law. No man is allowed to introduce anomalies into the ranks under which the population of the state is ranged and classified by its constitution and laws."[24]

The creation of an artificial entity, whether the civil body, the legal slave, or the felon rendered dead in law, takes place in a world where legal discernment remains inseparable from spiritual authority. As I said earlier, pro-slavery judges took their cue from Calvinist orthodoxy, repackaging its doctrines of innate depravity and divine determinism. The portrayal of slaves as the non-elect, but also as beings who had no free will, whose destiny was predetermined, servile, ineradicable, naturally lent support to arguments against their capacity to choose their future. Manumission, even as it became more severely restricted, or perhaps because of these restrictions, preserved this trade-off between matter and spirit, the saved and the damned.

Williamson v. Coalter, decided by the Supreme Court of Appeals in Virginia immediately after *Bailey* in May 1858, affirmed the inability of slaves to choose, but in terms that left no uncertainty about the gravity of manumission, its unavailability except through the master's express directive. The court defined it as "an act by which property is renounced and extinguished.... The moment the deed or will, the instruments alone by which slaves can be manumitted, takes effect, he is, in legal contemplation, transformed into a new being; no property in him can exist." We recall Blackstone's description of the king's pardon of an attainted felon: a metamorphosis from civil death into life that made the offender "a new man" with renewed "credit and capacity." Slaves not only are marked by their servile status, but also, in a fascinating way, are placed outside the Pauline injunction to be glorified in the body. Instead, they are degraded in their body. Not only because of various somatic bonds of subjection—a certain kind of hair and skin color—but more importantly, as Cobb suggests in his *Inquiry into the Law of Negro Slavery*, because of something more conclusive, the operations of law itself.[25]

"He can be reached only through his body," Cobb wrote, "and, hence, in cases not capital, whipping is the only punishment which can be inflicted." Why, one might ask, can he *not* be reached through his mind? The answer, it turns out, involves some of the most astute and thoughtful of southern judges in a dizzying array of examples that demonstrate the legal destruction of the person. Not only did manumission nearly cease to be legal in the Virginia courts, but the possibility of such putative rebirth begs the question: What would the *new man* do? Where could he live? And, compelled to leave Virginia within a year, where would he go? On the eve of the Civil War, following the decisions in *Bailey* and *Williamson*, only 277 slaves were freed out of a slave population of a half million.[26]

In the background of the argument against Poindexter stands the resurrected body. The admonition to "cast off the works of darkness" and "put on the armor of light" (Romans 13:12) becomes in the law of this case a drama that returns us to the rationale of civil death I discussed in chapter 2. To take on the skin of the civil and thus be protected by law, a human being must die to the natural order and be born again as a civil person. "It is sown in corruption; it is raised in incorruption" (1 Corinthians 15:42). But this Pauline ritual of the perishable body putting on imperishability takes on even greater resonance when applied to the dispossession necessitated by slavery. These newly reclaimed and unnatural persons, once acknowledged as perishables, relinquish their minds and retain only their bodies. Ineradicably tainted, forever resistant to the claims of the spirit, they bear a stigma that can never be removed. Judge Joseph Henry Lumpkin concluded in *Bryan v. Walton* (1853) in the Supreme Court of Georgia that even with manumission, "social and civil degradation, resulting from the taint of blood, adheres to the descendants of Ham in this country, like the poisoned tunic of Nessus."[27]

Can this person that remains either the object of the civil rights of others or the subject of property statutes *choose* to resurrect himself as emancipated and thus change his status from slave to free, from chattel to citizen? Howard wondered how this chattel, comparable to an ox or horse, could suddenly be endowed with civil rights and civil capacity, and thereby perform "that great, transcendent act of supreme civil dignity and sovereign power, the transformation of himself from a thing into a person, from a chattel to a man clothed with all the high attributes of a citizen." Later, concluding the argument on behalf of the heirs, Judge William Daniel explicitly states: "Any testamentary effort of a master to clothe his slave with such a power [to elect manumission], is an effort to accomplish a legal impossibility." The sacred metaphors of transformation—donning a new garment, putting on incorruption, or being "sown a natural body ... raised a spiritual body" (1 Corinthians 15:44)—became instead the necessary proofs of a status that would never change.[28]

"CHATTELS, SERVANTS, NEGARS, CATTLE OR ANY OTHER THING"

In the *Bailey* decision, the remnants of old taxonomies and codes, though present, were not as important as the need to maintain what had ended in the Caribbean and to confront the rancorous onslaught of abolitionist propaganda.[29] Slavery ended in Haiti after the successful slave revolution and creation of the republic in 1804. In Martinique and Guadeloupe, slavery was abolished in 1848. Emancipation in the West Indies, though gradual, was finally decreed in 1834. The establishment as well as the inventiveness of chattel slavery in the South owed a great deal to the tailoring of law to the demands of ownership. The resulting laws were unique. Paul Finkelman has written that they created a "racially based slavery," "both peculiar and damaging, not only to the slaves and masters of the time, but to the entire society then and now." Nothing so extensive as this "slave society" existed in the Caribbean.[30]

In *Bailey*, Howard admitted: "It is a curious fact, that there is no statute directly reducing negroes into slavery." The presumed racial inferiority of blacks, whether free or slave, made the curse of color synonymous with enslavement. A legal dispensation, however, was necessary to rationalize this enduring legacy of stigma so as to stamp out once and for all the possibilities of freedom for what Taney in *Dred Scott* had called "that class of persons." There being no legal limitation to human bondage, the conceptual scheme buttressed the project of certifying place, position, and rank. It sustained a manner of speaking about a void that could never be filled. In support of this unrelieved incompetency, the judges in *Bailey* not only justified slavery but also invited evidence that the utter negation of civil existence was both necessary and just.[31]

A new type of legal history was promulgated especially for slaves. Daniel quotes a passage from Chancellor James Kent's *Commentaries on American Law*, where he noted that the condition of southern slaves has more resemblance to "the slaves of the ancients than to that of the villeins of feudal times, both in respect to the degradation of the slaves, and the full dominion and power of the master." There was no legal precedent in Roman law. Though slaves remained mere chattels (*res*), and the products of mixed-status unions followed the condition of the mother (*partus sequitur ventrem*), comparisons with the Roman law of slavery are misleading. There were limits to dehumanization. Roman slaves could acquire property, they could be educated, could free themselves, and once freed, lose the taint of servitude, since it was not tied to inheritable blood or to race. Further, as we have seen, the feudal *villein* in England, though unprotected in his property, was *unfree* only in relation to his master.[32]

The next authority cited by Daniel, Judge Henry St. George Tucker, was even more explicit about the slaves' absolute incapacity, their legal disability as a "distinct class of *persons*," in the appendix to his edition of Blackstone's *Commentaries* (1803). Leaving aside the broad contours of Tucker's impassioned argument against that "partial system of morality which confines rights and injuries, to particular complexions," Daniel underscores the uniqueness of slavery:[33]

> [I]n all civilized nations all free persons, whether citizens or aliens; males or females; infants or adults; white or black, of sound mind, or idiots and lunatics, have their respective social rights according to the customs, laws and usages of the country. "Slaves only, where slavery is tolerated by the laws, are excluded from social rights."[34]

The persistent effort to underscore this exclusion made possible the hierarchy that put slaves outside the order of free, white individuals. Tucker, one of the few politicians in Virginia publicly to propose an end to slavery, emphasized how irreconcilable is the state of slavery with "the principles of a democracy" and "the bill of rights," which grants "enjoyment of life and *liberty*, with the means of *acquiring* and *possessing property*." To read Tucker's condemnation of slavery is to know how troubling the institution remained to a southerner, lawyer, and legal scholar. But Tucker was more than a southerner. He was also a West Indian. Born in Bermuda in 1752, he moved to Virginia at nineteen, enrolling as a student at the College of William and Mary. He took the side of the colonies during the Revolution. Back in Bermuda, he engaged in illicit trade with American rebels. Throughout his life, he remained unequivocal about the moral incoherence of a country that fought "to live free, or die," only to legalize a condition "ten thousand times more cruel than the utmost extremity of those grievances and oppressions" it had struggled against.[35]

In 1796, Tucker published *A Dissertation on Slavery: With A Proposal for the Gradual Abolition of It, in the State of Virginia*, which would later be incorporated into the appendix of his two-volume edition of Blackstone. It was fitting that this tract was appended to Blackstone's "Of the Rights of Persons," for Tucker gives a history to a jurisprudence gone awry. Slavery threatened the foundations of civil society; it spawned laws so extreme and unjust that their justification could only succeed by actions more anthropological than legal. Since no one has a right to insult, mistreat, or maim "*inferiors*," no matter their complexion, the only way to reconcile laws that allow such unnatural behavior with democratic principles is to sequester these persons from society. "It would be hard," he argues, "to reconcile reducing the negroes to a state of slavery ... unless we first degrade them below the rank of human beings, not only politically, but also physically and morally." The legal fictions that accommodated such degradation, once set in motion, had no conceivable limit.[36]

These deeply troubling, if not pathological, definitions of status advanced by some appellate judges followed Taney's decision in *Dred Scott*. How can human materials be legally hollowed out? It is in this light that we must see the responses of the lawyers who speak for Poindexter's heirs. Their lengthy ruminations go far beyond the necessities of the case and plunge us into a tangle of suppositions. Their reasoning adumbrates the fixed hierarchy that sustains the image of legal slaves as incurably unfit. A juristic curiosity becomes real and viable. The dicta amount to nothing less than a legal metaphysics that goes behind the scenes to show how the law gives birth to a new entity in body and mind. Moreover, such discriminations coin a new definition of body and give another meaning to mind. Here, in this disposition of human property, there are some very real limits to recognizing personhood.

These rhetorical efforts are framed with reference to questions of status, right, and legal capacity. Once Poindexter has died, the heirs' attempt to invalidate his will not only negates the master's dubious gift to his slaves, but also nullifies the testator's own will, both literally and figuratively. In these delicate calibrations of the master's dominion and the slave's person, the dead master Poindexter is himself deprived of legal capacity. Since civil status customarily referred to property—the power of suing for it, acquiring it, holding it—as the singular right of the master, the master who has willed his slaves the right of election must no longer be master of his will.

Either Poindexter did not understand the law of slavery or he knew it too well. On the one hand, he committed to paper what the majority would hold was a legal impossibility. On the other hand, since he had given his personal slaves—those he named in the will—to his nephew, was this clause of election Poindexter's way of saying that free or slave, manumitted or kept, blacks in the South could never be redeemed from servility? Their services, in one form or another, would always be for sale. They would always be redeemable, but at a cost that could never be met. Was his legacy a caustic demonstration, at the slaves' expense, of the irredeemable stigma of slavery? Perhaps he did not care at all what became of his slaves. Judge John Patton, arguing on behalf of the executors of Poindexter's will—and his argument is the only one reported, the only record we have of counsel, for that side—construes the will by beginning with what Poindexter might have said, "'I am indifferent, so far as my own wishes go'"; only to interject "(though I have no doubt he wished them to be free)"; and then concludes, again in the testator's voice, "'whether my slaves are emancipated or not; but I wish them to have their choice of being free.'"[37]

RIDDLING SLAVES, KITTENS, AND POTATOES

Which analogies, ultimately, are used to govern the case? After the appeal from the circuit court, all that remains in the record of the appellees—those arguing in favor of the slaves—is some of John M. Patton's argument, which is then rebutted by William Robertson. Both Patton and Robertson concentrate on the testamentary method known as manumission "in futuro," which meant that the master's last will and testament gave slaves their freedom at a specified time *after* his death. Usually, this freedom depended upon some act or condition of the slave or on some event before emancipation could be granted. Poindexter's will made the choice or election of the slaves the condition of their freedom, once his wife died. Until this appeal, such wills were treated by the courts as valid. In order to argue that Poindexter's intention should be respected, Patton makes utterly insignificant the wishes of slaves in order to show how wrongheaded is Howard's obsession with the slaves' ability to choose.

Patton argues that no matter what the slave wishes, emancipation is the testator's act. The "validity of the act of emancipation" is not affected by the conditional "if they [my slaves] wish." The appeal to their choice is "'idle wind'" because wholly irrelevant to the question. Emancipation, he argues, has nothing to do with the slaves' personal will. The hypothetical fable that

160

Patton tells makes choice a subterfuge: a semblance of cause and effect that has no effect. Granted, the condition of being a slave is unconditional. So it should be obvious, he implies in a series of hypothetical *if* clauses, that the words apparently giving them the right to election are meaningless. Only the testator's wishes count, for only the master can choose.

> If a testator by his will declared during the late presidential election, If Fremont is not elected president of the United States, then I wish all my slaves to be free. Or, if I make a crop of one hundred bushels of potatoes, I wish all my slaves to be emancipated; Or, if my wife's cat kittens between this and Christmas, I will all my slaves to be free; otherwise not: In all these cases, I presume, if the wills were admitted to probate, the right to freedom, on the happening of the event, would be clear; and would be ineffectual if they did not happen. Yet it would hardly be contended, that Buchanan by defeating Fremont; the potatoes; or the cat by having her litter in the time prescribed, had emancipated the slaves; or that the bequest was void because one man cannot emancipate another man's slaves; because potatoes are merely property; or a cat has no legal status, and cannot do any legal civil act!!! [38]

What stays in our minds after reading through the arguments of *Bailey* is that slaves were always implicitly analogous to "potatoes" and "kittens." The analogies matter greatly, perhaps not to the outcome but to the depiction of a certain kind of person. Each time the array of cats, kittens, and potatoes comes up, each time another reference is made to Patton's original hypothetical by lawyers for the heirs, something more is suggested about the slaves, about their rank in the order of things.

Robertson responds to Patton by restating the conditions— "if a testator should make the freedom of his slaves to depend on the election of Fremont as president; on his (the testator's) making one hundred bushels of potatoes; on his wife's cat kittening before Christmas"—and agreeing that in these cases, the will would be granted. He explains that no matter how ridiculous these conditions may be, they are not *unlawful*: "The law of God and nature allows it; and there is no clause in the constitution, or special statute, known to me, which forbids it." But to give slaves the "right or privilege" of choosing freedom remains "incompatible with the status of slavery."[39]

Though Patton's original point is eroded, and the slaves lose their possibility of freedom, something else endures. His example, which made irrelevant Poindexter's words about the slaves' wishes, fades away. What remains is a series of terms for understanding what it means to be a slave. Robertson grants that had the master freed the slave "on condition that his wife's cat may have kittens or the slave herself may have a male child before that time," this would have been legal. "The parturition of the cat or of the slave is, in the course of nature, unprohibited by law." In the kitchen, just as the wife's cat has kittens, so the wife's slave, in exquisite correspondence, has a child who takes on bondage in perpetuity, and transmits slavery to her own issue. That is the analogy that matters: between slaves and breeding pets.[40]

Robertson first adopts Patton's conditions of Fremont's election, potatoes, or kittens, only to up the ante. Moving away from a testator's mere whim or fancy, he introduces stereotypical propensities that threaten to overturn authority and unhinge the carefully calibrated protection of slaves. Without directly invoking the fear of numerous freed slaves roaming uncontrolled in Virginia, slightly defective and perfectly idle, he represents slaves as a new species without ascertainable age or detectable understanding. Yet they are willful in their body, potentially guilty of heinous crimes, capable of rape or assault. Had Poindexter actually emancipated his slaves, Robertson argues, they would have been free no matter what they did: "[I]t matters not … how absurd the reason, nor how unlawful the act on which the freedom may have been granted; if it were carnal connection with a white woman, or for assaulting a white man, the grant being consummated, would be effectual, and the title to freedom a vested right." But Robertson knew that this right was merely hypothetical; it could never be exercised, since the slave would be liberated only to be punished.[41]

Robertson makes the very idea of manumission foolhardy if not inconceivable in a series of desperate but effective suppositions. He does not need to appeal to Justice Taney's "indelible marks" that separate blacks from whites or to the "stigma of the deepest degradation." Instead, Robertson summons up varying scenarios of disenchantment: blacks bereft of moral sense and threatening whites. These dangerous characters stick in the mind and make legally meaningful the deficiency that becomes essential to the logic of slavery.[42]

HIERARCHIES OF IMPAIRMENT

A gift of manumission can depend upon any number of things —the birth of kittens or carnal conquest—but not the slave's choice. Such a choice, Robertson argued, is not only legally impossible but also of dubious logic. For what is freedom to a slave? When will this gift take effect? At what age? Can the legal mind, once vacated from the slave's person, be returned? Given the legal incapacities of slaves, a thing like liberty must remain uncertain, its character unknowable. As the arguments in the case continue, it is not enough to say that slaves have no legal mind, but the lawyers for the heirs go further still: even if slaves legally had the right to choose freedom, they could not be expected to know how to make such a choice, or what to do with such freedom once granted. The negative comparisons with infants, lunatics, or wives find their fullest expression in analyses of incapacity by Robertson. In his grid of comparable disabilities that range from infants to idiots to wives, slaves alone suffer permanent incapacity.[43]

These discussions of comparative disabilities convey the paternalistic concern for persons whose mental capacity could not be adequately judged. In his final argument, and sometimes with downright hostility, Robertson seems not to qualify the mind of slaves so much as to remove it. Uday Mehta in *Liberalism and*

163

Empire (1999) demonstrates how liberal universals are founded on a set of "anthropological capacities" that determine what it means to be human. The "anthropological minimum" for attaining moral personhood is the capacity to reason. But in legal relations, as I mentioned before, slaves are nothing more than what Edward Long portrayed as mindless effigies of the human, "mere matter, unanimated with a thinking principle."[44]

The slaves' incapacity is infinite. Not only can they not wish, choose—or, so it seems, hope—for anything, but no one can wish *for them*. No court, no commissioner, no guardian, no mother or father can bequeath to them. Though idiots and lunatics, Robertson writes, must "be well apprised of their rights, and the consequences of that election," no one can "instruct these ignorant slaves, to make them understand the benefits or evils of different plans for their future condition and residence."[45]

They are not only legally but also medically incompetent to choose. But how does Robertson describe the impairment of mind that can be held civilly deficient but criminally responsible? Does it differ from the standard medical categories of incapacity—insanity, lunacy, or unsoundness of mind? The exclusion of slaves from the civil order is based on something graver than the legal or natural incapacity of idiots, which is unrecoverable, impaired from birth; than the status of lunatics, who suffer only intermittent madness; or that of children, or married women, those disabled under law from full personhood. If a woman is judged *non compos mentis*, then the courts allow for interdiction: a judicial decree that deprives a person judged insane of the exercise of her civil rights. Like a dead person, she becomes legally a cipher; and like a slave, she cannot impose her will upon her life. She does not exist except through her guardian, in whom she lives, moves, and has her being.

Introducing the case on behalf of the heirs, Howard granted slaves the mental prerequisites of legal responsibility, but only up to a point. Recall that there are two scales: criminal and civil. As natural persons, slaves might have intellectual, moral, and volitional power. On this scale, they rank higher than infants, idiots, or lunatics. But as civil persons, slaves are utterly bereft of any relation to property, or any claim to it. Idiots, lunatics, or infants can own thousands of slaves, "inherit or be inherited from ... be the objects of devises or bequests, though they cannot devise and bequeath." In this hierarchy of legal incapacity, however, wives and slaves become analogous: "A married woman," Howard explained, "may commit a crime and will be punished for it, though she has no power to make a contract, and her civil being is absolutely merged in that of her husband." Like the slave, she is excluded from all public functions: "her civil relations are very different things from the relation she sustains to the criminal law."[46]

The use of women to clarify the status of slaves is part of the argument against Patton. Robertson, unlike Howard, denies that any "analogies" to slaves can be found in the law. Following Blackstone's exception of slaves from social rights, he distinguishes slaves from free persons, whether they are male or female, child or adult, sane or mad. Married women, he argues, have legal discretion and can inherit property by deed or will, as do "infants even in ventre sa mere, or idiots, or lunatics: They are all free persons, though under partial or temporary disabilities. To reason in favor of similar powers, rights or capacities in slaves, on the ground of analogy, is to plunge into a labyrinth of error." Slaves occupy the lowest rung of the ladder in terms of legal capacity. Not even the goodwill or capabilities of the slave—no matter how special or loyal—gave the slave legal rights as a person. What about the value of an efficiently performing slave? Does that not prove mental competency, or as Robertson asks, can that performance be considered a "civil act"? Only if the service of "a well-trained and sagacious dog," in bringing his owner meat in a butcher's basket, could "in a legal sense" be understood as "a civil act of the dog."[47]

Robertson portrays slaves as dead to law, except when committing a crime. Then he goes further. Slaves are unknown to the law; no one can choose for them. Even if they are unable to make decisions, they have no natural right to guardians.

Who can wish for them? ... Suppose there be infants of tender age without mothers or known fathers: who then is to wish for them? Their grand mothers or grand fathers? Perhaps in their dotage. Who are to choose or wish for idiots, if any, or lunatics, or doting old men and women? Say they are held incapable one or all, to judge for themselves, and that commissioners shall be appointed to choose for them.

But in the case of slaves who should assume such a power of choice, "on the one hand to condemn to perpetual slavery, or on the other to perpetual exile"? As for adult slaves, he asks: "[I]s it not every way probable, that many among them may be utterly incapable of making a sound and discreet decision?"[48]

Careful to cover the continuum of mental incapacity in both medical and legal terms, Robertson moves from idiots, lunatics, the aged, to those less legally impaired, but equally impression-able and easily confounded. Their mind is off-limits, a void wait-ing to be filled by whites, either for or against slavery. These descriptions of incapacity lead to examples of victimization. Both characterizations apply to the legal situation of slaves: "Their minds have been impressed by abolitionists perhaps on the one side, or interested claimants on the other." Or perhaps not empty, but deranged by their misfortunes and inebriated by whisky: "They have been menaced, frightened out of their pro-priety, by the terrors of the lash, at home; the dread of misery and starvation abroad; or poisoned by indulgence in whisky ... till their wits, if any they had, are unsettled."

OLD TOM'S HAUNT

In willing that his slaves exercise their will, Poindexter's legacy is void. In his will, the slaves, according to Robertson, not only are left with a choice of freedom or slavery, but they are to choose "whether they will be emancipated or sold publicly." How can this happen, when slaves have no legal capacity, no matter their age? It is a logical impossibility. "There is no such thing as lawful age to be predicated of slaves." Their condition remains the same no matter their age. Then he turns to "mental capacity." But, he wonders, how can one judge what is unsound when applied to slave minds? In *Elder v. Elder*, decided in 1833, two years before Poindexter made his will—and perhaps on Poindexter's mind when he considered making his last will—the Supreme Court of Appeals of Virginia allowed slave mothers to choose for all children under twenty-one. But what if that mother is "drunken, superannuated, or ignorant and reckless," Robertson asks, "swayed either way for a bottle of whisky"?[49]

"Over and above," the institution of slavery, wrote Harriet Beecher Stowe in *Uncle Tom's Cabin* (1852), "there broods a portentous shadow—the shadow of *law*." *Bailey* offers a response to Stowe's *Uncle Tom's Cabin*, *A Key to Uncle Tom's Cabin* (1853), and *Dred: A Tale of the Great Dismal Swamp* (1856). The law of slavery was sustained by literary fictions as well as its own. As many have recognized, the good nature and martyrdom of Tom, while turning him into a Christ figure, do nothing for his status. By the end of the novel, Stowe reserves the responsibility for race uplift to the light-skinned George. But even he must go to Liberia, and there found a nation in the image of the Anglo-Saxon idea.

Uncle Tom's Cabin tells many stories. The exposition of the generous Augustine St. Clare's premature death and the subsequent failed manumission of Uncle Tom and Tom's sale downriver to Simon Legree set the other plots in motion. Just a year before Stowe's *Dred*, Frederick Douglass published *My Bondage and My Freedom*. Yet it is neither the rebel slave Dred nor the escaped slave turned writer and orator Douglass, but Uncle Tom, called "'Old Tom'" (and Robertson marks his representativeness with quotation marks), who matters to the conclusion of *Bailey*.[50]

Robertson's recasting of Stowe's tale as exemplum occupies two paragraphs of his response. A literary figure supplies the context for the qualified capacity to reason, the indisposition, unfitness, or contrariety of mind that necessitates a slave's legal

167

condition. Robertson's characterization of Tom and the provisional, ever-contingent promise of freedom might at first seem to take what white antislavery writers such as Harriet Beecher Stowe and Lydia Maria Child lamented as tragic turns in their plots—failed emancipation—and make it the legal proof of incapacity.[51]

But perhaps Robertson appreciated the character Stowe had created. Miss Ophelia describes Stowe's good slave Tom, locked in the precincts of service, lying supine on the veranda in order to be close to the dying Eva, as "sleeping anywhere and everywhere, like a dog." Tom, put in the proper domestic setting, becomes the medium by which perfect submission becomes equivalent to the rule of law. It was Robertson, after all, who had earlier used a dog to prove the slave's civil nonexistence. The dog goes to the butcher, gets the meat, and brings it to the master, but none of these acts grants legal personality. Just so, no slave can will anything at all unless he acts explicitly as the instrument of the will of his owner.

> A man may call up his sons, and say to them, you shall have between you, Tom, Dick and Harry, as "Old Tom" shall desire, choose, or appoint: and on learning that desire, may consummate the gift by a deed on that express ground. But he cannot by his contract make a valid disposition of this kind to take effect *in futuro*.

The first story begins as if it is a fairy tale with a master, three boys—unidentified except for the sarcastic labels "Tom, Dick, and Harry"—and "Old Tom," the father of the slaves. The master makes a gift of slaves not freedom in this fable. But besides the dark fiction, Robertson means to deny Patton's argument that the choice is really Poindexter's, and insists instead on the illegality of manumission *in futuro*. "It is a legal solecism to speak of such election or renunciation as any thing short of civil acts— civil acts of the highest character." Only while the master lives can his will be passed on to the slave, can the slave obey the command to "desire, choose, or appoint."

The next anecdote puts Tom in his cabin with his sons, a privilege that depends on the master's whim, so long as he lives. "A master might say to 'Old Tom,' 'that shall be your cabin during life. Your sons Tom, Dick and Harry shall live with you and work for you as long as you choose;' and Old Tom might be permitted to enjoy these privileges as long as his master lived. But they would impose upon the master no obligation." Once the master dies, he cannot bequeath to Tom the right to choose for himself or his sons, nor can any permission of the master, once dead, remain in effect: not "permission to occupy the cabin," to remain with his sons, or send them to Liberia, or go there himself—"the bequests would all, in a legal sense, be nullities," unless enforced by executor, heir or devisee.[52]

MONCURE'S MIND

If, in regard to civil rights and relations, slaves are what constitutional and statute law makes them, and nothing more, then once we enter the realm of feeling or attachment, these objects of law undergo strange and paradoxical metamorphoses. For on one hand they must be kept in their proper place of absolute civil nonentity, and on the other they must be deemed, when it serves the owner's needs, peculiar kinds of property: "creatures" that engender sentiments of friendship, affection, and esteem. Legal thought relied on a set of fictions to sustain such concepts as the absolute idea of property and the changing distinction of slaves as things or persons, depending on whether the context was civil action (as article of property, utterly deprived of civil capacity) or criminal action (as capable of crime, hence recognized as a willful being with a consciousness that extended through time).[53]

In July 1856, when *Summers v. Bean* was brought before the Supreme Court of Appeals of Virginia—a year and a half before the arguments in *Bailey*—Judge Richard Cassius Lee Moncure insisted on the qualities of the slave as a unique legal creature and ordered the performance of a contract for delivery of slaves

169

in a court of equity. For Moncure, the Bible was the basis for the law: not the stories of Ham and the dark blight on the African race, but the hope of the Scriptures, and the disciplined ritual of the Book of Common Prayer. A vestryman in the Episcopal Church for forty years, Moncure was known as an independent judge who remained unmoved by the extremism of other jurists at mid-century. He wrestled with the ramifications of Enlightenment thought while remaining fascinated by the limits of moral responsibility in the context of legally ordained deprivation. For Moncure, masters as well as slaves were caught up in the radical qualifications of legal identity that the peculiar institution demanded.[54]

Moncure finally ruled that there was no remedy at law for the nondelivery of slaves, summoning in his support *Young v. Burton* (1841), an earlier case involving the transport and loss of slaves.[55] Damages based on market value could not substitute for this "peculiar species of property": in this case, two slaves, thirteen-year-old Caroline and eleven-year-old McKendry. Moncure turned to a transcendent ideal of conscience rather than the practical rules of law. Only a court of equity could come to the relief of the plaintiff and enforce the carrying out of the contract, not a law court.[56] This was the first time the Supreme Court of Virginia had to decide a case of this kind, to consider, as Moncure explained, "[w]hether a court of equity will specifically execute a contract for the sale or delivery of slaves ... or that adequate compensation for them cannot be obtained at law."[57]

Moncure based his decision on "the nature of the subject," "the peculiar species of property under consideration." Although we might be tempted to dismiss him as yet another southern antebellum judge who thought it wise to place as much value as possible on a piece of human property, I choose rather to accept the consequences of his ethically loaded valuation of personhood. The persuasive effects of these words matter a great deal. They offer a limited but unambiguous insight into the import and the fragility of his attempt to grant rational faculties to slaves while adhering to the *special* nature of this human property. Moncure cites an English case, *Pearne v. Lisle* (1749), regarding delivery of slaves on the island of Antigua. When lost or stolen, an irreplaceable slave was considered as something like "a cherry-stone very finely engraved" or "an extraordinary wrought piece of plate" rather than "diamonds," where "one may be as good as another." But this case is no precedent. Lord Hardwicke in *Pearne* failed to add, Moncure argues, that slaves were also human beings.[58]

In the confused and contentious past of slavery, the division of slaves into real and personal property mattered greatly to the necessary rituals of possession. As Howard pointed out in *Bailey* (recalling *Boyce v. Anderson*), a carrier transporting slaves is liable for their loss, since they are "intelligent beings" and "living men," not "common goods" or "inanimate matter." As property, a slave could be bought and sold. Animated property, she could be forced to work and even breed like a domestic animal. But this being still needed special restraints and care. Damages at law, Moncure argued in *Summers v. Bean*, cannot remedy the situation. Money cannot replace the uniqueness of this property, which must be returned bodily to the plaintiff, just as in "the specific execution of contracts concerning real estate." While fixing slaves on the land which depended upon them, he adds: "Slaves are not only property but rational beings; and are generally acquired with reference to their moral and intellectual qualities."[59]

Why does he mention real estate here? Not only because slaves worked the earth and remained close to the soil, but because their very being was determined both as movable, and, in some unusual cases of testamentary trust, as fixed to the land, like trees or buildings. Slaves occupied and cultivated the earth. They worked on the land—and, in an incalculable sense, lived through it and for it. Though they could not own it, they became it. Their existence was entangled with what bound them in labor.[60]

Moncure's position in the Virginia Supreme Court of Appeals was a difficult one. By the time he served as judge in *Bailey*, he realized how serious the question of emancipation had become. Unwilling to support the prevailing rationale of the court, he resisted the severity of its argument, especially the characterization of slaves as elaborated by Daniel, who dwelled on the disabilities inherent in "the true condition here of the class of persons to which they belong." Moncure argued that increasing public pressure to maintain slavery should not sway judges.[61]

Deadly serious, without rhetorical flourishes, literary references, or jokes, Moncure attempted to found an ethical relation in the context of slavery—a cautious attentiveness to the character of the enslaved as something more than what Daniel judged "the mere creatures of the master." He asserted that even within that institution, a master could develop a relation that mattered, and could, in making his will, ordain that it be recognized in law. To treat Poindexter's will as something to be ignored, or, worse, rendered null—by giving legatees the power to question his final wishes for his slaves—would be to deny or overlook the solidity of the attachments and sentiments that Poindexter's relationship might have engendered.[62]

There were no statutes or precedent cases that could justify the *Bailey* decision, Moncure argued. "That a master may emancipate his slaves upon a condition precedent, if there be nothing unlawful in the condition, is a proposition which will not be denied." Without taking up and joining the trivializing ripostes about kittens and potatoes, he concluded that "no condition however unreasonable or even capricious would, on that account merely, be unlawful." Moncure attempts to capture the psychological and emotional condition of individuals who also happen to be slaves. He takes up the argument of incapacity made by Judge Daniel and the lawyers for the heirs, and then modestly undercuts it. Daniel, agreeing with Howard and Robertson, negated Poindexter's wish, since he "endeavored to clothe his slaves with the uncontrollable and irrevocable power of determining for themselves whether they shall be manumitted." Moncure responds that even if slaves are "incapable of making a discreet choice, and could merely guess what was best for them, there would be nothing in that incapacity which would make the condition unlawful.... [A] condition is not unlawful, merely because unreasonable or even capricious."[63]

Refusing to reduce slaves to unthinking automata unable to will, except as "an instrument or medium" for the master, as Daniel had argued, Moncure carefully adds: "But slaves have some capacity to choose, though it may, generally, be very weak and imperfect." Further, without referring directly to his colleagues' repeated denials of capacity and declarations of legal incompetence, he turns to the conditions of slaves once freed. Instead of emphasizing how unfit they are for freedom—locked in their servile status—Moncure not only affirms their legal capacity in criminal law but also insists on their judgment and discrimination. Once freed, they have minds able to partake in civil society: "[T]hey are legally capable, without any increase of intelligence, of making contracts, buying and selling property, and doing other acts which require the exercise of mental faculties." Choice matters. They can elect to return to slavery, and they can choose freedom.[64]

Moncure emphasizes the most crucial part of his argument: that if a slave can only become free by the act of his master, prescribed by law, in his last will and testament, then once effectively done in that way, freedom "may be made to depend on the willingness of the slave as well as upon any other condition." This is a striking claim to make, given the arguments of his opponents. Moncure refuses at any point to negate the will of a slave. If a slave has the capacity to distinguish good from evil—and hence can be punished for crime—then a slave has the ability to choose. That Poindexter had recognized that ability to choose, the capacity to prefer, is not to be punished by the court. Instead, Moncure insists that what really matters in this case is the apparent retribution against a master who chooses to be considerate: who does not "wish to force freedom upon them against their will." There is pathos in Moncure's final appeal: "Ought we now to frustrate his will, and award the slaves unconditionally to those to whom he gave them only on condition that the slaves reject the boon of freedom which he offers them?" Further, Moncure argues the illogicality of the court's reasonable consensus: "A master may emancipate his slaves *against* their consent. Why may he not make such consent the condition of emancipation?"[65]

What Moncure focuses on is the charity of a master who wants to give the slave a chance to stay with his family, to remain home, not to be separated from what he loves. But it is this very care that William Daniel and his fellow conservative judges George N. Lee and J. J. Allen will not allow. By the time Moncure hears the case of *Williamson v. Coalter*, four months later in 1858, which further restricted bequests of freedom, he fiercely elaborates his rejection of the *Bailey* decision. As I noted earlier, the critical exchange between liberals and conservatives in the Virginia Court of Appeals centered on contrasting characterizations of the self, whether of the master or of the slave. In *Bailey*, the bequest and the choice were tied together in the same clause of the will—indeed, in the same sentence. In *Williamson v. Coalter*, however, Hannah Coalter introduces two separate clauses. One clearly directs emancipation on a specific date, January 1, 1858; in the other, her executors are instructed to raise a fund from her estate to send the slaves to Liberia or any other free state or country where they might wish to live. "I further direct, that if any of my said servants shall prefer to remain in Virginia, instead of accepting the foregoing provisions, it is my desire that they shall be permitted by my executors to select among my relations their respective owners." This second clause led the court to declare null and void Coalter's bequest of freedom. Citing *Bailey*, the court said, "[A]s there can be no intermediate condition between slavery and freedom in the *status* of the negro, so neither can there be an intermediate condition as to civil rights and capacities."[66]

Moncure, in his strongly worded dissent, wrote that he would have held the manumission valid and the later clause invalid, as the manumission was clear and was not made dependent on the slave's choice. Moncure recognizes that Hannah Coalter's slaves were "among the chief, if not the chief, objects of her bounty." The counsel for the appellants, who claimed the slaves against her wishes, deemed Coalter's will invalid

> not because she has not emancipated her slaves in plain and mandatory terms, but because, in her anxiety to provide for their comfort and happiness, she has superadded other terms which in effect give to them an election between freedom and slavery, instead of freedom absolutely.

Moncure attempts again to grasp the ethical relation in this most venal of suits against the dead. In trying to arrange for her slaves' comfort, Coalter had left an opening, which the relatives used to claim the slaves and their value for themselves. Solicitousness for them resulted in the very loophole that would most damage her slaves: their sale. Moncure's dissent focuses on shared intimacy—sentiments and attachments—between slaves and master. How, he wonders, can the second stage of her will, the force of her utterance, this moment of charity and care, negate everything that came before?[67]

At the core of the decision in *Bailey* lies a set of psychological and cognitive considerations—not only about the character of the slave but also about the perils of mastery. What must an owner be like in order to be recognized by law? By the end of these late Virginia cases, on the eve of the Civil War, it is clear that, as Jefferson had recognized in *Notes on the State of Virginia* (1787), the bond between master and slave is not only reciprocal. The laws of the state of Virginia saw to it that both were to be changed ineradicably because of this relationship. Moncure's effort to depict some deeper level of causation between the law's language and narrative presumes the relative cognitive and affective forms individuality can take, for both masters and slaves.[68]

Sympathy was off-limits for masters—just as rationality was unrecognized in slaves. Most lawyers readily recognized affect in slaves—the "animal" emotions, desires and appetite, even loyalty—but they were less generous when it came to reason. In the case of slave owners, jurists recognized the rational capacities but not possible kindness, sympathy, or love. What was legally recognized as the character of blacks was legally invisible in whites. This trade-off in law seeped into the assumptions or beliefs of daily life. Legal decisions and the forms of language necessary to make them stick were never cordoned off from experience. Those who made the law understood how their principles shaped beliefs, stoked desires, and dispensed with normalcy. The semblance of subjectivity invented here remains capricious. But its fictions live on in patterns of degradation that define community, even as they create the stigma that adheres to and sustains radical states of nonbelonging.

WHO GETS TO BE WANTON?

The law ... is stricter on the face of things,
than morality.

—Frederick Pollock, *The Law of Torts* (1887)

SHOOTING A TIGER

ON CHRISTMAS DAY IN 2007, TATIANA, A 243-POUND SIBERIAN tiger, escaped from her grotto at the San Francisco Zoo. She scaled the twelve-foot-five-inch wall, killed seventeen-year-old Carlos Sousa Jr., and injured his two friends Amritpal ("Paul") and Kulbir Dhaliwal. When police arrived at the scene, Tatiana was guarding Kulbir as her prey. She was shot and killed as she turned, responding to their shouts. A year later, the four San Francisco officers who appeared at the scene of this misadventure were awarded the Gold Medal of Valor by the chief of police. The man who shot the tiger reminded his audience at the ceremony: "There's no training with respect to wild animals."[1]

In the aftermath of this encounter between the forces of law and the emblems of savagery—with the zoo in lockdown, while the teens negotiated a book deal—the intensity of the language of blame, transgression, guilt, and vengeance was remarkable. Thousands of on-line memorials on MySpace and Facebook lamented either the death of the tiger or the assault on the boys, or blamed the zoo for the inadequate enclosure of the grotto, four feet shorter than the height recommended by the Association of

Zoos and Aquariums.[2] Eulogies to Tatiana vied with accusations against the survivors.

Pine cones, rocks, sticks, and branches found in Tatiana's grotto hinted that she had been tormented, scared, or abused. One witness claimed the boys roared; others that they dangled their jackets, used slingshots, or pelted the tiger while standing on the railing. The spokesman for the zoo insisted that evidence suggested that the teens, drunk and high on marijuana, had abused the tiger. Tatiana seemed to have a problem with the holiday season. On December 22, 2006, she mangled a zookeeper's arm during feeding. "We don't know if there was any intent (to harm) on the tiger's part," explained Robert Jenkins, the zoo's director of animal care and conservation.[3]

Whether the e-mails and on-line posts blamed the boys' malice, the tiger's viciousness, or the zoo's negligence matters less than the violence of the responses themselves. Who were the savages—teens or tiger? The dichotomies invoked—barbaric and civilized, vulgar and noble—entangle humans and animal in an appeal that blurs the distinction between victim and victimizer.

Who or what bears the blame? Did Tatiana intend to kill Sousa? Were Sousa and his friends wanton and malicious? How do we judge guilt? In this tragedy, a wild animal no longer stands in for unruly human subordinates. Instead, the tiger, once confined in a zoo, is at the mercy of those who threaten: the socially excluded or the keepers of order. Some of the messages asserted the tiger's "natural" innocence diabolically corrupted by disorderly types who had a propensity to cruel, indeed criminal acts. For others, a splendid animal was sacrificed in order to save deviants who belong behind bars.

Thirty-five days after declaring the San Francisco Zoo a crime scene, police suspended their investigation, claiming that they had no evidence that the Dhaliwal brothers had committed a misdemeanor. Had charges been filed against them, they could have been punished by two and a half years in prison for taunting Tatiana. They were not legally liable—at least not for what happened at the zoo. Three months after the incident, on March

27, 2008, Paul and Kulbir Dhaliwal filed claims with the city of San Francisco, seeking compensation for their injuries and emotional harm. Hours later, Paul, who, along with his brother already had a criminal record, was arrested and charged with five felony counts for allegedly shoplifting electronic equipment and video games from Target stores in San Leandro, Hayward, and Livermore, California, between March 24 and March 27.[4]

In the trade-off between dignity and degradation, the rights of humans are pitted against the treatment of animals. Recall my earlier discussions of retribution for unnatural deaths in biblical and classical texts—the ox that gores must be stoned—and the medieval trials and executions of animals: the pigs who ate children, the dogs who bit, or the cats who spooked. In the distant past, animals were taken as seriously as humans, given the dignity of trial, even the recognition that comes with sudden agony. Highly unnatural religious fictions gave rise to issues of legality. Punishments ritually communicated to animals the horror of their deed. Treated as if rational beings, they were expected to take responsibility for their crime.

These legal rituals were granted, however, only to domesticated animals, not to the untamed, such as tigers. In the confrontation at the San Francisco Zoo, both the young men and the tiger are alternately cast as predators and victims. Human and tiger merge. Their reciprocal narratives provide the categorical terms for treatment of those inhabiting the peripheries of civilization. Humans considered deviant are locked up in cages like dangerous beasts but kept out of sight. Once we discern such spectacles of degradation, they not only gain cultural significance but also help to clarify a legal history that lays claim to persons deemed extraneous.

STATES OF MIND

How and when did the law (criminal and civil) come to presuppose the existence of intent? Is there a philosophy of personhood in the logic of law? As the concept of personhood shifted, judged increasingly in a secular rather than a religious context, spiritual battles were fought, not on the ground of something vaguely imagined as *soul* but on the exacting site of *mind*. Did the disappearance of the soul into the psychologized space of consciousness change the way the law articulated the exchange or slippage between objects and persons, lifeless and living chattels?

As modern law appeared to scrutinize the medieval religiosity that underpinned secular law, objects or things lost their ability to commit wrong, to be cursed. Yet old rules maintain themselves. It was as if in a world teeming with wantonness, where persons and things interacted in mutually adaptable—even if belligerent—ways, another kind of law came into being. In removing the liability that once adhered to things or beasts, the law became harsher, but the claims of civility were intensified. So let us not forget how the vengeance wreaked upon the deodand or offending object survives in the stories we tell ourselves in order to warrant repression, to manipulate and control.[5]

Recall that Locke's person is a moral agent. Guilt and punishment on earth act as a kind of shadow play to the ultimate judgment of God. A drunken man, in one of Locke's famous examples, is punished for what the sober man does not remember. On this earth, within the limits of human law, where we cannot distinguish "what is real, what is counterfeit," innocence by reason of drunkenness is not accepted as a plea. "Humane Judicatures justly punish him," Locke writes, "because the Fact is proved against him, but want of consciousness cannot be proved for him." But on the "great Day," when bodies rise up, "the Secrets of all Hearts shall be laid open" and divine justice revealed.[6]

Haunting the history of penal justification, whether earthly or heavenly, in the law court or in the final justification on the Day of Judgment, is, once again, the concept of the deodand, the liability of the cursed thing. In its attachment of blame to the object or animal doing the damage, whether the body is that of a horse, boat, dog, or slave, legal remedy (Mosaic or Roman or common) ordained in the least expected of places the convertibility of temporal and spiritual persuasions.

The deodand with its associated belief in "evil influence" or "evil nature" is a direct bridge to the legal theory of *mens rea*, a "guilty mind."[7] We must reconsider the place of intent in determining criminality. Instead of the unreasoning thing moving to the death of a *reasonable* creature, the mental awareness necessary for criminal liability depends on a subjective test of liability: generally put, reasonableness gone reckless. This difficult standard, once applied—not to criminals but to their keepers—in cases concerning Eighth Amendment violations in prison, shifts the terminology of intent to the person meting out the treatment. When human responsibility is transferred to those who inflict the damage on the incarcerated, the codes of law skirt attention to actual suffering inflicted. In the process, the object of harm in this logic is denied interiority. Emptied of agency, the object is no longer even a victim but instead "a pile of blood, bone and meat that is unhappy," as Coetzee puts it so remarkably in his novel *Waiting for the Barbarians*.[8]

So the mutations generated by law become part of the logic of punishment. It is not indifference to the category of personhood, but rather an obsession with it, that introduced another kind of person, anomalous and somehow extraneous to civil society. My analysis of personhood takes seriously the law as its model and looks closely at the connections among the offending animal or inanimate object, the slave, the prisoner, and the newly targeted terrorist or detainee. In giving these entities some defining characteristics within the categories of reason and unreason, human and nonhuman, living and dead, I turn to case law.

A MORE ARDENT LAW

Since the eighteenth century, "cruel" and "unusual" have been coupled in lasting intimacy in our legal language and courts, yet they have been vexed by a rhetorical ambiguity that alternately has been used to protect prisoners and legitimize violence against them. First appearing in the English Bill of Rights of 1689, drafted by Parliament at the accession of William and Mary, the phrase "cruel and unusual punishment" seems to have been directed against punishments unauthorized by statute, beyond the jurisdiction of the sentencing court, or disproportionate to the offense committed. The American colonists included the principle in some colonial legislation, and after much debate the formula was incorporated into most of the original state constitutions. It became part of the Bill of Rights in 1791 as the Eighth Amendment to the U.S. Constitution.

Though brief, the Eighth Amendment is the only provision of the Bill of Rights that is applicable by its own terms to prisoners. It reads, "Excessive bail shall not be required, nor excessive fines imposed, nor cruel and unusual punishments inflicted." As a limit on the state's power to punish, the importance of this negative guarantee expands in the prison context. On the ruins of the rack, the thumbscrew, the wheel, the iron boot, an "enlightened" age redefined atrocity. The opposition between barbarism and civility, the key poles in eighteenth-century jurisprudence, retains its strategic force in today's legal terrain, even if the distinction is not as indisputable as we like to believe.[9]

The American draftsmen intended that the phrase apply to "tortures" and other "barbarous" methods of punishment, such as pillorying, disemboweling, decapitation, and drawing and quartering. In other words, what mattered in the American context was unusual cruelty in the *method* of punishment. The purpose of the amendment was not the prohibition of excessive punishments.[10] The lesson of this debate about technique is clear. Increasingly inhuman and degrading treatment becomes legitimate insofar as it is sanitized. Dark and dirty cells are replaced with clean, well-lighted cages. The flames and gas of the electric chair and gas chamber are superseded by the illusion of medically proficient and painless killing by lethal injection.[11]

Those who put their faith in the cultivated evolution of legal principles may think it proper to make a sharp division between

the courts' so-called hands-off era (1776–1965) and the height
of the "prisoners' rights" movement (1965–86). It is reassuring
to believe that, after ignoring the dank holes, vermin, and beat-
ings, the courts responded to the harsh treatment of inmates in
a triumph of enlightenment. But in Eighth Amendment cases,
in particular, it has become clear over time that though physically brutal treatment has been prohibited by the Supreme
Court, psychological harm has been disregarded.[12]

Because the courts have defined horrific abuse out of recognition, inhuman treatment continues. As early as 1968, just two
years before his appointment to the Supreme Court, Judge Harry
Blackmun, then a member of the U.S. Court of Appeals for the
Eighth Circuit, argued that debates over the language of cruel
and unusual were nothing more than a pretext for continued
excess. In *Jackson v. Bishop*, tired of the court's exhaustive attention to terminology, hairsplitting definitions that permitted obvious violations to continue, Blackmun wrote, "We choose to
draw no significant distinction between the word 'cruel' and the
word 'unusual' in the Eighth Amendment." Citing court decisions that had authorized whipping with a strap as punishment
—whether limited to ten lashes, or carried out in the fields, or
within twenty-four hours of an earlier whipping—Blackmun
asked, "[H]ow does one, or any court, ascertain the point which
would distinguish the permissible from that which is cruel and
unusual?"[13]

Later Eighth Amendment cases broadened its protections, yet
displays of cleanliness, as well as appeals to constitutional min-
ima, basic needs, and humane treatment, allowed severe sensory
deprivation and enforced isolation to evade Eighth Amendment
claims. Through an often ingenious technical legalism, the court
has paved the way for cruelty that passes for the necessary incidents of prison life. Extreme verbal qualifications make deprivation or injury matter only when "sufficiently serious," when
involving "more than ordinary lack of due care," or inflicting
"substantial pain." Recent cases also permit punishments that do
not necessarily leave scars or perceptible proof of injury. Instead,

as Justice Blackmun warned in his concurrence in *Hudson v. McMillian* (1992), they place "various kinds of state-sponsored torture and abuse—of the kind ingeniously designed to cause pain but without a tell-tale 'significant injury'—entirely beyond the pale of the Constitution." We are permitted to fracture the mind in the way that we once broke bones.[14]

Words like *decency* and *dignity* jockey for preeminence in these late twentieth-century cases and alternate with less expansive phrases like *basic human needs* or *minimal civilized measure of life's necessities*. The involvement of the law in prisoners' rights provided the terms by which apparent legitimacy masked conditions of incarceration. In miming the language of the law, these terms ensured that old abuses and arbitrary actions would continue. The formulaic call for *humane treatment* played easily into the hands of penal bureaucrats, only too ready to embrace such rhetorically powerful terms for their own purposes.

The notion of "evolving standards of decency" and the "dignity of man" in *Trop v. Dulles* (1958) asserted a very sharp distinction, albeit later repudiated, between the civilized and inhumane treatment of prisoners. Chief Justice Earl Warren's opinion in *Trop* emphasized a flexible interpretation of the Eighth Amendment, recognizing mental suffering or anguish as crucial to the meaning of cruel and unusual punishment. He ruled that it was unconstitutional for the government to deprive Albert Trop of citizenship as penalty for desertion from the army. Though there had been "no physical mistreatment, no primitive torture," Warren emphasized that involuntary expatriation was far worse, for it meant "the total destruction of the individual's status in organized society." Had the government's position been upheld, Trop would have "lost the right to have rights." But during the years of the Rehnquist court (1986–2005) and since that time, most judges have ignored mental anguish, as well as the enduring consequences of degradation.[15]

Chronologies of progress are always unreliable, especially when these narratives are told by the free in the name of the bound. The terminology of human rights is not natural. It has a history, both paradoxical and vexing, as Arendt explained:

> No paradox of contemporary politics is filled with a more poignant irony than the discrepancy between the efforts of well-meaning idealists who stubbornly insist on regarding as "inalienable" those human rights which are enjoyed only by citizens of the most prosperous and civilized countries, and the situation of the rightless themselves.[16]

Despite claims to universality, humanity and rights are not shared. Unseemly tensions characterize the rhetoric of human rights, and nowhere do the duplicities or the claims of civilization become as obvious as in the recent uses of such terms as *dignity* or *decency* to justify the most extreme suffering. In *Baze v. Rees* (2008), for example, the Supreme Court upheld Kentucky's method of execution by lethal injection. The state's lethal injection protocol, the Court argued, did not violate the Eighth Amendment's ban on cruel and unusual punishments. Chief Justice John G. Roberts's opinion demonstrates how the argument regarding "the dignity of the procedure"—actually nothing more than the veneer of dignified death—masks excruciating pain. The paralyzing drug pancuronium bromide risks leaving an improperly sedated inmate conscious but unable to breathe, move, or cry out. This method of lethal injection, Roberts explains, is more humane, more dignified than others. In other words, it is less disturbing to witnesses.[17]

Everything depends on the object of humane treatment: the legal protection of slaves, for example, never prohibited mutilation or "correction *even* unto death," words that would be echoed in the "torture memos" of the Bush White House on the legal limits of interrogation. Humanitarian claims and benign moral rectitude have always permitted the torments of continued servitude. Just as with slavery, the language in prison cases undergoes unusual permutations: words no longer mean what they usually do. When you deal with persons labeled as anomalous and extraneous to civil society—whether slaves, animals, criminals, or detainees—they "do not have *rights* as the term is normally used," the legal scholar Gary Francione observes in *Animals, Property, and the Law.* What is normally considered "'humane' treatment" or "'unnecessary' suffering may," he explains, "differ considerably from the ordinary-language interpretation of those terms."[18]

WHAT'S IN A WORD?

Oliver Wendell Holmes warned, "We are not studying etymology, but law."[19] But the legal history of the word "wanton" is crucial to the case law concerning cruel and unusual punishment. Its use targets the power and privilege enjoyed by agents administering torturous treatment, whether prison correctional officers or interrogators of alleged "enemy combatants." In the spectacle of lust and shame recorded in the Abu Ghraib photos; the shackles, dogs, "restraint chairs," and permanent solitary confinement at Guantánamo Bay; and the treatment in supermax confinement in the United States, the drama of degradation turns on the relation between those who get to be wanton and others who count only as something of nonvalue: conceptually no longer *persons* who suffer cruelty or torture.[20]

How could these treatments be legal? The answer lies in the extraordinary latitude that prison guards and officials enjoy, thanks to enabling Supreme Court decisions. Beginning in the 1980s with a series of cases challenging inadequacies in medical care, use of force, and conditions of confinement, the Court turned to a novel translation of *malice aforethought* for murderers into the *maliciously wanton* standard for prison officials. The full force of mental volition is transferred to the person of the prison official. The requirement that aggrieved prisoners show *deliberate* indifference by their keepers when claiming cruel and unusual punishment permits untoward rationalizations. This reasoning measures cruelty not by the pain and suffering inflicted but by the intent of the person who inflicts them. In the vain search for intent, the official who commits the act is vindicated while the object of harm is ignored.

In their discussion of ancient criminal law in 1898, Pollock and Maitland explained: "A mean must be found between these two extremes—absolute liability for all harm done, and liability for harm that is both done and intended." This attempt "to detect and appreciate the psychical element in guilt and innocence," they acknowledge, is doomed to failure.[21] We will see that the Eighth Amendment cases of the Rehnquist court and the torture memos of 2002 and 2003 written by lawyers for the Bush administration, however, depend on the concept of intention. Moreover, the switch to a focus on intent drastically transformed Eighth Amendment cases, and the attribution of both moral responsibility and legal liability constitutes the background against which the disfigurement of prisoners and detainees must be understood.

"Wanton" means you cannot be shamed; you cannot be humiliated. It applies only to the dominating, not to the subordinated. The latter are completely powerless before this word that curiously mixes caprice and wickedness: a profligate and maleficent magic. What does this term's applicability—to what kind of persons can it be applied—say about thought and feeling, cognition and affect? Before parsing and elaborating the language of wantonness in U.S. prison cases that have turned on the legal meaning of the Eighth Amendment prohibition on "cruel and unusual punishments," I examine whether qualitative distinctions, not simply dictionary definitions of "wanton," can illuminate the standards invoked by its use.

But, first, two approaches to wantonness: one describing assault and battery in John Bouvier's *Law Dictionary* (1856) and the other lascivious behavior and punishment in Isaiah. Bouvier defines "wantonness" by telling a tale of a hat and a hand:

A licentious act by one man towards the person of another without regard to his rights; as, for example, if a man should attempt to pull off another's hat against his will in order to expose him

187

to ridicule, the offence would be an assault, and if he touched him it would amount to a battery. In such a case there would be no malice, but the wantonness of the act would render the offending party liable to punishment.

Here, wantonness and malice are separated, as they are not in later legal definitions.

The sense of "lasciviousness" or "lewdness," something more serious than mere dalliance, appears in Isaiah (3:16–17). Charged with sin, the haughty and immodest daughters of Zion will be punished for their deceiving and amorous glances, which are offenses to God:

> Moreover the Lord saith, Because the daughters of Zion are haughty, and walk with stretched forth necks and wanton eyes, walking and mincing as they go, and making a tinkling with their feet: Therefore the Lord will smite with a scab the crown of the head of the daughters of Zion.

Their heads were cast high in pride, so God will bring them low: consuming their flesh with disease, stripping their bodies of finery, and leaving baldness, sackcloth, and stink where there had been tresses, finery, and perfume.

The history of punishment is also a history of language. According to the *Oxford English Dictionary* (OED), "wanton" etymologically links *wan* (meaning "lacking") + *togen* (past participle of *teon*, meaning "to discipline"): hence, undisciplined. If we put the example of the man wantonly pulling off the hat of someone on the street, or daring to touch him, next to the mincing and unchaste women of Zion, we get a sense of the wide range of this word—its wayward character, the confounding of legal and moral bearing by a sexuality that is ever close to the surface, lurking beneath the modern attribution of moral responsibility and legal liability.

Wantonness signals the animation of mind rising in its highest pitch to *legal malice*, which in statutory law means much more than in common language. Combined with "unnecessary," the word "wanton" suggests reckless sportiveness more than malign intent: something gratuitous but as inexcusable as knocking the hat off someone's head. There is a lot of history in this word, in its tinge of depravity, effeminacy, frivolity, excess. Thus, Shakespeare's Henry IV portrays his "unthrifty son," Prince Hal, the "young wanton and effeminate boy," or Hamlet warns his mother, in a call for abstinence that revels in intemperance: "Not this by no means I bid you do: / Let the bloat king tempt you again to bed, / Pinch wanton on your cheek, call you his mouse / And let him for a pair of reechy kisses, / Or paddling in your neck with his damned fingers, / Make you to ravel all this matter out."[22]

But the term also refers to the exercise of brutality, savagery, and pitilessness. Glee and malice work together in the abuse of those targeted for humiliation. In the reports following the first leaks of the Abu Ghraib photos, press descriptions insisted upon the merging of "chastisement and caprice," "punishment and amusement," "wantonness and cruelty." A naked man pulled on a leash by a swaggering Lyndie England. The smiling Charles A. Graner, Jr. and a human pyramid of seven naked, hooded detainees. "A certain amount of violence was to be expected," said Guy Womack, Graner's lawyer, adding, "Striking doesn't mean a lot. . . Breaking a rib or a bone—*that* would be excessive." Of the leashed prisoner, Womack concluded: "If it hurt his little psyche, it could have been a lot worse."[23]

An early case sets the scene for the spirit of wantonness. Though *Louisiana ex rel. Francis v. Resweber* (1947) concerns a botched execution, its reliance on the distinction between purpose and accident became the controlling precedent for later cases that analyzed how one might apply the "cruel and unusual punishments" standard to prisoners' conditions of confinement. Willie Francis, a "colored citizen," was sentenced to death by a Louisiana court. When the electrocution failed due to mechanical difficulties, Francis petitioned the Supreme Court, arguing that a second attempt to execute him would be unconstitutionally cruel. Justice Stanley Reed's ruling against Francis resorts to a language that is resigned to a merciless arbitrariness, while it commits to familiar standards of necessity and reasonableness. In order to argue that a repeated execution would not be "any more cruel in the constitutional sense than any other execution," Reed unhinges the meaning from ordinary words, making the question of *cruelty* itself pointless, if not trifling. "The cruelty against which the Constitution protects a convicted man is cruelty inherent in the method of punishment, not the necessary suffering involved in any method employed to extinguish life humanely."[24]

In order to legally narrow the meaning of cruelty in such a way that actual harm can be ignored, Reed makes apparent exactness the cue for wrangling over the obvious. While granting that the Eighth Amendment prohibits "the wanton infliction of pain" and conceding that Francis now must again undergo the mental anguish of preparing for death, Reed turns Francis's torment into a matter of no significance. Reed pursues the argument of necessity. He gives legal weight to both the executioner's state of mind and the state's intent. No one proposes "to inflict unnecessary pain," nor does the method of execution promise "any unnecessary pain." This mishap suggests no "malevolence": "The situation of the unfortunate victim of this accident is just as though he had suffered the identical amount of mental anguish and physical pain in any other occurrence, such as, for example, a fire in the cell block."[25]

TRIALS OF DEFINITION

The use of the word "wanton" in the current enterprise of degradation and punishment prompts us to consider how the ethical framework of judicial practice becomes darker, more doubtful, and more mysterious rather than more reasonable and more enlightened. More crucial perhaps than the decisions themselves is the language in which they are rendered. The compulsion to define grants a license for ambiguity. Quibbling over terms contributes to the pose of judicial caution, as it generates the hyperlegality that institutes judicial novelties the Eighth Amendment was designed to prohibit. As we observe the extension of legal reasoning into antiquated domains of reference, we must ask how bound the law is to redress harm if words can define it away.[26]

In recent cases that judge challenges to conditions of confinement, it is striking that the trade-off between illegal and legal torment is also between those who administer discipline and those who lack it. But though the root meaning of "wanton" is lacking discipline, only officers who guard, order, train, and control—whose job is to impose control—are capable of wantonness. The insufferable becomes legal and torment legitimate through the manipulation of language. Judges like Antonin Scalia and Clarence Thomas, especially, obsessed as they are by the legal history of words, preempt the reality that those words label and describe. The more obsessive their task of definition, the more murky is the intelligibility of their arguments. From that opacity the law takes its power. Shifting the language of subjective blameworthiness to prison or governmental officials, the legal decisions I discuss testify to the thorough calibration of the relationship between persons and things, between those capable of intent and the presumed unthinking recipients of punishment.[27]

In 1986 Pearly Wilson, an inmate at the Hocking Correctional Facility in Ohio, brought a *pro se* lawsuit—that is, one in which he represented himself—alleging that conditions in the prison, including overcrowding, excessive noise, inadequate heating and ventilation, unsanitary dining facilities, and lack of protection from communicable disease, violated the Eighth Amendment. When *Wilson v. Seiter* finally reached the Supreme Court four and a half years later, it was a pivotal event in prisoners' rights: the first conditions-of-confinement case since *Rhodes v. Chapman* (1981). In *Rhodes*, Justice Lewis Powell, writing for the majority, found no constitutional mandate for "comfortable prisons" and argued that conditions such as prison overcrowding do not fall within the scope of a "serious deprivation of basic human needs" by contemporary standards. The double celling of inmates was not serious enough to violate the constitutional standard: "To the extent that such conditions are restrictive and even harsh, they are part of the penalty that criminal offenders pay for their offenses against society." Without specifying the degree of severity that would violate the Eighth Amendment, he suggested a policy of deference to the expertise of prison officials.[28]

In *Wilson*, the plaintiff argued that if prisoners are deprived of "the minimal civilized measure of life's necessities," the Eighth Amendment is violated regardless of anyone's intent. But Justice Scalia, giving the intent requirement its fiercest play, raised the threshold of harm to the point where it ceased to be legally relevant. Writing for the five-member majority in the sharply divided decision—joined by Chief Justice Rehnquist and Justices O'Connor, Kennedy, and Souter—Justice Scalia focused on the meaning and extent of *punishment*. He noted Judge Richard Posner's return to the legal history of the term in *Duckworth v. Franzen* (1985), where Posner invokes Samuel Johnson's *A Dictionary of the English Language* (1755): "'Any infliction or pain imposed in vengeance of a crime'":

> The infliction of punishment is a deliberate act intended to chastise or deter.... [I]f [a] guard accidentally stepped on [a] prisoner's toe and broke it, this would not be punishment in anything remotely like the accepted meaning of the word, whether we consult the usage of 1791, or 1868, or 1985.[29]

In order to limit judicial interference in prison administration, Scalia shifted attention—and the court's definitional proclivities—to the analysis of *punishment*.

In *Wilson*, Scalia construes a legal idiom that makes the definition of punishment an excuse for depersonalization. If deprivations are not a specific part of a prisoner's sentence, they are not *really* punishment unless imposed by prison officials with a "guilty mind." No matter how much actual suffering is experienced by a prisoner, if the intent requirement is not met, then the effect on the prisoner is not a matter for judicial review. "The source of the intent requirement," Scalia reasons, "is not the pre-dilections of this Court, but the Eighth Amendment itself, which bans only cruel and unusual *punishment*." If it is not meted out by the sentencing judge, then "some mental element must be attributed to the inflicting officer before it can qualify."[30]

The Court thus requires not only an objective component ("was the deprivation sufficiently serious?"), but also a separate subjective component ("did the officials act with a sufficiently culpable state of mind?") in all Eighth Amendment challenges to prison practices and policies. In order to meet the second criterion, Scalia maintains that "the offending conduct must be *wanton*," a term that even he admits is slippery in the con-text. Undeterred, he returns to *Whitley v. Albers* (1986) and the necessarily hasty response to a prison riot in which a prisoner—Albers—was shot by a guard. Even if "the conduct is harmful enough to satisfy the objective component of an Eighth Amend-ment claim, whether it can be characterized as 'wanton' depends upon the constraints facing the *official*."[31]

Adopting the subjective-component standard of *Estelle v. Gamble* (1976), which concerned the "deliberate indifference to serious medical needs," Scalia went further. The court in *Wil-son* decided that *Estelle*'s deliberate indifference standard should apply to all conditions of confinement claims. In this agent-centered psychodrama, Scalia moved along the scale of blame by ranking degrees of culpability. As Souter would later state in *Farmer v. Brennan* (1994), deliberate indifference "entails some-thing more than mere negligence," but "less than acts or omis-sions for the very purpose of causing harm or with knowledge that harm will result."[32]

In appealing to a mentalist language of law, Scalia lingered on the word *wanton*. Once wantonness has become the test whereby prisoners may demand their constitutional rights, the objects of attention become state agents whose judgment can be neither predicted nor controlled. Prison officials are thus endowed with will, reason, and foresight. They might choose to be unreason-able. They might act maliciously in spite of what they know to be just. But they remain actors—agents in the difficulties and dangers of correctional life.

It is their concerns, thoughts, inclinations, fears, lapses, and strain that occupy the pages of this opinion, not the effects of their actions on the incarcerated. During an emergency situation, such as a prison riot that "poses significant risks to the safety of inmates and prison staff" and necessitates "excessive force" (*Whitley*), "wantonness consist[s] of acting 'maliciously and sadistically for the very purpose of causing harm,'" but in the context of inadequate medical care (*Estelle*), the standard for judging unconstitutionality does not depend on that "very high state of mind." Deliberate indifference will do. In *Wilson*, Scalia sees "no significant distinction between claims alleging inadequate medical care and those alleging inadequate 'conditions of confinement'" and applies the *Estelle* standard: "Since, we said, only the 'unnecessary and wanton infliction of pain' implicates the Eighth Amendment, a prisoner advancing such a claim must, at a minimum, allege 'deliberate indifference.'"[33]

The obsession—recall my discussion of mens rea and the deodand—with mentalist instead of behavioral explanations for crime has now resurfaced in the strangest of places. Obvious signs of violence disappear in quest of the unseen: What was the official, who also happens to be the malefactor, thinking? Was he "deliberately indifferent"? Did he have a "sufficiently culpable state of mind"? In this spectacle of deference to prison authorities, the Court seeks grounds and reasons after the fact. Evidence resides in the most obscure and unverifiable place: the private thoughts of prison officials. If the objective severity of conditions is judged unconstitutional only when the subjective intent of those in control is present, Eighth Amendment violations are wholly impossible to prove in practice. Justice Byron White, in a concurrence agreeing only in the judgment, joined by Justices Marshall, Blackmun, and Stevens, objected that previous decisions insisted that "the conditions are themselves *part of the punishment*, even though not specifically 'meted out' by a statute or judge." "Not only is the majority's intent requirement a departure from precedent," he concluded, but "it will likely prove impossible to apply in many cases. Inhumane prison conditions often are the result of cumulative actions and inactions by numerous officials inside and outside a prison, sometimes over a long period of time."[34]

What is the legal personality of the criminal, once caught between the decision decreed by the sentencing judge and the intent of the inflicting officer? In the insistent verbal distinctions of *Wilson*, the intangible self—the *thinking thing*—becomes detached from the prisoner, while his body comes forth as focus. Only the physical harm arising from conditions of confinement —an "injury that requires medical attention or leaves permanent marks"—is legally recognized, as Justice Blackmun insisted in *Hudson v. McMillian*, nearly a year after *Wilson*. If we follow the logic of *Wilson*, the full possession of the mental faculty (it gets to be wanton, malicious, obdurate, and willful) is transferred to the person of the official, while the mind of the prisoner, lost to the subtleties of legal interpretation, is eliminated. Literally stripped of the right to experience suffering, to know fear and anguish, the plaintiff becomes a nonreactive, defenseless object, for whom harsh or even intolerable conditions—such as indefinite supermax isolation—are not legally an issue unless they leave a bruise.

By the time Blackmun wrote his qualification to the decision in *Farmer v. Brennan* (1994), the year he resigned from the Court, he did not mince words about the dangers of Scalia's reasoning in *Wilson*, especially the narrow delimitation of punishment to the inmate's sentence by a judge. "The Court's analysis is fundamentally misguided; indeed it defies common sense. 'Punishment' does not necessarily imply a culpable state of mind on the part of an identifiable punisher." He argued that intentionality, requiring "an easily identifiable wrongdoer with poor intentions" guaranteed that "barbaric conditions," if not "a reign of terror," could continue, unmitigated and without redress.[35]

In *The Problems of Jurisprudence*, Richard Posner praises Oliver Wendell Holmes's *The Common Law* for "standing the concept of the deodand on its head." As Posner put it, instead of "treating dangerous objects as people," Holmes proposed "to treat dangerous people as objects." Let us take this further. If civilized good sense teaches us that "we cannot discover thoughts" or "peer into people's minds," why do our federal courts not only expect but also demand this *primitive* or *unreasonable* ability? In concentrating on the culpable mind of the punisher—and the attribution of responsibility that comes with it—this judicial reasoning, in making inmate claims ineligible, does not so much objectify as depersonalize the prisoner: the animate object given up to the state.[36]

The insistence on mental elements in determining criminality is not new, given that the purview of early English law was confined to intentional wrongs. Yet the stakes of legality become disquieting when justices translate wrongdoing in criminal cases into wanton intention in civil law. Once states of mind characterized as "indifferent," "unreasonable," or "malicious" are ascribed to those who harm without liability to punishment, something vicious is done to the object of harm, now reduced to a mere body controlled by administrative power. Subjectivity, though it takes its definition from criminal law, is the privilege of those in control: not only the prison officials, but the judges whose linguistic maneuvering has lethal effects on those whose lives depend on their words.

DALLYING WITH WORDS

In laying down the limits of torture, the lawyers of the Bush White House left its meaning more unintelligible and the perpetrators less accountable. This legal procedure staged a public ritual of evasion and complicity. In Australia on October 18, 2003, when asked in a television interview whether two Australian nationals held in U.S. custody in Guantánamo Bay were being tortured, President George W. Bush offered a categorical denial. His words make him *wanton* in the sense of "insolent" or "reckless of justice and humanity," a definition that the *OED* notes as obsolete by the end of the seventeenth century, but, as we are now aware, is quite appropriate to the twenty-first century.[37] "We don't torture people in America. And people who make that claim just don't know anything about our country."[38]

It is clear that the United States continues to torture detainees, under the specious legal cover of the previous governmental memoranda approving it or the current justification of inhumane conditions in Patrick M. Walsh's Department of Defense (DoD) review ordered by President Obama in a January 22, 2009, executive order. Detainees—whether "ghost detainees" disappeared into secret CIA "black sites," or locked up in Guantánamo or the U.S.-occupied Bagram air base in Afghanistan— recount being subjected to permanent shackling, prolonged standing to induce stress, beating and kicking, sleep deprivation, isolation, and "environmental manipulation." Abuses continue to be reported by the Center for Constitutional Rights, the American Civil Liberties Union (ACLU), Amnesty International, Human Rights Watch, the International Red Cross, and by released detainees.[39]

In the cases of those labeled "terrorists," punishment is legally recognized as torture only if it *deliberately* or *intentionally* inflicts severe and lasting physical or psychological pain approximating organ failure or death. What began as unquestionable becomes doubtful. One of the best ways to produce ambiguity is to clarify obsessively. The legal scholar Jeremy Waldron warns against the pernicious effort to clarify the meaning of torture on a continuum of brutality: "There are some scales," he writes, "one really should not be on, and with respect to which one really does not have a legitimate interest in knowing precisely how far along the scale one is permitted to go." The Bush administration sought to distinguish humiliation from torture and to narrow the definition to the deliberately malicious infliction of the most extreme form of pain possible short of death. The memos describe evidence of torture—bruises, maiming, scars, and subsequent psychological trauma—as "mild non-injurious physical contact," the result of "enhanced interrogation techniques."

197

Further, the memos encouraged techniques that leave less visible marks and hence are harder to document.[40]

Though the legal narratives associated with prisoners, their status, and conditions of confinement are ignored in most classes on constitutional law, they were studied carefully by lawyers of the Bush White House. The concept of intention underpins the torture memos of August 1, 2002, "Standards of Conduct for Interrogation" (written by Assistant Attorney General Jay S. Bybee and sent to then White House counsel Alberto Gonzales) and of March 6, 2003, the "Working Group Report on Detainee Interrogations in the Global War on Terrorism: Assessment of Legal, Historical, Policy and Operational Considerations" (drafted by the Department of Defense Legal Task Force and known as the Pentagon memo). The latter, drawing heavily on the Bybee memo, established interrogation policies for U.S. military personnel in Iraq, Afghanistan, and Guantánamo Bay.[41]

Both memos not only narrowly define torture, but formulate how interrogators, if innocent of the *intent* to torture, are not liable. The labyrinthine legal rationale of the Bybee memo, for example, excuses acts that are unreasonable, or even torturous, as long as interrogators had no intent to harm.

> If the defendant acted knowing that severe pain or suffering was reasonably likely to result from his actions, but no more, he would have acted only with general intent.... As a theoretical matter, therefore, knowledge alone that a particular result is certain to occur does not constitute specific intent.... Thus, even if the defendant knows that severe pain will result from his actions, if causing such harm is not his objective, he lacks the requisite specific intent even though the defendant did not act in good faith. Instead, a defendant is guilty of torture only if he acts with the express purpose of inflicting severe pain or suffering on a person within his custody or physical control.[42]

Whether an interrogator has maimed, blinded, or killed a detainee does not matter unless the interrogator *intended* to maim, blind, or kill. Not just *generally* but *specifically* intended. Definitional sleights of hand diminish the effects of torture, making torturous treatment—such as water boarding, wall slamming, extended sleep deprivation, and use of insects—nothing more than rogue or abusive horseplay: nothing more wanton than knocking a hat off someone's head.

A subsection of the Pentagon memo entitled "Specifically Intended" explains that violation of the federal "torture statute" (18 U.S.C. 2340) "requires that severe pain and suffering must be inflicted with specific intent," meaning that the defendant "must have expressly intended to achieve the forbidden act." If an act caused death, it was legal as long as it was not meant *expressly* to cause harm. The interrogator even gets another loophole: his intent can be nullified if he had "a good faith belief" that whatever he did would not result in mutilation or death. The results—a mutilated, blind, or dead body—get defined away by the vain search for intent, and the defendant who committed the act is (if the jury cooperates) vindicated.[43]

The Bush lawyers understood how the arbitrary formalism of words and phrases could by deliberate subterfuge leave an individual vulnerable to acts of extraordinary and random brutality. They also knew that they could use those words to shelter government agents from prosecution. In part III of the Pentagon memo, under "Domestic Law," the Working Group refers explicitly to recent Supreme Court cases that deal with the Eighth Amendment in its application to prisoners. In addition to the legal language and logic of the Bybee memo, the Working Group relies on a series of cases in the 1980s and 1990s, especially *Wilson v. Seiter.* These pages on the penal practices legitimated by courts in the United States present in powerfully condensed form the Eighth Amendment standards analyzed and thereby establish the precise legal foundation for evading the character of punishment. The only difference is that now the hypothetical plaintiffs are not criminals but alleged terrorists, who have not even been charged with, let alone convicted of, any crime. Whether the Eighth Amendment has been violated depends not on the cruel and inhumane treatment of prisoners but on the motivation or intention of prison officials—and, in this context, on the intent of military police guards. The Pentagon memo also reiterates the unprecedented demand in *Wilson* that all prison-condition claims under the Eighth Amendment follow the "deliberate indifference" standard of *Estelle v. Gamble.*[44]

Both memos use verbal qualifiers to gut the substance of suffering in favor of increasingly rarefied rituals of definition. The imprecision of such qualifiers not only neutralizes the obvious but also trivializes abuse. The legal analysis relies particularly on the definition of the term *severe* in the Torture Statute in Federal Criminal Law (18 U.S.C. 2340), enacted in 1994. Torture is defined as any *"act committed by a person acting under the color of law specifically intended to inflict severe physical or mental pain."* Since the word "severe" is not defined in the statute, the authors of the memos decided to "construe a statutory term in accordance with its ordinary or natural meaning." Their turn to dictionary definitions is a crucial gesture repeated throughout the memos. The pileup of references—to *Webster's New International Dictionary, The American Heritage Dictionary of the English Language*, and *The Oxford English Dictionary*—introduces the next section on "severe mental pain or suffering," which then leads to a list of what constitutes "prolonged mental harm," which ushers in the further equivocation of "prolonged" or "lasting" but not "necessarily permanent damage." Once schooled in these rituals of redefinition, these writers parse words to a degree that goes far beyond the practice of the courts in order to derive legal standards of interrogation that are wanton and unsteady in their application.[45]

The Pentagon memo, while analyzing the meaning of the Eighth Amendment proscription against cruel and unusual punishments, also discusses at length the U.S. Reservation to Article 16 of the United Nations Convention Against Torture and Other Cruel, Inhuman, or Degrading Treatment or Punishment (proposed by the United Nations in 1984 and ratified by the United States in 1994). The prohibition against torture in Article 16 is binding "only in so far as the term 'cruel, inhuman, or degrading treatment or punishment'" means—and is, therefore, limited to the phraseology of cruel and unusual punishment— "prohibited by the 5th, 8th, and 14th Amendments to the U.S. Constitution." In refusing to include the words "inhuman" and "degrading" in its definition—arguing that the meaning of the term "degrading treatment" is vague and ambiguous—the United States lowers the bar of acceptable treatment. According to Amnesty International's *Briefing for the UN Committee Against Torture* (May 2000), the reservation to Article 16 "has far-reaching implications and can apply to any US laws or practices which may breach international standards for humane treatment but are allowed under the US Constitution, for example, prolonged isolation or the use of electro-shock weapons."[46]

The United Nations Commission on Human Rights issued a devastating report on February 15, 2006, criticizing the Bush administration for using domestic standards to define away its human rights obligations under international law. Calling for the immediate release of the detainees held at Guantánamo, the five authors (experts appointed by the commission) were especially concerned that the United States deliberately positioned itself to employ "certain interrogation techniques that would not be permitted under the internationally accepted definition of torture." In their report, the experts explained the United States' legal obligations and condemned arbitrary and ineffective confinement, "prolonged isolation," "cultural and religious harassment," "sensory deprivation," "intimidation," use of "excessive force," and "prolonged detention in Maximum Security Units."[47]

What Bush called "alternative sets of procedures" (and the *New York Times* "Bush's shadow penal system") are not illegal. Instead, the rationales of terror nurture the working magic of the law. Guantánamo, Abu Ghraib, "black sites" or secret prisons, and other detention centers throughout the world are not regions in legal limbo.[48] In this politically oriented persecution, there is no escape from the principles and procedures of legality. Politics is not so much beset as abetted by legal proprieties.[49]

A TORTIOUS TOUCH

Too much defining qualifies words out of existence. The search for euphemism or the intricate specifications of terms evacuate the obvious. Even a word like "torture," once submitted to perplexing disputes, makes language signify either nothing at all or whatever the legal expositors please. In making the reasonable arbitrary, verbal wantonness can be "employed," as Locke complained, "to darken Truth and unsettle People's Rights; to raise Mists, and render unintelligible both Morality and Religion."[50]

On December 29, 1983, Keith Hudson, an inmate at the state penitentiary in Angola, Louisiana, sued three corrections officers for punching him in the eyes, mouth, chest, and stomach. The bruises were minor, but his face, mouth, and lip were swollen. The officers also cracked his dental plate and loosened his teeth. The supervisor on duty watched the beating of the handcuffed and shackled Hudson and advised his officers to not "have too much fun." The United States District Court for the Middle District of Louisiana ruled that guards used unnecessary force and violated the Eighth Amendment. So Hudson was entitled to damages, an award of $800. The Fifth Circuit Court of Appeals reversed, finding that an inmate must demonstrate "significant injury" in order to claim cruel and unusual punishment.[51]

When *Hudson v. McMillian* reached the Supreme Court in 1992, Justice Sandra Day O'Connor wrote for the 7–2 majority. Justice Thomas, joined by Scalia, dissented. Given the officers' malicious, wanton, and sadistic intent, the use of excessive physical force, the opinion argued, could constitute cruel and unusual punishment even though no "serious injury" resulted. The *Hudson* Court held that "[w]hen prison officials maliciously and sadistically use force to cause harm, contemporary standards of decency always are violated."[52]

Even though the majority opinion rejected the federal appeals court's assertion of a "significant injury" requirement (requiring medical attention or leaving permanent marks), the victory for prisoners was qualified. The language in which *Hudson* is argued renders the personhood of inmates suspect. Their mental life is consistently ignored. But more than devising a new kind of entity that exists *only* to be punished, *Hudson* and the other cases I have described set the stage for the verbal quibbles, fastidious distinctions, and indiscriminate parsing of definitions that characterize the memoranda prepared for the "war on terror."

Justice Thomas, joined by Scalia, wrote in his dissent in *Hudson* that the judgment had not only ignored the "significant injury" requirement but also wrenched the Eighth Amendment and the word "punishment" itself "from its historical moorings." If we accept the rack, the thumbscrew, the wheel, and other ingenious forms of mutilation as the context for the constitutional guarantee, then even a beating, an "entirely physical" injury, could fail to be "sufficiently serious." He insists again that the meaning of "punishment" must be narrowed to "penalties meted out by statutes or sentencing judges," not a "broad range of prison deprivations." Clarifying the kind of injury that is not subject to an Eighth Amendment claim, he invokes harm that is not *torturous* but *tortious*. He writes: "A use of force that causes only insignificant harm to a prisoner may be immoral, it may be tortious, it may be criminal, and it may even be remediable under other provisions of the Federal Constitution, but it is not cruel and unusual punishment." In his argument, Thomas resorts to the concept of tortious liability: a touch both offensive and purposely aggressive.[53]

THE LAND OF TORT

Even a dog distinguishes between being stumbled over
and being kicked.

—Oliver Wendell Holmes, *The Common Law* (1881)

What is the landscape of liability and harm? Who gets to commandeer its liturgies, to survey the scene of negligence, the remnants of wrong and damage? In a world teeming with injury, vengeance vies with compensation, retribution with redemption. In the old land of tort, cows munch a neighbor's grass, dogs bite sheep, a snail lies decomposed in a bottle of ginger beer. With the Industrial Revolution, tort law confronted the mania of technology and the machine, specifically the railroad. As trains increased economic growth, they wreaked devastation. They "roared through the countryside, killing livestock, setting fire to crops, smashing passengers and freight." Torts and trains, as Lawrence Friedman explains, "grew up ... together." In the contemporary terrain, teens taunt tigers, a zoo's agents defame teens. To live in society is to reckon with all kinds of injuries. Some cause emotional distress, some physical harm, others loss of money or reputation.[54]

To commit a crime is to be punished. The state removes the criminal from society, as if a sinner. A civil affront, whether it is assault, libel, or deceit, is not the same as a crime, and the drama of pursuit—by the lawyers for the person injured—lets the law into unexpected domains. Criminal outrage is nothing like the sometimes-vulgar indecency of tortious acts. Not only does tort displace legal action from punishing the agent of injury to redressing persons who are damaged or their kin, but it attends to and listens for any affront to civil society, the nuances of civility and propriety. In torts, ordinariness trumps the extraordinary, as the unusual must become commonplace for the law to intercede. Ordinary caution, or the vague standard of the "reasonable man," becomes the criterion for judging conduct negligent, the most common basis for tort liability. In judging conduct reasonable, legal decisions typecast the unreasonable. Law not only regulates social conduct, but in doing so erases individual personality. Though persons with physical disabilities are granted exceptions for their incapacity, surprisingly, the mentally deficient in civil actions are held to the same legal standard of reasonableness as everyone else.[55]

"But he who is intelligent and prudent does not act at his peril, in theory of law." In a world of threat, where all humans act at their peril, to contradict Holmes, law becomes necessity. Yet its effects are sometimes disheartening, especially in determining incapacity or defect. If behavior is judged along a continuum from ideal–average–prudent to sullied–delinquent–reckless, it risks classifying the weak, racially suspect, and politically unpopular. General legal standards often become the foundation for vile practices.[56]

Law words and legal fictions work wonders on the commonsense world of experience outside the courtroom. In the process of defining harm, assessing damages, or assigning blame, legal reasoning sometimes deforms the individuals in its purview, or gives them a negative status in the civil order. Hierarchies of value matter most in cases of personal injury. Once the realities of ownership and mastery are brought before the courts, they become suspect, if not downright malignant. Where nonhuman animals are concerned, especially, notions of personhood and the meaning of atrocity are sorely tested.

Intent and inadvertence, foresight and blame are very much part of the terminology and principle of torts. In *Trauerman v. Lippincott* (1890), the Court of Appeals of Missouri defined wanton acts in an action of trespass:

> [I]f one intentionally does a wrongful act and knows at the time that it is wrongful, then he does it wantonly, by which word I understand is meant causelessly, without restraint and in reckless disregard.... When one intentionally commits a wrong, he does it from an evil spirit and bad motive. Good motive or spirit does not impel the commission of willful wrongs.

Yet Holmes reminded his readers that although "the law of torts abounds in moral phraseology," it is not about individual "moral short-coming." Pushing interiority out of legal interpretation, and emphasizing that "law only works within the sphere of the senses," Holmes managed to both deindividualize and externalize tort law. Without bearing a person ill will or malice, one can still be guilty of tortious intent. But *wanton or willful* misconduct does not require proof of the intent to injure.[57]

How does the *normal* or *average* person understand the law of torts, the thicket of manner and motive—and even morals— that are remade in legal reckonings? From the outside looking in, as a nonlawyer surveying the terrain of torts, I appreciate its power and pervasiveness, its fluidity and indeterminacy. A secular world replaced the problem of evil with that of injury. What is fascinating about contemporary torts is how dichotomies such as public and private, personal and impersonal, subjective and objective become blurred. Sometimes arbitrary decisions and indefensible distinctions greatly enhance the meaning of *good* or *bad* person, and nowhere as rigorously as in deliberations about tort liability. Tortious, unlike criminal, acts are crucial to civil life, to defining what those granted a place in a social world are not only capable of but also deserving of. So, what kind of world is this? If one is not civilly dead but civilly alive, how does law define morality, teach us about responsibility, and make us liable? [58]

G. Edward White, in concluding *Tort Law in America*, emphasizes its conflicting purposes and doctrinal complexities: to be "admonitory" or "compensatory," a "private law subject" (arising out of "injuries to individual citizens") or "public law in disguise" ("a mechanism for allocating the costs of injuries in modern American society"). In a society of risk—whether from industry, random animals, private individuals, or government officials— where justice is so distinctly inequitable, where the experience of legal decisions is so radically distinct for different persons, the difficulty of law language—its ability to make words mean more or less than in common parlance—matters greatly. In the gradations of intentional wrongs, negligence, and strict liability, the rules of tort cover most of the pleasures, distress, and danger of quotidian life. Their opacity and omnipresence give this law a place equal to the divine, to the God or gods of an earlier time.[59]

Tort law began as a response to trespass, which changed over time from transgression—violent invasions by marauders, assault and thievery, and other enormities—to the lesser evil of encroachment on land, most easily understood as the wandering of a cow into some yard, trampling flowers, or onto the highway and causing an accident. According to early common law, wild animals were excluded as objects of larceny, as were "peacocks and sporting dogs," which were "luxury articles without economic value." But if one has what Holmes calls "a valuable property" in an animal—such as a cow or sheep—then one is "'bound to take care that it does not stray into the land of [one's] neighbor.'" Since a dog "is not the subject of property," it does not harm by simply crossing the land of others than its owner.[60]

Harm is judged according to property value and also determined by the "nature" or "propensities" of an animal, whether luxury or useful, tame or wild. Crucial also to this judgment is what can be known by a human about an animal, or what can never be known or understood or foreseen. In early twentieth-century English law, anyone who keeps a "wild animal of a savage kind, or even a domestic animal which is known to him to be savage … will be liable for damage done by it, whatever care he may have used to keep it safely." If a dog that had already bitten a human being bit again, the owner is liable for the offense. Even if an owner had no knowledge of the dog's propensity to harm, he was liable for damage it did to cattle or poultry.[61]

Torts were not concerned only with animals, of course. Novel taxonomies of persons flourish in the history of torts. The collision of persons and things, animate and inanimate, hides behind the form of logical arguments from precedents. Tortious examples of errant cattle, stray dogs, and fierce tigers form the backdrop to the wanton, mischievous, and willful actions of humans. What can the straying of animals tell us about the treatment of persons judged most vulnerable or bestial in their community? Let us return to the San Francisco Zoo and the legal consequences of the encounter between Tatiana the tiger and the humans who visited her during Christmas 2007. A tiger, restrained in its liberty, is confined in a zoo for the amusement of humans. It escapes, mauls, and kills. The escape of wild animals from owners is one of the few areas of law clearly governed by strict liability—meaning liability for injury, regardless of fault (either intentional conduct or negligence). Yet a public zoo is different. Some courts, aware that the abnormally dangerous activity of keeping a tiger is in this instance normally and socially sanctioned, have been unwilling to use strict liability against zoos. In the case of Tatiana, however, Mark Geragos, the lawyer for the Dhaliwal brothers, argues a strict liability analysis. "One who possesses or harbors a dangerous animal, whether wild or domesticated, is absolutely liable for injuries inflicted by it, where he or she knows or should know of its dangerous propensities."[62]

By looking at the most extreme cases of outrage, as well as trifling antisocial acts, committed either deliberately or carelessly, we begin to understand the expectations of civil and the coercions of social life. The language of torts and its fittest locales are commentaries on prejudice, justice, and the way humans act toward other species, as well as toward their own kind. The sometimes inconspicuous little rituals of daily life harbor the threat of damage, as well as the legal personifications through which recompense can be made. No matter how amorphous the language of tort—its chains of wide-ranging adjectives such as *willful*, *wanton*, or *malicious*; *reckless*, *oppressive*, or *fraudulent*—it prevents, courts, and inspires violence. The domain of justice and injustice, dependent as these are on each other, inevitably leads to judgments about civilization and barbarism. No matter how general, predictable, or objective the law's standards are—or perhaps because they aim not to be value judgments—they judge defects and capacity, and supply the terms for inclusion and ostracism.

SKIN OF THE DOG

It is the judges (as we have seen) that make the
common law. Do you know how they make it? Just as
a man makes laws for his dog. When your dog does
anything you want to break him of, you wait till he
does it, and then beat him for it. This is the way you
make laws for your dog: and this is the way the judges
make law for you and me. They won't tell a man
beforehand what it is he *should not do*—they won't
so much as allow of his being told: they lie by till he
has done something which they say he should not
have done, and then they hang him for it.

—Jeremy Bentham, *Truth versus Ashhurst,
Or Law As It Is* (1792)

A DOG IS BEING STOLEN

NOT ALL LAWS COMMAND THE SAME ASSUMPTIONS ABOUT PERSON-
hood and property, nor can we be sure how far case law can be
understood to offer insight into worth and insignificance. If we
were challenged to write a legal history of dispossession, we
could find no better examples, both profound and ancient, than
in the taxonomies of personhood when bounded and enlivened
by the dog kind. Only with dogs before us and beside us can we
understand the making or unmaking of *the idea of persons*.

Does ownership mean the same thing for all citizens? Perhaps one way to approach questions of value is to consider the

position of dogs in the law of property. History offers an exemplum. In the story of Katrina dogs, many left behind in New Orleans or taken from the arms of their possessors, we see how the fate of dogs entangles with the treatment of the poor, the persons desperate to escape catastrophe. Out of the rags and flotsam of civil life came images of loss. An old man perished on a chaise longue in the middle of the road. Around the corner, outside the Convention Center in New Orleans, an elderly woman lay dead in her wheelchair, covered by a blanket. Another corpse was beside her wrapped in a sheet. "I don't treat my dog like that," forty-seven-year-old Daniel Edwards remarked. "I buried my dog. But we're out here like animals. We don't have help."

The sight of citizens turned refugees in their own country made me think about abandoned dogs. Not because I want to equate people with dogs, but because the proximity between them helps us to grasp the relationship between legal status and proprietary interests. Like homeless dogs, later shot or dying in the streets of New Orleans, these persons had no names, they could seek no reprieve. They were alone, although they were surrounded by people. They had claims on our sympathy, but nonetheless remained powerless, prey to the vagaries of coercion, legality, and control.

The nature and status of dogs as defined by law are crucial to understanding the limits of restitution and the uneven application of remedy to persons who must answer to or reckon with the law. Old-time forfeiture, the guilt and surrender of inanimate or nonhuman objects, lives on in narratives of dogs seized and dispatched. The imputed guilt of the deodand lives on in the treatment of dogs deemed expendable. Though hurricane Katrina was an emergency, separating humans from dogs and owners from their property seemed harsh as officers led distressed citizens to safety and left their dogs to drown or starve.

In legal judgments, an obsolete justice is repackaged in unexpected ways. One of the more vexing issues in prosecutions for larceny is whether dogs are subjects of property. If they are

not, then their loss through thievery cannot be a cause for restitution in law. I return to the history of criminal and civil law in
order to extend the fate of Katrina dogs—and their owners'
loss—to larger questions of judicial interpretation and its consequences. Actions against or unconcern with dogs are related
to the giving or withholding of legal personality from human
animals.

Dogs were once subject to the legal fiction that they had no
value. They were judged to be either ignoble or trivial, kept only
for pleasure and caprice and not for sustenance or service. Blackstone explains that "a man may have a base property therein,
and maintain a civil action for the loss of them, yet they are not
of such estimation, as that the crime of stealing them amounts
to larceny." The ambiguous identity of dogs—sources of indulgence and delight but otherwise useless or wild—was institutionalized in the common law.[1]

Filow's case (1520), heard in the Court of Common Pleas during the reign of Henry VIII, decided for the first time that dog
stealing can be judged wrongful. William Filow, a knight, brought
an action of trespass ("brief de Transgressioun") against J——,
who had beaten his servant and taken his bloodhound. Several
of the judges who voted in the majority argued that if a dog is
private property, its owner can maintain trespass for the loss of
it, since its utility for the owner's pleasure is an adequate element of value. Though "this dog is a thing of pleasure, still he is
profitable for hunting or recreation," argued John Newport and
John Newdigate. But John Roe preferred the outlawry of dogs
to the punishment of thieves: "[F]or the taking of a dog one will
not have an appeal of felony, though it be taken with felonious
intent, since there is no reason why one should have judgment
of life or limb for a dog which is of no value." In other words, a
man should not hang for a dog. This singular antipathy to dogs
was supported by the Church. The dissenting judge Richard
Eliot distinguished beasts that were once "savage" and "now docile," such as sheep, cattle, and horses, from dogs. Dogs were so
contemptible that he equated them with "vermin," along with

"apes and monkeys." Hence, "dogs and cats are not tithable; for the spiritual law does not desire that vermin should be tithable." And the owner's pleasure? Nothing but a trifling concern. If "a lady who has a little dog is unwilling to sell this for a great sum of money, and if I take it, there is no reason why she shall have an action for the pleasure that she had in it." [2]

Justice Richard Brooke's argument acknowledged the propriety of possession and gave value to the dog as long as he bore proof of his master's training. Once tamed, a dog gains legal value, even if not the status of *absolute* property. Brooke analyzes the appropriation of animals as nothing less than Edenic dispensation, which he renders in terms of rebellion and submission.

> For at the commencement of the world all the beasts were obedient to our first father Adam, and all the four elements were obedient to him; but after that he broke the commandment of our Lord God, all the beasts commenced to rebel and become savage; and this was for the punishment of his crime, and now they are in common and belong to the occupant, as fowls in the air and fish in the sea and beasts of the land. When I have taken a wild fowl and by my industry have tamed him and deprived him of his liberty, now I have a special property in him, because he has become obedient to me by my labor.

In thus invoking the glories of property and possession, another justice, Lewis Pollard, waxes poetic: "[M]y hound is my treasure, for he takes game for my pleasure." The rigors of affectionate appropriation have a domino effect. His transformative sweep moves from "this hound" in "my possession" to this hound in "the possession of my servant," concluding the paean to control with "then here this possession of my servant is my possession." Even when praised as docile and devoted, and hence rising in status, dogs are prized not for themselves but as proofs of their owners' right to possess. [3]

The human dominion over things became fixed in law as the criterion of civilization. Although early legal historians, most notably Theodore Plucknett, reasoned that "the institution of slavery … left little mark on our law," in fact the common law of personal property laid out the terms for reducing human chattels to things worth possessing.[4] The terminology of occupation (rather than ownership) made what had been the property of no one—*res nullius*—the framework for the conversion of persons into things, reclaimed out of wildness into obedience, whether by restraint or cultivation. These reflections on industrious appropriation demonstrate the juridical creation of a servile order. What makes the worthless worthy of being possessed— and its loss recoverable in damages—is the labor of the person who acquires, subdues, and enhances for himself what was nugatory.

To be owned, then, is to be special. For certain entities, held as property, there is a status to be reckoned with, from high to low. The question is *how* you are owned, the success of domestication. In the matter of ownership alone lies your fate. If labor has been expended, then the entity is reclaimed from the wild. Once you have turned an animal from wild to docile, from misbehavior to obedience, you gain the right to claim it as personal property. The fact of this discipline in *Filow's* case made the theft a trespass.

Glanville Williams argues in his *Liability for Animals* (1939) that by the nineteenth century, the rules of law put "the dog upon a much higher level in the scale of ownership." Law began to recognize property in dogs, and criminal action as well as civil remedies could be sought against someone convicted of dog stealing. Yet if dogs were no longer as legally insignificant as before, they continued to be subject to the rigor of civil law: judged as either harmless or dangerous, accused of damage or injury, impounded or killed. They became worthless insofar as they lapsed from their servile status. To be no longer obedient was to be no longer special, not worth keeping and easily disposed of. Their representation and treatment—whether stolen, cared for, beaten, or ignored—are limit cases in the extravagance of status-making in law: at what point are dogs legally recognizable, and when do they cease to count?[5]

At common law, as we have seen, a human could not be punished for stealing a dog, and archaic fictions held that "it had no intrinsic value" and that "it was not fully domesticated,—but by nature base."[6] Implied here is an obligation to assess a dog's value and usefulness, an obligation that was maintained in American legal practice. In this intermediate, imperfect state, dogs are neither wild nor domesticated, neither profitable nor worthless. In the absolute sense, they were simply not property as were other chattels, including slaves. This legal representation of ambivalent status is distinct from that of the slave. As numerous southern courts decreed, it was legally impossible that human chattels occupy a state in between freedom and servitude or between worth and uselessness. If they had no value as instruments of labor or procreation, then they literally had no reason for being and no legal protections against neglect or mutilation, maiming or death.

Slaves had no legal personality in civil law but gained it in criminal law. Dogs, on the other hand, had no property value in criminal law but were granted it in civil law. What both dogs and slaves have in common, however, is their standing outside the concerns of civil life. Let us recall the striking example of *Bailey v. Poindexter* (1858). A master's last will and testament requesting that his slaves be given the option to elect freedom was judged null and void because slaves had no legal capacity to choose. Although the court granted value to the individual slave who performs a job well, this performance was not considered a "civil" act. The rationale depended on an analogy with a dog: only if the service of a "well-trained and sagacious dog," in bringing his owner meat in a basket from a butcher, could "in a legal sense" be understood as "a civil act of the dog" could a slave's services be considered a civil act.[7]

The involvement of dogs in the lives of humans was questioned, documented, and parsed by the law, though dogs were usually entitled to less legal regard and protection than other animals. Dogs became the center of cases of slander, assault, trespass, negligence, or nuisance. In *Findlay v. Bear* (1822), the Supreme Court of Pennsylvania decided that there could be no action of slander for the words "Daniel Bear pilfered a dog, and peddled the dog through the county, and then sold him to John Levingood for five dollars." Even if Bear stole the dog, even if he sold the dog, the law privileges fiction over fact. Since the dog cannot be stolen in law, the words are not slander. Though they might have a basis in reality, they have none in law.[8]

As law became more concerned with dogs, the applicable field of legal ritual expanded. The processes that created the legal personalities of ghosts and humans—either as endowed with rights or as slaves and convicts and other categories of deprivation and undesirability—now extended to dogs.

In some later cases, legal considerations of value granted dogs their status as property. Two opinions by Judge Robert Earl of the New York Court of Appeals exemplify how these rituals could be variously applied to people and dogs in the construction of legal personalities. We have already encountered one, *Avery v. Everett* (1888), in which Earl would enter the fogs and fictions of civil death and advocate its strict application in the case of a prisoner held for life by the state. He was severe in his dissent, pronouncing the litany of dispossession that applied not only to rights and duties but also to the fact of a legal oblivion that knew no exceptions and brooked no compromise.

Seven years earlier, in *Mullaly v. The People of the State of New York* (1881), Earl considered whether a prisoner convicted of stealing a dog worth less than $25 was rightly condemned. Showing far greater sympathy to dogs than to convicts, he sought to reexamine the common-law precedent that "[w]hile it was not larceny to steal a dog, it was larceny to steal the skin of a dead dog." He countered claims of dogs' baseness and their use as things kept "for the mere whim and pleasure of their owners" with stories that illustrate how "inapplicable to modern society" is the "artificial reasoning" upon which old common-law rules are based:

When we call to mind the small spaniel that saved the life of William of Orange and thus probably changed the current of modern history … and the faithful St. Bernards, which after a storm has swept over the crests and sides of the Alps, start out in search of lost travelers, the claim that the nature of a dog is essentially base and that he should be left a prey to every vagabond who chooses to steal him will not now receive ready assent.

Ultimately, he held that dogs were "personal property" as defined in the New York Revised Statutes.[9]

Though Earl's opinions were very different in these two cases—in *Avery* he negated legal personality, while in *Mullaly* he brought a creature into legal existence—in each he demonstrated the law's extraordinary power to define and the wide field of existence over which it could be exercised. The law makes things on its own terms, terms that may or may not be accountable to experience depending on the whim and prejudice of a jurist.

Law thus became an influential element in shaping a new understanding of the relation between dogs and humans. In *Hamby v. Samson* (1898), Judge C. J. Deemer of the Supreme Court of Iowa also relates the history of canine law in order to rule that dogs can be the subject of larceny. Were dogs to be included within the definition of chattels, or were they simply imperfect or qualified property, he asked? Dogs were in fact to be deemed "chattels," he argued, in contrast to strict common-law rules. So the dog thief before him was guilty of larceny. Deemer reversed the district court decision that had wrongly discharged the thief. In considering the evolution of property in dogs, he recognized them as ownable: they are taxed, owners are liable for damages they cause, and civil proceedings recognize them as property. And though these regulations could be considered simply as part of the police power of the states and not a legal dispensation, Judge Deemer concludes: "Surely, it was not the intent of the legislature to recognize dogs as property for the purposes of taxation, and yet leave them to the mercy of thieves."[10]

Should a person die for stealing dogs? Sir Edward Coke, chief judge of the Common Pleas (1606–13), aware that death was punishment for taking property worth twelve pence, suggested that such a punishment was inappropriate. But "those ancient law-givers," Earl continues in *Mullaly v. People*, "thought it not unfit that a person should die for stealing a tame hawk or falcon." Past artifices of law that pitch falcons and hawks, once reclaimed, into the service "of princes and of noble and generous persons" are relinquished in favor of a new paradigm of nobility: the bestowing of property status on dogs.

> In nearly every household in the land can be found chattels kept for the mere whim and pleasure of the owner, a source of solace after serious labor, exercising a refining and elevating influence, and yet they are as much under the protection of the law as chattels purely useful and absolutely essential.

In this argument on behalf of the negligible but delightful, the salutary if useless dogs find a home in lawfully ordained servility.[11]

WHY DOGS?

If a dog goes missing, she must be found. In Nashville you drive to a place that houses both criminals and dogs. The large concrete sign at the entrance announces "Sheriff's Correctional Complex." Below is the emblem of a sheriff's badge and in bold black letters the words "OFFENDER RE-ENTRY CENTER." Underneath in equally prominent letters it reads "METRO ANIMAL CONTROL." The juxtaposition marks the precarious status of two kinds of being: dogs being sheltered until claimed or euthanized and humans being welcomed back into the restraints of law. Whereas dogs were surrendered to the chance of being reclaimed or the certainty of death, offenders were being sheltered during incarceration so that they could get help finding jobs and housing. A promise of reclamation in counterpoint to the threat of disposal. In both cases, this is the place where the lost can be found, but there is always the risk of surrender to the state.

No country kills more dogs or imprisons more people than the United States. Inmates and dogs find themselves together in situations that are matters of life and death—and the ambiguous space in between. After Katrina, the Humane Society in Gonzales, Louisiana, sent more than two hundred dogs to temporary quarters on the grounds of two prisons there, where inmates cared for them. The correspondence between dogs and prisoners, however, is not always as heartening.

At the height of the move to "get tough on prisoners" in 2000, the infamous Sheriff Joe Arpaio of Maricopa County, Arizona, converted a section of the First Avenue Jail in Phoenix into a kennel for abused and neglected animals. He understood the trade-off between dignity and degradation. Ten dogs who were victims of abuse remained in the jailhouse kennel while a criminal investigation of their owners was conducted. Cared for by inmates, the dogs lived in air-conditioned cells, slept on blankets, and, as one news story reported, were "treated to good food and music specially designed to have a calming effect on animals." Arpaio contrasted his treatment of human inmates—tent cities, posses, "last chance chain gangs," foul green bologna, pink underwear, bread and water diets—and his care of abused dogs. In the many e-mail exchanges following what one critic called Arpaio's "dog and pony show," some writers reflected on "poor dogs" versus "the dregs of society," others emphasized the abuse of prisoners versus the benevolence toward dogs.[12]

Dogs take their place alongside persons targeted for coercion, control, or worse. A young soldier smiles into the camera in the corridor of Abu Ghraib. In the background are two army dog handlers in camouflage combat gear restraining two German shepherds. The dogs bark at a man. It is difficult to see, since the soldier partially blocks our view. Another image shows the naked Iraqi prisoner. He leans against the cell door, hands clasped behind his neck, crouching in terror. The dogs bark just a few feet away. In another, taken a few minutes later, the prisoner lies on the ground, writhing in pain. A soldier sits on top of him and presses his knee to his back. Blood streams from the prisoner's leg. The final shot in these photos of incremental degradation is a close-up of the naked prisoner lying on the floor, just his waist to his ankles in sight. A bite or deep scratch is on his right thigh. There is a larger wound on his left leg covered in blood.

The use of unmuzzled military working dogs, sometimes called "war dogs," to intimidate prisoners during interrogation at Abu Ghraib was approved by military intelligence officers at the prison. They received instructions from Army Major General Geoffrey D. Miller, who had also told the guards that "you're treating the prisoners too well. You have to treat prisoners like dogs." Miller later denied that he ever discussed using dogs during interrogations, acknowledging only that he knew "there's a cultural fear of dogs in the Arab culture." He claimed that their use was limited to the custody and control of detainees.[13]

But though the media focus on the use of dogs in prisons like Abu Ghraib and Guantánamo, they have generally ignored the common practice of using dogs to conduct cell extractions in U.S. prisons. In October 2006, Human Rights Watch published the report "Cruel and Degrading: The Use of Dogs for Cell Extractions in U.S. Prisons." "The use of a fierce animal to control an imprisoned person is inherently humiliating, denying an inmate's personhood. Terrifying an inmate into compliance also denies his personal integrity. It reduces the inmate himself to an animal crouched in fear in the face of an attack." In Arizona, Terry Stewart, then director of the Department of Corrections, started the practice of "dog frights" in order to protect staff, or so he testified to the Arizona legislature. The training video *Open Pod Extractions* was made in 1998. Unseen dogs bark in the background, as the voiceover advises no more force than is "reasonable and necessary." Then, with upbeat music playing, we see the German shepherd held on a long leash, straining toward the cell, as his handler restrains him. We hear the order, "Cuff up or I'll release my dog, and he will bite you." The dog pants, the "inmate" refuses to obey. The cell door is opened, the dog charges toward the dummy of a prisoner, jumps on him, and takes hold of his leg with his teeth. When the handler pulls the dog's leash, the prisoner is pulled out with him, like a bone. As a correctional officer later told me, "It's pretty funny to see the prisoner pee on himself. I think even the dog can't stand the smell. Between the foam on his mouth and the pee on the floor, you can't tell which one's the dog."[14]

Something about dogs makes them the subject of jokes as well as a source of terror, not only in sites of torture or abuse but also in cases of law. Dogs are sometimes amusing, sometimes ferocious. In 1856 in the Supreme Court of New York, Judge W. F. Allen responded vigorously to an appeal of a judgment that had awarded damages to the plaintiff whose trespassing dog had died from injuries sustained in a fight with the defendant's dogs and the defendant's subsequent blows. In *Wiley v. Slater*, Allen admits that he has never been asked before to apply the law to the vicissitudes of dog life, certainly not to judge the legal effects of a "pure dog fight."

> I am constrained to admit total ignorance of the code duello among dogs, or what constitutes a just cause of offense and justifies a resort to the *ultima ratio regem* [*sic*], a resort to arms, or rather to teeth, for redress; whether jealousy is a just cause of war, or what different degrees and kinds of insult or slight, or what violation of the rules of etiquette entitle the injured or offended beast to insist upon prompt and appropriate satisfaction, I know not.

He argues that fighting—settling scores and taking revenge—is one of the few privileges left to these animals in their domesticated state. Given this "semi-divine right of dogs to fight," there is no law "human or divine, moral or ceremonial, common or statute" that has ever regulated barking and biting. No rule exists that gives the owner of the losing dog satisfaction from the owner of the victor. Allen reversed the judgment of the county court that had awarded damages to the plaintiff whose dog had died, but not without a final quip: "The owner of the dead dog would, I think, be very clearly entitled to the skin, although some, less liberal, would be disposed to award it as a trophy to the victor."[15]

The English common law, especially when reinvigorated in the United States in the nineteenth century, was hard-pressed to find classifications for dogs as they lived in and were evaluated by human society. Old law conceits about dogs were repeated in modern judgments on dog stealing. *State v. Langford* (1899) in the Supreme Court of South Carolina, in considering an indictment for stealing a dog from a doghouse, recalls the Statute of 10 George III and "the reasoning satisfactory at that day": "[I]t was larceny to steal a tame hawk, but not larceny to steal a tame dog, although it was larceny to steal the hide of a dead dog." Why would a dead dog's skin be worth more than the dog alive? The labor of tanning the skin, making goods from it, and the possibility of profit from their sale—all make something out of nothing. But the South Carolina court decided that a stolen dog should be included in the law of larceny, as well as provided for in civil remedies.[16]

By the 1890s, tort cases began to describe, evaluate, and judge the limits of canine injury and death. In the courtrooms of America, dog owners sued for damages when their dogs were wrongfully killed. Going beyond the rule that dogs were imperfect property, as in earlier common-law examples, bereft owners described and judged their dogs' uniqueness. Some argued their dogs were special, indeed irreplaceable, so that recovery in damages could not be limited by their actual market value. Though the vast majority of appellate courts held property in dogs to be restricted, if not negligible, sometimes jurists took account of a dog's inestimable worth. Testimonies of admirable qualities and lineage were recounted in ways that tested the patience of defendants—carriers, railroad and street car companies, and individuals. In *Citizens' Rapid Transit Co. v. Dew* (1898), the Supreme Court of Tennessee held that a street railway company may be liable in damages for negligently running over and killing a dog. A valuable retriever was running along the turnpike in front of his owner's vehicle when "little birds flying up" attracted his attention. He stopped to "set" or "point them," and the street-car ran over him. Seeing that his dog was fatally injured, the owner shot him to put him out of his suffering.[17]

In his decision, the judge affirmed that dogs were now personal property, subject to larceny, with an elevated standing before the law.

> Large amounts of money are now invested in dogs, and they are extensively the subjects of trade and traffic. They are the negro's associates, and often his only property, the poor man's friend, and the rich man's companion, and the protection of women and children, hearthstones and henroosts.

Then he referred to the dog's pedigree. A "blue blood," belonging "to the inner circles of the four hundred, a member of the F.F.T., or first families of Tennessee ... of English descent." He also accepted as testimony the dog's reputation as trusted house dog and wide ranger, "thoroughly broken" and "a fine retriever from land or water." Anticipating complaints from those who described the intricacies of dog law as gibberish, he explained: "In the earlier law books it was said that 'dog law' was as hard to define as was 'dog Latin.' But that day has passed, and dogs have now a distinct and well established status in the eyes of the law."[18]

A COMMON NUISANCE

In spite of evidence throughout the nineteenth century of concern for dogs and compensation to their owners, in the towns and cities of the United States dogs still walked at great risk. A dog without a collar could be killed with impunity. A dog without a license faced death by gunshot or beating not just from the police, who were entitled to destroy any threat to public welfare, but from anyone else. Dogs knew adversity, rejection, and scorn. Their disposability was enshrined in legal judgments. A festering odor, smoke from a chimney, the screeching of cockerels or dogs barking in the night—all could be considered a nuisance at common law.[19]

In the case of dogs howling, the English cases are significantly less harsh than the American. In *Street v. Tugwell* (1800), Lord Kenyon held that while six or seven pointers howling in a kennel night and day caused a disturbance, their owner could not be held liable for nuisance. Accordingly, though no evidence was given in support of the owner, the jury declined to order him to pay damages. Kenyon refused the distraught neighbor's motion for a new trial. American dogs (and their owners) were less fortunate. Forty years later in *Brill v. Flagler* (1840), the Supreme Court of New York reversed a similar verdict by a lower court in favor of a dog owner. A neighbor, desperate to silence an English setter that had been wandering outside his home incessantly "barking and howling," shot and killed the dog. Though the dog's owner "was fully advised of this mischievous propensity of the animal," he "willfully neglected to confine him." The dog's market value and the possibility of restitution for its loss were wholly irrelevant in "a case of serious and intolerable nuisance."[20]

When can a dog offensive to humankind be legally killed? And what is the nature of the offense? Defendants are justified in killing a dangerous dog that the owner knowingly allows to run at large. As the court decided in *Putnam v. Payne* (1816) in the Supreme Court of New York, the owner's negligence could be punished by destroying the nuisance: "Such negligence was wanton and cruel, and fully justified the defendant in killing the dog as a nuisance," but judges were careful to note that "killing more useful and less dangerous animals"—such as sheep or cattle—was not acceptable. In *Brown v. Carpenter* (1854), the Supreme Court of Vermont decided that there was no remedy for the killing of a dog known to growl, jump on and bite people, for "such a dog is *hostis communis*, the common enemy, and may be killed by any one." The court, citing previous cases in New York, argued that such a dog must be treated "as an outlaw and a common nuisance, liable to destruction." Later, a Kentucky appellate court refused to spare even harmless dogs that happened to wander into a neighbor's yard unattended—"even though it be for the propagation of his species, his innocence is no protection to him … his life is forfeited, if the owner of the premises on which he is found will exact the penalty, and chooses to execute the sentence."[21]

In *Woolf v. Chalker* (1862), the Supreme Court of Connecticut awarded damages to a traveling peddler who came, unannounced and uninvited, into a customer's sitting room and was bitten by the family dog. Though the dog was protecting his owner's wife and children, the court based its judgment on findings of the dog's ferocity: "A man may not, in this country, use dangerous or unnecessary *instruments* for the protection of his property against trespassers. Such instruments may be used in England, but the principles on which their decisions purport to rest are not sustainable or applicable here." The court's language was especially severe when it came to arguing about the dog's propensities: "Thus a ferocious dog accustomed to bite mankind is a common nuisance, and may be destroyed by any one." Addicted to biting mankind, and suffered to run at large, a dog could be killed, even if there was no evidence that it was doing or threatening injury at the time of the killing. The definition of actionable nuisance was broad enough to accommodate barkers as well as biters: "The dog is a *noisy* animal, and may in that way become a nuisance and be destroyed."[22]

In these judgments of wrongs, dogs not only act but live *at their peril*. For who is to judge ferocity? How violent must a dog be to cause enough alarm to be labeled "dangerous"? Are evil propensities known by a bite or the apparent desire to injure? Does a single bite justify liquidation? Some later decisions questioned the necessity of such legalized violence against dogs and their owners. In August 1894, William Shand asked the Supreme Court of New York to prevent James G. Tighe, a police justice, from enforcing the fine he had placed on Shand for refusing to kill his dog after it bit a man. In an article entitled "Dogs Must Be Respected," the *New York Times* reported that "Justice William J. Gaynor … yesterday rendered a unique decision in a dog case, which should endear to him every dog-owner in Brooklyn. He lays down the rule that a dog is property, and as such is entitled to the same consideration as any other kind of property."[23]

In the course of an accomplished though now forgotten life, William Gaynor (1849–1913) reshaped New York law, as well as politics, crusading for reform as a journalist, attorney, judge, and ultimately mayor of New York City from 1910 to 1913. During his first year as mayor, he was shot by a disgruntled city employee, the only New York mayor to be the target of an assassination attempt. The bullet remained lodged in his throat until his death three years later. He referred to the injury when he wanted to avoid discussing a sensitive issue: "Sorry, can't talk today. This fish hook in my throat is bothering me." For three years he fought patronage and the machinations of Tammany Hall and rooted out corruption from the police department. He pushed for the construction of a citywide subway and condemned arbitrary government wherever he found it. Gaynor had two mottos: "Ours is a government of laws not man" and "The world does not grow better by force or by the policeman's club."[24]

Written by "an intimate who knew him," the *New York Times* obituary praises Gaynor, "a farmer's boy," and his "unyielding commitment to civil liberties." "To Mayor Gaynor there were no outlaws. Even the vilest man and woman had rights under the Constitution and the laws." A later biographer described how police oppression moved Gaynor to fury, recalling his words: "Human liberty never was so cheap. The charge of vagrancy was trumped up.... If such outrages are to pass quietly, it will come to pass, that no citizen is safe at the hands of the police." Gaynor condemned outlawry as the barbaric relic of an earlier, rude history. He knew that deprivation, taint, and incapacity lived on. Let us recall that as slavery was gradually abolished in New York, civil death for felons stirred to new life in harsher statutes. Speaking about "distributive justice," he cautioned his audience: "[S]o look to it that your own calling does not dwarf your minds.... An animal lives in a little circle, as I know every time I look at my dog, or my horse or my cow or my pig, or even my goose, and within that horizon that animal knows more than we do."[25]

Not only humans but also dogs were entitled to something more than summary execution. Gaynor's opinion in *People v. Tighe* exemplified its author's warm sensitivity to dogs that bore the brunt of prejudice and police power. Gaynor begins his opinion with the ordinance passed by the common council of Brooklyn:

> If any dog shall "attack a person" at any place except on the premises of his owner, upon a complaint being made to the mayor, or a police justice, he shall inquire into the complaint, "and if satisfied of its truth, and that such dog is dangerous, he shall order the owner or possessor of such dog to kill him immediately;" and if the owner refuses to obey the order within forty-eight hours he shall forfeit ten dollars, and also five dollars more every forty-eight hours thereafter until the dog is killed.

Gaynor proceeds to demolish the complaint of the bitten man, Thomas Croke. The dog had not attacked, Gaynor said. Instead, reading Croke's complaint, Gaynor saw that Croke had sworn the dog was on the street with "the owner's boy," and "that (to use his exact words) 'I got hold of the boy and the dog bit me,' so that instead of the dog making an attack, Croke seems to have attacked the boy and the dog defended him." Gaynor therefore not only invalidated Tighe's order that Shand's collie be killed but also granted a writ that prevented enforcement of the fine. In doing so, he vindicated dogs from their degraded status, making potent reference to the common-law rule that "a dog was not property. It was no larceny to steal a dog, though it was larceny to steal a dead dog's hide."[26]

Repudiating the rule, Gaynor opined: "But the world moves and these crudities no longer exist, and in this state a dog is property," as was decided thirteen years earlier in *Mullaly v. People.* Gaynor described the dog "from the beginning" as "the friend and solace of man." "The law," he wrote, "has only recognized the testimony of human nature, history and poetry in withdrawing [dogs] from outlawry." The opinion draws upon Motley's *Rise and Fall of the Dutch Republic*, Thomas Moore's *Life of Byron*, and Homer's *Odyssey*. In making the dog full and absolute property, Gaynor demanded that any order to kill a dog must give the dog's owner due process: "Property may not be taken, affected or destroyed except by due process of law, which requires notice of hearing to the owner and opportunity to be heard." Dismissing such "oddities" as valuing a dog's hide or a tame hawk more than a living dog, he attacks the Brooklyn ordinance as "one of those absurdities which we often encounter." But he goes further. He singles out the interference of the police justice as unwarranted. "This ordinance is a fair sample of too much law and government, like many others enacted in Brooklyn, one of which is that no householder shall allow his chimney to take fire." [27]

We must recognize that Gaynor's enthusiasm for dogs is rare in that particular domain of justice and injustice we think of as law. The necessity of subordinating both humans and dogs to external authority and its rules varied from state to state, but most courts and legislatures came to see dogs increasingly as disturbances or threats. Tougher regulations began to demonstrate the peculiar vigilance of the modern era. In response to this severity, organizations were formed to "protect" and "care for" dogs.

In 1866 the state legislature of New York passed the country's first anticruelty law. In the same year, it issued An Act to Incorporate the Society for the Prevention of Cruelty to Animals and granted it power in vague terms: "An Act for the prevention of cruelty to animals, and empowering certain societies for the prevention of cruelty to animals to do certain things."

These "certain things" creditably included arresting anyone who tortured, tormented, deprived of necessary sustenance, or beat, mutilated, or killed "any living creature." But that was not all. In 1894 a new law gave the ASPCA in New York control over stray and unwanted animals. Along with this responsibility, it was granted the power to order a license tax on dogs and the right to seize and dispose of dogs it had not licensed. A few years later, a New York court in *Fox v. Mohawk and Hudson River Humane Society* ruled against this authority, since no state could delegate a private corporation to levy or collect taxes. The statute at issue was thus unconstitutional "so far as it requires the owner of a dog to pay a license fee to the defendant for its own use." Such a requirement—and the profits that followed—gave the Society a special immunity and privilege not granted to others.

But on appeal the court upheld the statute. Though recognized as a private organization, this humane society was now legally authorized to enforce the law, to levy canine taxes, and to impound and destroy unlicensed dogs without notice to the owner and without any judicial proceeding.[28]

The state's power over dogs expanded in tandem with its empowerment of the newly established societies for "humane treatment." Anticruelty statutes came to operate like the flip side of police measures. They worked together. Even today, in Humane Society protocol, dogs labeled as "dangerous" are subject to disposal without a hearing, despite the recognition that they are property. There is also the "potentially dangerous" dog that "chases or approaches a person ... in a menacing fashion or apparent attitude of attack" or that has "a known propensity, tendency or disposition to attack unprovoked." In her analysis of these Humane Society instructions, poet, philosopher, and dog trainer Vicki Hearne, who spent the last years of her life writing against breed bans, explained: "The phrase 'otherwise threaten the safety of human beings or domestic animals' does a magnificent job of including any dog alive in the category 'dangerous,' since existence itself is bound to be a nuisance to someone."[29]

To untangle the philosophy of personhood embedded in the rules of law, we must let the legal force of canine disposal speak for itself. In these cases of discrimination and damage, the potent rituals of law come to light. Pushed to define value, property, and process when judging dogs in human society, the law goes to great lengths to enshrine the ferocity and mischief that turns them from "high-status animal to low-status person."[30]

CANINE FICTIONS

What a load dogs must bear. In the Old Testament, dogs are always hungry. They feast on Jezebel. They devour meat mangled by beasts in the field. They lick up the blood of evildoers or devour the kin of Jeroboam and Baasha. In one of Jeremiah's many curses, the Lord selects four kinds of destroyers: "the sword to slay, and the dogs to tear, and the fowls of the heaven, and the beasts of the earth, to devour and destroy" (Jeremiah 15:3).

Matthew (15:21–28) tells a dog story that has not received much attention. It is found with some changes in Mark (7:24–30). Here, for the only time in the Old or New Testament, dogs have something to do with salvation. They are the most ignoble thing, at the opposite extreme from holiness, so they wait. Their stillness leads the way, thus becoming the medium for a new kind of sanctity. A parable it is not, for it sets dogs in a precise and imaginable relation to salvation.

A Canaanite woman from the district of Tyre and Sidon, in other words a Gentile, shouts: "Have mercy on me, O Lord, thou Son of David; my daughter is grievously vexed with a devil." As is often the case, Jesus refuses to recognize the source of recognition. The Canaanite comes and kneels at his feet, "Lord, help me." Instead of immediately answering her plea, he responds: "It is not meet to take the children's bread, and cast it to the dogs."

"Truth, Lord," she replies, "yet the dogs eat of the crumbs which fall from their masters' table." (In Mark the dogs are positioned explicitly "under the table.") We confront the delicacy of submission, that of both the woman and her dogs. Jesus answers her: "O woman, great is thy faith: be it unto thee even as thou wilt," and her daughter is healed, no longer possessed. How did her answer prove her faith? According to Matthew Henry in his *Commentary on the Whole Bible* (1828), those whom Christ means most to honor, he first humbles. The Gentiles, unlike the chosen, the children of Israel, come forth as unworthy as dogs. But so satiated are God's privileged children that they throw away both meat and sweetness, leaving the refuse as crumbs for those ready to receive, and be redeemed.[31]

The Church did not follow this merciful lead. In medieval France and Germany, Jews were suspended by their feet "together with a dog (or dogs) who, depending on local custom, may have been either dead or alive." In the later Middle Ages, Christians called Jews dogs, as Marlowe knew. In *The Jew of Malta*, Barabas confesses, "We Jews can fawn like spaniels when we please / And when we grin, we bite." In Shakespeare, both Shylock and Othello's circumcised Turk are dismissed as dogs; and Shylock in *The Merchant of Venice* warns: "Since I am a dog, beware my fangs."[32]

Powerful metaphors for the extremities of abuse, adoration, and prejudice, dogs define the possibilities of fantasy and madness, but in a way that is not altogether inconceivable. Out of the accursed islands of the Encantadas, where tortoises drag under a weight of sun, Melville tells two stories of dogs and their owners: the Chola Widow and the Dog-King. In both stories the dogs die. The action takes place in lands so wrecked that they must be enchanted: "In no world but a fallen one could such lands exist." The Chola Widow Hunila lives alone, stranded on Norfolk Island since her husband's death with "ten small, soft-haired, ringleted dogs, of a beautiful breed." Helped by mariners, she plans to return to her native Payta in Peru. Since all the dogs cannot board the ship, she takes only two and leaves the rest behind on the shore to die. "They did not howl, or whine; they all but spoke." When the Creole, whom Melville names "the Dog-King," takes over St. Charles's Island, he is accompanied by a "cavalry of large grim dogs." A mutiny occurs, and the rabble who had been kept in check by the "cavalry body-guard of dogs" fight them to the death. The mutineers are victors, and "the dead dogs ignominiously thrown into the sea."[33]

In Pliny's *Naturalis Historia*, "dog-soldiers" inhabit what is now Libya, and on the Canary Islands "Dog-People" have a dog for a king. But Melville probably brings these legends closer to home. The Dog-King could be Melville's rendering of Donatien Marie Joseph de Vimeur, vicomte de Rochambeau, who arrived in Saint-Domingue with a pack of dogs in February 1802 to become the brutal commander of a French army in tatters. Though Melville's "adventurer from Cuba" remains unnamed ("—I forget his name—," he writes), his dogs become the crux of Melville's fiction. They are reborn as the Dog-King's "canine regiment." Though "of a singularly ferocious character" and possessed of "severe training," the dogs are docile.

According to some historians, what became known as "Rochambeau's dogs" had been brought from Havana by the genteel aristocrat Louis Marie, vicomte de Noailles. When they appeared on the scene, they sported silks, ribbons, and feathered headdresses. In the arena set up in the courtyard of an old Jesuit monastery, Rochambeau used these dogs to torment, mutilate, and kill his enemies. Starved and forced to eat black males, these dogs, most probably mastiffs, did not always perform appropriately. Sometimes the French unleashed the dogs, only to be attacked by them. Other stories recount how these very dogs became food for starving French soldiers.[34]

The dog becomes absolutely necessary to the demands of servitude. In "Benito Cereno," Captain Delano meditates on benign "naked nature" and the servant Babo, who is as loyal and affectionate as a Newfoundland dog. Melville's dogs also bear witness to the devious taxonomies of natural histories, supported as they are by cultural fantasies. They lay bare the pressures of personhood. In *The Confidence-Man*, Melville extends his comparison. Here the dog is not so much personified as materially bound but not subordinate to the human. Der Black Guinea's crippled legs not only give him "the stature of a Newfoundland dog," but the man's "knotted black fleece" literally becomes the dog itself, no longer someone else's icon of "good-natured" and "honest" affection. George Orwell also gets into the fray. In "A Hanging," only the dog described as "half Airedale half pariah" has the range of emotions we would identify with persons. His responses, from excitement, joy, and compassion to shame, sorrow, and guilt (it is "conscious of having misbehaved itself"), track the progress of the narrative. Orwell's dog, its response to the hanging, marks the limits of the inhuman, for it is the consummate person.

This iconography has a logic that can easily turn worth into rubbish. Bearing the brunt of the most extreme denigration and at the same time enjoying the greatest affection, dogs are in a precarious space—so ignoble that they are the least cared for and so good that they are the most loved. In the law, this seeming paradox becomes the working definition of dog: so empty of substance that it can accrue to itself all kinds of projections. The excesses of sentiment are as dangerous to the lives of dogs as their cruel treatment by humans.

This double-sided meaning is rendered, undercut, and exceeded in J. M. Coetzee's *Disgrace* (1999), his dark and uncompromising novel about post-apartheid South Africa. Here is the conversation between David Lurie and his daughter Lucy, who has put herself outside the bounds of civil life. She chooses to live "with nothing. Not with nothing but. With nothing. No cards, no weapons, no property, no rights, no dignity." "Like a dog," her father, David Lurie, says. "Yes," she agrees, "like a dog." When she is raped, her dogs are killed. But what counts in this story of brutalization is Lurie's dedication to the shelter dogs that are to be euthanized. To the dogs, especially the dead, Lurie gives dignity, putting them in garbage bags with a solemnity that turns bags into shrouds. He gives these dog bodies, which otherwise might be broken, thrown away like refuse, another kind of burial, something that approaches holiness. That is his salvation, though Coetzee is too wise to present it as such. It is not salvation but grace when he quietly surrenders his favorite dog to death. "Bearing him in his arms like a lamb," Lurie gives up the last sweet thing he might have possessed.[35]

Literary fictions of dogs are increasingly the center of our attention. And the fictions connected to dogs' sensibility and their often unimaginable torment by humans put them in relation to the habits of law. Because dogs are vessels for the most ardent outpourings of human emotion, when the subject is a dog, questions of good and evil, blame and fault are brought to life in the sharpest relief: a drama of vested interests, conflicts, and affiliations with a long history.

DOG LAW

In early criminal law the thing doing the damage was liable, and through the thing the owner was made accountable. Under the name of deodand, as we have seen, the offending object was forfeited to the victim's kin or the Crown: surrendered for retribution. But this order of things changed radically in modern law. The progress from thing-liability to human responsibility meant that law, as Holmes put it, "is becoming more refined by the increased attention to the culpability of the person charged." If the thing that caused death or injury happened to be a dog, for example, both owner and dog suffered blame and answered for the deed. But the form this justice took must be understood as part of the history of legally induced forfeiture and dispossession.[36]

Indiscriminate liability belonged, as the legal scholar John H. Wigmore assured his readers, to "primitive times." It "stands for an instinctive impulse," he explained, "guided by superstition, to visit with vengeance the visible source, whatever it be,—human or animal, witting or unwitting,—of the evil result." This confusion about or unconcern with innocence or guilt, which he allied with archaic beliefs or the "irrational spirit" that inspired "the jural doings of primitive society," was for Wigmore a remnant of what Holmes also saw as an early stage in the progress of law "from barbarism to civilization." Although it is comforting to imagine that the "path of law" has moved out of darkness into the light, I have been suggesting that the claims of reason have never proved enlightenment. Rules of evidence, judicial enquiry, and legal reasoning have not prevented even torture.[37]

The power of law to sustain, or, rather, summon up archaic debris emerges clearly in what we might call *dog law*: the standards of larceny, liability, and cruelty that apply to dogs in human society. The legal fictions associated with dogs recall an enchanted world where voiceless and presumably mindless things were first personified and then surrendered, forfeited, or exterminated. When it comes to dogs, the instinct of vengeance lingers still. And in their treatment we also see how the law's understanding of tortious acts is an assumption about status.

If proof of a crime depends on establishing mens rea—a criminal intent that was also granted animals in ancient criminal law—an owner's liability for his animal's wrongdoing also came to depend on a strange and, for some legal historians, absurd mode of proof called *scienter* (knowingly). It is a procedure not entirely unconnected to the archaic belief in thing-liability. To recover for injuries caused by a domestic animal, the plaintiff had to prove not only that the animal had a vicious propensity to do the injury, but also that the owner *knew* of this dangerous or mischievous propensity, that he *knowingly* kept or harbored such a creature.

In *The Law Relating to Dogs* (1888), Frederick Lupton thought this rule "consonant neither with moral justice or common sense," and hoped that the law of England might soon adopt the "more reasonable doctrine" of other countries.[38] At the time he wrote, only injuries to sheep and cattle made an owner liable without having to prove *scienter*. Glanville Williams was less critical of the *scienter* action.

> The general principle in present-day English law is that, apart from cases in cattle-trespass and the ordinary torts of nuisance, negligence, and so on, liability for damage caused by one's animal depends on previous knowledge of its vicious nature. Such knowledge had originally to be proved in all cases, but in modern law it is presumed if the animal in question is one of the

dangerous class. The principle is known as the scienter principle (from the words scienter retinuit in the old form of the writ), and proof of knowledge is called, somewhat ungrammatically, proof of scienter.

Williams admits that such a rule "may at first sight be thought over-refined," since it calls upon us "to examine the mental state of animals, and to pass judgment upon its transgressions in accordance with the ethical standards of human beings." Reasonable ground must be shown by the plaintiff that the dog's ferocious character is known to the owner. Yet in practice, he argues, this "vice," "viciousness," or "malevolence" was not difficult to apply. It did mean, however, that a certain understanding was assumed between owners and dogs, and recognition of that intimate relationship by law. Liability thus determined meant awareness from previous observation or evidence that the animal is "accustomed to bite mankind," as pleading ran in the case of dogs.[39]

As in other legal issues, however, the dog becomes the exception to the normal assumptions about this proof. In recent American law, knowledge goes out the window when assumptions of ferocity come into play. And under the harsh measures of contemporary statutes, an owner is held strictly liable for his dog's actions with no regard for knowledge or evidence of viciousness. Instead of asking whether or not the owner knew of a dog's propensity to bite, for example, it is enough to presume that a dog had a bad nature, or manifested a threatening attitude or intended to attack. And this intuition or good-faith belief is enough. No proof of *scienter* is necessary. Once a dog is labeled "dangerous"—not by the owner, but by neighbors, police, or anyone else—the owner can be liable for damages and the dog killed without redress.

Numerous cases in the late nineteenth and early twentieth centuries give us examples of the extremity of rhetoric used in judging character but not necessarily behavior: "a threat to mankind," "a fierce and mischievous nature," "a vicious disposition toward mankind." Let us return briefly to *Woolf v. Chalker.* Here, dogs are deemed "'base,' inferior, and entitled to less regard and protection than property in other domestic animals." Any dog suspected of being mad, liable to become mischievous—"*noisy, and a private nuisance*"—ferocious, or a biter may be destroyed by anyone, at any time. This "discrimination against dogs," the court writes, "results legitimately from their proneness to mischief, their uselessness and liability to hydrophobia, and the consequent base character of property in them."[40]

What constitutes knowledge of an animal's vicious propensity? Statutes making the owners of dogs liable regardless of *scienter* or of negligence, though quite commonplace, varied greatly in detail. Depending on the circumstances, canine characteristics veered between the poles of domestic and wild. Ferocity could at any time break through what some courts judged as nothing more than the veneer of tameness. A great range of dog regulations were considered the legitimate exercises of the state's police power. Immediate, indefinite, and absolute, the police power depended on the control and coercion of alleged threats to civil order—to the safety, welfare, or morality of citizens— whether animal or human. In all the slaveholding states, for example, "a body of men" called "the patrol" exercised "certain police powers, conferred by statute, for the better government of the slave, and the protection of the master."[41] The actions of these patrols, described so powerfully by Bryan Wagner, were concerned "with the slave, first and foremost, as potential threat." The historical range of the police power is immense. Granting virtually unlimited power to state governments, this preemptive justice, the disposal of threats to public welfare "by any means necessary," was to have unfortunate implications in canine-control laws. [42]

Appeals courts upheld canine-control ordinances based on the principle that the state's police power to manage, sequester, and dispatch dogs was virtually unlimited. The act "to regulate and license the keeping of dogs" was "an exercise of the police, and not of the taxing power of the state" and was "constitutional," a

Wisconsin court ruled in *Carter v. Dow* (1862). The financial and social consequences of such police regulations—a tax on dogs to remunerate sheep owners that could just as easily become a license to ban dogs entirely—were recognized and sustained in *McGlone v. Womack* (1908). The Kentucky appellate court upheld a statute making *everyone* who owns dogs pay a tax for the benefit of those whose sheep had been killed. Thus, in order "to promote the sheep industry," dogs and their owners were held responsible for any canine predator:

> [T]he regulation of dogs is within the police power of the State, and … it is competent for the Legislature to prohibit the keeping of dogs entirely, or, if it is necessary for the public welfare, any other regulation may be adopted which to the Legislature may seem most expedient for the promotion of that end.[43]

The question of canine outlawry focused on injury or killing, especially when the dog's victims were moneymaking sheep or cattle. In 1855 Lord Cockburn observed in a manner that betokened a generosity mostly lacking from American assessments of injury: "[E]very dog is entitled to have at least one worry." Under early common law, every dog was entitled to "one free bite."[44] Yet the one-bite or first-bite rule at common law was more complicated than the term might suggest. On one hand, the rule was an absolving principle that required a prior bite to prove knowledge of a dog's aberrant habits. On the other, the law based liability not only on the owner's knowledge but also on his culpability. In other words, liability did not relate to the number of bites allowed before punishment became due, but rather depended on both *culpa* and *scientia*. "Blame can only attach to the owner," Lord Cranworth argued, "when, after having ascertained that the animal has propensities not generally belonging to his race he omits to take proper precautions.... [T]he culpa or negligence of the owner is the foundation on which the right of action against him rests."[45]

Let us consider the legal evolution of the "one-bite rule," now seen as outmoded and hence absent from the dog-bite or "strict liability" statutes of most states in America.[46] Is this an advance in justice? An injured person does not have to prove *scienter* or that the dog owner did anything wrong. In a state with "vicious dog" or "dangerous dog" laws, which are often enforced arbitrarily, a dog sometimes has little chance to survive a wrong. In "Fault and Liability: Two Views of Legal Development" (1918), Nathan Isaacs questioned the divide between absolute liability in the archaic law of injuries and a measure of culpability based on the culprit's intention. The best example he found for instances of strict liability without fault is a dog owner's liability. He argued that the law instead of moving forward appears to slip backward into the absolute liability of an allegedly more vengeful time. "Statutes and ordinances raising a presumption of negligence, sometimes 'conclusive' in law as well as in fact ... are creeping into the books."[47]

These surviving fictions are "mere euphemisms for 'liability without fault'": "The liability of the owner of a dog is being placed by statute squarely on the ground of ownership independently of negligence even to a greater extent than it was in King Alfred's day." In his note, Isaacs contrasted the graduated punishments of a biting or killing dog in Alfred's *Ancient Laws and Institutes of England*—for the first "misdeed" of biting or killing, six shillings; for the second twelve shillings; for the third thirty shillings—with the summary killing and strict liability in the General Code of Ohio, 1910: "A dog that chases, worries, injures or kills a sheep, lamb, goat, kid, domestic fowl, domestic animal or person, can be killed at any time or place." And whereas the keeper of the dog in Alfred's Code must pay the money or give up the dog, as well as pay compensation proportionate to the damage inflicted, the Ohio law reads: "The owner or harborer of such dog shall be liable to a person damaged for the injury done."[48]

As others have argued in writing about the deodand or thing-liability, summary executions of dogs by the state and their more considered euthanasia by owners demonstrate, in William Ewald's words, not that we are "more humane" nor that we have "a greater underlying kindness, or a greater respect for the moral personality of animals," but rather "a greater indifference and a shift in metaphysics."[49]

The regulatory politics of the state and the legal categories emerging from it provided the tacit motive for claims of humanitarian enlightenment. A restructuring of categories of stigma and subjugation occurred at the same time as private property was enmeshed in the idea of the public good. As we have seen, dogs help us to understand how old forms of brutality were transfigured. They were recast through judicial fictions that led to arbitrary discrimination. Owners had no recourse to constitutional rights of due process, and dogs were abandoned to the subterfuges of the state. Usually, courts did not interfere with the carrying out of the police power and the statutes that enforced the law.

The aftereffects of slavery cast a long shadow over dog law. In the late 1890s, courts witnessed a dramatic increase in legal actions against or on behalf of dogs. Landmark cases redefining the state's power over dogs, their regulation, disposal, and licensing by newly established humane societies were decided alongside constitutional challenges to African Americans' right to equality of accommodations and integration on railroads. The Supreme Court's decision in *The Civil Rights Cases* in 1883 marked the end to federal intervention in the ongoing racial discrimination of southern states while creating a new figurative entity: "a mere citizen." The act of an innkeeper or a common carrier in refusing equal accommodation, the Court argued, did not impose "onerous disabilities and burdens" nor a "badge of slavery or servitude" but instead involved only "an ordinary civil injury."[50]

In 1896 a case on appeal from the court of appeals in the Parish of Orleans in the State of Louisiana reached the U.S. Supreme Court. *Sentell v. New Orleans and Carrollton Railroad Company* (1897) is unique, since it began with a dog—a "Newfoundland bitch" known as Countess Lona, killed by a streetcar in New Orleans—but soon involved the owner who sought damages for her death. By the time he delivered his opinion in

1897, Justice Henry Billings Brown felt it necessary to supplement his decision in favor of the railroad with a formidable disquisition on dogs' standing as property and their necessary control by the state. The modern conception of the dog as personal property did very little to advance its position in law, since cases such as this not only promoted the ancient view that dogs are imperfect property but also subjected dogs to the repressive classification and discrimination of a subjugated population.[51]

Justice Brown delivered this striking opinion on April 26, 1897, nearly a year after his decision in *Plessy v. Ferguson*. In *Plessy* the Supreme Court upheld the constitutionality of racial segregation, mandating separate but equal accommodations for blacks and whites in public facilities—especially railroads. Rejecting Homer Plessy's claim that the East Louisiana Railroad had denied him his rights under the Thirteenth and Fourteenth amendments, the Court denied that "the enforced separation of the two races stamps the colored race with a badge of inferiority." Instead, stigma existed "solely because the colored race chooses to put that construction upon it." State-sanctioned segregation, once joined with the stubborn residues of scientific racism, gave birth to a newly vacuous legal person. Once recognized as citizens, blacks were dispossessed of any personal claim they might have to that very citizenship. Nominal civil and political equality brought with it social ostracism and personal insult. Individuals could thus practice discrimination behind the mask of constitutional guarantees, while state power remained free to enforce racial mandates with increasing violence. The Fourteenth Amendment, Judge Brown argued, had nothing to do with social equality, private choices, even bad conduct, which were beyond the power of law, but only with political and legal equality.[52]

Although arguing for the new dispensation of freedom, Justice Brown reinforced the allegedly superseded badges and incidents of involuntary servitude. The legal historian Rebecca Scott has engaged with the deviousness of his argument: "The damage thus done was both practical and doctrinal, formalizing the sleight of hand that portrayed an aggressive program of state-imposed caste distinctions as the mere ratification of custom."[53] The exclusionary language of *Plessy*, necessary for the degradation of blacks, gains additional impact and heft when Brown turns to the subject of property, the limits of redress, and the uncertain status of dogs.

Read together, *Sentell* and *Plessy* mark the convertibility between species usually considered distinct. I do not suggest that what happens to dogs is an injustice equal to segregation, but that law can be used to make men dogs and dogs trash. Although the connection might appear simply provocative, Brown's ruling on segregation, harmful property, and strays bears out that link. Such a near wonder occurs when for one reason or another the benefits and privileges usually reserved for persons are extinguished, and a new understanding of personhood is required.

On the morning of March 15, 1893, Mr. George W. Sentell's purebred Countess Lona, registered in the American Kennel Stud Book, followed him on a walk through the streets of New Orleans. Bred to the stud "Young Malcolm" two months before, she was to give birth a week or so later. Sentell had already booked orders for the puppies from that litter. When she stopped "to relieve herself" on the track of a streetcar, "heavy with young" and "not possessed of her usual agility," she was "caught by the car and instantly killed." Sentell sued the railroad for wanton negligence and carelessness in the Civil District Court, and the jury awarded him damages in the amount of $250. He also challenged the Louisiana statute, Act 107 of 1882, which among other things, conditioned recognition of dogs as personal property upon registration of their value with and payment of taxes to the local government. The district court agreed that this statute was unconstitutional. The dog was property, and both the Fifth and Fourteenth amendments prohibit the government from depriving anyone of "life, liberty, or property, without due process of law."[54]

The Court of Appeals, however, reversed the decision, claiming on one hand that the accident was largely caused by the owner's lack of prudence and due care. He should have known that her condition made it risky to take her on a busy thoroughfare "without exercising the greatest care and vigilance." The court also argued that Sentell had not complied with state law, which required that his dog be recorded on the assessment rolls. She was due no consideration as property and no legal protection in civil law. Therefore, Sentell was not entitled to damages for his loss. The court also ruled that the Louisiana statute was not in conflict with the Fourteenth Amendment.[55]

When *Sentell v. New Orleans and Carrollton Railroad Company* reached the Supreme Court, Justice Brown argued that constitutional liberties such as due process can be suspended for the public good without in any way harming core principles of liberty and justice. State directives in this class of cases trumped the Constitution. If a dog was a stray, a person a vagrant, then the state had the responsibility to unleash familiar practices of discrimination and control in the name of a newly dispensed equality. This dispensation was undercut by a threat that depended on "legislation of a drastic nature," as Brown put it, as well as the redefinition of property and persons that came along with it.

> ... in determining what is due process of law we are bound to consider the nature of the property, the necessity for its sacrifice, and the extent to which it has heretofore been regarded as within the police power. So far as property is inoffensive or harmless, it can only be condemned or destroyed by legal proceedings, with due notice to the owner; but so far as it is dangerous to the safety or health of the community, due process of law may authorize its summary destruction.

He returns to the old common-law precedent that dogs are unprotected by criminal laws, since "property in dogs is of an imperfect or qualified nature." Dogs stand between wild animals in which there is no property right and those in which the property right is complete, such as economically useful farm animals. But once money is paid for a license and a tag put on the dog's collar, the right to property is granted. The dog gains value—and protection—and recompense can be made for her death.[56]

Legalized violence against animals for the benefit of public welfare relies on the same legal calisthenics that produced legalized segregation. Brown's analysis testifies to the pervasive prejudice of the 1890s, since the categories of exclusion necessary to legalize Plessy's assignment to a separate railroad car also applied to dogs. The competition between private and public interests— or individual satisfaction and communal good—became the legal form through which slavery could be reconstructed and the curse of color reinvigorated. In both cases, it was as if the proof of an industrializing world, the railroad, became the instrument for moral disaster. Something harmful, bad, and shocking occurred in both cases, and their judgments depended on the compelling if dubious trade-off between persons and property.

Attorneys for the state of Louisiana in both *Plessy* and *Sentell* presented discrimination as a mere exercise of the state's legitimate police power. Justice Brown not only agreed, but he also provided the logic behind which this injustice could hide. In *Sentell* he countered the claim of property and the desire for recognition with a rationale for valuation, marking, and expense that separates bad dogs from good, worthy from disposable, errant from law-abiding. In Brown's holding, birth and rank are exquisitely applied to dogs, but in a way that echoed, reaffirmed, and ultimately perpetuated other kinds of subjugation, such as those experienced by persons deemed racially inferior. It has never been specifically overruled.

> ... dogs are not considered as being upon the same plane with horses, cattle, sheep and other domesticated animals, but rather in the category of cats, monkeys, parrots, singing birds and similar animals kept for pleasure, curiosity or caprice.... Unlike other domestic animals, they are useful neither as beasts of burden, for draught (except to a limited extent), nor for food. They are peculiar in the fact that they differ among themselves more widely than any other class of animals, and can hardly be said to have a

characteristic common to the entire race. While the higher breeds rank among the noblest representatives of the animal kingdom, and are justly esteemed for their intelligence, sagacity, fidelity, watchfulness, affection, and, above all for their natural companionship with man, others are afflicted with such serious infirmities of temper as to be little better than a public nuisance. All are more or less subject to attacks of hydrophobic madness.

Even those of good breeding can become threats. No one can be sure about dogs, since it is difficult to distinguish among them. They must be registered. They cannot stray. They must be claimed or owned. Brown summarizes at length previous cases that affirmed the right of *any* person at *any* time to kill *any* dog found without a collar or seen without a license. He also relies on a Nantucket statute of 1743, which guaranteed the right to kill "any dog or bitch whatsoever that shall at any time be found there."[57]

He goes further. Even if dogs are considered property in "the fullest sense of the word"—and, he implies, even if they are licensed—they can be destroyed if necessary for public protection. In this instance, dogs are comparable to rotten "meats, fruits, and vegetables." If decayed, he writes, they "do not cease to become private property," but "it is clearly within the power of the State to order their destruction in times of epidemic, or whenever they are so exposed as to be deleterious to the public health." What counts as disposable, and when can due process be surrendered? Disposables can be simply "rags and clothing," which must be destroyed if "they become infected and dangerous," or quite literally society's cast-offs, "vicious, noisy and pestilent" dogs, and—we can surmise—persons dressed in rags, reduced to pauperism, without a home, without work or known means of livelihood. They are liable to extermination if their very destitution signals danger.[58]

Dogs thus legally disabled take their place along with vagrants and criminals. Who or what can be permitted to roam the streets? Around 1900, courts rallied to support legislative acts that led not only to reenslavement through convict lease and chain gangs, but also to vigilante justice. Police departments used tramp acts or loitering and vagrancy laws to control persons that the public viewed as nuisances. A vagrant was defined as one without visible means of support: in other words, anyone who could not afford to pay the licensing tax—in this case for themselves, not their dogs. And the language of what would become excuses for legal terror against the allegedly noxious was the same whether the subject was human or animal. The suspicion against racial or ethnic minorities was legitimated and exercised through ever more stringent police regulations against dogs.

The law made little effort to suppress righteous wrath. Instead, it tried to regulate it, to use it against those singled out for repression and hate. Brown argued that "a ferocious dog" is looked upon as an outlaw that must be banished from society, with "no right to his life which man is bound to respect." So dogs alleged to be bad were granted legal personality but were not the subject of rights. The familiar argument of reasonableness and necessity was made whenever the argument concerned a risk to society: those entities put outside its protection. The phrase "no right to his life" was repeated countless times when justice was called upon to guard a community against the depredations of vagabonds, paupers, drunkards, prostitutes, or criminals.[59]

Though it may seem odd, even problematic, that I suggest a connection between dogs and persons, or more particularly a Newfoundland dog and an African American—as does Melville's benighted and dangerous Captain Delano in *Benito Cereno*—I want to push this analogy. Perhaps Bryan Wagner's discernment is useful: what matters "is not the idea that the negro is an animal. It does not matter whether the negro is human or animal; that is the racism."[60] In other words, we can no longer avoid the historical cohabitation of the dog-kind and humans thought too base to be part of civil community. Whether blacks or other persons imaginatively tarred with the same brush, they are de-humanized and excluded. And once put outside the valuable discriminations of personhood, their claims become nugatory, insignificant, unreal.

Legal language makes possible such a compulsion for analogy: its choice of images, its reiterated terms and punishing effects. It is through the law that persons gain or lose definition, become victims of discrimination or inheritors of privilege. So a report for the West Virginia Bar Association wondered about the reason for the *Sentell* court's relapse into medieval judgments about dogs. Wondering why the court argued for "a maimed right of property in a dog," the writer reflects on places where dogs are eaten or dogs drag sleds, and decides:

> The only partially valid reason for refusing to dogs such proud equality as might come from ranging them with thoroughly domesticated animals, like common pigs and "setting" hens, has never been urged by any lawyer or court. Dogs are so humanly intelligent that to give their owners full right of property in regard to them might seem too much like a revival of slavery.[61]

In legal rationales, realities are created. As we have seen, old inequalities and racial discrimination are repackaged in unexpected forms. And these inventions succeed only because they reflect "the emotional approval of the community."[62] Brown makes the link between unidentifiable dogs and their derelict owners. Both are anonymous as they wander the streets under cover of darkness: "As their depredations are often committed at night, it is usually impossible to identify the dog or to fix the liability upon the owner, who, moreover, is likely to be pecuniarily irresponsible."[63] Such rationalizations, bound up as they are with "the existence of social control and valuation," are very much part of the pretense of law's objectivity. Whether the subject is human, animal, or an "imagined spirit," and "whether or not it possesses a personality," law can either make an entity the subject of rights or deprive it of the right to have rights.[64]

AFFECTIONATE APPROPRIATION

If it is necessary to correct a wayward animal, then it can be beaten, overworked, mutilated, and killed. Though slavery had ended, its legal rhetoric of protection and allowable injury had not. It is in the treatment of dogs that we see how easily a disquisition on personhood—individual qualities and propensities—and even the consideration of status can not only sustain prejudicial harm but lead to an order for extermination.

When dogs became pets, the law was quick to make amends for previous judgments about their character. The modern conception of dogs as personal property is embodied in both legislative enactments and judicial decisions. A miniature dachshund named Heidi, tethered in her owner's yard, was killed when a garbage collector wantonly threw the emptied trash can at her, laughing as he departed. In *La Porte v. Associated Independents, Inc.* (1964), the Supreme Court of Florida awarded damages for this intentional harming of the dog. "Without indulging in a discussion of the affinity between 'sentimental value' and 'mental suffering,'" the opinion read, "we feel that the affection of a master for his dog is a very real thing." To have human qualities like attachment or devotion, however, is not to be granted legal consideration. While the offending garbage collector and the bereft owner are recognized by the court, the dead dog exists only in so far as it elicits human feeling. When not suspected of ferocity or baseness, therefore, dogs rise in legal estimation but only as a form of "sentimental" property. They thus take their place somewhere between legal personality and domestic chattel. But what kind of creature is this? We read stories about dogs drugged, dressed up, overbred, cloned, or made monstrous as popular hybrid breeds. At some point, too much care becomes cruel.[65]

Once ordained as domesticated and objects of love, dogs are recognized as deserving protection. But their ambiguous status remains, even if reconfigured. Theirs is always an uneven disposition of privilege. "A pet is not just a thing but occupies a special place somewhere in between a person and a piece of personal property," the Civil Court of the City of New York, Queens County, writes in *Corso v. Crawford Dog and Cat Hospital* (1979). Inhabiting this intermediate space between person and property, between the most loved and the most disdained, the dog exists nowhere in itself. In the law this seeming paradox becomes the working definition of dog: so empty of substance that it can accrue to itself all kinds of properties, no matter that they are paradoxical, even nonsensical. The flesh-and-blood dog that cares, suffers, reacts, and remembers no longer exists. In Port-au-Prince I often heard the proverbial "This is Haiti, where even the dogs commit suicide." As friends explained, "Here dogs jump out of windows, run under cars, and walk into the sea."[66]

Perhaps the more a dog is loved, the more it is perceived as higher in rank or pedigree, the more excessive and immediate the reaction when its fierceness breaks through. Or the more necessary becomes the distinction between beloved, high-status pets and mistreated, lowborn dogs. As we see in bite laws and breed bans, the laws against dogs—even if admired and seen as full property, or perhaps because of this—are repressive, and the label "dangerous" becomes equivalent to proof. And as in early modern inquisitorial procedure, which depended on testimonies about character, not evidence, the current jural doings are pervaded by an essentially superstitious and irrational spirit. Without evidence of wrong done, hunches about the essence, nature, or type of creature result in statutes that condemn them to death and criminalize their owners.

The much-publicized "dog bite epidemic" demonstrates society in the act of turning specific breeds of dogs into what their labels proclaim. With dogs subject to breed-specific legislation, condemned as inherently dangerous or vicious, we see how much the law impinges on and transforms our expectations of what life has to offer. Though legal classifications vary from one city to the next, the police power, as we saw in turn-of-the-century cases, determines how dogs become victims of exemplary punishment: summarily seized and exterminated when considered threats to public welfare. In May 2005, to take just one example, animal control units in Denver began to round up all pit bulls within city limits. Dogs were taken from their homes and killed without regard to their disposition or demeanor. Pit bull ordinances in other states, though they do not dispose automatically of such dogs, nevertheless single out this breed as objects of stringent control.[67]

Today's pit bull bans tell us more about ourselves than about the breed: about the rituals and the illusions that have become necessary to our survival. The drive to label, condemn, and exterminate has become a moral enterprise. No wonder the stories about pit bulls—at once labeled "vicious" and brutalized by those who so label them—confound the ability to know right from wrong, to judge injury, to discriminate between victims and predators, cruelty and care.

The classification of dogs as "dangerous," like that of prisoners as "security threat" or detainees in the ongoing "war on terror" as "terrorist," is a situation-oriented, highly arbitrary, legislative act. Evidence for the legality of political action loses significance in relation to a general presumption of dangerousness. What is decisive is the status the dog possesses in society: its suspected "innate character" or "vicious propensity" replaces objective characteristics, and even evidence of wrongdoing, thus making the uncertain boundaries between legal and illegal, necessary and arbitrary still more indeterminate.[68]

Severe dog bite laws and breed bans now coexist also with the promotion of kinder, gentler training methods. As police measures against dogs have increased, Americans have eagerly embraced the proof of their affectionate appropriation: pet loss hotlines, pet grief homilies, pet memorial gardens, and pet cemeteries. The yoking together of ruthlessness and kindness, gentleness and brutality, is made effective through the blurring of the distinction between human and nonhuman.

THE LAWS

Let us think about the special world created by law's ritual, which means asking how dogs, so meaty and substantial, became spectralized—the palpable but ghostly fictions of law, as well as the idealized objects of human affection. Though dogs in common law seemed to be the exceptions to every rule, they also prove how the exception becomes commonplace, ever extendable to the disabled, outlawed, civilly dead. Dogs are the vessels that hold the substance of the ancient law. The residues of its history surface intermittently through their bodies.

Gradations of personhood are articulated in law—whether stigmatized bodies or stolen minds. Though the master's dominion judged otherwise, law was not beyond the ken of slaves or their descendants, but something that obsessed them. Nor do its artifices escape the understanding of persons most oppressed by legal narratives. They understand its power and know that the elements of law had a great deal to do with the making of gods and spirits—and political authority. To say that law uses and represents history is to know how it becomes a site of commemoration. How does law materialize memory? As a locus of embodied history, laws become crucial to understanding what it meant when slaves, formerly property, were freed into another kind of status that simply exchanged one kind of bondage for another.

The skin of the civil was assumed to be white, the material envelope that allowed access to respect, rights, and sometimes even life. Since in the old days dogs had no legal value while their skins did, the physical envelope gained precedence and attention over the substance. The laws thus created entities in their own image. In the minds of some, these dogs without skin return. They roam in the night. Recognized as rapacious, predatory, or mischievous, the dogs seek vengeance and push to the limits the meaning of inhuman.

The summary justice of the police power regulates the keeping of dogs, as it once did the possession of slaves and, after emancipation, the criminalization of indigents, derelicts, and other disenfranchised individuals. The move from nuisance to predator was easy and assured. Preventive measures never ceased. The amorphous fear of outsiders always found new bodies of residence. Statutes historically allowed the immediate destruction of dogs, as we have seen, if owners had not licensed, tagged, or muzzled them. The "base nature" or ferocity of dogs though legally condemned easily became instrumental in hunting down errant slaves, even as they remained subject to the inequities of the police power. At the mercy of the very forces that turned them into tools of terror, dogs were an ambiguous force in the law's arsenal.

The Black Code of Georgia (1732–1899), assembled by W.E.B. DuBois for the Negro exhibit of the American section of the Exposition Universelle in Paris in 1900, includes in the list of prohibited acts of cruelty against slaves: "cruelly and unnecessarily biting or tearing with dogs." No mutilation or death that occurred during the canine capture of fugitive slaves was judged illegal if it was unintended and necessary.

> How in de name of de Lawd could slaves run away to de North wid dem Nigger dogs on their heels? I never knowed any one to run away. Patterollers never runned me none, but dey did git after some of de other slaves a whole lot.[69]

When it came to disposing of threats, dogs embodied swift, necessary action: whether the dogs that accompanied the "paterollers" in hunting down slaves, or later those tracking down all manner of vagrants or suspected criminals. Even today, bluetick hounds and redbone hounds, the best tracking dogs in Arizona, scent out escapees—and never lose a quarry.

What is the common terror of peaceable citizens? Not one dog but all dogs, and the persons who return in their bodies seeking vengeance. Noxious creatures, they incarnate the judgment that held them perverse and dangerous. They take chances. They appear in the form of the enemy, in the skin of whiteness, the envelope of the civil, and haunt the communities of the unsuspecting. They give flesh and blood to the law, but without the rationalization, the veneer of justice or claims of civilization.

When I grew up in Atlanta, the police were known as "the laws." I grew up hearing about the "meat that takes directions from someone." The laws were as terrifying and unknowable as evil spirits. They controlled and judged. I heard stories of the paterollers who could get you if you were found walking outside at night.

> The law was angry
> The law was rabid
>> It came upon you in the night
>> The paterollers
>>> Seeking you out
> They always came with a white dog
> They were white dogs
> With their white cone hoods
> And their white capes
> Ghosts in the night

No pateroller caught you as long as you stayed at home. But the paterollers helped along by their dogs soon merged into them, reinforcing an old history of intimacy and threat. So I was warned not to walk alone at night, to beware of the flash of white, the dog that could devour, its fiery eyes fixing you in place. The white dog, I was told, "steals your soul, tears at your flesh, and thieves your mind."

The ghosts of the ancestors always return. What is abused and damaged rises up to haunt. Persons judged outside the law's protection and marked as enemies of the community resort to an alternative understanding of law. Degraded and socially excluded, they interpret legal precepts and proscriptions for themselves and reconceive the rules: not the opposite of law but its haunting. So out of the grit and press of death comes the white dog. Both lawful and spectral, this dog is the lure, putting law squarely in the courts of sorcery and permitting magic to find itself in the temple of law.

ACKNOWLEDGMENTS

THIS BOOK BEGAN WHEN I SAW CHAIN GANGS ON THE ROADS AND IN the prisons of Tucson, Arizona in May 1995. I was fortunate to meet Michael A. Arra, at that time the spokesperson for the Arizona Department of Corrections. He made possible my initial visits to the death house, death row, Cell Block 2 in the Arizona State Prison Complex–Florence, and later, to Special Management Units 1 and 2 in the Arizona State Prison Complex–Eyman. In the prisons there I owe an immense debt to the inmates I interviewed and to those who wrote letters to me under conditions that became increasingly difficult and risky. In particular, I thank Mark Koch for his legal acuity and courage. The officials who were part of the punitive regime I would soon devote myself to exposing granted me both time and access. For that, I thank those who were very much a part of my initial research: Terry Stewart, at the time the director of the Arizona Department of Corrections; Charles ("Chuck") Ryan, then senior warden of the Arizona State Prison Complex–Florence/Eyman; and James Mc-Fadden, who granted me interviews when he was the deputy warden of Special Management Unit 2.

On my first visit to Florence, Arizona, I met the late Della Meadows. Working at the Arizona State Prison–Florence, from March 1, 1948, until her retirement on December 31, 1983, she introduced me to a kinder, gentler time before the retributive practices of the nineties. Not only did she make available necessary archival materials, but her great good warmth softened my encounter with hard labor, lockdown, and chain.

The late judge Carl Muecke, for twenty of his thirty years on the federal bench, ruled in favor of prisoners in cases ranging from prison overcrowding to the overturning of the Arizona death penalty statute and the granting of access to law libraries for the incarcerated. The summer before his retirement from the United States District Court in Arizona in 1997, he let me use his offices, as well as the court transcripts and depositions that revealed the dark underbelly of public rites of degradation. That summer changed the course of my work.

Mary Murrell was an inspiration from the beginning, when she was editor at Princeton University Press and encouraged me to give flesh and blood to the law. Since then, in many ways, large and small, she has been present—reading the manuscript and giving me feedback during the final push toward publication. My editor at Princeton, Hanne Winarsky, believed in this book when it was supposed to be only about prisons and the law, and her passion grew with each revised outline of my plans and at every stage of the project. She was there: guiding, thinking, challenging, shepherding. I am in her debt.

Stephan Palmié and Avery Gordon—visionary thinkers and writers—hovered over this writing, even when I did not rise to their demands. Saidiya Hartman, Stephen Best, Cheryl Harris, and members of the Sawyer Seminar, University of California Humanities Research Institute (April 28, 2003), challenged me in rigorous debate. Since that seminar, my conversations with Stephen Best have been a necessary provocation.

The inexhaustible Austin Sarat, who first asked me to speak about prison law, has been the intellectual companion who pushed me to delve further into the death-dealing facts of law. Over the years of writing, I had lively discussions with many friends, colleagues, and students, some of whom also read the manuscript, talked me through problems, or heartened me during lonely moments. These include Diane Marie Amann, Daphne Brooks, Vincent Brown, Sharon Cameron, Gabe Cervantes, Eric Cheyfitz, Stuart Clark, Jay Clayton, Jerry Couretas, Natalie Davis, Lynn Enterline, Celia Fassberg, Kenneth Gross, Nasser Hussein,

Andrew Krichels, Fred Moten, Dana Nelson, Lisa Paransini-Gebert, Kathryn Schwarz, and David Wood. And I thank Ronald Paulson, always my most constructive critic. I owe much to the work of Angela Davis, Ruthie Gilmore, and Dylan Rodriguez for their exhilarating blend of activism and scholarship on the ground. Their attempt to bend thought to practical ends makes their work on slavery, incarceration, and the ongoing ruination of a society's war on particular categories of persons the lodestone of my continued inquiry.

I am not a lawyer, so I owe a huge debt to the lawyers and legal scholars who provided feedback, critique, or simply exemplary engagement: Jamil Dakwar, director of the American Civil Liberties Union's (ACLU's) Human Rights Program; David Fathi, formerly at the ACLU's National Prison Project and now director of the U.S. Program at Human Rights Watch; Kemal Mericli, Pennsylvania's senior deputy attorney general; Jeremy Waldron and David Cole. Daniel Pochoda, now legal director of the ACLU of Arizona, made this book possible in ways too numerous to relate. From our first meeting in the summer of 1997, when he had completed his work as federal Special Master in the lengthy case that became *Lewis v. Casey*, his acuity and perseverance throughout the difficult legal setbacks that turned the Arizona prison system into one of the most oppressive in the country set the example for many of us. He was never too busy to answer my questions, to make materials available—and, quite simply, to educate me, spending hours talking through and righting my ideas.

For assistance in my research I thank Andrew Doolen, Jennifer Ellis, Donald McNutt, Justine Murison, Eliot Polinsky, Catherine Vidler, and Sarah Helen White. Julie Miller, first as my research assistant at Vanderbilt and then as reader of the manuscript in its final stages, provided incalculable expertise. I thank her for her support and for her legal brilliance.

Numerous institutions and foundations awarded me fellowships and sabbatical leave to support my research and writing. This book began at the University of Arizona, which supported

255

what then seemed like work very distant from the English department's purview: chain gangs and supermaxes in the Arizona State Prison System. The Princeton Program in Law and Public Affairs supported archival work; and the sharp observations and unrelenting questions of colleagues in 2000–2001 made this a very different book from what it might have been. Chris Eisgruber, Dirk Hartog, Stephen Macedo, and Diane Orentlicher were generous in their critique. I thank both the University of Pennsylvania and Vanderbilt University for their belief in the book and the leave time that allowed me to bring it to fruition. I am indebted to the Guggenheim Foundation for a grant to study slavery and the law of persons in 2005–6. The book was completed at Princeton in 2009. As the partner of a fellow at the Davis Center for Historical Studies, I was granted a phantom presence in Dickinson Hall, where Dan Rodgers, Jennifer Houle, and Judy Hanson fostered my most productive work year.

Deb Chasman, my editor at the *Boston Review*, helped me to frame and edit my first article connecting local prison practices to the exigencies of global torture—as well as other articles—all made sharper because of her readings. In the final year of revising the manuscript for publication, Simon Waxman, with real brilliance—both theoretical and stylistic—helped me to rethink parts of the argument and rewrite whole sections that lacked precision and punch. The readers for the press, Mark Greif and one anonymous, offered supportive and penetrating criticisms of the manuscript.

Over the years, parts of this book were presented at various seminars and as lectures. Its preliminary stages were first tested at the Barker Center at Harvard University; at the Clark Library at the University of California, Los Angeles; and as the John Hope Franklin Seminar lecture, cosponsored with the Atlantic Studies Group, at Duke University. I am grateful to Ian Baucom and members of the Duke Atlantic Studies Seminar. And to David Lloyd, I owe a huge debt for his invitations to USC and for much talk and encouragement. Later, seminars and workshops at Berkeley, Columbia, Cornell, NYU, Irvine, University of California–Santa Barbara, UCLA, Princeton, the Institute for the Humanities–University of Illinois, and the Vanderbilt History Seminar pressed me to sharpen my thoughts. I give thanks to Stephan Palmié for his invitation to speak at the Center for the Study of Race, Politics, and Culture at the University of Chicago. In "From the Plantation to the Prison: Incarceration and U.S. Culture," at Yale University, Caleb Smith and Naomi Paik provided a lively forum for debate. Donna Haraway invited me to present a chapter at the Center for Cultural Studies, UC Santa Cruz. Her questions and the promptings of Carla Frecerro and Gina Dent led me to reassess the limits of this project.

Finally, I thank the production team at Princeton University press, especially Ellen Foos and Joan Giseke, for their help and discernment in bringing the book to completion.

The white dog in my title owes something more to Vicki Hearne's novel *The White German Shepherd* and her deep sense of the "evocation by the dog of the dog within the dog" than to Romain Gary's *White Dog*, used as a metaphor for the excesses of racism in the United States. In other ways, too, this book owes a great deal to the memory of Vicki's passion, wit, and wonder at the person in the dog.

And to David Wasserstein, I dedicate this book, again, in thanks for his presence, his eagle-editing eye, and his unstinting attentiveness to me—and the dogs.

NOTES

CHAPTER 1. HOLY DOGS, HECUBA'S BARK

1. *Stambovsky v. Ackley*, 169 A.D. 2d 254, 256 (1991). I thank Stephan Palmié for bringing this case to my attention. In *Wizards and Scientists: Explorations in Afro-Cuban Modernity and Tradition* (Durham, NC: Duke University Press, 2002), Palmié exhumes the haunts of modernity. This visitation of "pasts," once invoked, not only disrupts illusions of normalcy and the pretences of social life, but also invokes another kind of knowledge —one that transforms the meaning of history as it stakes out the brutal plot of politics as usual.

   After Rubin's decision, the parties settled out of court. Stambovsky paid Ackley $5,000, and she withdrew the contract. (Personal communication with Israel Rubin, May 22, 2009.) *Stambovsky* made headlines around the world, and once the house was returned to the market, numerous potential buyers called. It sold a few months later for $20,000 less than the original asking price of $650,000. See Helen Herdman Ackley, "Our Haunted House on the Hudson," *Reader's Digest*, May 1977, 217–24. After the case, once Helen Ackley had moved to Oregon, the medium Glenn Johnson had some thirty conversations with the two ghosts—Sir George and his housekeeper Margaret—and interviewed Ackley, as well as her ghosts, publishing the results in Bill Merrill and Glenn Johnson, *Sir George: The Ghost of Nyack* (Beaverton, OR: Deer, 1995), 5. For other comments and reactions to the case, see Haunted America Tours, http://hauntedamericatours.com/hauntedhouses/disclose, and The Kavanagh Home Page, "The Ghost of Nyack," authored by a person who claims to be married to someone who lived in the house, at http://home.comcast.net/~subwaymark/Ghost/ghost-court.htm; Linda Zimmermann, *Ghost Investigator*, vol. 1, *Hauntings of the Hudson Valley* (New York: Lightning Source, 2003); and the *New York Times* articles once the house was back on the market: James Barron, "Phones Ringing (Eerily?) for Nyack Spook Home," March 20, 1990, B2, and "Let Buyer Beware? Indeed!" July 19, 1991, B3.
2. *Stambovsky*, 257, 256, 260.
3. J. H. Baker, *An Introduction to English Legal History*, 2nd ed. (London: Butterworths, 1979), 89.

4. *Stambovsky*, 258, 256.
5. *Stambovsky*, 258.
6. Joseph Ferrara, "A New York Ghost Story," Sellsius° Real Estate Blog, October 29, 2006, http://blog.sellsiusrealestate.com/2006/10/29/a-new-york-ghost-story/.
7. *Platner v. Sherwood*, 6 Johns. Ch. 118, paragraph 2 of argument of Butler and Henry, counsel for plaintiff Platner (1822). *Avery v. Everett*, 110 N.Y. 317 (1888). In his *Commentaries on American Law* (1826; repr., Boston: Little, Brown, 1873), 5:37, 386, Kent admits how difficult it is to accommodate the federal abolition of corruption of blood and forfeiture of property with the continuing strict civil death enacted by statute in various states. Kent presided over two cases concerning civil death in the early nineteenth century: *Troup v. Wood*, 4 Johns. Ch. 228 (1820), and *Platner v. Sherwood*. He realized in *Platner* that his decision in *Troup* had to be revised: "personal rights" had to remain in spite of a sentence to life imprisonment. In his striking admission, he explains that although in *Troup* he had been "induced to think ... that every person attainted of felony was accounted in law *civiliter mortuus*" (128), he now wanted to reconsider "this very unusual question of law." He asked whether imprisoned persons could be utterly divested of their property. In a sentence that would be much quoted in later cases, Kent wrote: "As there was to be no forfeiture of estate, the law would not be consistent with itself if it held the party alive for the purpose of being sued and charged in execution, and yet dead as to the purpose of transmitting his estate to his heirs" (*Platner*, 131).
8. For the unsurpassed interpretation of the legal fiction of civil death and its very real effects, see Kim Lane Scheppele, "Facing Facts in Legal Interpretation," *Representations* 30, no. 1 (Spring 1990): 42–77.
9. *Stambovsky*, 259, 256, 260.
10. Stuart Clark, *Thinking with Demons: The Idea of Witchcraft in Early Modern Europe* (New York: Oxford University Press, 1997), 396. In "Witchcraft and Racecraft: Invisible Ontology in its Sensible Manifestations," in *Witchcraft Dialogues: Anthropological and Philosophical Exchanges*, ed. George Clement Bond and Diane M. Ciekawy (Athens, OH: Ohio Center for International Studies, 2001), 291–92, Karen Fields argues that *witchcraft* and *racecraft*, once brought together, reveal their similarities to each other. Both "presuppose invisible, spiritual qualities underlying, and continually acting upon, the material realm of beings and events." In Cheryl I. Harris, "Whiteness as Property," *Harvard Law Review* 106, no. 8 (June 1993): 1709–91, we see how powerfully the invisible demands of a racist state are made not only visible but real. See also Margaret Jane Radin, "Property and Personhood," *Stanford Law Review* 34, no. 5 (May 1982): 957–1015; Stephanie Rosenbloom, "Some Buyers Regret Not Asking: Anyone Die Here?" *New York Times*, April 30, 2006, J1; and Peter G. Miller, "What Is Stigmatized Property?" *Realty Times*, at http://realtytimes.com/rtguide/rtcpages/What_Is_Stigmatized_property."

11. Andrew Lang, in "Ghosts Before the Law," *Blackwood's Magazine* 155, February 1894, 220–21, writes that although no records from this French suit exist, the pleadings are preserved in Pierre Le Loyer's *Discours des Spectres*. He wrote this article to repair what he saw as a fault in Sir Walter Scott's essay "Ghosts Before the Law"—Scott's statement about the lack of "apparition-evidence" in the courts. See also Lang, *Cock Lane and Common-Sense* (1894; repr., Charleston, SC: BiblioBazaar, 2007), for stories of ghosts, hauntings, and other paranormal phenomena. Lang's description of the case is retold in William White Ackerly's "Law and Apparitions," *Case and Comment: The Lawyer's Magazine* 21 (November 1914): 457.

12. Andreas Becker, *Disputatio Juridica de Jure Spectrorum*, Jena, 1745, in Henry Charles Lea, *Materials toward a History of Witchcraft*, arr. and ed. Arthur C. Howland (Philadelphia: University of Pennsylvania Press, 1939), 3:1411–15. I owe this reference to Stuart Clark. *The Works of Jeremy Bentham*, published under the supervision of his executor, John Bowring (Edinburgh: William Tait, 1838–43), 1:426. For Bentham on solitary confinement, see Janet Semple, *Bentham's Prison: A Study of the Panopticon Penitentiary* (Oxford: Clarendon Press, 1993), 129–33.

13. Edward Peters, *The Magician, the Witch, and the Law* (Philadelphia: University of Pennsylvania Press, 1978), 185.

14. Avery F. Gordon, *Ghostly Matters: Haunting and the Sociological Imagination* (Minneapolis: University of Minnesota Press, 1997), 207.

15. *Carnahan v. Hamilton*, 265 Ill. 508, 522 (1914). Blewett Lee, "Psychic Phenomena and the Law," *Harvard Law Review* 34, no. 6 (April 1921): 625–38, 627. The court in *Carnahan* recognized degrees of thinking between "the highest degree of rationality" and "the wildest dreams of superstition" (522), and the decision included a wonderful summary of previous cases regarding personal property, testamentary capacity, and the supernatural.

16. *McClary v. Stull*, 44 Neb. 175, 189–90 (1895). *Irwin v. Lattin*, 29 S.D. 1, 12 (1912), citing *O'Dell v. Goff*, 149 Mich. 152, 158 (1907) (emphasis added by *Irwin*). On the construction of wills and analyses of personhood, see Robert E. Heinselman, "Effect of Superstitious Beliefs or Insane Delusions upon Competency," *Case and Comment* 21, no. 6 (November 1914): 459–63; and E. Vine Hall, "Wills and Ghosts," *Case and Comment* 21, no. 6 (November 1914): 464–67. On testamentary incapacity, see especially Susanna L. Blumenthal, "The Deviance of the Will: Policing the Bounds of Testamentary Freedom in Nineteenth-Century America," *Harvard Law Review* 119, no. 4 (February 2006): 959–1034; and "The Default Legal Person," *UCLA Law Review* 54, no. 5 (June 2007): 1135–265.

17. Robert Cover, "Violence and the Word," *Narrative, Violence, and the Law: The Essays of Robert Cover*, ed. Martha Minow, Michael Ryan, and Austin Sarat (Ann Arbor: University of Michigan Press, 1992), 203.

18. These words attributed to Thomas Reed Powell, professor of American constitutional law at Columbia and Harvard Law School, have been recalled often since his death on August 16, 1955. See, for example, Robert Livingston Schuyler, ed., introduction to *Frederic William Maitland, Historian: Selections from His Writings* (Berkeley: University of California Press, 1960), 10–11; Aviam Soifer, *Law and the Company We Keep* (Cambridge, MA: Harvard University Press, 1995), 104–5; and Marc Galanter, *Lowering the Bar: Lawyer Jokes and Legal Culture* (Madison: University of Wisconsin Press, 2005), 51. Three moving tributes to Thomas Reed Powell by Felix Frankfurter, Henry M. Hart Jr., and Paul A. Freund were published in *Harvard Law Review* 69, no. 5 (1956): 797–805.

19. *Ruffin v. Commonwealth*, 62 Va. 90, 795 (1871). John Locke, *An Essay Concerning Human Understanding*, edited with an introduction by Peter H. Nidditch (Oxford: Oxford University Press, 1975), 2.1.19:115. Nidditch bases his text on the fourth edition, published in 1700. I use this version throughout.

20. Jeremy Bentham, *Memoirs*, cited in C. K. Ogden, ed., *Bentham's Theory of Fictions* (1932; repr., London: Routledge, 2001), xi, and Bentham, *Works*, vol. 9, 83–84, also cited in Ogden, *Bentham's Theory*, xvi. Herman Melville, *Moby-Dick, or the Whale*, ed. Harrison Hayford, Hershel Parker, and G. Thomas Tanselle (Evanston, IL: Northwestern University Press, 2001), 195, 193.

21. William Blackstone, *Commentaries on the Laws of England* (1765–69; repr., Chicago: University of Chicago Press, 1979), 3:267–68. See Jeremy Bentham, *A Comment on the Commentaries and A Fragment on Government*, ed. J. H. Burns and H.L.A. Hart (1776; repr., London: Athlone Press, 1977), 119–20. Bentham, *Constitutional Code* in *Works*, vol. 9, 77–78, quoted in Ogden, *Bentham's Theory*, cxvi.

22. Ogden, *Bentham's Theory*, xviii, and *Constitutional Code*, quoted in Ogden, *Bentham's Theory*, cxvi.

23. Jeremy Bentham, *The Panopticon Writings*, ed. Miran Božovič (London: Verso Books, 1995), 20–22. See also Slavoj Žižek, *Jacques Lacan: Critical Evaluations in Cultural Theory* (London: Taylor and Francis, 2003), 269. The most far-reaching and ambitious study of Bentham's obsession with fictions is Philip Schofield's "Real and Fictitious Entities" in his *Utility and Democracy: The Political Thought of Jeremy Bentham* (Oxford: Oxford University Press, 2006), 1–27. I thank Stephen Engelmann for his indispensable counsel on Bentham, ghosts, and fictions.

24. Bentham, *Commentaries*, 411. Bentham, *Rights, Representation, and Reform: Nonsense upon Stilts and other Writings on the French Revolution*, ed. Philip Schofield, Catherine Pease-Watkin, and Cyprian Blamires (New York: Oxford University Press, 2002), 321–22. See Hannah Arendt's hesitation about the rights-giving language that gives birth to the citizen in *Origins of Totalitarianism* (1951; repr., New York: Schocken Books, 2004), 377–82.

25. Friedrich Nietzsche, *Thus Spoke Zarathustra*, ed. Adrian Del Caro and Robert Pippin (Cambridge: Cambridge University Press, 2006), 126.

26. David Gordon White, *Myths of the Dog-Man* (Chicago: University of Chicago Press, 1991), 5. This breathtaking journey into the world of ghosts, demons, and foreigners coalesces in the form of dogs. See also his "Dogs" in *Encyclopedia of Religion*, vol. 4, 2nd ed., ed. Lindsay Jones (Detroit: Macmillan Reference USA, 2005), 2392–94. In *The Holy Greyhound: Guinefort, Healer of Children since the Thirteenth Century*, trans. Martin Thom (1979; repr., Cambridge: Cambridge University Press, 1983; Paris: Editions de la Maison des Sciences de l'Homme, 1983), Jean-Claude Schmitt writes the "historical anthropology" or "ethnohistory" of the dog martyr Saint Guinefort, a rite of memory and veneration by the peasants of the Dombes, which though brutally repressed by the Church survived well into the twentieth century.

27. Jean Rhys, *Wide Sargasso Sea* (1966; repr., New York: W. W. Norton, 1982), 128.

28. On the ambiguous status of Hecuba and her transformation, see especially P.M.C. Forbes Irving, *Metamorphosis in Greek Myths* (Oxford: Clarendon Press, 1990), 207–10; and Judith Mossman, *Wild Justice: A Study of Euripides'* Hecuba (Oxford: Clarendon Press, 1995). Mossman presents Euripides' play as infested with dogs and dog behavior, and turning to Hecuba's revenge, she explores the function of Hecuba's metamorphosis into a dog. On Hecuba see also Robert Graves, *The Greek Myths* (1955; repr., Mt. Kisco, NY: Moyer Bell, 1988).

29. *The Metamorphoses of Ovid*, trans. Allen Mandelbaum (New York: Harcourt, 1993), 452–53.

30. On the confusing origins of the poem, its date, and background, see the entry on two writers with the name of Lycophron in *The Oxford Classical Dictionary*, 3rd ed., ed. Simon Hornblower and Antony Spawforth (Oxford: Oxford University Press, 1996), 895–97; and Arnaldo Momigliano, "The Locrian Maidens and the Date of Lycophron's *Alexandra*," *Classical Quarterly* 39, no. 1–2 (January–April 1945): 49–53; Elizabeth Kosmetatou, "Lycophron's 'Alexandra' Reconsidered: The Attalid Connection," *Hermes* 128, no. 1 (2000): 32–53; and E. D. Phillips, "Odysseus in Italy," *Journal of Hellenic Studies* 73 (1953): 53–67; and Graves, *Greek Myths*, 267. In a poem of 1,474 lines, there are approximately 500 words that do not occur anywhere else in the whole of extant Greek literature. See Henri-Charles Puech, "A propos de Lycophron, de Rab et de Philon d'Alexandrie," *Revue des Etudes Grecques* 46, no. 217 (July–September 1933): 311–33.

31. I use George W. Mooney's translation in *The Alexandra of Lycophron: With English Translation and Explanatory Notes* (London: G. Bell and Sons, 1921), which I much prefer to that of A. W. Mair in *Callimachus: Hymns and Epigrams/Lycophron* (Cambridge, MA: Harvard University Press, 1921).

32. E. R. Dodds, *The Greeks and the Irrational* (Berkeley: University of California Press, 1951), 138–40. For Homer's conception of *psyche* see also Bruno Snell, *The Discovery of the Mind in Greek Philosophy and Literature* (1953; repr., New York: Dover, 1982), 8–9. On the tripartite structure of

Haitian identity and "personality" or "thinking matter," see Colin Dayan, *Haiti, History, and the Gods* (Berkeley: University of California Press, 1995), 67–68. I am inspired in these reflections, indeed pushed "beyond the boundaries of the human," by Eduardo Kohn's "How Dogs Dream: Amazonian Natures and the Politics of Transspecies Engagement," *American Ethnologist* 34, no. 1 (February 2007): 3–24; and by Sharon Cameron's *Impersonality: Seven Essays* (Chicago: University of Chicago Press, 2007).

33. Erna Brodber, *Myal* (London: New Beacon Books, 1988), 108.

34. Mary Midgley, "Is a Dolphin a Person?" in *The Animal Ethics Reader*, ed. Susan Jean Armstrong and Richard George Botzler (London: Routledge, 2003), 169.

35. In this book I do not discuss the plight of immigrants in the United States. With Secretary Janet Napolitano supporting and even expanding the Bush administration's 287 (g) program of the Department of Homeland Security, which gives local law enforcement and corrections agencies the power to enforce immigration law, the chance of further abuse, even ethnic cleansing of neighborhoods, becomes certainty. This policing function encourages racial profiling and indiscriminate "crime sweeps," as William Finnegan has described in his *New Yorker* profile of Sheriff Joe Arpaio, "Sheriff Joe," July 20, 2009. See also the *New York Times* editorial "Immigrants Criminalized," November 27, 2009, A38. See also Tom Barry, "A Death in Texas: Profits, Poverty, and Immigration Converge," *Boston Review*, November–December 2009.

36. Avery Gordon, "The Prisoner's Curse," in *Toward a Sociology of the Trace*, ed. Herman Gray and Macarena Gómez-Barris (Minneapolis: University of Minnesota Press, forthcoming). I thank Avery Gordon for sending me the manuscript.

37. John T. Noonan Jr., *Persons and Masks of the Law: Cardozo, Holmes, Jefferson, and Wythe as Makers of the Masks* (New York: Farrar, Straus and Giroux, 1976), 4. In his revealing account of the "magic of legal rule," Noonan concentrates on the disguises and accommodations necessary to the negative personification of slavery.

38. Alexander Nékám, *The Personality Conception of the Legal Entity* (Cambridge, MA: Harvard University Press, 1938), 8–11, 20–27. See also the influential treatment of Justice Douglass's dissent in *Sierra Club v. Morton*, 405 U.S. 727 (1972), and the *legal considerableness* of the inanimate object in Christopher D. Stone's *Should Trees Have Standing? And Other Essays on Law, Morals and the Environment* (Dobbs Ferry, NY: Oceana, 1996); and Miguel Tamen, *Friends of Interpretable Objects* (Cambridge, MA: Harvard University Press, 2001).

39. Cited in Clive Stafford Smith, *Bad Men: Guantánamo Bay and the Secret Prisons* (London: Weidenfeld and Nicolson, 2007), 209, from Shaker Aamer's diary, November 21, 2005.

40. Abdelli Feghoul is still at the time of this writing in solitary confinement, though he has been cleared for release since at least 2006, according to

"Current Conditions of Confinement at Guantánamo: Still in Violation of the Law," Center for Constitutional Rights, February 23, 2009, 4. See also the center's "Solitary Confinement at Guantánamo Bay," available at http://ccrjustice.org/learn-more/faqs/solitary-confinement-guantanamo -bay.

41. Stafford Smith, *Bad Men*, 214–15.
42. Julian E. Barnes, "Military Says Special Chair Stops Gitmo Hunger Strikes," *US News.com*, February 22, 2006, http://www.usnews.com/usnews/news/ articles/060222/22gitmo.htm. On June 10, 2006, 3 of the 460 prisoners held at Guantánamo hanged themselves. Navy Rear Admiral Harry Harris grasped the nature of this collective resistance. After he accused them of having "no regard for life, either ours or their own," he declared, "I believe this was not an act of desperation, but an act of asymmetrical warfare waged against us." See "Guantanamo Suicides a 'PR Move,'" *BBC News*, June 11, 2006, http://news.bbc.co.uk/2/hi/americas/5069230.stm; and Sara Wood, "Three Guantánamo Bay Detainees Die of Apparent Suicide," U.S. Department of Defense, American Forces Press Service, June 10, 2006, http://www.defense.gov/news/newsarticle.aspx?id=16080.
43. U.S. Department of Defense, "Review of Department Compliance with President's Executive Order on Detainee Conditions of Confinement," Arlington, VA, February 23, 2009, 56–57. Guantánamo's purpose might well be to test the limits of "forcible contamination," as Erving Goffman describes self-defilement in *Asylums: Essays on the Social Situation of Mental Patients and Other Inmates* (1961; repr., New York: Doubleday Anchor, 1990), 48.
44. Stafford Smith, *Bad Men*, 207.
45. Sabin Willett, Testimony to the House Committee on Foreign Affairs' Subcommittee on International Organizations, Human Rights and Oversight, May 20, 2008, in "Current Conditions of Confinement at Guantánamo: Still in Violation of the Law," Center for Constitutional Rights, February 23, 2009. See also the blog posted by Jamil Dakwar, "Pentagon Report Whitewashes Gitmo Abuses," Human Rights Program, ACLU, February 24, 2009, at http://blog.aclu.org/2009/02/24/pentagon-report -whitewashes-abuses-at-gitmo/.
46. See Clive Stafford Smith, "Guantánamo Suicides Report," June 13, 2006, Reprieve, http://www.reprieve.org.uk/memosuicidesatguantanamo.
47. Frederick Pollock and Frederic William Maitland, *The History of English Law Before the Time of Edward 1*, 2 vols. (1898; repr., Cambridge: Cambridge University Press, 1968): 1:476, 2:580, 2:449.
48. William Glaberson, "U.S. May Permit 9/11 Guilty Pleas in Capital Cases," *New York Times*, June 6, 2009, A1.
49. Lynn White, "The Legacy of the Middle Ages in the American Wild West," *Speculum* 40, no. 2 (April 1965): 199, quoted in Peters, *The Magician, the Witch, and the Law*, 192. I am indebted to Peters's analyses of how past judicial torture remains contemporaneous with the present legal universe.

In the history of Western law, "torture plays a role that seems to echo at once both a remote and archaic legal universe and ... an appallingly contemporary one" (184).

50. Sheryl Gay Stolberg, "Obama Would Move Some Terror Detainees to U.S," *New York Times*, May 21, 2009, A1. See also William Glaberson, "President's Detention Plan Poses Fundamental Test: Absence of Trials Challenges a Principle," *New York Times*, May 23, 2009, A1. For labeling and incapacitation according to status, see Colin Dayan, "Due Process and Lethal Confinement," *South Atlantic Quarterly* 107, no. 3 (Summer 2008): 485–507, reprinted in *States of Violence: War, Capital Punishment, and Letting Die*, ed. Austin Sarat and Jennifer L. Culbert (Cambridge: Cambridge University Press, 2009), 127–50.

51. The White House, Office of the Press Secretary, "Remarks By the President on National Security." My recognition of the institutionalized witchcraft of the state and the psychic cannibalism it practices is indebted to Misty L. Bastian, "'Bloodhounds Who Have No Friends': Witchcraft and Locality in the Nigerian Popular Press," in *Modernity and Its Malcontents: Ritual and Power in Postcolonial Africa*, ed. Jean Comaroff and John L. Comaroff (Chicago: University of Chicago Press, 1993), 133–34. Bastian describes the witches' contempt for, while retaining uncanny intimacy with, their victims: "She becomes a psychic cannibal, worse than a murderer, because she treats other human beings as though they were meat and her prey."

52. J. M. Coetzee, *Waiting for the Barbarians* (New York: Penguin, 1982), 78.

53. For the legal history of questions of property in the human body, especially corpses buried, unburied, envaulted, or cremated and the rights attached to "human tissue," see Paul Matthews's "Whose Body? People as Property," in *Current Legal Problems*, ed. Lord Lloyd of Hampstead and Roger W. Rideout with Jacqueline Dyson (London: Stevens and Sons, 1983), 36:193–239.

54. I take the term "magicalities" from Jean Comaroff's and John Comaroff's introduction to *Modernity and Its Malcontents*, xxx; Ralph A. Austin, "The Moral Economy of Witchcraft," 90, in *Modernity and Its Malcontents*. In "The Legal Status of Human Materials," *Drake Law Review* 44, no. 2 (1996): 195–260, Philippe Ducor tackles the problems of ascertaining the differences between subjects and objects, and the legal extension of rights to fetuses, embryos, corpses, and other creatures. The most brilliant analysis of what he calls "marooned body parts"—thinking of "transplant failure as the incomplete physiological appropriation of alienated tissue, or, phrased differently: as a re-assertion of biotic individuality on the part of its (by then disembodied) former 'owner'"—is Stephan Palmié's "Thinking with *Ngangas*: Reflections on Embodiment and the Limits of 'Objectively Necessary Appearances,'" *Comparative Studies in Society and History* 48, no. 4 (October 2006): 852–86, 876.

55. *Bailey v. Poindexter's Executor*, 55 Va. 132, 35 (1858), available at 1858 WL

3940. I refer to the ghoulish memoranda authored mainly by John C. Yoo, Jay S. Bybee, and Steven G. Bradbury, which authorized the methods of interrogation. While limiting the definition of "severe pain and suffering" to whether or not the interrogator intended to torture, they also narrowed the definition of torture to the deliberately malicious infliction of the most extreme possible form of pain. To rise to the level of torture, the interrogator must cause "prolonged mental harm" or "lasting, though not necessarily permanent damage." Anything is allowable unless it causes "organ failure" or death. As this book went to press, more than a year after President Obama signed the order to close Guantánamo, the abominations inaugurated there by President Bush have not changed in a significant way.

56. Blackstone, *Commentaries on the Laws of England*, 4:236. See also 2:429: "[T]hough the heir has a property in the monuments and escutcheons of his ancestors, yet he has none in their bodies or ashes; nor can he bring any civil action against such as indecently at least, if not impiously, violate and disturb their remains, when dead and buried." For a spirited, lengthy disagreement with the notion that dead bodies cannot be stolen as property, see Matthews, "Whose Body?" 36:197–205. In "Thinking with *Ngangas*," 868, Stephan Palmié discusses the importance of legal and magical practice in creating what he calls "uncanny hybrids," where divisions such as persons or things are not only challenged but remade.

57. See *Meagher v. Driscoll*, 99 Mass. 281 (1868); *Pierce v. Proprietors of Swan Point Cemetery*, 10 R.I. 227 (1872); *Weld v. Walker et al.*, *American Law Review* 14, no. 1 (1880): 57–66.

58. E. P. Evans, *The Criminal Prosecution and Capital Punishment of Animals* (London: William Heinemann, 1906), 82, discusses Bougeant's rationalization of cruelty toward billions of beasts wandering the earth. See the discussion of Bougeant's "little devils" who are indistinguishable from a "multitude of persons" in William Ewald, "Comparative Jurisprudence (I): What Was It Like to Try a Rat?" *University of Pennsylvania Law Review* 143, no. 6 (June 1995): 1889–2149, 1907–8.

59. Melville, *Moby-Dick, or the Whale*, ed. Harrison Hayford, Hershel Parker, and G. Thomas Tanselle (Evanston, IL: Northwestern University Press and the Newberry Library, 2001), 185.

60. *Philostratus. The Life of Apollonius of Tyana*, 2 vols., ed. and trans. Christopher P. Jones (London: Loeb Classical Library, 2005), 2.6.43:206–09. On Apollonius of Tyana see E. L. Bowie, "Apollonius of Tyana: Tradition and Reality," *Aufstieg und Niedergang der roemischen Welt*, ed. Hildegard Temporini and Wolfgang Haase (Berlin: de Gruyter, 1978), 2.16.2, 1652–99; Maria Dzielska, *Apollonius of Tyana in Legend and History*, trans. Piotr Pienkowski (Rome: "L'Erma" di Bretschneider, 1986); Graham Anderson, *Sage, Saint and Sophist: Holy Men and Their Associates in the Early Roman Empire* (London: Routledge, 1994). Glenn Most in *Doubting Thomas* (Cambridge, MA: Harvard University Press, 2005), 245, notes that since

1832 the relation between Philostratus's account of Apollonius and New Testament accounts of Jesus "has been an unsolved problem for historical scholarship."

61. Philostratus, *The Life of Apollonius of Tyana*, 2.6.43–57:206–9.

CHAPTER 2. CIVIL DEATH

1. Ruth Wilson Gilmore, *Golden Gulag: Prisons, Surplus, Crisis, and Opposition in Globalizing California* (Berkeley: University of California Press, 2007), 244.

2. In "Wounded Names: The Medieval Doctrine of Infamy," in *Law in Mediaeval Life and Thought*, ed. Edward B. King and Susan J. Ridyard (Sewanee: The Press of the University of the South, 1990), 43–89, Edward Peters discusses the passage of *infamia* from its earliest Roman usage to its indispensable juridical significance well into the nineteenth century. Not only did it penalize criminals but it also stigmatized and controlled "the lives of those whose character is doubtful and whose reputation is bad," thus inflicting dishonor and shame whether in court or in public opinion. Distinguishing between infamy and outlawry, Peters shows how the Roman *infamis* like the Greek legal category of *atimia* while "[r]emaining in the community" is "disabled from the most significant forms of community life."

3. William Blackstone, *Commentaries*, 4 vols. (1765–69; repr., Chicago: University of Chicago Press, 1979), 1:121.

4. Peters, "Wounded Names," 48 n. 9.

5. Orlando Patterson, *Slavery and Social Death: A Comparative Study* (Cambridge, MA: Harvard University Press, 1982), 22, 45.

6. Patterson, *Slavery and Social Death*, quoting from Claude Meillassoux, ed. *L'esclavage en Afrique précoloniale* (1975), 38.

7. See Frederick Cooper, *Colonialism in Question: Theory, Knowledge, History* (Berkeley: University of California Press, 2005), 17; and especially Vincent Brown's "Social Death and Political Life in the Study of Slavery," *American Historical Review* 114, no. 5 (December 2009): 1231–49, for an assessment of the vagaries of social death that dangerously consumes or petrifies the slaves' "collective forms of belonging and striving" (1236). The term, according to Brown, is a motive for disguise, an instrument of monumental history that defeats particularity and change over time.

8. Patterson, *Slavery and Social Death*, 3.

9. See Blackstone, *Commentaries*, 2:121; 4:374–81; 1:128–29. On civil death, see Walter Matthews Grant et al., "The Collateral Consequences of a Criminal Conviction," *Vanderbilt Law Review* [1942] 23, no. 5 (October 1970): 929–1242; "Civil Effects of Sentence to Life Imprisonment," *American Law Reports, Annotated* 139 (1942): 1308–25; Alec C. Ewald, "'Civil Death': The Ideological Paradox of Criminal Disenfranchisement Law in the United States," *Wisconsin Law Review* 5 (2002): 1045–137.

On early American definitions of civil death, see especially John Bouvier's *A Law Dictionary Adapted to the Constitution and Laws of the United States of America; and of the Several States of the American Union, with References to the Civil and Other Systems of Foreign Law*, 2 vols., 6th ed. (Philadelphia: Childs and Peterson, 1856), where "civil death" is simply defined as "that change of state of a person which is considered in the law as equivalent to death. See DEATH."

10. Blackstone, *Commentaries*, 2:256, 254, 253, 254.
11. In *The Prison and the American Imagination* (New Haven, CT: Yale University Press, 2009), Caleb Smith uses the legal mechanism of civil death, augmenting my earlier work, to underpin his haunting analysis of solitary confinement and the literary gothic medium it inspired.
12. Blackstone, *Commentaries*, 1:125.
13. Blackstone, *Commentaries*, 1:129; 4:373.
14. Thomas Blount, *Nomo-lexikon, a Law Dictionary: Interpreting Such Difficult and Obscure Words and Terms As Are Found Either In Our Common or Statute, Ancient or Modern Lawes: With References to the Several Statutes, Records, Registers, Law-books, Charters, Ancient Deeds, and Manuscripts, Wherein the Words are Used: and Etymologies, Where They Properly Occur* (England: In the Savoy; printed by Thomas Newcomb for John Martin and Henry Herringman, 1670).
15. In *The Anthropology of Slavery: The Womb of Iron and Gold* (Chicago: University of Chicago Press, 1991), 107, 109, Claude Meillassoux describes the violence of the servile idiom which incapacitated slaves in two ways: through "de-socialization" and "de-personalization."
16. Nathan Bailey, *An Universal Etymological English Dictionary; and An Interpreter of Hard Words* (London: Printed for J. Buckland, J. Beecoft, W. Strahan, J. Hinton, 1773). Bailey defines "Taint" as "a Conviction, a Spot or Blemish in Reputation," links "to Taint" to the meaning of "to corrupt, to spoil, to bribe, to attaint," then finds another definition of "Taint" in "corrupted as Meat, smelling rank," and, finally, gives stench to the criminal, as he defines "Tainted" as "convicted of a Crime, having an ill Smell."
17. A.W.B. Simpson, writing about the doctrine of escheat following a felony, noted that "later, lawyers attributed the escheat in cases of felony to the biologically absurd notion that the felon's blood was 'corrupted,' whatever that may mean, so that inheritance was impossible through him" (*A History of the Land Law* [Oxford: Clarendon Press, 1985], 20). "Attain" and "attainder" come through Norman French from Latin *attingo, attingere, attigi, attactum* (the base of which is the Latin *tango*, etc., meaning to touch, strike, attack), which was then subsequently changed in its meaning by erroneous association with the French *taindre, teindre*, which has a different Latin etymology from "attain" and "attainder," from *tingo* (or *tinguo*), *tingere, tinxi, tinctum*, meaning to dye or to color (captured in the English *taint* and *tinge*). See John Cowell's singular exception in *The Interpreter: or Book Containing the Signification of Words* (London: F. Leach, for

distribution by Hen. Twyford, Tho. Dring, and Io. Place, 1658), where he recognizes the source of attainted (*attinctus*) in the French *teindre*, with a further link to the French *estre attaint* and *vayncu en aucuncas:* "Which maketh me to think that it rather commeth from (*attainder*) as we would say in English catched, overtaken, or plainly deprehended" (n.p.).

18. Modes of specifically racial anti-Semitism also evolved in terms of blood, turning what was legal or metaphorical into the natural and scientific.

19. Winthrop D. Jordan, *White over Black: American Attitudes toward the Negro, 1550–1812* (1968; repr., New York: W. W. Norton, 1977), 15.

20. Blackstone, *Commentaries*, 4:395.

21. *Somerset v. Stewart*, 98 Eng Rep 499, 502 (1772).

22. Alexis de Tocqueville, *Democracy in America* (1835–40; repr., New York: Everyman's Library, 1994), 169, 166–67.

23. Tocqueville, *Democracy in America*, 357–58.

24. Virginia R. Dominguez, *White by Definition: Social Classification in Creole Louisiana* (New Brunswick, NJ: Rutgers University Press, 1986), 24. For a discussion of the taxonomic intricacies and legal effects of French colonial mixing, see Jean-Luc Bonniol, *La couleur comme maléfice: Une illustration créole de la généalogie des "Blancs" et des "Noirs"* (Paris: Albin Michel, 1992); Dayan, *Haiti, History, and the Gods*; and Yvan Debbasch, *Couleur et liberté: Le jeu du critère ethnique dans un ordre juridique esclavagiste* (Paris: Librairie Dalloz, 1967). Bryan Edwards, *The History, Civil and Commercial, of the British Colonies in the West Indies*, 2 vols. (Dublin: Luke White, 1793), 2:17–18; *Journals of the Assembly of Jamaica*, 3, 124, of March 30, 1733, cited in Edward Brathwaite, *The Development of Creole Society in Jamaica, 1770–1820* (Oxford: Clarendon Press, 1971), 167–68.

25. James Kent, discussing the "Rights of Persons" in *Commentaries on American Law* (1826; repr., Boston: Little, Brown, 1873), vol. 2, part 4, lect. 25, 72–73, considers the one-eighth rule in Louisiana, the French colonies, and South Carolina. Here, he reveals the logic necessary to prove—without observable color—that one is part of the adulterated race: "A remote taint will not degrade a person to the class of persons of color; but a mere predominance of white blood is not sufficient to rescue a person from that class…. If the admixture of African blood does not exceed the proportion of one eighth, the person is deemed white." See also Cheryl I. Harris, "Whiteness as Property," *Harvard Law Review* 106, no. 8 (June 1993): 1707–91.

26. In British colonial law, according to Elsa Goveia, *The West Indian Slave Laws of the 18th Century* (Barbados: University of the West Indies, 1970), 25, the respect for the rights of private property resulted in harsher treatment of slaves: the slave was recognized as "a person in a sphere far more limited than that allowed him [in] either Spanish or French law."

27. Jonathan A. Bush, "Free to Enslave: The Foundations of Colonial American Slave Law," *Yale Journal of Law and Humanities* 5, no. 2 (1993): 417–70, 426, 432–33, 420.

28. See Kent, *Commentaries*, vol. 2, part 4, lect. 32, 250–51, for his distinction between villeinage and slavery: "No person in England was a villein in the eye of the law, except in relation to his master.... To all other persons he was a freeman, and as against them he had rights of property; and his master, for excessive injuries committed upon the vassal, was answerable at the king's suit."

29. Thomas Cobb, *An Inquiry into the Law of Negro Slavery in the United States of America* (1858; repr., New York: Negro Universities Press, 1968), 84.

30. *The State of Mississippi v. Isaac Jones*, 1 Miss. 83, 84, 85 (1820).

31. *State of Mississippi*, 85.

32. *Avery v. Everett*, 110 N.Y. 317, 334 (1888). See the analysis of this case in the examination of civil death in Scheppele, "Facing Facts in Legal Interpretation,"42–77.

33. *Avery*, 331, 335.

34. Blackstone, *Commentaries*, 1:132..

35. My early analyses of the legal forms for the incapacitation of life in civil death were the originating impulse for this book: Dayan, "Held in the Body of the State," in *History, Memory, and the Law*, ed. Austin Sarat and Thomas R. Kearns (Ann Arbor: University of Michigan Press, 1999), 183–249. Dayan, "Legal Slaves and Civil Bodies," in *Materializing Democracy: Toward a Revitalized Cultural Politics*, ed. Russ Castronovo and Dana D. Nelson (Durham, NC: Duke University Press, 2002), 53–94.

36. For the origins of the phrase "badges and incidents of slavery," see George Rutherglen, "The Badges and Incidents of Slavery and the Power of Congress to Enforce the Thirteenth Amendment" (Working Paper 68, University of Virginia Law School Public Law and Legal Theory Working Paper Series, 2007), http://law.bepress.com/cgi/viewcontent.cgi?article=1108& context=uvalwps.

37. Kent, *Commentaries*, vol. 2, part 4, lect. 32, 256–57; vol. 2 part 4, lect. 28, 155–57.

38. *Platner v. Sherwood*, 6 Johns. Ch. 118 (1822); *Troup v. Wood*, 4 Johns. Ch. 228 (1820). Later cases such as *In re Zeph's Estate* (20 N.Y. St. Rep. 382, 1888), *Avery v. Everett* (110 N.Y. 317, 1888), *Riggs v. Palmer* (115 N.Y. 506, 1889), and *In re Lindewall's Will* (287 N.Y. 347, 1942) attest to the staying power of civil death. As a "creature of law" (*Holmes v. King*, 216 Ala. 412, 415 (1927), civil death continues to haunt persons convicted of crime.

39. *Civil Rights Cases*, 109 U.S. 3, 26, 31, 33, 48, 60, 61 (1883).

40. Jamie Fellner and Marc Mauer, "Losing the Vote: The Impact of Felony Disenfranchisement Laws in the United States," Human Rights Watch and the Sentencing Project, 1998, http://www.sentencingproject.org/ doc/File/FVR/fd_losingthevote.pdf. In "'Civil Death': The Ideological Paradox of Criminal Disenfranchisement Law in the United States," *Wisconsin Law Review* 5 (2002): 1045–132, Alec. C. Ewald traces the disenfran-

chisement of criminal offenders, the overwhelming majority of whom are African Americans. It is striking that in some states, disenfranchisement laws apply not only to convicted felons who are incarcerated and those who were incarcerated and are now released under parole supervision, but also to those felons sentenced to probation—thus never incarcerated—as well as ex-felons. See Jeff Manza and Christopher Uggen, "Punishment and Democracy: Disenfranchisement of Nonincarcerated Felons in the United States," *Perspectives on Politics* 2, no. 3 (September 2004): 491–505. On the legal history of American felon disenfranchisement laws, see Robin L. Nunn, "Lock Them Up and Throw Away the Vote," *Chicago Journal of International Law* 5, no. 2 (Winter 2005): 763–84; and Pamela A. Wilkins, "The Mark of Cain: Disenfranchised Felons and the Constitutional No Man's Land," *Syracuse Law Review* 56, no. 2 (2005): 85–144. In "The Modern-Day Literary Test? Felon Disenfranchisement and Race Discrimination," *Stanford Law Review* 57, no. 2 (2004): 611–55, Daniel S. Goldman links felon disenfranchisement laws to the discriminatory purpose of literacy tests, a continuation of racial stigma and political exclusion. See also the 2009 report of the Sentencing Project, "Felony Disenfranchisement," in *Sentencing Project News*, http://www.sentencing project.org/template/page.cfm?id=133.

41. *Ruffin v. Commonwealth*, 62 VA 790, 792, 796, 794, 793, 796 (1871). It is not surprising that *Ruffin* acted as a memorial recalled by Justices Thurgood Marshall, William Brennan, and John Paul Stevens, as if exhuming for the Rehnquist Court the state-sanctioned slavery that the Court refuses to name. See, for example, the dissents in *Jones v. North Carolina Prisoners Labor Union, Inc.*, 433 U.S. 119 (1977) (Marshall dissenting, joined by Brennan); *Meachum v. Fano*, 427 U.S. 215 (1976) (Stevens dissenting, joined by Brennan and Marshall); *Lewis v. Casey*, 518 U.S. 343 (1996) (Stevens dissenting).

42. Alfred Avins, *The Reconstruction Amendments' Debates* (Richmond: Virginia Commission on Constitutional Government, U.S. Congress, 1967), 258.

43. Sumner in Avins, *Reconstruction*, 258. For examinations of this inventive reenslaving, see David M. Oshinsky's *"Worse than Slavery": Parchman Farm and the Ordeal of Jim Crow Justice* (New York: Free Press, 1996); and Alex Lichtenstein's *Twice the Work of Free Labor: The Political Economy of Convict Labor in the New South* (London: Verso, 1996); and the story of imprisonment as crucial to understanding the American experience of democracy in Scott Christianson's *With Liberty for Some: Five Hundred Years of Imprisonment in America* (Boston: Northeastern University Press, 1998).

44. See Giorgio Agamben, *Remnants of Auschwitz: The Witness and the Archive*, trans. Daniel Heller-Roazen (New York: Zone Books, 1999), 73–74.

45. United Kingdom, House of Commons, "Report on the Penitentiaries of the United States, Addressed to His Majesty's Principal Secretary of State

for the Home Department," prepared by William Crawford, August 11, 1834, 26–27.

46. Beaumont and Tocqueville, *On the Penitentiary System in the United States*, trans. Francis Lieber (Philadelphia: Carey, 1833), 5, 15. Elisha Bates, *The Moral Advocate: A Monthly Publication on War, Duelling, Capital Punishments, and Prison Discipline* (Mt. Pleasant, OH: Printed by the Editor, 1821–22), 1:171.

47. Charles Dickens, *American Notes* and *Pictures from Italy* (1842; repr., New York: Oxford University Press, 1957), 99–100.

48. William Roscoe, *A Brief Statement of the Causes Which Have Led to the Abandonment of the Celebrated System of Penitentiary Discipline in Some of the United States of America* (Liverpool: Harris, 1827). Roberts Vaux, "Letter on the Penitentiary System of Pennsylvania, Addressed to William Roscoe, Esquire" (Philadelphia: Printed by Jesper Harding, 1827), 9.

49. Lieber in Beaumont and Tocqueville, *On the Penitentiary System*, xii, xviii, xix.

50. Benjamin Rush, *Essays: Literary, Moral, and Philosophical*, edited with an introductory essay by Michael Meranze (1806; repr., Schenectady, NY: Union College, 1988), 86, 88.

51. Rush, *Essays*, 99–100.

52. Beaumont and Tocqueville, *On the Penitentiary System*, 39–40. Although I disagree with his sense of "Quaker technique," see Michel Foucault's well-known analysis of "absolute isolation" in Philadelphia in *Discipline and Punish: The Birth of the Prison*, trans. Alan Sheridan (New York: Vintage, 1995), 238–39.

53. See C. G. Goen's excellent introduction to his edition of Jonathan Edwards, *The Great Awakening* (New Haven, CT: Yale University Press, 1972), which includes the text of Edwards's *A Faithful Narrative of the Surprising Work of God* (1736). On what Puritans called "conviction" of sin or "humiliation," see also Edmund S. Morgan, *Visible Saints: The History of a Puritan Idea* (Ithaca, NY: Cornell University Press, 1963), 66–69, Edwards, *Faithful Narrative*, in Goen, *The Great Awakening*, 163–71.

54. John Locke, *The Reasonableness of Christianity, As Delivered in the Scriptures* in *The Works of John Locke*, 10 vols. (1695; repr., London: Printed for Thomas Tegg; W. Sharpe and Son; etc., 1823), 7:6.

CHAPTER 3. PUNISHING THE RESIDUE

1. Hannah Arendt, *Origins of Totalitarianism* (1951; repr., New York: Schocken Books, 2004), 371, 373, 372.

2. For a bracing discussion of the hyperlegality of contemporary practices of detention, as well as the justifications of torture that accompany them, see Nasser Hussain, "Beyond Norm and Exception: Guantánamo," *Critical Inquiry* 33, no. 4 (Summer 2007): 734–53.

3. Arendt, *Origins of Totalitarianism*, 383, 365, 383.

NOTES TO CHAPTER 3

4. In an interview with Arizona Department of Corrections spokesperson Mike Arra in June 1995, I was told that the state-of-the-art super–maximum security units were built to house the "worst of the worst." For an example of Bush administration labeling, see Katharine Q. Seelye, "Threats and Responses: The Detainees; Some Guantánamo Prisoners Will Be Freed, Rumsfeld Says," *New York Times*, October 23, 2002.

5. In *Laboratories of Virtue: Punishment, Revolution, and Authority in Philadelphia, 1760–1835* (Chapel Hill: University of North Carolina Press, 1996), 199, Michael Meranze, following Michael Foucault in *Discipline and Punish*, describes solitary confinement as a "regime imposed by a self upon itself." The self produced by solitary complicates the philosophical definition of "person." See Margaret Jane Radin's "Property and Personhood," *Stanford Law Review* 34, no. 5 (1982): 957, on conceptualizations of the person that clarify the double affliction of the supermax prisoner: deprived not only of the rights consequent upon imprisonment but also of self-consciousness and memory.

6. What I refer to as "society's refuse," "human materials," or "human waste," the humans contained or quarantined in the global need for security and order, recalls Zygmunt Bauman's description of the poor and the stigmatized in *Wasted Lives: Modernity and Its Outcasts* (Cambridge, UK: Polity Press, 2004). What he describes as "the human waste disposal industry," which defines disposable waste as "[r]efugees, the displaced, asylum seekers, migrants, the *sans papiers*," is both essential to and the result of globalization. The prison, as Loïc Wacquant and David Garland have also emphasized, is essential to this project of dumping and containment, the neutralization and incapacitation of persons deemed noxious or useless to society. See Loïc Wacquant, "Deadly Symbiosis: When Ghetto and Prison Meet and Mesh," *Punishment and Society* 3, no. 1 (2001): 95–133; and David Garland, *The Culture of Control: Crime and Social Order in Contemporary Society* (Chicago: University of Chicago Press, 2001).

7. I interviewed Harold ("Hal") Whitley, deputy warden of SMU 1, on October 21, 1996. He began his career at the age of twenty-one as a correctional officer at Oregon State Penitentiary. Captain Whitley was the original defendant in *Whitley v. Albers*, 475 U.S. 312 (1986). On June 27, 1980, Captain Whitley, the "prison security manager," ordered an officer to fire warning shots in order to free a hostage during a riot. Inmate Gerald Albers was shot in the knee and brought a case against Whitley. The majority of justices found the use of deadly force justified in an emergency. James McFadden, former deputy warden of SMU 2—the most astute prison administrator that I interviewed—supervised the design, construction, and opening of SMU 2. My interviews with him took place at SMU 2 on June 7, 1996, and October 21, 1996.

8. The supermaxes' use of severe sensory deprivation and enforced idleness has been condemned since the 1980s by the United Nations Committee Against Torture, Human Rights Watch, Amnesty International, the Amer-

274

ican Civil Liberties Union, and the Center for Constitutional Rights. In April 2006, the ACLU presented the Committee Against Torture with its detailed report "Enduring Abuse: Torture and Cruel Treatment by the United States at Home and Abroad," asserting a link between torture and abuse at Guantánamo, Afghanistan's Bagram Air Base, Abu Ghraib, the CIA's "black sites," and the barbarous practices in the prisons and jails of the United States, especially in units reserved for prolonged or indefinite detention.

9. Interviews (names withheld), SMU 1, June 3, 1996, and October 21, 1996.

10. The lockdown at Marion State Penitentiary in 1983 initiated the use of widespread lockdown and solitary confinement as a means to punish political prisoners. In "Resisting Living Death at Marion Federal Penitentiary, 1972," *Radical History Review* 2006, no. 96 (Fall 2006): 58–86, Alan Eladio Gómez focuses on the political awakening that led to "the prison authority's deployment of living death as a strategy to control radical inmates." I thank Marie Gottschalk for alerting me to this article and to the threat posed by the radical prisoners' rights movement as impetus for current death-in-life supermax conditions. See also Jamie Fellner and Joanne Mariner, *Cold Storage: Super-Maximum Security Confinement in Indiana* (New York: Human Rights Watch, 1997), http://www.hrw.org/reports/1997/usind/; Lorna Rhodes, *Total Confinement: Madness and Reason in the Maximum Security Prison* (Berkeley: University of California Press, 2004); the special issue on supermax prisons in *The Prison Journal* 88, no. 1 (March 2008); and Dylan Rodríguez's *Forced Passages: Imprisoned Radical Intellectuals and the U.S. Prison Regime* (Minneapolis: University of Minnesota Press, 2006) for his analysis of the site of incarceration as ground for a new understanding of radical politics. Judged incorrigible and rendered anonymous, the imprisoned demand through their activism and resistance—a redefinition of the very terms of personal and social identity.

11. *Hutto v. Finney*, 437 U.S. 678 (1978).

12. Personal correspondence (name withheld), July 16, 1999.

13. Interview (name withheld), Arizona State Prison–Florence, August 25, 1995.

14. Interview with James McFadden, June 7, 1996.

15. Interview with McFadden, October 21, 1996.

16. On the unique involvement of the courts in the development of the supermax prison see James Robertson, "Houses of the Dead: Warehouse Prisons, Paradigm Change, and the Supreme Court," *Houston Law Review* 34, no. 4 (Winter 1997): 1003–65.

17. *Bell v. Wolfish*, 441 U.S. 520 (1979). For my previous writings on this legal redefinition of the contours of injury and the renovation of civil death in the Rehnquist years, especially, see Dayan, "Held in the Body of the State: Prisons and the Law," *History, Memory, and the Law*, ed. Austin Sarat and Thomas Kearns (Ann Arbor: University of Michigan Press, 1999); and

Dayan, *The Story of Cruel and Unusual* (Cambridge, MA: MIT Press, 2007). On the erosion of due process rights for prisoners in the United States as preliminary to the elimination of due process for prisoners at Guantánamo, see "Due Process and Lethal Confinement," *Killing States: Lethal Decisions/Final Judgments*, ed. Jennifer L. Culbert and Austin Sarat, special issue of *South Atlantic Quarterly* 107, no. 3 (Summer 2008): 485–507, reprinted in *States of Violence: War, Capital Punishment, and Letting Die*, ed. Austin Sarat and Jennifer L. Culbert (Cambridge: Cambridge University Press, 2009), 127–50.

18. Interview with William Bailey, classifications specialist, Arizona Department of Corrections, Phoenix, August 14, 1996. The Offender Classification system is based on the Correctional Classification Profile (CCP). The two major scores are the public-risk score and the institutional-risk score: the first is based on the crime and the second on management decisions within the prison. It is the latter score that qualifies the inmate for incapacitation in a supermax. Those deemed "security threats" risk indefinite confinement without redress, since their assignment to a supermax is usually based on judgments that have nothing to do with behavior or evidence of wrongdoing. On the erosion of due process protections in the context of gang classification and status-based penology, see Scott N. Tachiki, "Indeterminate Sentences in Supermax Prisons Based upon Alleged Gang Affiliations: A Reexamination of Procedural Protection and a Proposal for Greater Procedural Requirements," *California Law Review* 83, no. 4 (July 1995): 1115–49. This domestic practice became the precedent for the antiterrorist law of the Patriot Act: a person can be indefinitely detained for an immigration-related violation, for example, if he or she is "certified" as a terrorist. This certification requires the minimal "reasonable grounds to believe" standard.

19. Personal correspondence (name withheld), January 26, 2000.

20. Interview (name withheld), October 21, 1996.

21. *Ruffin v. Commonwealth*, 62 Va. 790, 796 (1871).

22. René Descartes, *Meditations on First Philosophy* in *The Philosophical Writings of René Descartes*, 2 vols., trans. John Cottingham, Robert Stoothoff, and Dugald Murdoch (Cambridge: Cambridge University Press, 1985), 16.

23. Correctional officers (names withheld), Special Management Unit 1, October 21, 1996.

24. Telephone interview with Michael A. Arra, spokesperson for the Arizona Department of Corrections, August 25, 1995.

25. Complex Detention Unit, Arizona State Prison Complex, Tucson, Arizona, June 12, 1995.

26. Telephone interviews with Michael A. Arra, May 26 and May 28, 1995.

27. Interview with officer (name withheld), Arizona State Prison Complex, Tucson, August 10, 1995.

28. Interview with Michael Arra, June 12, 1995.

29. *In Re Medley*, 134 U.S. 160, 168–71 (1890).

30. Stuart Grassian, *Lee v. Coughlin*, 26 F. Supp. 2d 615, 637 (1998) and Grassian, "Psychiatric Effects of Solitary Confinement," *Washington University Journal of Law and Policy* 22 (2006): 325–84, 333, 354.

31. Stuart Grassian, interview by Mike Wallace, *60 Minutes*, January 15, 1995. This interview followed and updated his first interview on Pelican Bay prison, "California's High Tech Maximum Security Prison Accused of Torture and Mental Abuse," *60 Minutes*, September 12, 1993.

32. "N.M. Repeals Death Penalty," *Los Angeles Times*, March 19, 2009. Cost was also cited as a factor in the decision to repeal. See Ian Urbina, "Citing Cost, States Consider End to Death Penalty," *New York Times*, February 24, 2009 and Solomon Moore, "Number of Life Terms Hits Record," *New York Times*, July 23, 2009. See, especially, Ashley Nellis and Ryan S. King, "No Exit: The Expanding Use of Life Sentences in America," The Sentencing Project (July 2009): 1–45 at http://www.sentencingproject.org/doc/publications/publications/inc_noexitseptember2009.pdf.

33. Alfred McCoy, *A Question of Torture: CIA Interrogation, From the Cold War to the War on Terror* (New York: Henry Holt, 2006), 8.

34. Personal correspondence (name withheld), December 15, 1999.

35. John Locke, *An Essay Concerning Human Understanding*, ed. Peter H. Nidditch (1700; repr., New York: Oxford University Press, 1975), 2:27:22, 344.

36. Locke, *Essay*, 2.27.17:341; 2.27.26:346.

37. Locke, *Essay*, 2.2.21.117, 2.1.22.117. Rush, *Essays*. See Michael Meranze's history of punishment in the late colonial and early republican periods: *Laboratories of Virtue*. On Rush and solitary confinement, see also Smith, *Prison and the American Imagination*, 8–9, 10, 17, 54–55, 90–91.

38. Locke, *Essay*, 2.27.10: 336.

39. William James, *The Principles of Psychology* (1890; repr., New York: Cosimo Classics, 2007), 1:293–94.

40. *Laaman v. Helgemoe*, 437 F. Supp. 269, 325 (1977). A year earlier, in the landmark case *Pugh v. Locke*, 406 F. Supp. 318, 323, the judge described Alabama's prisons as "wholly unfit for human habitation" and considered the totality of unconstitutional conditions that made rehabilitation impossible and reform unlikely.

41. *Laaman*, 293, 325, 293.

42. In *Harsh Justice: Criminal Punishment and the Widening Divide Between America and Europe* (Oxford: Oxford University Press, 2003), James Q. Whitman, building on Harold Garfinkel and Erving Goffman's work, argues that the peculiarly vehement rites of degradation in America not only pertain to the inferior status of offenders but also aim to cultivate inferiority.

43. Correctional officer (name withheld), Special Management Unit 1, October 21, 1996.

44. Interview with deputy warden (name withheld) in Cell Block 6, the old death row, also called "row of the dead," Arizona State Prison, June 13, 1996.

45. Interview with Charles ("Chuck") Ryan, then senior warden of Arizona State Prison–Florence, August 25, 1995.

46. *Beard v. Banks*, 548 U.S. 521 (2006). *Hamdan v. Rumsfeld*, 548 U.S. 557, 630, 631, 632 (2006).

47. These cases, which decided when punishments are judged as cruel and unusual, are *Estelle v. Gamble*, 429 U.S. 97 (1976); *Rhodes v. Chapman*, 452 U.S. 337 (1981); *Whitley v. Albers*, 475 U.S. 312 (1986); *Wilson v. Seiter*, 501 U.S. 294 (1991); *Hudson v. McMillian*, 503 U.S. 1 (1992); *Farmer v. Brennan*, 511 U.S. 825 (1994); and *Hope v. Pelzer*, 536 U.S. 730 (2002).

48. *Beard v. Banks*, 525, 526.

49. *Beard*, 526, *Beard v. Banks* Respondent's Brief, 2006 WL 403662, 5.

50. *Beard*, 533 (quoting *Overton v. Bazzetta* 539 U.S. 126, 134 (2003)).

51. *Procunier v. Martinez*, 416 U.S. 396, 413, 416 (1974).

52. *Procunier*, 423, 426, 427, 428.

53. *Turner v. Safley*, 482 U.S. 78, 89 (1987).

54. *O'Lone v. Shabazz*, 482 U.S. 342, 352 (1987).

55. *O'Lone*, 354, 356.

56. *O'Lone*, 354, 355; *Turner*, 84.

57. *Lewis v. Casey*, 518 U.S. 343 (1996); *Overton v. Bazzetta*, 539 U.S. 126 (2003).

58. *Overton*, 139, 143. *In re Medley*, 134 U.S. 160 (1890).

59. *Overton*, 132.

60. For accounts of the Verizon/MCI monopoly on inmate phone calls, see "Case Challenges Verizon/MCI Monopoly On Inmate Phone Calls," *North Country Gazette*, September 21, 2006, http://www.northcountrygazette .org/articles/092106PhoneMonopoly.html. In 2007, after years of pressure from the Center for Constitutional Rights, the New York State legislature, in the Family Connections Bill, prohibited the state from profiting from any future telephone contract. In 2009, the New York State Court of Appeals in *Walton v. New York State Department of Correctional Services* (13 N.Y. 3d 475 (2009)) rejected the claims of prisoners' families seeking compensation for years of overcharging. The scandal continues in many other states.

61. *Overton*, 135, 137.

62. *Overton*, 139, 138.

63. *Banks v. Beard*, 399 F.3d 134 (2005). Telephone interview with Kemal Mericli, July 23, 2007.

64. *Banks*, 138, 144, 142, 141, 142.

65. *Banks*, 148, 149, 148.

66. *Banks*, 147.

67. *Banks*, 145.

68. *Banks*, 143.

69. *Beard v. Banks* Oral Argument, March 27, 2006, 2006 WL 909420, 7, 41.

70. *Beard*, Oral Argument, 3.

71. *Beard*, Oral Argument, 5, 6, 9.
72. *Beard*, Oral Argument, 20, 19, 20.
73. *Beard*, Oral Argument, 21, 22, 26.
74. *Beard v. Banks* Respondent's Brief, February 16, 2006, 2006 WL 403662, 4, 25.
75. *Beard*, Oral Argument, 47, 48, 49, 38.
76. *Beard*, Oral Argument, 40, 51, 49.
77. *Beard v. Banks*, 525 (quoting *Overton*, 132), 531(quoting *Turner*, 95), 533 (quoting *Overton*, 134).
78. *Beard*, 537, 539, 540.
79. Brief of the American Civil Liberties Union, ACLU of Pennsylvania, The Legal Aid Society, People for the American Way Foundation, American Friends Service Committee, and California Prison Focus as Amicus Curiae in Support of Respondents, *Beard v. Banks*, 548 U.S. 521 (2006), February 16, 2006, WL 448206, 11.
80. Telephone interview with David Fathi, June 16, 2007.
81. *Beard v. Banks*, 552, 546, 555, 551.
82. Craig Haney, "Mental Health Issues in Long-Term Solitary and 'Supermax' Confinement," *Crime and Delinquency* 49, no. 1 (January 2003): 124–56, 139, 141, 139.
83. Telephone conversation with Kemal Mericli, July 23, 2007.
84. *Beard v. Banks*, 552–553, 543. Personal correspondence, July 19, 2007.

CHAPTER 4. TAXONOMIES

1. Herman Melville, *Israel Potter: His Fifty Years of Exile*, ed. Harrison Hayford, Hershel Parker, and G. Thomas Tanselle (Evanston, IL: Northwestern University Press and the Newberry Library, 1982), 154, 158, 159
2. Melville, *Israel Potter*, 161–64.
3. Melville, *Israel Potter*, 164.
4. Melville, *Israel Potter*, 164–65.
5. Bernard Mandeville, *The Fable of the Bees: Or, Private Vices Publick Benefits* (London: Printed for J. Roberts, near the Oxford Arms in Warwick Lane, 1714), 157.
6. The phrase is from *Bartleby, the Scrivener*, a "Story of Wall Street," *The Piazza Tales and Other Prose Pieces, 1839–1860*, ed. Harrison Hayford, Alma A. MacDougall, and G. Thomas Tanselle et al. (Evanston, IL: Northwestern University Press and the Newberry Library, 1987), 21.
7. Herman Melville, "Benito Cereno," *Piazza Tales*, 116.
8. Georges-Louis Leclerc, comte de Buffon, *Oeuvres complètes de Buffon*, ed. Frédéric Cuvier (Bruxelles: Chez Th. Lejeune, Libraire-éditeur, 1828–30), 1:72.
9. Edward Long, *The History of Jamaica, or General Survey of the Antient and Modern State of That Island*, 2 vols. (London, 1774; repr., New York, Arno Press, 1972), 2.3.1: 356, 372, 358.

10. Locke, *Essay* (New York: Oxford University Press, 1975), 3.6.12:447, 3.6.38:463.

11. Locke, *Essay*, 3.6.13:447, 3.6.23:452. See Daniel Carey, "Locke, Travel Literature, and the Natural History of Man," *Seventeenth Century* 11, no. 2 (1996): 259–80.

12. Locke, *Essay*, 3.6.23:451. Long, *History of Jamaica*, 2.3.1:360, 364. Locke, *Essay*, 3.6.17:449, 3.6.22:450, 3.6.23:451, 3.6.22:45.

13. Locke, *Essay*, 3.6.26:453, 3.6.27, 454.

14. Long, *History of Jamaica*, 2.3.1:358, 365, 363, 371, 370.

15. Long, *History of Jamaica*, 2.3.1:375–76.

16. Locke, *Essay*, 2.1.10:109, 3.8.1:474. The twenty-seventh chapter of the second book of Locke's *Essay*, "Identity and Diversity" (added in the second edition in 1694), caused numerous theological debates, most famously with Edward Stillingfleet, bishop of Worcester.

17. Locke, *Essay*, 2.7.10:132, 2.1.12:111, 2.1.11:110, 2.1.19:115, 2.1.11:110.

18. Locke, *Essay*, 2.1.12:111.

19. Locke, *Essay*, 2.27.8:333, 4.4.14:569–70, 4.4.15:571.

20. Locke, *Essay*, 2.27.26:346, 2.27. 6:332.

21. Long, *History of Jamaica*, 2.3.1:372. Locke, *Essay*, 4.3.6:541.

22. Locke, *Essay*, 2.27.17:341.

23. Long, *History of Jamaica*, 2.3.1:371.

24. The story of Atlantic slavery has been told by David Brion Davis in numerous works, most recently, *Inhuman Bondage: The Rise and Fall of Slavery in the New World* (New York: Oxford University Press, 2006). For an exhaustive study of slavery in the New World, its thoroughly commercial character and imperial ideology, see Robin Blackburn, *The Making of New World Slavery: From the Baroque to the Modern, 1492–1800* (London: Verso, 1997).

25. Cobb, *Inquiry into the Law of Negro Slavery*, 85.

26. Pollock and Maitland, *History of English Law*, 2:149, 151.

27. Long, *History of Jamaica*, 2.3.5:486, 488.

28. For a detailed discussion of trials and punishment of lifeless things, animals, and slaves, see Edward Payson Evans, *The Criminal Prosecution and Capital Punishment of Animals* (London: William Heinemann, 1906; New York: E. P. Dutton, 1906); and Jacob J. Finkelstein, "The Goring Ox: Some Historical Perspectives on Deodands, Forfeitures, Wrongful Death, and the Western Notion of Sovereignty," *Temple Law Quarterly* 46, no. 2 (Winter 1973): 169–290. See also Paul Schiff Berman, "Rats, Pigs, and Statues on Trial: The Creation of Cultural Narratives in the Prosecution of Animals and Inanimate Objects," *New York University Law Review* 69, no. 2 (1994): 288–326. In "An Anthropological Approach to Modern Forfeiture Law: The Symbolic Function of Legal Actions Against Objects," *Yale Journal of Law and the Humanities* 11, no. 1 (1999): 1–45, Berman links "the supposedly senseless origins of forfeiture" in the English common law to the

acceptance of the practice in the U.S. Supreme Court's justifications for civil forfeiture.

29. See Finkelstein, "Goring Ox," for the distinction between "biblical" punishment and "noxal surrender" and "the real rationale for the deodand institution" which "lay in the assumption by the state" of sacred authority. In his words, "the offending animal is not 'offered to God'—let alone to the kin of the victim—but is killed by stoning" (180–83).

30. Pollock and Maitland, *History of English Law*, 2:474 n. 4. William Ewald in "Comparative Jurisprudence (I): What Was It Like to Try a Rat?" *University of Pennsylvania Law Review* 143, no. 6 (June 1995): 1889–2149, 1910–12, distinguishes Blackstone's discussion of the deodand from Pollock and Maitland's extensive discussion in order to carry his stunning query further into the metaphysics of animal trials: why was the legal ritual of a trial necessary, and what does it tell us about our assumptions of personhood and animality, brutality, and civility?

31. Pollock and Maitland, *History of English Law*, 2:472.

32. Pollock and Maitland, *History of English Law*, 2:472.

33. For a detailed account of the transformative antics of *lougawou* in Haiti, see my *Haiti, History, and the Gods*, 264–65.

34. Goveia, *West Indian Slave Laws*, 20–22. *Somerset v. Stewart*, 98 E.R. 499 (1772).

35. Blackstone, *Commentaries*, 4:373; Edward Long, "An Abstract of the Jamaica *Code Noir*, or Laws affecting Negroe and other Slaves in that Island," in *History of Jamaica*, 2:3.1.556, 365–70. For an incisive account of colonial slave law, especially in Jamaica, see David Barry Gaspar, "'Rigid and Inclement': Origins of the Jamaica Slave Laws of the Seventeenth Century," *The Many Legalities of Early America*, ed. Christopher L. Tomlins and Bruce H. Mann (Chapel Hill: University of North Carolina Press, 2001), 78–97.

36. Long, *History of Jamaica*, 2.3.5:487n.

37. Orlando Patterson, *Slavery and Social Death: A Comparative Study* (Cambridge, MA: Harvard University Press, 1982), 22, 38; Vincent Brown, *The Reaper's Garden: Death and Power in the World of Atlantic Slavery* (Cambridge, MA: Harvard University Press, 2008), 127–28. See also Thomas Morris, *Southern Slavery and the Law: 1619–1860* (Chapel Hill: University of North Carolina Press, 1996), 337–38, for a discussion of the "tensions, inconsistencies, and variations within the codes" regarding the ownership of property.

38. See Brown's discussion of Edmund Burke's elaboration of how slaves might acquire property as part of their preparation "for their eventual assumption of British liberties and responsibilities" in his "Sketch of a Negro Code" sent to the Home Secretary Henry Dundas in 1792, 122–23; Cobb, *Inquiry into the Law of Negro Slavery*, 238. *Dred Scott v. Sandford*, 60 U.S. 393, 409 (1857).

39. Jonathan A. Bush, "Free to Enslave: The Foundations of Colonial American Slave Law," *Yale Journal of Law and the Humanities* 5, no. 2 (1993): 422.

40. *Dred Scott*, 410, 421.

41. On *Dred Scott*, see Austin Allen, *Origins of the Dred Scott Case: Jacksonian Jurisprudence and the Supreme Court, 1837–1857* (Athens: University of Georgia Press, 2006); Mark A. Graber, *Dred Scott and the Problem of Constitutional Evil* (New York: Cambridge University Press, 2006); Don E. Fehrenbacher, *The Dred Scott Case: Its Significance in American Law and Politics* (Oxford: Oxford University Press, 1978). For an exhaustive discussion of citizenship and social compact theory from *Dred Scott* to the Fourteenth Amendment, see Douglas G. Smith, "Citizenship and the Fourteenth Amendment," *San Diego Law Review* 34, no. 2 (1997): 681–808.

42. *Dred Scott*, 409, 413, 416, 403, 450.

43. Abraham Lincoln, "Speech at Peoria, Illinois." The text can be found at http://www.lincolnbicentennial.gov/uploadedFiles/Lincolns_Life/Words_and_Speeches/Speech-at-Peoria.pdf.

44. Blackstone, *Commentaries*, 2:390–95. A favorite text in the antebellum South, Blackstone's *Commentaries* appeared in a new edition by St. George Tucker in 1803. According to Robert M. Cover in *Justice Accused: Antislavery and the Judicial Process* (New Haven, CT: Yale University Press, 1975), "More than 1,000 textual footnotes updated the law, and more than 800 pages of appendices, consisting of essays, refuted or supplemented the *Commentaries* on major issues" (37). For a discussion of the demand for Blackstone's work and its influence on American law generally, see Anthony F. Granucci, "'Nor Cruel and Unusual Punishments Inflicted': The Original Meaning," *California Law Review* 57, no. 4 (1969): 839–65, 862. "In 1775," Granucci writes, "Edmund Burke is reported to have told the House of Commons that almost as many copies of the *Commentaries* had been sold in America as in the whole of England."

45. Blackstone, *Commentaries*, 2:390.

CHAPTER 5. A LEGAL ETHNOGRAPHY

1. Frederic William Maitland, *Domesday Book and Beyond: Three Essays in the Early History of England* (1897; repr., Cambridge: Cambridge University Press, 1988), 9.

2. Maitland, *Domesday Book*, 27, 341, 28.

3. Bryan Wagner, *Disturbing the Peace: Black Culture and the Police Power after Slavery* (Cambridge, MA: Harvard University Press, 2009), 74.

4. Thomas D. Morris, *Southern Slavery and the Law, 1619–1860* (Chapel Hill: University of North Carolina Press, 1996), 57. In *Scenes of Subjection: Terror, Slavery, and Self-Making in Nineteenth-Century America* (New York: Oxford University Press, 1997), 94, Saidiya Hartman focuses on the na-

ture of the "captive person in law," the mutilated subjecthood that "intensified the bonds of captivity and the deadening objectification of chattel status."

5. A. E. Keir Nash in his provocative article, "Reason of Slavery: Understanding the Judicial Role in the Peculiar Institution," *Vanderbilt Law Review* 32, no. 1 (1979): 7–218, wrote: "It is hard to be sufficiently critical of the majority's behavior ... the Virginia court was narrowly but surely in the hands of unabashed pro-slavery extremists" (183). *Bailey* is also discussed by A. Leon Higginbotham Jr. and Barbara K. Kopytoff, "Property First, Humanity Second: The Recognition of the Slave's Human Nature in Virginia Civil Law," *Ohio State Law Journal* 50, no. 3 (1989): 511–40. Nash's article is a response to Mark Tushnet's "The American Law of Slavery, 1810–1860: A Study in the Persistence of Legal Autonomy," *Law and Society Review* 10, no. 1 (Autumn 1975): 119–84. See also Tushnet, *American Law of Slavery, 1810–1860: Considerations of Humanity and Interest* (Princeton, NJ: Princeton University Press, 1981).

6. *Bailey v. Poindexter's Executor*, 55 Va. 132, 1 (1858), available at 1858 WL 3840.

7. *Bailey*, 1.

8. The *Richmond Recorder* warning is quoted by John H. Russell in "The Free Negro in Virginia: 1619–1865," *Johns Hopkins University Studies in Historical and Political Science*, ser. 31, no. 3 (1913): 42–87. According to Russell, this "Act to Amend the Several Laws Concerning Slaves," passed on January 25, 1806, was a cruel ruse. It provided for the removal of free blacks but provided no place for them to go; it offered a freedom that had no domicile. "A refugee slave," Russell writes, "was far more likely to meet with hospitality in the Northern States than was a free negro" (72). Richard Hildreth, thirteen years after publishing *The Slave, or Memoirs of Archy Moore* (Boston: John H. Eastburn, 1836)—the first antislavery novel, though unmentioned by Stowe—wrote in *The History of the United States of America*, 6 vols. (New York: Harper and Brothers, 1849), 3:392, that manumissions after the "Act to Authorize the Manumission of Slaves" in 1782 were so numerous that had the restrictive act of 1806 not been passed, "the free colored population of Virginia might now exceed the slaves." See also Higginbotham and Kopytoff, "Property First, Humanity Second," 535.

9. *Bailey*, 2. Apparently, Poindexter meant the thousand dollars to be divided among the slaves.

10. James Stephen, *The Slavery of the British West India Colonies Delineated, as It Exists Both in Law and Practice, and Compared with the Slavery of Other Countries, Antient and Modern*, 2 vols. (1824; repr., New York: Kraus Reprint, 1969), 378. Morris in *Southern Slavery and the Law*, 380–81, writes that though legally slaves lacked will and therefore could not enter into contracts, some masters did "enter into agreements" that allowed slaves

to purchase freedom, but such conduct "would not create an enforceable legal obligation."

11. On manumission, see especially Cobb, *Inquiry into the Law of Negro Slavery*, 279–305; and Morris, *Southern Slavery and the Law*, 372–423.

12. Cobb, *Inquiry into the Law of Negro Slavery*, 302.

13. In *Creswell's Executor v. Walker*, 37 Ala. 229, 233–34, 236 (1861), Judge James B. Clark followed *Bailey* in deciding that a master cannot "by his will" give his slaves the power to change by election their own civil status. Juridically making and unmaking the idea of the person, Clark gives a "legal mind" to slaves only insofar as they err, only when committing a crime.

14. *Bailey*, 10.

15. Cobb, *Inquiry into the Law of Negro Slavery*, 21.

16. In *Whispered Consolations: Law and Narrative in African American Life* (Ann Arbor: University of Michigan Press, 2000), 61–64, Jon-Christian Suggs argues that "slaves were not *legal* persons, but were *moral* entities," with "no contractual existence." Though this is an excellent and much-needed reminder that the courts and their language differed in their representation of the slaves' personhood, the substitution of the moral for the legal threatens to erase the peculiar tension so necessary to the invention of a new class of persons, with a status that gives new meaning to life: lived in such a way as to redefine morality and law.

17. *Bailey*, 2, 4, 5.

18. *Bailey*, 6.

19. The history of unsoundness of mind or *non compos mentis* and contract law is fascinating; see, e.g., Blackstone's *Commentaries*, 2:291; Kent, *Commentaries*, 2:451; *A New Abridgment of the Law*, by Matthew Bacon, with large additions and corrections, by Sir Henry Gwyllim and Charles Edward Dodd—to which are added *Notes and References to American Law and Decisions* by John Bouvier (Philadelphia: Thomas Davis, 1846), 1:154–55; and Theophilus Parsons, *The Law of Contracts*, 6th ed. (Boston: Little, Brown, 1873), 1:383–87. My lead throughout has been the formidable work of Susanna L. Blumenthal, "The Default Legal Person," *UCLA Law Review* 54, no. 5 (2006–7): 1135–265; Blumenthal, "The Deviance of the Will: Policing the Bounds of Testamentary Freedom in Nineteenth-Century America," *Harvard Law Review* 119, no. 4 (2006): 960–1034; and Blumenthal, "The Mind of a Moral Agent: Scottish Common Sense and the Problem of Responsibility in Nineteenth-Century American Law," *Law and History Review* 26, no. 1 (2008): 99–160.

20. *Bailey*, 7.

21. "Primitive Notions in Modern Law," *American Law Review* 10 (1876–81): 422, in *The Collected Works of Justice Holmes*, ed. Sheldon M. Novick (Chicago: University of Chicago Press, 1994), 3:8; *Bailey*, 10.

22. *Boyce v. Anderson*, 27 U.S. 150, 154–55 (1829).

23. *Bailey*, 9.

24. *Bailey*, 35.
25. *Williamson v. Coalter*, 55 Va. 394, 398–99 (1858); Blackstone, *Commentaries*, 4:395.
26. Cobb, *Inquiry into the Law of Negro Slavery*, 266; Kenneth M. Stamp, *The Peculiar Institution: Slavery in the Ante-Bellum South* (New York: Knopf, 1956), 192.
27. *Bryan v. Walton*, 14 Ga. 185, 198 (1853).
28. *Bailey*, 7, 35.
29. Alden T. Vaughan in "Blacks in Virginia: A Note on the First Decade," *William and Mary Quarterly*, 3rd ser., 29, no. 3 (1972): 469–78, 477, discusses how white Virginians viewed blacks during the first decade—1619 to 1629—of African bondage. Their views were harsh; as Governor Sir George Yeardley's will demonstrates, "Negroes" are listed between servants and cattle: "To his heirs Sir George left 'goode debts, chattels, servants, negars, cattle or any other thing.'" See also Thomas D. Morris, "'Villeinage ... as it existed in England, reflects but little light on our subject': The Problem of the 'Sources' of Southern Slave Law," *American Journal of Legal History* 32, no. 2 (1988): 95–137, 100.
30. Paul Finkelman, "The Centrality of the Peculiar Institution in American Legal Development," *Chicago-Kent Law Review* 68, no. 3 (1993): 1010–12. Finkelman argues for the innovativeness of southern slavery, as well as its influence on "the social, political, and legal structure of the Nation" (1010).
31. *Bailey*, 4. *Dred Scott v. Sandford*, 403.
32. *Bailey*, 31. See Kent, *Commentaries*, 2.4.32:250–51. Discussing the "severity or degradation" of "domestic slavery," he contrasts the "feudal villain of the lowest order" with the "Greek, Roman, or West India slave": "No person, in England, was a villein in the eye of the law, except in relation to his master. To all other persons he was a freeman." In "'Villeinage ... as it existed in England,'" Morris gives an overview of the competing principles and ideological struggles which contributed to the southern law of slavery.
33. St. George Tucker, *Blackstone's Commentaries: With Notes of Reference to the Constitution and Laws, of the Federal Government of the United States, and of the Commonwealth of Virginia* (1803), with an introduction by Paul Finkelman and David Cobin, 5 vols. (Union, NJ: The Lawbook Exchange, 1996), vol. 2, appendix, 54, 31 n. H.
34. *Bailey*, 31.
35. St. George Tucker, *Blackstone's Commentaries*, 2, appendix, 31 n. H. See C. T. Cullen, "St. George Tucker and Law in Virginia, 1772–1804" (Ph.D. dissertation, University of Virginia, 1971).
36. St. George Tucker, *A Dissertation on Slavery: With a Proposal for the Gradual Abolition of It, in the State of Virginia* (Philadelphia: Printed for Mathew Carey, no. 118, Market-Street, 1796), reprinted in Tucker, *Blackstone's Commentaries*, 2, appendix, 31, 54–55 n. H.
37. *Bailey*, 12.

38. *Bailey*, 14, 12, 13, 14.
39. *Bailey*, 19.
40. *Bailey*, 22.
41. *Bailey*, 21.
42. *Dred Scott v. Sandford*, 410, 409.
43. Stereotypes of slaves—as vicious, idle, drunken, or insane—mattered greatly in the legal reckonings of slavery, as demonstrated by Ariela J. Gross in *Double Character: Slavery and Mastery in the Antebellum Southern Courtroom* (Princeton, NJ: Princeton University Press, 2000). Especially pertinent is her discussion of the "merging of moral and medical," or alleged "mental perturbation" that removed "agency—and honor—from slaves" (146–52). See also William W. Fisher III, "Ideology and Imagery in the Law of Slavery," *Chicago-Kent Law Review* 68, no. 3 (1993): 1051–86.
44. Uday Singh Mehta, *Liberalism and Empire: A Study in Nineteenth-Century British Liberal Thought*, 2nd ed. (Chicago: University of Chicago Press, 1999), 47, 52. Although I disagree with Mehta's argument that Locke's texts "have an effectively exclusionary thrust"—for I think the *Two Treatises on Government*, for example, must be read as distinct from the *Essay* in their treatment of personal and political identity—I value greatly his trenchant critique of liberal universalism. Long, *History of Jamaica*, 2.3.1:371.
45. *Bailey*, 27.
46. *Bailey*, 10.
47. *Bailey*, 20, 23.
48. *Bailey*, 26.
49. *Bailey*, 25. *Elder v. Elder's Executor*, 31 Va. 252 (1833); *Bailey*, 25.
50. Reviewed by the South's most prominent reviewer, and, later, professor of history, political economy, and international law at William and Mary College, George Frederick Holmes, in the *Southern Literary Messenger* 18 (December 1852), *Uncle Tom's Cabin* was widely read throughout the South. See "Uncle Tom's Cabin," *Southern Literary Messenger* 18 (December 1852): 721–31, in *Slavery Defended: The Views of the Old South*, ed. Eric L. McKitrick (Englewood Cliffs, NJ: Prentice-Hall, 1963), 99–111.
51. In *Race, Citizenship, and Law in American Literature* (New York: Cambridge University Press, 2002), 77–80, Gregg Crane argues for further exploration of the jurisprudential aims and results of Stowe's writing, quite rightly making the case for moving her literary efforts squarely "into the precincts of politics and law," which is the space the novel occupied and transformed when it appeared.
52. *Bailey*, 22.
53. *Bailey*, 35.
54. I thank the Virginia Historical Society for sending me biographical information on Moncure, as well as a copy of the catalog of books from Moncure's library, sold at auction April 3, 1883.
55. *Young v. Burton*, McMul. Eq. 255 WL 2598 (1841).

56. Chancery courts became crucial to the law. Though restitution of chattel or personal property in common law was rare, courts of chancery in their exercise of equitable jurisdiction sometimes compelled restitution of a specific chattel when it was of exceptional value. In "Building the Pyramid: The Growth and Development of the State Court System in Antebellum South Carolina, 1800–1860," *South Carolina Law Review* 24, no. 3 (1972): 357–79, Donald Senese traces the complex evolution of courts of equity along with the common-law courts of South Carolina.

57. *Summers v. Bean*, 54 Va. 404, 412 (1856); Morris, *Southern Slavery and the Law* 19; *Summers*, 410.

58. *Summers*, 410, 412; *Pearne v. Lisle*, 27 E.R. 47 (1749); *Summers*, 411 (quoting *Pearne*, 49). Judges Moncure and Daniel opposed each other in *Bailey*, in regard to the slave's capacity to make an election, but they agreed in *Summers*. What was it about the latter that brought together the conservative Daniel and liberal Moncure—one of the few cases in which they agreed?

59. *Bailey*, 9; *Summers*, 411, 412–13.

60. For a discussion of judicial rulings concerning chattel personal or real estate, see Morris, *Southern Slavery and the Law*, 77–80.

61. *Bailey*, 31.

62. *Bailey*, 35.

63. *Bailey*, 37, 35, 37.

64. *Bailey*, 35, 37.

65. *Bailey*, 38, 41, 37.

66. *Williamson v. Coalter*, 401, 397–98.

67. *Williamson*, 408.

68. Thomas Jefferson, *Notes on the State of Virginia*, 2nd American ed. (Philadelphia: Printed for M. Carey, 1797), 236.

CHAPTER 6. WHO GETS TO BE WANTON?

1. CBS Channel 5, San Francisco, "SF Honors Officers in Zoo Tiger Escape Shooting," February 4, 2009, http://cbs5.com/pets/tiger.mauling.officers .2.926929.html (accessed April 2010).

2. On inadequacy of the enclosure, see Carolyn Marshall, "Wall Isolating Tiger Habitat Is Shorter than Zoos Advise," *New York Times*, December 28, 2007.

3. Michael Taylor and Patricia Yollin, "San Francisco: Zoo Keeper Hurt in Tiger Attack," SFGate.com, December 23, 2006, http://www.sfgate.com/ cgi-bin/article.cgi?f=/c/a/2006/12/23/TIGER.TMP.

4. In November 2008, the Dhaliwal brothers followed up their initial filing with a new suit in federal court which accused city and zoo officials of defamation for suggesting the young men had provoked the tiger, in addition to a claim of negligence for the incident itself. For the criminal prosecutions of

Kulbir and Paul Dhaliwal, see Henry Lee, "2ⁿᵈ Brother Attacked by Tiger Is Sentenced," *San Francisco Chronicle*, December 11, 2008, http://articles .sfgate.com/2008-12-11/bay-area/17129909_1_kulbir-dhaliwal-christmas -day-tiger-attack-police-officer.

5. On the deodand and public spectacles of blame and sacrifice see Colin Dayan, "The Dogs," *Southwest Review* 88, nos. 2 and 3 (2003): 183–199.

6. Locke, *Essay*, 2.27.22:343–44.

7. On the definition and theory of *mens rea*, I still find the most useful, detailed analysis of its meaning from early to modern law is F. B. Sayre, "Mens Rea," *Harvard Law Review* 45, no. 6 (1932): 974–1021. In "The Origin of the Doctrine of Mens Rea," *Illinois Law Review* 17, no. 2 (1922–23): 117–37, 120, Albert Lévitt suggests that "the existence of the law of deodand is a beginning of our law of mens rea." John Wigmore in his three-part article, "Responsibility for Tortious Acts," *Harvard Law Review* 7, nos. 6–8 (1893–94), distinguishes contemporary law, "standing on a rational basis," from "the indiscriminate liability of primitive times … guided by superstition" (no. 6:314–16). Rather than simply affirming the "extremes" of rational and irrational, civilized and savage, however, he attempts to trace the transition from the "irrational spirit which pervaded the jural doings of primitive society," the "development in the realm of Agency" (no. 8:441) and, finally—through the precedents of 1300–1800 —to "make out *the subjective course of legal thought* in its progress towards the accepted standards of today" (emphasis, added, no. 8:442).

8. Coetzee, *Waiting for the Barbarians* (Boston: Penguin Books, 1982), 83.

9. See *The Story of Cruel and Unusual* for my analysis of the history of Eighth Amendment jurisprudence from slavery to imprisonment to the meaning of "torture" in the Bush administration's war on terror and the memos written to evade punishment for torture.

10. For the still-unsurpassed analysis of the adaptation of the "cruel and unusual" punishment clause to the exigencies of colonial America, see Anthony F. Granucci's "'Nor Cruel and Unusual Punishments Inflicted': The Original Meaning," *California Law Review* 57, no. 4 (1969): 839–65.

11. Conditions of confinement are my subject here, however, not the Supreme Court's progressive opinions on the death penalty (judging the execution of the retarded [*Atkins v. Virginia*, 536 U.S. 304 (2002)] and those under the age of eighteen at the time of their capital crime [*Roper v. Simmons*, 543 U.S. 551(2005)]). It is notable that the compelling evidence of torturous suffering during lethal injection due to the faulty three-drug protocol was not judged cruel and unusual in *Baze v. Rees* (128 S. Ct. 1520 [2008]). Chief Justice Roberts wrote the decision in words that resonate with the Bush lawyers' torture memos (August 1, 2002, and March 6, 2003): "[T]o constitute cruel and unusual punishment, an execution method must present a 'substantial risk of serious harm' or 'objectively intolerable risk of harm'" (*Baze*, 1531, quoting *Farmer v. Brennan*, 511 U.S. 825, 842, 846 [1994]). See especially the concurrences of Scalia and

Thomas for the invocation of past atrocities of a barbaric time as counter to the argument that lethal injection causes "excruciating pain" (*Baze*, 1561, Thomas, joined by Scalia), harrowing for the inmate though invisible to the witnesses. As Jeremy Waldron warns in "Torture and Positive Law: Jurisprudence for the White House," *Columbia Law Review* 105, no. 6 (2005): 1681–750, to define precisely the word "torture" is to be on a slippery slope of language where rituals of definition allow precisely those practices that such a search for meaning ostensibly is designed to prohibit.

12. State prisoners could not claim the protection of the Eighth Amendment until *Louisiana ex rel. Francis v. Resweber*, 329 U.S. 459 (1947). The Court clarified that the Fourteenth Amendment prohibited "by its due process clause execution by a state in a cruel manner" (463). But while procedural due process asks whether there is a liberty or property interest that has been interfered with by the state—and, if so, whether the procedures attendant upon the deprivation were constitutionally sufficient—it is the Eighth Amendment that gauges the seriousness of the violation. Treatment *during* detention is not met by the question of due process, since there remains the issue of how extreme are harsh or inhuman conditions. The extent of the deprivation of the formulaic "basic human needs" (*Rhodes v. Chapman*, 452 U.S. 337, 347 [1981]) is not my concern; rather, I am interested in how such a narrow definition of *human* ignores the disintegration of personal identity that occurs during incarceration.

13. *Jackson v. Bishop*, 404 F. 2d 571, 580 (1968).

14. *Hudson v. McMillian*, 503 U.S. 1, 13–14 (1992) (Blackmun concurring). Linda Greenhouse in *Becoming Justice Blackmun: Harry Blackmun's Supreme Court Journey* (New York: Times Books / Henry Holt, 2005) ignores Blackmun's concern with prisoners, and with conditions that are "potentially devastating to the human spirit," as Blackmun writes in his concurrence in *Farmer v. Brennan*, 511 U.S. 825, 853 (1994), the year he left the Supreme Court. Increasingly outspoken in his later years on the Court, he spoke powerfully against *Wilson v. Seiter*, 501 U.S. 294 (1991), arguing that the Court's "unduly narrow definition of punishment blinds it to the reality of prison life" (*Farmer v. Brennan*, 855).

15. *Trop v. Dulles*, 356 U.S. 86, 101, 100, 101, 102 (1958).

16. Hannah Arendt, *The Origins of Totalitarianism* (1951; repr., New York: Schocken Books, 2004), 355.

17. *Baze v. Rees*, 128 S.Ct. 1520, 1535 (2008).

18. Gary L. Francione, *Animals, Property, and the Law* (Philadelphia: Temple University Press, 1995), 4–5.

19. Oliver Wendell Holmes, Jr., *The Common Law* (1881; repr., New York: Dover, 1991), 215.

20. Throughout this analysis, I am in dialogue with Jeremy Waldron's "Inhuman and Degrading Treatment: A Non-Realist View," New York University Public Law Colloquium, New York, April 23, 2008, which takes seriously

my attention to terminology in *The Story of Cruel and Unusual* and acutely expands on it to include the meaning of the words "cruel, inhuman, or degrading" in the prohibitions of the Universal Declaration of Human Rights of 1948 and the International Covenant on Civil and Political Rights (ICCPR), 1976.

21. Pollock and Maitland, *History of English Law*, 2:475, 474.

22. Shakespeare, *Richard II*, 5.3:1–12; *Hamlet*, 3.4:165–70.

23. Scott Higham and Joe Stephens, "Punishment and Amusement: Documents Indicate 3 Photos Were Not Staged for Interrogation," *Washington Post*, May 22, 2004; Adam Liptak, Michael Moss, and Kate Zernike, "Accused G.I.'s Try to Shift Blame in Prison Abuse," *New York Times*, May 16, 2004.

24. *Louisiana ex rel. Francis v. Resweber*, 329 U.S. 459, 460, 464 (1947).

25. *Louisiana*, 463, 464, 463, 464.

26. The focus on terminology and the opacity of law language are crucial to the history of the common law. In *A Concise History of the Common Law*, 4th ed. (1929; repr., London: Butterworth, 1948), Theodore Plucknett memorably attests to the devious history of legal formulas in his discussion of "the very troublesome word 'malice'.... It is best regarded as a traditional form which only occasionally coincided with the natural meaning of the word" (419). If legal fictions fly in the face of fact, Plucknett argues that *legal forms*—better known as *terms of art*—have a life quite independent of what they ordinarily mean. Perhaps obvious, but what is most striking in his pages is how in early modern law, words were left to be vague and hoary, gaining force in their repetition and apparently profiting from their ambiguity.

27. Justice Thomas's concurrence in the *Baze v. Rees* (2008) judgment, joined by Scalia, exemplifies the return to a history of atrocity in order to reinvent the nature of suffering in the present. Thomas's focus on "historical practices" with old "tools" of intensifying death reads like a litany of horrors—disemboweling alive, burning at the stake, public dissection, to name just a few—and aims to prove the un-cruel and un-atrocious nature of lethal injection. What the pages and pages of examples do instead is to make us question the nature of "terror," reminding us of the inmate who suffers and not just the kind of punishments inflicted (*Baze*, 1556–57).

28. *Wilson v. Seiter*, 501 U.S. 294 (1991); *Rhodes v. Chapman*, 452 U.S. 337, 349, 347 (1981).

29. *Wilson*, 298 (quoting *Rhodes*, 347). *Duckworth v. Franzen*, 780 F.2d 645, 652 (7th Cir. 1985). *Wilson*, 300 (quoting *Duckworth*, 652).

30. *Wilson*, 300. In *The Story of Cruel and Unusual*, I analyze how the words themselves—from slavery and imprisonment to the torture memos of the Bush administration—in their combination of generality and emptiness ensure that old abuses continue, made legitimate by vague standards.

31. *Wilson*, 298, 302. *Whitley v. Alpers*, 475 U.S. 312 (1986). *Wilson*, 303.

32. *Estelle v. Gamble*, 429 U.S. 97, 106 (1976). *Farmer v. Brennan*, 511 U.S. 825, 835 (1994).

33. *Whitley*, 320, 327; *Wilson*, 302 (quoting *Whitley*, 320–21); *Wilson*, 302, 303, 297 (quoting *Gregg v. Georgia* 428 U.S. 153, 173 (1976) and quoting *Estelle* 106. The joint opinion in *Gregg v. Georgia*, which overturned *Furman v. Georgia*, 408 U.S. 238 (1972) and reinstated capital punishment, coined the phrase "unnecessary and wanton infliction of pain."

34. *Wilson*, 306, 310.

35. *Farmer v. Brennan*, 854, 857, 855, 853 (Blackmun concurring). The legal nonrecognition of mental or emotional injury due to prolonged detention in maximum security units is demonstrated in *Madrid v. Gomez*, 889 F. Supp. 1146 (1995), a case heard by Chief Judge Thelton Henderson in the United States District Court for the Northern District of California. Though Henderson admits that confinement in the special housing unit "may well hover on the edge of what is humanly tolerable for those with normal resilience," he held that such conditions remain within the limits of permissible pain for inmates not in the "specific population subgroups identified in this opinion" (1280). In *Wilkinson v. Austin*, 545 U.S. 209 (2005), the Supreme Court questioned whether the procedures used by the Ohio State Prison administrators to assign inmates to super–maximum security prison violate their constitutional right to due process. While the Court found that prisoners have a due process liberty interest in avoiding supermax placement, it upheld the written policy that includes annual review of such placement as comporting with due process. Most significantly, there is no substantive limitation on prison officials' ability to put prisoners in supermaxes in the first place.

36. Richard A. Posner, *The Problems of Jurisprudence* (Cambridge, MA: Harvard University Press, 1990), 168.

37. I thank Kathryn Schwarz for this definition of "wanton."

38. As former assistant attorney general Jay S. Bybee wrote at the beginning of what has become known as the Bybee memo (August 2002): "[C]ertain acts may be cruel, inhuman, or degrading, but still not produce pain and suffering of the requisite intensity to fall within ... [the] proscription against torture" (172). All references to these memos are to *The Torture Papers: The Road to Abu Ghraib*, ed. Karen J. Greenberg and Joshua L. Dratel (Cambridge: Cambridge University Press, 2005): 172–218, 241–86.

39. See especially the recent "Current Conditions of Confinement at Guantánamo: Still in Violation of the Law," Center for Constitutional Rights, February 23, 2009, http://ccrjustice.org/files/CCR_Report_Conditions _At_Guantanamo.pdf; Jamil Dakwar, "Pentagon Report Whitewashes Gitmo Abuses," Human Rights Program at ACLU, February 24, 2009, http://blog.aclu.org/2009/02/24/pentagon-report-whitewashes-abuses -at-gitmo/; Mark Danner's ongoing revelations in "Tales from Torture's Dark World," *New York Times*, March 15, 2009, http://www.nytimes.com/ 2009/03/15/opinion/15danner.html?_r=1&pagewanted=print; and "US Torture: Voices from the Black Sites," *New York Review of Books*, April 9, 2009, 69–77. For the earlier reports, see ACLU, "Enduring Abuse: Torture

and Cruel Treatment by the United States at Home and Abroad," http://
www.aclu.org/safefree/torture/25354pub20060427.html; Center for Constitutional Rights, "Report on Torture and Cruel, Inhuman, and Degrading
Treatment of Prisoners at Guantánamo Bay, Cuba," July 2006, http://
ccrjustice.org/files/Report_Report OnTorture.pdf; Human Rights Watch,
"Supplemental Submission to the Committee Against Torture," June 2006,
http://www.hrw.org/en/news/2006/05/03/human-rights-watch-supple
mental-submission-committee-against-torture. Amnesty International's
report, "United States of America: Updated Briefing to the Human Rights
Committee on the Implementation of the International Covenant on Civil
and Political Rights," can be found at http://www.amnestyusa.org/document.
php?id=ENGAMR511112006&lang. The revelations of complicity with torture in high places continue. See "Lawyers Agreed on the Legality of Brutal
Tactic," *New York Times*, June 7, 2009, which shows how none of the Justice
Department lawyers—including Jack Goldsmith—who reviewed the legality of torturous interrogation argued that the methods were clearly illegal.
Instead, they acquiesced in water boarding and other harsh practices.

40. The Bybee memo (August 2002) redefines torture as the intentional infliction of severe physical pain "equivalent in intensity to the pain accompanying serious physical injury, such as organ failure, impairment of
bodily function, or even death" (172), or severe mental pain which pro-
duces "lasting, though not necessarily permanent, damage. For example ...
the development of a mental disorder such as posttraumatic stress disorder, which can last months or even years, or even chronic depression,
which also can last for a considerable period of time if untreated" (177).
It distinguishes torture from "cruel, inhuman, or degrading treatment or
punishment" (172) and insists that an interrogator must have the "specific
intent" (174) to cause such severe pain in order for his or her methods to
be defined as torture. See Jeremy Waldron, "Torture and Positive Law:
Jurisprudence for the White House," *Columbia Law Review* 105, no. 6
(2005): 1701.

41. The *New York Times* guide to the memos is available at http://www.ny
times.com/ref/international/24MEMO-GUIDE.html?scp=1&sq=torture
%20memos&st=cse. The best edition of the torture memos, as well as the
full texts of the legal memoranda that sought to redefine what constituted
torture—what Anthony Lewis in his introduction called "an extraordinary
paper trail to moral and political disaster" (xiii)—is Greenberg and Dratel's *The Torture Papers*, which I use here; see also Mark Danner, *Torture
and Truth: America, Abu Ghraib, and the War on Terror* (New York: New
York Review of Books, 2004); and Sanford Levinson, ed., *Torture: A Collection* (New York: Oxford University Press, 2004).

42. Bybee memo, August 2002, 174–75.

43. Pentagon memo, March 2003, 245–46. The two "torture memos" were later
withdrawn from operational use after they became public. See my discus-

sion of the memo repudiating and replacing the previous memos, the memorandum "for James B. Comey, Deputy Attorney General" (December 30,
2004), written by Daniel Levin, the head of the Justice Department's office
of legal counsel, in *The Story of Cruel and Unusual*, 82–84. The forms of
"extreme conduct" enumerated in the Levin memorandum lie, as I say, "at
the outer limits of the barbarous. Any lesser atrocity is permitted."

44. See Pentagon memo, March 2003, 268–71.
45. Bybee memo, August 2002, 173, 176–77 and Pentagon memo, March
2003, 244, 247–48. Torture is defined in the Convention Against Torture
and Other Cruel, Inhuman, or Degrading Treatment or Punishment as
"any act by which severe pain or suffering, whether physical or mental, is
intentionally inflicted on a person" in order to extract information or a
confession. Terms such as *torture, inhuman*, and *degrading treatment or
punishment*, though sometimes thought to be placed in a hierarchy, are
interlinked in Article 3 of the European Convention for the Protection of
Human Rights and Fundamental Freedoms, which prohibits in absolute
terms torture or inhuman or degrading treatment or punishment. Intention is irrelevant to the prohibition. See John Cooper, *Cruelty: An Analysis
of Article 3* (London: Sweet and Maxwell, 2003).
46. Pentagon memo, March 2003, 243. For my extended discussion of the
reliance of the United States government on the delimitation of the Eighth
Amendment and its reservation to Article 16 (the prohibition against
"acts of cruel, inhuman or degrading treatment or punishment") of the
United Nations Convention Against Torture (UNCAT) and the appearance of Secretary of State Condoleezza Rice's legal adviser John B. Bell-
inger III before UNCAT on May 5 and May 8, 2006, where he again insists
on the reservation, see Dayan, *The Story of Cruel and Unusual*, 65–85.
47. The text of the report can be found at http://www2.ohchr.org/english/
bodies/hrc/docs/ngos/woflu.pdf.
48. On February 19, 2010, the Department of Justice released the Office of
Professional Responsibility's report on whether government lawyers who
wrote two Office of Legal Counsel memos in 2002 violated professional
ethics. The 260-page OPR report harshly condemns the torture memos
and recommends discipline for the lawyers who wrote them. But senior
DoJ attorney David Margolis rejected the office's recommendations; and
in a sixty-nine-page memo, he excused John Yoo and Jay S. Bybee, noting
that after the scare of 9/11, they wrote in a hurry and exercised "poor
judgment," so "these memos contain some significant flaws." The bars of
which these lawyers are members have so far refrained from acting.
49. Editorial, "Rushing Off a Cliff," *New York Times*, September 28, 2006.
50. Locke, *Essay*, 3:10:131.
51. *Hudson v. McMillian*, 929 F. 2d 1014, 1015 (5th Cir. 1990).
52. *Hudson v. McMillian*, 503 U.S. 1, 9 (1992).
53. *Hudson*, 21, 26, 21, 18 (Thomas, joined by Scalia, dissenting).

54. G. Edward White in *Tort Law in America: An Intellectual History* (1980; repr., New York: Oxford University Press, 2003), opens his book by announcing: "Torts was not considered a discrete branch of law until the late nineteenth century. The first American treatise on Torts appeared in 1859; Torts was first taught as a separate law school subject in 1870; the first Torts casebook was published in 1874"(3). "'Tortious' wrongs were, in their early history, merely wrongs not arising out of contract and giving rise to civil liability" (14). There is disagreement about the origin of crime and tort and the relationship between them: it depends on how one defines criminal law. If defined as a law that imposes a fine or punishment, this is not distinct from wrongs, broadly defined. If, however, criminal law is defined as imposed by the state or society at large, this is a later development. See, especially, John H. Wigmore, "Responsibility for Tortious Acts," *Harvard Law Review* 7, nos. 6–8 (1893–94): 315–43, 383–405, 441–63; and Paul Hyams, "Does It Matter When the English Began to Distinguish between Crime and Tort?" in *Violence in Medieval Society*, ed. Richard W. Kaeuper (Woodbridge, Suffolk: Boydell Press, 2000), 107–29. On torts generally, see Holmes, *Common Law*, 77–163; Frederick Pollock, *The Law of Torts: A Treatise on the Principles Arising from Civil Wrongs in the Common Law* (1886; repr., Philadelphia: Blackstone, 1887); Plucknett, *Concise History of the Common Law*, 397–99, 428–34; Lawrence Friedman, *History of American Law* (New York: Simon and Schuster, 1973), 410, 428–34; Morton Horwitz, *The Transformation of American Law, 1870–1960*, vol. 2 (New York: Oxford University Press, 1992); and more recently, Barbara Welke's extraordinary *Recasting American Liberty: Gender, Race, Law, and the Railroad Revolution, 1865–1920* (New York: Cambridge University Press, 2001).

55. In *Ancient Law: Its Connection with the Early History of Society and Its Relation to Modern Ideas* (1861; repr., Boston: Beacon Press, 1963), Henry Sumner Maine explains that "the penal Law of ancient communities is not the law of Crimes," but "the law of Wrongs, or, to use the English technical word, of Torts." Although, he says, the person not the state is addressed as the object of wrong, "it is not to be supposed that a conception so simple and elementary as that of wrong done to the State was wanting in any primitive society." For the fascinating elucidation of the "ancient conception of crime," see Maine, *Ancient Law*, 359–62. Joseph W. Glannon in *The Law of Torts*, 3rd ed. (New York: Aspen, 2005), 74–76, in discussing the "fictitious construct" of the reasonable person, discusses the refusal to consider individual personality in the judgment of the mentally ill, who are held to the same standard as everyone else.

56. Holmes, *Common Law*, 108.

57. *Moses Trauerman v. M.V. Lippincott*, 39 Mo. App. 478, 488 (1890); Holmes, *Common Law*, 79, 110. In civil action, as opposed to criminal, fault was not generally equated with the subjective intent to cause harm.

58. In *The Hidden Holmes: His Theory of Torts in History* (Cambridge, MA: Harvard University Press, 1995), 4, David Rosenberg argues against the description of Holmes as a legal formalist who favored a universal negligence rule instead of strict liability, which protected damages done by industry. In *History of American Law,* Friedman explains that though new tort law in the Gilded Age favored industry over workers, as sympathy for labor increased, tort law was "never a perfect engine of oppression" (416–17).

59. White, *Tort Law in America,* 291–92.

60. Plucknett, *Concise History of the Common Law,* 422. Holmes, *Common Law,* 22–23. See also Thomas Chambers, *A Course of Lectures on the English Law, 1767–1773,* ed. Thomas M. Curley, 2 vols. (Oxford: Clarendon Press, 1987), 2:190, for a discussion of the "several gradations" of animals as property: "some being naturally more susceptible of appropriation than others."

61. W. M. Geldart, *Elements of English Law* (1911; repr., Oxford: Oxford University Press, 1938), 168.

62. See Restatement, 2nd, Torts 507, 509, 6 Witkin Summary of California Law, ch. 9, sec. 1403, quoted in Geragos's letter to Dennis Harara and James Hannawalt, Office of the City Attorney, January 6, 2008. On May 29, 2009, the San Francisco Zoo resolved the Dhaliwal brothers' claims against the city, the zoo, and Sam Singer, the public relations spokesperson. The Dhaliwals were awarded $900,000.

CHAPTER 7. SKIN OF THE DOG

1. Blackstone, *Commentaries,* 4:236.

2. *Filow's* case, Year Book, Trinity Term, 12 Henry VIII, plea number 3, trans. Theodore W. Dwight in *The Columbia Jurist 2,* no. 23 (March 4, 1886): 266–68, and cited in Glanville L. Williams, *Liability for Animals: An Account of the Development and Present Law of Tortious Liability for Animals, Distress Damage Feasant and The Duty to Fence, In Great Britain, Northern Ireland and the Common Law Dominions* (Cambridge: Cambridge University Press, 1939), 138–40, and 138, n. 7. *Filow's* case also available at Boston University School of Law, "Legal History: The Year Books; Report #1520.003ss." http://www.bu.edu/phpbin/lawyearbooks/display.php?id =22103. See also Theodore William Dwight, *Commentaries on the Law of Persons and Personal Property,* ed. Edward F. Dwight (Boston: Little, Brown, 1894), 450 n. 3.

3. *Filow,* trans. Dwight, 267, 268. In the First Treatise [1680] of his *Two Treatises of Government,* ed. Peter Laslett (1689; repr., Cambridge: Cambridge University Press, 1988), 9.92:209, Locke includes animate beings—animals—as the first item in his list of kinds of personal property; indeed, the "original" property right is the "right a man has to use any of the inferior creatures, for the subsistence and comfort of his life."

4. Plucknett, *Concise History of the Common Law*, 443.
5. Williams, *Liability for Animals*, 140. See also Chambers, *A Course of Lectures on the English Law, 1767–1773* (Oxford: Clarendon Press, 1986), 2 vols., 2.3.15:190–91.
6. *Hamby v. Samson*, 105 Iowa 112 (1898).
7. *Bailey v. Poindexter*, 55 Va. 132, 23 (1858).
8. *Findlay v. Bear*, 8 Serg. & Rawle 571, 1 (1822), available at 1822 WL 1966, 1.
9. *Avery v. Everett* 110 N.Y. 317 (1888). *Mullaly v. The People of the State of New York* 86 N.Y. 365, 367, 368 (1881).
10. *Hamby v. Samson*, 105 Iowa 112, 115 (1898). Deemer's recognition of dogs as chattels refers to the opinion in *Commonwealth v. Hazelwood*, 84 Ky. 681 (1887) in the Court of Appeals of Kentucky, which recognized dogs as chattel and therefore the subject of larceny.
11. *Mullaly*, 367.
12. Since 2007, Arpaio's no-kill animal shelter, MASH, has housed and cared for animals that have been abused or neglected by their caretakers. Rescued by the Animal Cruelty Investigative Unit and taken to what was once the First Avenue Jail, the dogs and cats are fed and cared for by prisoners. Lindsay Isaacs, "Q&A: Unorthodox Management Defines Maricopa Jail," *American City and County*, October 1, 2001, http://americancity andcounty.com/mag/government_qaunorthodox_management_defines/: "It costs $1.15 a day to feed the dogs and only forty cents a day to feed the inmates, but that's the way it goes around here."

    Arpaio's kindness to animals contrasts with his brutal treatment of prisoners. From 2004 through November 2007, he was the target of 2,150 lawsuits in U.S. District Court. See John Dickerson, "Inhumanity Has a Price," *Phoenix New Times*, December 20, 2007, http://www.phoenixnew times.com/2007-12-20/news/inhumanity-has-a-price/1. The harsh treatment of pretrial detainees and the injuries and deaths in Arpaio's jails have been criticized by the ACLU and Amnesty International. See "Ill-Treatment of Inmates in Maricopa County Jails, Arizona," Amnesty International, August 1, 1997, http://web.amnesty.org/library/index/engAMR 510511997?open&of=eng-2am. See my early account of Arpaio's packaging of spectacles of punishment and his depersonalization through terror, as well as an account of my visits to Phoenix and interviews with him in 1995 and 1996 in "From the Plantation to the Penitentiary: Chain, Classification, and Codes of Deterrence," in Doris Y. Kadish, ed., *Slavery in the Caribbean Francophone World: Distant Voices, Forgotten Acts, Forged Identities* (Athens: University of Georgia Press, 2000), 198–208. See also William Finnegan's profile, "Sheriff Joe," *New Yorker*, July 20, 2009, 42–48.
13. See "Abu Ghraib Dog Use 'Lacked Rules,'" *BBC News*, March 16, 2006, http://news.bbc.co.uk/l/hi/world/americas/4812366.stm; Peter Spiegel, "General Testifies at Abu Ghraib Trial," *Latimes.com*, May 25, 2006, http:// articles.latimes.com/2006/ma/25/nation/na-abuse25; Eric Schmitt, "Army

Dog Handler Is Convicted in Detainee Abuse at Abu Ghraib," *New York Times*, March 22, 2006. See also Thom Shanker, "General in Abu Ghraib Case Retires after Forced Delay," *New York Times*, August 1, 2006.

14. "Cruel and Degrading: The Use of Dogs for Cell Extractions in U.S. Prisons," Human Rights Watch, October 2006. Also at the Human Rights Watch website, see "How Dogs Are Used in Cell Extractions," http://hrw.org/reports/2006/us1006/3.htm; "Policy and Practice in Seven States," http://hrw.org/reports/2006/us1006/4.htm; "Views of Corrections Professionals and Experts," http://hrw.org/reports/2006/us1006/5.htm; "Standards Governing Use of Force in Prisons," http://hrw.org/reports/2006/us1006/6.htm. In March 2006, the new director of the Arizona Department of Corrections, Dora Schriro, prohibited the practice of using dogs for cell extractions. The Arizona training video is no longer available on the web. Conversation (name withheld), May 28, 1998.

15. *Wiley v. Slater*, 22 Barb. 506 n.p. (1856).

16. *State v. Langford*, 55 S.C. 322, 324 (1899). In this light, dogs are seen as *ferae naturae* like tigers, who are not considered subjects of property until they are killed or subdued.

17. *Citizens' Rapid Transit Co. v. Dew*, 100 Tenn. 317, 319 (1898).

18. *Citizens' Rapid Transit Co. v. Dew*, 323–24, 326, 327, 324. See also *McCallister v. Sappingfield*, 72 Ore. 422 (1914).

19. *Bradford v. McKibben*, 67 Ky. 545 (1868). In *Commonwealth v. Markham*, 70 Ky. 486, 487 (1870), an owner was forced to pay a fine for the lack of "a brass collar, duly stamped" on a dog, who, ultimately, was executed. At the turn of the century, many states authorized "any person to kill a dog which had no collar on, even though licensed" (*Fox v. Mohawk and Hudson River Humane Society*, 165 N.Y. 517, 521 [1901]), referring to *Morewood v. Wakefield*, 133 Mass. 240 (1882); see also *Morey v. Brown*, 42 N.H. 373 (1861); *Tenney v. Lenz*, 16 Wis. 566 (1863); *Mitchell v. Williams*, 27 Ind. 62 (1866); *Ex parte Cooper*, 3 Tex. App. 489 (1878); and *Jenkins v. Ballantyne* 8 Utah 245 (1892).

20. *Street v. Tugwell* (1800) 2 Selw. N.P. (9th ed. 1838) 1138; *Brill v. Flagler*, 23 Wend. 354, 357, 359 (1840).

21. *Putnam v. Payne*, 13 Johns. 312, 313 (1816). *Brown v. Carpenter*, 26 Vt. 638, 642, 643 (1854). *Bradford v. McKibben*, 546.

22. *Woolf v. Chalker*, 31 Conn. 121, 131, 130, 129 (1862).

23. "Dogs Must Be Respected: Justice Gaynor Rules That They Are Property," *New York Times*, September 2, 1894, discusses the case *The People ex rel. Shand v. Tighe* 9 Misc. 607 (1894).

24. Henry Mann, "William Jay Gaynor as an Intimate Knew Him: The Lawyer, the Judge, the Mayor, and the Man, Described by a Noted Editor-Author Whose Friendship with Him Covered a Long Period," *New York Times*, September 21, 1913; C. J. Sullivan, "William Jay Gaynor, NYC Mayor 1910 to 1913, Has Been Forgotten, Along with His Statue," *New York Press*, July 24, 2001, http://www.nypress.com/article-4511-william

-jay-gaynor-nyc-mayor-1910-to-1913-has-been-forgotten-along-with
-his-statue.html.; The Bowery Boys: New York City History, "Know Your
Mayors: William Jay Gaynor," March 4, 2008, http://theboweryboys.blog
spot.com/2008/03/know-your-mayors-william-jay-gaynor.html.

25. Lately Thomas, *The Mayor Who Mastered New York: The Life and Opinions of William J. Gaynor* (New York: William Morrow, 1969), 92–95.

26. *The People ex rel. Shand v. Tighe*, 9 Misc. 607, 608, 609 (1894).

27. *People v. Tighe*, 609, 610.

28. *Fox v. Mohawk and Hudson River Humane Society*, 165 N.Y. 517 (1901). This extraordinary sequence of cases—from the Supreme Court of New York, Albany County (trial court), to the Supreme Court, Appellate Division, New York (intermediate court), to Court of Appeals of New York (high court)—tests a group of dog owners' right to due process, as well as the right of a private corporation to exercise the power of taxation and dispose of those owners' canine property without due process of law. *Fox v. Mohawk and Hudson River Humane Society* (March 1897); *Fox v. Mohawk and Hudson River Humane Society* (January 1898); *Fox v. Mohawk and Hudson River Humane Society* (February 1901).

29. Vicki Hearne, *Bandit: The Heart-Warming True Story of One Dog's Rescue from Death Row* (1991; repr., New York: Skyhorse, 2007), 159. See also Colin Dayan, "Dead Dogs: Breed Bans, Euthanasia, and Preemptive Justice," *Boston Review*, March–April 2010.

30. James Serpell, ed., *The Domestic Dog: Its Evolution, Behaviour and Interactions with People* (Cambridge: Cambridge University Press, 1995), 254.

31. Matthew Henry, *Commentary on the Whole Bible*, 6 vols. (1828; repr., Peabody, MA: Hendrickson, 1991), 5:177–78.

32. I am indebted here to Elliott Horowitz's review essay, "Circumcised Dogs from Matthew to Marlowe," *Prooftexts* 27, no. 3 (2007): 531–45.

33. Herman Melville, "The Encantadas, or Enchanted Isles," in *Piazza Tales*, 148–49, 160–62.

34. See White, *Myths of the Dog-Man*, 51–53 and 59, for a discussion of these dog warriors, as well as others. For an account of the dogs' arrival in Saint-Domingue, see Thomas Madiou, *Histoire d'Haiti (1492–1846)*, 8 vols. (Port-au-Prince: Editions Henri Deschamps, 1989), 2:506; and Beaubrun Ardouin, *Etudes sur l'histoire d'Haïti*, 2nd ed. (1853–60; repr., Port-au-Prince: Chez l'éditeur, Francois Dalencour, 1958), 5:84–85. See Sir James Barskett, *History of St. Domingo* (London: Frank Cass, 1972), for his account of the bloodhounds the French were forced to eat in the last months of 1803.

35. J. M. Coetzee, *Disgrace* (New York: Penguin Books, 1999), 205, 220.

36. Oliver Wendell Holmes, "Primitive Notions in Modern Law," no. 1 (1876) in *The Collected Works of Justice Holmes: Complete Public Writings and Selected Judicial Opinions of Oliver Wendell Holmes*, ed. Sheldon M. Novick (Chicago: University of Chicago Press, 1995), 3:10.

37. Wigmore, "Responsibility for Tortious Acts," 316–17, part 1 of three-part article; Holmes, *Common Law*, 5.

38. Frederick Lupton, *The Law Relating to Dogs* (London: Stevens and Sons, 119 Chancery Lane, 1888), 4–5, 7–13. The Dog Act of 1865 (28 & 29 Vict. C. 60), held the owner strictly liable for injury to sheep and cattle, but not to humans.

39. Williams, *Liability for Animals*, 273.

40. *Woolf v. Chalker*, 127, 128, 129.

41. Cobb, *Inquiry into the Law of Negro Slavery*, 107.

42. See Wagner, *Disturbing the Peace*, 7–20. The "police power," as Wagner argues, was coined by Chief Justice John Marshall in *Brown v. Maryland*, 25 U.S. 419 (1827), but was critically delineated in *Mayor, Alderman, and State of New York v. Miln*, 36 U.S. 102 (1837), and *Commonwealth v. Alger*, 61 Mass. 53 (1851). For a discussion of how the legal definition of police power increased in the late nineteenth century as state governments regulated a great number of public institutions, see Gary Gerstle, "The Resilient Power of the States Across the Long Nineteenth Century: An Inquiry into a Pattern of American Governance," in *The Unsustainable American State* (New York: Oxford University Press, 2009), 61–88.

43. *Carter v. Dow*, 16 Wisc. 298, 303 (1862); *McGlone v. Womack &c.*, 129 Ky. 274, 277, 284 (1908).

44. Lord Cockburn in the Scottish appeal of *Fleeming v. Orr*, 2 Macq. 14 (1855). Most dangerous-dog laws are local, and they differ significantly from state to state.

45. Lord Cranworth in *Fleeming v. Orr*, discussed in E.O.S., "Injuries by Domestic Animals," *Journal of the Society of Comparative Legislation* 1, no. 1 (March 1899): 54–61, 57–58.

46. Although a majority of states have some form of strict liability rule for harm caused by pet dogs, not all states have eliminated the scienter doctrine, or some modern version of it. See J. Hoult Verkerke, "Notice Liability in Employment Discrimination Law," *Virginia Law Review* 81, no. 21 (1995): 278 n. 10. Approximately thirty-four states and the District of Columbia apply the strict liability standard for dog bites or other personal injury done by dogs. See Animal Legal and Historical Center at Michigan State University College of Law, "Quick Overview of Dog Bite Strict Liability Statutes," http://www.animallaw.info/articles/qvusdogbiteslstatutes.htm.

47. Nathan Isaacs, "Fault and Liability: Two Views of Legal Development," *Harvard Law Review* 31, no. 7 (1918): 961. Melville M. Bigelow, *Leading Cases on the Law of Torts: Determined by the Courts of America and England* (Boston: Little, Brown, 1875), 491. These states alone maintain the "one-bite rule": Alaska, Arkansas, Colorado, Delaware, Georgia, Idaho, Kansas, Maryland, Mississippi, Missouri, Nevada, New Mexico, New York, North Carolina, North Dakota, Oregon, South Dakota, Tennessee, Texas, Vermont,

Virginia, and Wyoming. See Mary Randolph, *Every Dog's Legal Guide: A Must-Have Book for Your Owner*, 6th ed. (Berkeley, CA: Nolo, 2007), 235.

48. Nathan Isaacs, "Fault and Liability," 961 and 961 n. 15. See also Wigmore, "Responsibility for Tortious Acts," part 1, 325–26; Bigelow, *Leading Cases on the Law of Torts*, 491. Some legal historians have argued that no one in Anglo-Saxon times would have thought a dog worth even six shillings. "A choice between giving up the animal and paying for its damage would thus have been no choice at all." So Alfred's largesse was moot.

49. Williams, *Liability for Animals*, 271–73. Isaacs, "Fault and Liability," 961 n. 5. Ewald, "What Was It Like to Try a Rat?" 1889–2149, 1915, esp. 1891–975. See Piers Beirne, "The Law Is an Ass: Reading E. P. Evans, 'The Medieval Prosecution and Capital Punishment of Animals,'" *Society and Animals: Journal of Human-Animal Studies* 2, no. 1 (1994): 27–46; Marilyn Katz, "Ox-Slaughter and Goring Oxen: Homicide, Animal Sacrifice, and Judicial Process," *Yale Journal of Law and the Humanities* 4, no. 2 (Summer 1992): 249–78; Jen Girgen, "The Historical and Contemporary Prosecution and Punishment of Animals," *Animal Law* 9 (2003): 97–133, part 3, 122–33.

50. *Civil Rights Cases*, 109 U.S. 3, 25, 37 (Harlan dissenting), 24 (1883).

51. *Sentell v. New Orleans and Carrollton Railroad Company*, 166 U.S. 698, 700 (1897).

52. *Plessy v. Ferguson*, 163 U.S. 537, 551 (1896).

53. Rebecca J. Scott, "The Atlantic World and the Road to *Plessy v. Ferguson*," *Journal of American History* 94, no. 3 (December 2007): 726–33, 731. For Scott's later analysis, see "Public Rights, Social Equality, and the Conceptual Roots of the *Plessy* Challenge," *Michigan Law Review* 106, no. 5 (March 2008):777–804, 800: "The language of the majority decision thus incorporated a key tenet of white supremacist ideology—the sleight of hand through which *public rights* were re-characterized as importunate *social claims*." For two other recent analyses of the legal discrimination of *Plessy v. Ferguson*, see Saidiya Hartman, *Scenes of Subjection: Terror, Slavery, and Self-Making in Nineteenth-Century America* (New York: Oxford University Press, 1997), 193–26; and Barbara Young Welke's analysis of *Plessy* within the ever-widening law of racial segregation and railroads in *Recasting American Liberty: Gender, Race, Law, and the Railroad Revolution, 1865–1920* (New York: Cambridge University Press, 2001), 323–75.

54. *Sentell v. New Orleans and Carrollton Railroad Company* (decided April 26, 1897), 700, 705. The quotations are also taken from the transcript of record, Supreme Court of the United States, October term, 1896, with briefs for defendant and plaintiff in *U.S. Supreme Court Records and Briefs*. Act 107 is the Rev. St. La. § 1201 as amended July 5, 1882.

55. *Sentell* (decided April 26, 1897), 700. After the passage of the Fourteenth Amendment (1868), cases such as *Slaughter-House* (1873) and *The Civil*

Rights Cases (1883) whittled away at due process by attacking equal access to "life, liberty, or property."

56. *Sentell*, 706, 705, 701.
57. *Sentell*, 701, 703.
58. *Sentell*, 704, 705.
59. *Sentell*, 702. See *Ruffin v. Commonwealth*, 62 Va. 790 (1871).
60. Wagner, *Disturbing the Peace*, 20.
61. West Virginia Bar Association, Executive Council, "The Legal Disabilities of Dogs," *West Virginia Bar Association* 4, no. 7 (1897): 131. Opening the discussion of the case with "On Monday the Supreme Court of the United States gave a decision... ," the report bears the date 1896, presumably a misprint.
62. Alexander Nékám in *The Personality Conception of the Legal Entity* (Cambridge, MA: Harvard University Press, 1938), 9–10, 25–26, discusses how anything "can become a subject—a potential center—of rights, whether a plant or an animal, a human being or an imagined spirit" (29). He should be read in conjunction with Christopher Stone's "Should Trees Have Legal Standing?" in *Should Trees Have Standing? And Other Essays on Law, Morals and the Environment* (Dobbs Ferry, New York: Oceana, 1996), 1–49.
63. *Sentell*, 705–6.
64. Nékám, *Personality Conception*, 10, 26.
65. *La Porte v. Associated Independents, Inc.*, 163. So. 2d 267, 269 (1964). The phrase "sentimental property" is coined in El Tribunal Supremo de Puerto Rico in *Infante v. Leith*, 85 D.P.R. 26 (1962), a particularly gruesome case of dogs in Puerto Rico seized from their owners and thrown off bridges to their deaths. In "The Legal Status of Animals Under Animal Welfare Law," *Environmental and Planning Law Journal* 9 (February 1992): 20–30, Philip Jamieson describes the excess of care as oblivious to the suffering or death of the animal while privileging the human: attending either to the "guilty mind" of the offender or to the monetary loss and mental distress of the master. On drugged cats and dogs, see James Vlahos, "Pill-Popping Pets," *New York Times Magazine*, July 13, 2008, 38–45, 54. On legal responses to such anthropomorphic biases, see Lynn A. Epstein, "Resolving Confusion in Pet Owner Tort Cases: Recognizing Pets' Anthropomorphic Qualities Under a Property Classification," *Southern Illinois University Law Journal* 26, no. 1 (Fall 2001): 31–52; Jerrold Tannenbaum, "Animals and the Law: Property, Cruelty, Rights," *Social Research* 62, no. 3 (Fall 1995): 539–607; Eric W. Neilsen, "Is the Law of Acquisition of Property by Find Going to the Dogs?" *Thomas M. Cooley Law Review* 15 (1998): 479–516. See also the Animal Welfare Act at U.S. Department of Agriculture, National Agricultural Library, http://www.nal.usda.gov/awic/legislat/awa.htm. For a daring redefinition of "[c]ompassionate action" and the "category making and unmaking" at stake in claiming dogs as "companions," see Donna J.

Haraway, *When Species Meet* (Minneapolis: University of Minnesota Press, 2008).

66. *Corso v. Crawford Dog and Cat Hospital,* 97 Misc. 2d 530, 531 (1979).

67. In 2005, Denver reinstated its pit bull ban. See "Denver's pit bull ban roils owners," *The Christian Science Monitor,* July 17, 2005. See also *Colorado Dog Fanciers, Inc. v. City and County of Denver,* 820 P.2d 644 (1991). In "The New Breed of Municipal Dog Control Laws: Are They Constitutional?" *University of Cincinnati Law Review* 53, no. 4 (1984): 1067–82, Lynn Marmer discusses the unconstitutionally vague pit bull ordinances and questions whether the passage of canine control laws is "a constitutionally legitimate exercise of a city's police power to protect the public's safety and welfare" (1067). Numerous pit bull owners tried to save their dogs from breed bans, and Vicki Hearne's experience following her rescue of Bandit is just one example of how the police and legislative ordinances single out not only the dogs but their owners as well—usually suspect because of race, ethnicity, or poverty—for vilification and harassment. In 1989, the U.S. District Court for the Southern District of Ohio in *Vanater v. Village of South Point,* 717 F. Supp. 1236, referred to *Sentell* and reaffirmed its discrimination based on the language of scientific racism: "The Court finds that the Ordinance is a reasonable response to the special threat presented by the Pit Bull dog breed based upon their phenotypical characteristics and the traits which have been bred into the breed by their owners" (1243). The ban against pit bulls and all manner of dogs randomly included in this designation continues. In January 2008, Responsible Owners of Arkansas Dogs (ROADS) filed a constitutional challenge in federal court against ordinances that regulate pit bulls, in this case in four Arkansas cities, described in a chilling website: DogsBite.org: Some Dogs Don't Let Go, at http://www.dogsbite.org/blog/2008/01/arkansas -group-appeals-to-federal-court.html.

68. There are some legal exceptions to dog bites and the death penalty. In *Phillips v. San Luis Obispo County Department of Animal Regulation,* 183 Cal. App. 3d 372 (1986), a court of appeal of California reversed the lower court and ruled that Missy—a black Labrador who had bitten at least three children—should not be destroyed, since owners had not been given notice and a hearing. The court declared that Missy "shall live and 'go out in the midday sun'" (374). For a sampling of Internet coverage of "Zero Tolerance: Dog Bites," see http://www.dogbitelaw.com/PAGES/ danger.htm and http://www.dogbitelaw.com/PAGES/crim.html.

69. W.E.B. DuBois, "The Black Code of Georgia," an exhibition at the Exposition Universelle, Paris, April 15–November 12, 1900; George P. Rawick, ed., "Elisha Doc Garey, Ex-Slave in Georgia, Age 76," in *The American Slave: A Composite Autobiography,* vol. 12 (1941; repr., Westport, CT: Greenwood, 1972). See also William Goodell, *The American Slave Code in Theory and Practice* (New York: American and Foreign Anti-Slavery Society, 1853), 237.

BIBLIOGRAPHY

CASES

Atkins v. Virginia, 536 U.S. 304 (2002)
Avery v. Everett, 110 N.Y. 317 (1888)
Bailey v. Poindexter's Executor, 55 Va. 132 (1858)
Banks v. Beard, 399 F.3d 134 (2005)
Baze v. Rees, 553 U.S. 35 (2008)
Beard v. Banks, 548 U.S. 521 (2006)
Bell v. Wolfish, 441 U.S. 520 (1979)
Boyce v. Anderson, 27 U.S. 150 (1829)
Bradford v. McKibben, 67 Ky. 545 (1868)
Brill v. Flagler, 23 Wend. 354 (1840)
Brown v. Carpenter, 26 Vt. 638 (1854)
Bryan v. Walton, 14 Ga. 185 (1853)
Burchill v. Hermsmeyer, 212 Tex. Civ. A. S.W. 767 (1919)
Carnahan v. Hamilton, 265 Ill. 508 (1914)
Carter v. Dow, 16 Wisc. 298 (1862)
Citizens' Rapid Transit Co. v. Dew, 100 Tenn. 317 (1898)
Civil Rights Cases, 109 U.S. 3 (1883)
Colorado Dog Fanciers, Inc. v. City and County of Denver, 820 P.2d 644 (1991)
Commonwealth v. Alger, 61 Mass. 53 (1851)
Commonwealth v. Hazelwood, 84 Ky. 681; 2 S.W. 489 (1887)
Commonwealth v. Markham, 70 Ky. 486 (1870)
Corso v. Crawford Dog and Cat Hospital, 97 Misc. 2d 530, 415 N.Y.S.2d 182 (1979)
Creswell's Executor v. Walker, 37 Ala. 233 (1861)
Dred Scott v. Sandford, 60 U.S. 393 (1857)
Duckworth v. Franzen, 780 F.2d 645 (7th Cir. 1985)
Elder v. Elder, 31 Va. 252 (1833)
Estelle v. Gamble, 429 U.S. 97 (1976)
Ex parte Cooper, 3 Tex. App. 489 (1878)
Farmer v. Brennan, 511 U.S. 825 (1994)
Findlay v. Bear, 8 Serg. & Rawle 571 (1822)
Fleeming v. Orr, 2 Macq. H.L. Sc. 14 (1855)

Fox v. Mohawk and Hudson River Humane Society, 46 N.Y. 232 (1897)
Fox v. Mohawk and Hudson River Humane Society, 165 N.Y. 517 (1901)
Fox v. Mohawk and Hudson River Humane Society, 25 N.Y. App. Div. 26 (1898)
Hamby v. Samson, 105 Iowa 112 (1898)
Hamdan v. Rumsfeld, 548 U.S. 557 (2006)
Helling v. McKinney, 509 U.S. 25 (1993)
Holmes v. King, 216 Ala. 412, 415 (1927).
Hudson v. McMillian, 503 U.S. 1 (1992)
Hudson v. McMillian, 929 F.2d 1014 (5th Cir. 1990)
Hutto v. Finney, 437 U.S. 678 (1978)
In re Lindewall's Will, 287 N.Y. 347 (1942)
In re Medley, 134 U.S. 160 (1890)
In re Zeph's Estate, 50 Hun. 523, 3 N.Y. (1888)
Infante v. Leith, 85 D.P.R. 26 (1962)
Irwin v. Lattin, 29 S.D. 1, 12 (1912)
Jackson v. Bishop, 404 F.2d 571 (1968)
Jenkins v. Ballantyne, 8 Utah 245 (1892)
Jones v. North Carolina Prisoners Labor Union, Inc., 433 U.S. 119 (1977)
La Porte v. Associated Independents, Inc., 163 So.2d 267 (Fla. 1964)
Laaman v. Helgemoe, 437 F. Supp. 269 (D.N.H. 1977)
Lee v. Coughlin, 26 F. Supp. 2d 615 (S.D.N.Y. 1998)
Lewis v. Casey, 518 U.S. 343 (1996)
Louisiana ex rel. Francis v. Resweber, 329 U.S. 459 (1947)
Madrid v. Gomez, 889 F. Supp. 1146 (N.D. Cal. 1995)
McCallister v. Sappingfield, 72 Ore. 422 (1914)
McClary v. Stull, 44 Neb. 175, 189 (1895)
McGlone v. Womack &c., 129 Ky. 274 (1908)
Meachum v. Fano, 427 U.S. 215 (1976)
Meagher v. Driscoll, 99 Mass. 281 (1868)
Mitchell v. Williams, 27 Ind. 62 (1866)
Morewood v. Wakefield, 133 Mass. 240 (1882)
Morey v. Brown, 42 N.H. 373 (1861)
Mullaly v. The People of the State of New York, 86 N.Y. 365 (1881)
O'Dell v. Goff, 149 Mich. 152, 158 (1907)
O'Lone v. Shabazz, 482 U.S. 342 (1987)
Overton v. Bazzetta, 539 U.S. 136 (2003)
Pearne v. Lisle, Amb. 75, 27 E.R. 47 (1749)
The People ex rel. Shand v. Tighe, 9 Misc. 607, 30 N.Y. Supp. 368 (1894)
Phillips v. San Luis Obispo County Department of Animal Regulation, 183 Cal.
    App. 3d 372 (1986)
Pierce v. Proprietors of Swan Point Cemetery, 10 R.I. 227 (1872)
Platner v. Sherwood, 6 Johns. Ch. 118 (1822)
Plessy v. Ferguson, 163 U.S. 537 (1896)
Procunier v. Martinez, 416 U.S. 411 (1974)
Putnam v. Payne, 13 Johns. 312, 313 (1816).

Rhodes v. Chapman, 452 U.S. 337 (1981)

Riggs v. Palmer, 115 N.Y. 506 (1889)

Roper v. Simmons, 543 U.S. 551(2005)

Ruffin v. Commonwealth, 62 Va. 790 (1871)

Sentell v. New Orleans and Carrollton Railroad Company, 166 U.S. 698 (1897)

Sierra Club v. Morton, 405 U.S. 727 (1972)

Somerset v. Stewart, 20 State Tr 1 (1772)

Stambovsky v. Ackley, 169 A.D.2d 254 (N.Y.A.D. 1991)

The State of Mississippi v. Isaac Jones, 1 Miss. 83 (1820)

State of New York v. Miln, 36 U.S. 102 (1837)

State v. Langford, 55 S.C. 322 (1899)

Street v. Tugwell, (1800) 2 Selw. N.P., 1138 (9th ed., 1838)

Summers v. Bean, 54 Va. 404 (1856)

Tenney v. Lenz, 16 Wisc. 566 (1863)

Trauerman v. Lippincott, 39 Mo. App. 478 (1890)

Trop v. Dulles, 356 U.S. 86 (1958)

Troup v. Wood, 4 Johns. Ch. 228 (1820)

Turner v. Safley, 482 U.S. 78 (1987)

Vanater v. Village of South Point, 717 F. Supp. 1236 (D. Ohio 1989)

Walton v. New York State Dept. of Correctional Services and MCI, 8 N.Y.3d 186 (2007)

Whitley v. Albers, 475 U.S. 312 (1986)

Wiley v. Slater, 22 Barb. 506 (1856)

Wilkinson v. Austin, 544 U.S. 74 (2005)

Williamson v. Coalter, 55 Va. 394 (1858)

Wilson v. Seiter, 501 U.S. 294 (1991)

Woolf v. Chalker, 31 Conn. 121 (1862)

Young v. Burton, 16 S.C. Eq. (McMul. Eq.) 255 (1841)

BOOKS

Agamben, Giorgio. *Remnants of Auschwitz: The Witness and the Archive*. Translated by Daniel Heller-Roazen. New York: Zone Books, 1999.

Allen, Austin. *Origins of the Dred Scott Case: Jacksonian Jurisprudence and the Supreme Court, 1837–1857*. Athens: University of Georgia Press, 2006.

Anderson, Graham. *Sage, Saint and Sophist: Holy Men and Their Associates in the Early Roman Empire*. London: Routledge, 1994.

Ardouin, Beaubrun. *Etudes sur l'histoire d'Haïti*. 1853–60. Reprint, Port-au-Prince: Chez l'éditeur, Francois Dalencour, 1958.

Arendt, Hannah. *The Origins of Totalitarianism*. 1951. Reprint, New York: Schocken Books, 2004.

Avins, Alfred. *The Reconstruction Amendments Debates*. Richmond: Virginia Commission on Constitutional Government, U.S. Congress, 1967.

Bacon, Matthew. *A New Abridgment of the Law*. Revised by Sir Henry Gwyllim, Charles Edward Dodd, and John Bouvier. Philadelphia: Thomas Davis, 1846.

Bailey, Nathan. *An Universal Etymological English Dictionary; and An Interpreter of Hard Words.* London: Printed for J. Buckland, J. Beecoft, W. Strahan, and J. Hinton, 1773.

Baker, J. H. *An Introduction to English Legal History.* 2nd ed. London: Butterworths, 1979.

Barskett, Sir James. *History of St. Domingo.* London: Frank Cass, 1972.

Bates, Elisha. *The Moral Advocate: A Monthly Publication on War, Duelling, Capital Punishments, and Prison Discipline.* Mt. Pleasant, OH: Printed by the Editor, 1821–22.

Bauman, Zygmunt. *Wasted Lives: Modernity and Its Outcasts.* Cambridge, UK: Polity Press, 2004.

Bentham, Jeremy. *Bentham's Theory of Fictions.* Edited by C. K. Ogden. 1932. Reprint, London: Routledge, 2001.

———. *A Comment on the Commentaries and a Fragment on Government.* Edited by J. H. Burns and H.L.A. Hart. 1776. Reprint, London: Athlone Press, 1977.

———. *Jeremy Bentham: The Panopticon Writings.* Edited by Miran Božovič. London: Verso Books, 1995.

———. *Rights, Representation, and Reform: Nonsense upon Stilts and Other Writings on the French Revolution.* Edited by Philip Schofield, Catherine Pease-Watkin, and Cyprian Blamires. New York: Oxford University Press, 2002.

———. *The Works of Jeremy Bentham.* Edited by John Bowring. Edinburgh: William Tait, 1838.

Best, Stephen. *The Fugitive's Properties: Law and the Poetics of Possession.* Chicago: University of Chicago Press, 2004.

Bigelow, Melville M. *Leading Cases on the Law of Torts: Determined by the Courts of America and England.* Boston: Little, Brown, 1875.

Blackburn, Robin. *The Making of New World Slavery: From the Baroque to the Modern: 1492–1800.* London: Verso, 1997.

Blackstone, William. *Commentaries on the Law of England.* 4 vols. 1765–69. Reprint, Chicago: University of Chicago Press, 1979.

Blount, Thomas. *Nomo-lexikon, a Law Dictionary: Interpreting Such Difficult and Obscure Words and Terms As Are Found Either In Our Common or Statute, Ancient or Modern Lawes: With References to the Several Statutes, Records, Registers, Law-books, Charters, Ancient Deeds, and Manuscripts, Wherein the Words are Used: and Etymologies, Where They Properly Occur.* England: In the Savoy; Printed by Thomas Newcomb for John Martin and Henry Herringman, 1670.

Bond, George Clement, and Diane M. Ciekawy, eds. *Witchcraft Dialogues: Anthropological and Philosophical Exchanges.* Athens: Ohio Center for International Studies, 2001.

Bonniol, Jean-Luc. *La couleur comme maléfice: Une illustration créole de la généalogie des "Blancs" et des "Noirs."* Paris: Albin Michel, 1992.

Bouvier, John. *A Law Dictionary Adapted to the Constitution and Laws of the United States of America; and of the Several States of the American Union, with*

References to the Civil and Other Systems of Foreign Law. 2 vols. 6th ed. Philadelphia: Childs and Peterson, 1856.

Brathwaite, Edward. *The Development of Creole Society in Jamaica, 1770–1820*. Oxford: Clarendon Press, 1971.

Brodber, Erna. *Myal*. London: New Beacon Books, 1988.

Brown, Vincent. *The Reaper's Garden: Death and Power in the World of Atlantic Slavery*. Cambridge, MA: Harvard University Press, 2008.

Buffon, Georges-Louis Leclerc, comte de. *Oeuvres complètes de Buffon*. Edited by Frédéric Cuvier. Bruxelles: Chez Th. Lejeune, Libraire-éditeur, 1828–30.

Cameron, Sharon. *Impersonality: Seven Essays*. Chicago: University of Chicago Press, 2007.

Castronovo, Russ, and Dana D. Nelson, eds. *Materializing Democracy: Toward a Revitalized Cultural Politics*. Durham, NC: Duke University Press, 2002.

Chambers, Robert, and Samuel Johnson. *A Course of Lectures on the English Law Delivered at the University of Oxford, 1767–73*. Edited by Thomas M. Curley. Oxford: Clarendon Press, 1987.

Christianson, Scott. *With Liberty for Some: Five Hundred Years of Imprisonment in America*. Boston: Northeastern University Press, 1998.

Clark, Stuart. *Thinking with Demons: The Idea of Witchcraft in Early Modern Europe*. New York: Oxford University Press, 1997.

Cobb, Thomas. *An Inquiry into the Law of Negro Slavery in the United States of America*. 1858. Reprint, New York: Negro Universities Press, 1968.

Coetzee, J. M. *Disgrace*. New York: Penguin Books, 1999.

———. *Waiting for the Barbarians*. Boston: Penguin Books, 1982.

Cole, David. *Enemy Aliens: Double Standards and Constitutional Freedoms in the War on Terrorism*. New York: The New Press, 2003.

Comaroff, Jean, and John L. Comaroff, eds. *Modernity and Its Malcontents: Ritual and Power in Postcolonial Africa*. Chicago: University of Chicago Press, 1993.

Cooper, Frederick. *Colonialism in Question: Theory, Knowledge, History*. Berkeley: University of California Press, 2005.

Cooper, John. *Cruelty: An Analysis of Article 3*. London: Sweet and Maxwell, 2003.

Cover, Robert M. *Justice Accused: Antislavery and the Judicial Process*. New Haven, CT: Yale University Press, 1975.

———. *Narrative, Violence, and the Law: The Essays of Robert Cover*. Edited by Martha Minow, Michael Ryan, and Austin Sarat. Ann Arbor: University of Michigan Press, 1992.

Cowell, John. *The Interpreter: or Book Containing the Signification of Words*. London: F. Leach, for distribution by Hen. Twyford, Tho. Dring, and Io. Place, 1658.

Crane, Gregg D. *Race, Citizenship, and Law in American Literature*. New York: Cambridge University Press, 2002.

Cusac, Anne-Marie. *Cruel and Unusual: The Culture of Punishment in America*. New Haven, CT: Yale University Press, 2009.

Danner, Mark. *Torture and Truth: America, Abu Ghraib, and the War on Terror.* New York: New York Review of Books, 2004.

Davis, Angela Y., *Are Prisons Obsolete?* New York: Seven Stories Press, 2003.

Davis, David Brion. *Inhuman Bondage: The Rise and Fall of Slavery in the New World.* New York: Oxford University Press, 2006.

———. *The Problem of Slavery in the Age of Revolution, 1770–1823.* New York: Oxford University Press, 1999.

Dayan, Colin. *Haiti, History, and the Gods.* Berkeley: University of California Press, 1995.

———. *The Story of Cruel and Unusual.* Cambridge, MA: MIT Press, 2007.

de Beaumont, Gustave, and Alexis de Tocqueville. *On the Penitentiary System in the United States.* Translated by Francis Lieber. Philadelphia: Carey. 1833.

de Tocqueville, Alexis. *Democracy in America.* 1835–40. Reprint, New York: Everyman's Library, 1994.

Debbasch, Yvan. *Couleur et liberté: Le jeu du critère ethnique dans un ordre juridique esclavagiste.* Paris: Librairie Dalloz, 1967.

Descartes, René. *Meditations on First Philosophy.* 1641. Reprint in *The Philosophical Writings of Descartes.* Translated by John Cottingham, Robert Stoothoff, and Dugald Murdoch. Cambridge: Cambridge University Press, 1985.

Dickens, Charles. *American Notes and Pictures from Italy.* 1842. Reprint, New York: Oxford University Press, 1957.

Dodds, E. R. *The Greeks and the Irrational.* Berkeley: University of California Press, 1951.

Dominguez, Virginia R. *White by Definition: Social Classification in Creole Louisiana.* New Brunswick, NJ: Rutgers University Press, 1986.

Dwight, Theodore William. *Commentaries on the Law of Persons and Personal Property.* Edited by Edward F. Dwight. New York: Little, Brown, 1894.

Dzielska, María. *Apollonius of Tyana in Legend and History.* Translated by Piotr Pienkowski. Rome: "L'Erma" di Bretschneider, 1986.

Edwards, Bryan. *The History, Civil and Commercial, of the British Colonies in the West Indies.* 2 vols. Dublin: Luke White, 1793.

Edwards, Jonathan. *The Great Awakening.* Edited by C. C. Goen. New Haven, CT: Yale University Press, 1972.

Evans, Edward Payson. *The Criminal Prosecution and Capital Punishment of Animals.* London: William Heinemann, 1906; New York: E. P. Dutton, 1906.

Fehrenbacher, Don E. *The Dred Scott Case: Its Significance in American Law and Politics.* Oxford: Oxford University Press, 1978.

Foucault, Michel. *Discipline and Punish: The Birth of the Prison.* Translated by Alan Sheridan. New York: Vintage, 1995.

Francione, Gary L. *Animals, Property, and the Law.* Philadelphia: Temple University Press, 1995.

Friedman, Lawrence. *History of American Law.* New York: Simon and Schuster, 1973.

Galanter, Marc. *Lowering the Bar: Lawyer Jokes and Legal Culture*. Madison: University of Wisconsin Press, 2005.

Garland, David. *The Culture of Control: Crime and Social Order in Contemporary Society*. Chicago: University of Chicago Press, 2001.

Geldart, W. M. *Elements of English Law*. 1911. Reprint, Oxford: Oxford University Press, 1938.

Gilmore, Ruth Wilson. *Golden Gulag: Prisons, Surplus, Crisis, and Opposition in Globalizing California*. Berkeley: University of California Press, 2007.

Glannon, Joseph W. *The Law of Torts: Examples and Explanations*. 3rd ed. New York: Aspen, 2005.

Goffman, Erving. *Asylums: Essays on the Social Situation of Mental Patients and Other Inmates*. 1961. Reprint, New York: Doubleday Anchor, 1990.

Goodell, William. *The American Slave Code in Theory and Practice*. New York: American and Foreign Anti-Slavery Society, 1853.

Gordon, Avery F. *Ghostly Matters: Haunting and the Sociological Imagination*. Minneapolis: University of Minnesota Press, 1997.

Gottschalk, Marie. *The Prison and the Gallows: The Politics of Mass Incarceration in America*. New York: Cambridge University Press, 2006.

Goveia, Elsa V. *The West Indian Slave Laws of the 18th Century*. Barbados: University of the West Indies, 1970.

Graber, Mark A. *Dred Scott and the Problem of Constitutional Evil*. New York: Cambridge University Press, 2006.

Graves, Robert. *The Greek Myths*. 1955. Reprint, Mt. Kisco, NY: Moyer Bell, 1988.

Greenberg, Karen J., and Joshua L. Dratel, eds. *The Torture Papers: The Road to Abu Ghraib*. Cambridge: Cambridge University Press, 2005.

Greenhouse, Linda. *Becoming Justice Blackmun: Harry Blackmun's Supreme Court Journey*. New York: Times Books / Henry Holt, 2005.

Gross, Ariela J. *Double Character: Slavery and Mastery in the Antebellum Southern Courtroom*. Princeton, NJ: Princeton University Press, 2000.

Haraway, Donna J. *When Species Meet*. Minneapolis: University of Minnesota Press, 2008.

Hartman, Saidiya V. *Scenes of Subjection: Terror, Slavery, and Self-Making in Nineteenth-Century America*. New York: Oxford University Press, 1997.

Hearne, Vicki. *Bandit: The Heart Warming True Story of One Dog's Rescue from Death Row*. 1991. Reprint, New York: Skyhorse, 2007.

Henry, Matthew. *Matthew Henry's Commentary on the Whole Bible*. 2nd rev. ed. Peabody, MA: Hendrickson, 1991.

Hildreth, Richard. *The History of the United States of America*. 6 vols. New York: Harper and Brothers, 1849.

———. *The Slave, or Memoirs of Archy Moore*. Boston: John H. Eastburn, 1836.

Holmes, Oliver Wendell. *The Collected Works of Justice Holmes: Complete Public Writings and Selected Judicial Opinions of Oliver Wendell Holmes*. The

Holmes Devise Memorial ed. Edited by Sheldon M. Novick. Chicago: University of Chicago Press, 1994.

———. *The Common Law*. 1881. Reprint, New York: Dover, 1991.

Hornblower, Simon, and Antony Spawforth, eds., *The Oxford Classical Dictionary*. 3rd ed. Oxford: Oxford University Press, 1996.

Horwitz, Morton J. *The Transformation of American Law, 1870–1960: The Crisis of Legal Orthodoxy*. New York: Oxford University Press, 1992.

Irving, P.M.C. Forbes. *Metamorphosis in Greek Myths*. Oxford: Clarendon Press, 1995.

James, William. *The Principles of Psychology*. 1890. Reprint, New York: Cosimo Classics, 2007.

Jefferson, Thomas. *Notes on the State of Virginia*. 2nd American ed. Philadelphia: Printed for M. Carey, 1797.

Jones, Lindsay, ed. *Encyclopedia of Religion*. 2nd ed. Detroit: Macmillan Reference USA, 2005.

Jordan, Winthrop D. *White over Black: American Attitudes toward the Negro, 1550–1812*. 1968. Reprint, New York: W. W. Norton, 1977.

Kadish, Doris Y., ed. *Slavery in the Caribbean Francophone World: Distant Voices, Forgotten Acts, Forged Identities*. Athens: University of Georgia Press, 2000.

Kent, James. *Commentaries on American Law*. 4 vols. 1826. 12th ed., Boston: Little, Brown, 1873.

Lang, Andrew. *Cock Lane and Common-Sense*. 1894. Reprint, Charleston, SC: BiblioBazaar, 2007.

Lea, Henry Charles. *Materials toward a History of Witchcraft*. 3 vols. Edited and arranged by Arthur C. Howland. Philadelphia: University of Pennsylvania Press, 1939.

Levinson, Sanford, ed. *Torture: A Collection*. New York: Oxford University Press, 2004.

Lichtenstein, Alex. *Twice the Work of Free Labor: The Political Economy of Convict Labor in the New South*. London: Verso, 1996.

Locke, John. *An Essay Concerning Human Understanding*. Edited by Peter H. Nidditch. 1700. Reprint, New York: Oxford University Press, 1975.

———. *Locke: Two Treatises of Government*. Edited by Peter Laslett. 1689. Reprint, Cambridge: Cambridge University Press, 1988.

———. *The Reasonableness of Christianity, As Delivered in the Scriptures*. 1695. Reprint in *The Works of John Locke*. London: Printed for Thomas Tegg; W. Sharpe and Son; etc., 1823.

Long, Edward. *The History of Jamaica, or a General Survey of the Antient and Modern State of That Island*. 1774. Reprint, New York: Arno Press, 1972.

Lupton, Frederick. *The Law Relating to Dogs*. London: Stevens and Sons, 119 Chancery Lane, 1888.

Lycophron. *The Alexandra of Lycophron: With English Translation and Explanatory Notes*. Translated by George W. Mooney. London: G. Bell and Sons, 1921.

Lynch, Mona. *Sunbelt Justice: Arizona and the Transformation of American Punishment*. Stanford: Stanford Law Books, 2010.

Madiou, Thomas. *Histoire d'Haiti, 1492–1846*. 8 vols. Port-au-Prince: Editions Henri Deschamps, 1989.

Maine, Henry Sumner. *Ancient Law: Its Connection with the Early History of Society and Its Relation to Modern Ideas*. 1861. Reprint, Boston: Beacon Press, 1963.

Maitland, Frederic William. *Domesday Book and Beyond: Three Essays in the Early History of England*. 1897. Reprint, Cambridge: Cambridge University Press, 1988.

———. *Frederic William Maitland, Historian: Selections from His Writings*. Edited by Robert Livingston Schuyler. Berkeley: University of California Press, 1960.

Maitland, Frederic William, and Sir Frederick Pollock. *The History of English Law Before the Time of Edward I*. 2 vols. 1898. Cambridge: Cambridge University Press, 1968.

Mandeville, Bernard. *The Fable of the Bees: Or Private Vices Publick Benefits*. London: Printed for J. Roberts, near the Oxford Arms in Warwick Lane, 1714.

McCoy, Alfred. *A Question of Torture: CIA Interrogation, from the Cold War to the War on Terror*. New York: Henry Holt, 2006.

McKitrick, Eric L., ed. *Slavery Defended: The Views of the Old South*. Englewood Cliffs, NJ: Prentice-Hall, 1963.

Mehta, Uday Singh. *Liberalism and Empire: A Study in Nineteenth-Century British Liberal Thought*. 2nd ed. Chicago: University of Chicago Press, 1999.

Meillassoux, Claude. *The Anthropology of Slavery: The Womb of Iron and Gold*. Chicago: University of Chicago Press, 1992.

Melville, Herman. "Bartleby, the Scrivener: A Story of Wall Street." 1856. Reprint in *The Piazza Tales and Other Prose Pieces, 1839–1860*. Edited by Harrison Hayford, Alma A. MacDougall, G. Thomas Tanselle et al. Evanston, IL: Northwestern University Press and the Newberry Library, 1987.

———. "Benito Cereno." 1856. Reprint in *The Piazza Tales and Other Prose Pieces, 1839–1860*. Edited by Harrison Hayford, Alma A. MacDougall, G. Thomas Tanselle et al. Evanston, IL: Northwestern University Press and the Newberry Library, 1987.

———. *Israel Potter: His Fifty Years of Exile*. Edited by Harrison Hayford, Hershel Parker, and G. Thomas Tanselle. Evanston, IL: Northwestern University Press and the Newberry Library, 1982.

———. *Moby-Dick, or the Whale*. Edited by Harrison Hayford, Hershel Parker, and G. Thomas Tanselle. Evanston, IL: Northwestern University Press and the Newberry Library, 2001.

Meranze, Michael. *Laboratories of Virtue: Punishment, Revolution, and Authority in Philadelphia, 1760–1835*. Chapel Hill: University of North Carolina Press, 1996.

Merrill, Bill, and Glenn Johnson. *Sir George: The Ghost of Nyack*. Beaverton, OR: Deer, 1995.

Morgan, Edmund S. *Visible Saints: The History of a Puritan Idea*. Ithaca, NY: Cornell University Press, 1963.

Morris, Thomas D. *Southern Slavery and the Law, 1619–1860*. Chapel Hill: University of North Carolina Press, 1996.

Mossman, Judith. *Wild Justice: A Study of Euripides' Hecuba*. Oxford: Clarendon Press, 1995.

Most, Glenn W. *Doubting Thomas*. Cambridge, MA: Harvard University Press, 2005.

Nékám, Alexander. *The Personality Conception of the Legal Entity*. Cambridge, MA: Harvard University Press, 1938.

Nietzsche, Friedrich. *Thus Spoke Zarathustra*. Edited by Adrian Del Caro and Robert Pippin. Cambridge: Cambridge University Press, 2006.

Noonan, John T., Jr. *Persons and Masks of the Law: Cardozo, Holmes, Jefferson, and Wythe as Makers of the Masks*. New York: Farrar, Straus and Giroux, 1976.

Oshinsky, David M. *"Worse than Slavery": Parchman Farm and the Ordeal of Jim Crow Justice*. New York: Free Press, 1996.

Ovid. *The Metamorphoses of Ovid*. Translated by Allen Mandelbaum. New York: Harcourt, 1993.

Palmié, Stephan. *Wizards and Scientists: Explorations in Afro-Cuban Modernity and Tradition*. Durham, NC: Duke University Press, 2002.

Parsons, Theophilus. *The Law of Contracts*. 6th ed. Boston: Little, Brown, 1873.

Patterson, Orlando. *Slavery and Social Death: A Comparative Study*. Cambridge, MA: Harvard University Press, 1982.

Peters, Edward. *Torture*. Expanded ed. Philadelphia: University of Pennsylvania Press, 1996.

Philostratus. *The Life of Apollonius of Tyana*. 2 vols. Edited and translated by Christopher P. Jones. London: Loeb Classical Library, 2005.

Plucknett, Theodore. *A Concise History of the Common Law*. 4th ed. 1929. Reprint, London: Butterworth, 1948.

Pollock, Frederick. *The Law of Torts: A Treatise on the Principles Arising from Civil Wrongs in the Common Law*. 1886. Reprint, Philadelphia: Blackstone, 1887.

Posner, Richard A. *The Problems of Jurisprudence*. Cambridge, MA: Harvard University Press, 1990.

Randolph, Mary. *Every Dog's Legal Guide: A Must-Have Book for Your Owner*. 6th ed. Berkeley, CA: Nolo, 2007.

Rhodes, Lorna A. *Total Confinement: Madness and Reason in the Maximum Security Prison*. Berkeley: University of California Press, 2004.

Rhys, Jean. *Wide Sargasso Sea*. 1966. Reprint, New York: W. W. Norton, 1982.

Rodríguez, Dylan. *Forced Passages: Imprisoned Radical Intellectuals and the U.S. Prison Regime*. Minneapolis: University of Minnesota Press, 2006.

Roscoe, William. *A Brief Statement of the Causes Which Have Led to the Abandonment of the Celebrated System of Penitentiary Discipline in Some of the United States of America*. Liverpool: Harris, 1827.

Rosenberg, David. *The Hidden Holmes: His Theory of Torts in History*. Cambridge, MA: Harvard University Press, 1995.

Rush, Benjamin. *Essays: Literary, Moral, and Philosophical*. Edited by Michael Meranze. 1806. Reprint, Schenectady, NY: Union College, 1988.

Sarat, Austin D., and Jennifer L. Culbert, eds. *States of Violence: War, Capital Punishment, and Letting Die*. Cambridge: Cambridge University Press, 2009.

Sarat, Austin, and Thomas R. Kearns, eds. *History, Memory, and the Law*. Ann Arbor: University of Michigan Press, 1999.

Schmitt, Jean-Claude. *The Holy Greyhound: Guinefort, Healer of Children since the Thirteenth Century*. 1979. Reprint, Cambridge: Cambridge University Press, 1983; Paris: Editions de la Maison des Sciences de l'Homme, 1983.

Schofield, Philip. *Utility and Democracy: The Political Thought of Jeremy Bentham*. Oxford: Oxford University Press, 2006.

Semple, Janet. *Bentham's Prison: A Study of the Panopticon Penitentiary*. Oxford: Clarendon Press, 1993.

Serpell, James. *The Domestic Dog: Its Evolution, Behaviour and Interactions with People*. Cambridge: Cambridge University Press, 1995.

Shakespeare, William. *Hamlet* [1603]. The Arden Shakespeare, third ser. Edited by Ann Thompson and Neil Taylor. London: Arden, 2006.

———. *Richard II* [1597]. The Arden Shakespeare, third ser. Edited by Charles R. Forker. London: Arden, 2002.

Simpson, A.W.B. *A History of Land Law*. Oxford: Clarendon Press, 1985.

Smith, Caleb. *The Prison and the American Imagination*. New Haven, CT: Yale University Press, 2009.

Snell, Bruno. *The Discovery of the Mind in Greek Philosophy and Literature*. 1953. Reprint, New York: Dover, 1982.

Soifer, Aviam. *Law and the Company We Keep*. Cambridge, MA: Harvard University Press, 1995.

St. George Tucker, ed. *Blackstone's Commentaries: With Notes of Reference to the Constitution and Laws, of the Federal Government of the United States, and of the Commonwealth of Virginia*. 5 vols. 1765–69. Reprint, Union, NJ: The Lawbook Exchange, 1996.

Stafford Smith, Clive. *Bad Men: Guantánamo Bay and the Secret Prisons*. London: Weidenfeld and Nicolson, 2007.

Stamp, Kenneth M. *The Peculiar Institution: Slavery in the Ante-Bellum South*. New York: Knopf, 1956.

Stephen, James. *The Slavery of the British West India Colonies Delineated, as It Exists Both in Law and Practice, and Compared with the Slavery of Other Countries, Antient and Modern*. 2 vols. 1824. Reprint, New York: Kraus Reprint, 1969.

Stone, Christopher D. *Should Trees Have Standing? And Other Essays on Law, Morals and the Environment*. Dobbs Ferry, NY: Oceana, 1996.

Suggs, Jon-Christian. *Whispered Consolations: Law and Narrative in African American Life*. Ann Arbor: University of Michigan Press, 2000.

Tamen, Miguel. *Friends of Interpretable Objects*. Cambridge, MA: Harvard University Press, 2001.

Thomas, Lately. *The Mayor Who Mastered New York: The Life and Opinions of William J. Gaynor*. New York: William Morrow, 1969.

Tomlins, Christopher L., and Bruce H. Mann, eds. *The Many Legalities of Early America*. Chapel Hill: University of North Carolina Press, 2001.

Tushnet, Mark V. *The American Law of Slavery, 1810–1860: Considerations of Humanity and Interest*. Princeton, NJ: Princeton University Press, 1981.

Wagner, Bryan. *Disturbing the Peace: Black Culture and the Police Power after Slavery*. Cambridge, MA: Harvard University Press, 2009.

Welke, Barbara Young. *Recasting American Liberty: Gender, Race, Law, and the Railroad Revolution, 1865–1920*. New York: Cambridge University Press, 2001.

White, David Gordon. *Myths of the Dog-Man*. Chicago: University of Chicago Press, 1991.

White, G. Edward. *Tort Law in America: An Intellectual History*. Expanded ed. 1980. Reprint, New York: Oxford University Press, 2003.

Whitman, James Q. *Harsh Justice: Criminal Punishment and the Widening Divide Between America and Europe*. Oxford: Oxford University Press, 2003.

Williams, Glanville L. *Liability for Animals: An Account of the Development and Present Law of Tortious Liability for Animals, Distress Damage Feasant and The Duty to Fence, In Great Britain, Northern Ireland and the Common-Law Dominions*. Cambridge: Cambridge University Press, 1939.

Zimmermann, Linda. *Ghost Investigator*. Vol. 1, *Hauntings of the Hudson Valley*. New York: Lightning Source, 2003.

Žižek, Slavoj, ed. *Jacques Lacan: Critical Evaluations in Cultural Theory*. London: Taylor and Francis, 2003.

BOOK CHAPTERS AND JOURNAL ARTICLES

"Annotation: Civil Effects of Sentence to Life Imprisonment." *American Law Reports, Annotated* 139 (1942): 1308–25.

Austin, Ralph A. "The Moral Economy of Witchcraft." In *Modernity and Its Malcontents: Ritual and Power in Postcolonial Africa*, edited by Jean Comaroff and John L. Comaroff, 89–110. Chicago: University of Chicago Press, 1993.

Bastian, Misty L. "'Bloodhounds Who Have No Friends': Witchcraft and Locality in the Nigerian Popular Press." In *Modernity and Its Malcontents: Ritual and Power in Postcolonial Africa*, edited by Jean Comaroff and John L. Comaroff, 129–66. Chicago: University of Chicago Press, 1993.

Beirne, Piers. "The Law Is an Ass: Reading E. P. Evans, 'The Medieval Prosecution and Capital Punishment of Animals.'" *Society and Animals: Journal of Human-Animal Studies* 2, no. 1 (1994): 27–46.

Blumenthal, Susanna L. "The Default Legal Person." *UCLA Law Review* 54, no. 5 (2007): 1135–265.

———. "The Deviance of the Will: Policing the Bounds of Testamentary Freedom in Nineteenth-Century America." *Harvard Law Review* 119, no. 4 (2006): 959–1034.

———. "The Mind of a Moral Agent: Scottish Common Sense and the Problem of Responsibility in Nineteenth-Century American Law." *Law and History Review* 26, no. 1 (2008): 99–160.

Bowie, E.L. "Apollonius of Tyana: Tradition and Reality." In *Aufstieg und Niedergang der Roemischen Welt*, edited by Hildegard Temporini and Wolfgang Haase, 2.16.2, 1652–99. Berlin: de Gruyter, 1978.

Brown, Vincent. "Social Death and Political Life in the Study of Slavery." *American Historical Review* 114, no. 5 (2009): 1231–49.

Bush, Jonathan A. "Free to Enslave: The Foundations of Colonial American Slave Law." *Yale Journal of Law and Humanities* 5, no. 2 (1993): 417–70.

Carey, Daniel. "Locke, Travel Literature, and the Natural History of Man." *Seventeenth Century* 11, no. 2 (1996): 259–80.

Dayan, Colin. "The Dogs." *Southwest Review* 88, nos. 2 and 3 (2003): 183–200.

———. "Due Process and Lethal Confinement." *South Atlantic Quarterly* 107, no. 3 (2008): 485–507. Reprinted in *States of Violence: War, Capital Punishment, and Letting Die*, edited by Austin Sarat and Jennifer L. Culbert, 127–49. Cambridge: Cambridge University Press, 2009.

———. "Held in the Body of the State: Prisons and the Law." In *History, Memory, and the Law*, edited by Austin Sarat and Thomas R. Kearns, 183–247. Ann Arbor, Michigan: University of Michigan Press, 1999.

———. "Legal Slaves and Civil Bodies." In *Materializing Democracy: Toward a Revitalized Cultural Politics*, edited by Russ Castronovo and Dana D. Nelson, 53–94. Durham, NC: Duke University Press, 2002.

———. "Legal Terrors," *Representations*, no. 92 (Fall 2005): 42–80.

Ducor, Philippe. "The Legal Status of Human Materials." *Drake Law Review* 44, no. 2 (1996): 195–260.

E.O.S. "Injuries by Domestic Animals." *Journal of the Society of Comparative Legislation* 1, no. 1 (1899): 57–58.

Epstein, Lynn A. "Resolving Confusion in Pet Owner Tort Cases: Recognizing Pets' Anthropomorphic Qualities Under a Property Classification." *Southern Illinois University Law Journal* 26, no. 1 (2001): 31–52.

Ewald, Alec C. "'Civil Death': The Ideological Paradox of Criminal Disenfranchisement Law in the United States." *Wisconsin Law Review* 5 (2002): 1045–137.

Ewald, William. "Comparative Jurisprudence (I): What Was It Like to Try a Rat?" *University of Pennsylvania Law Review* 143, no. 6 (1995): 1889–2149.

Finkelman, Paul. "The Centrality of the Peculiar Institution in American Legal Development." *Chicago-Kent Law Review* 68, no. 3 (1993): 1010–33.

Finkelstein, Jacob J. "The Goring Ox: Some Historical Perspectives on Deodands, Forfeitures, Wrongful Death, and the Western Notion of Sovereignty." *Temple Law Quarterly* 46, no. 2 (1973): 169–290.

Fisher, William W., III. "Ideology and Imagery in the Law of Slavery." *Chicago-Kent Law Review* 68, no. 3 (1993): 1051–86.

Frankfurter, Felix, Henry M. Hart Jr., and Paul A. Freund. "Thomas Reed Powell." *Harvard Law Review* 69, no. 4 (1956): 797–805.

Girgen, Jen. "The Historical and Contemporary Prosecution and Punishment of Animals." *Animal Law* 9 (2003): 97–133.

Goldman, Daniel S. "The Modern-Day Literacy Test? Felon Disenfranchisement and Race Discrimination." *Stanford Law Review* 57, no. 2 (2004): 611–55.

Gómez, Alan Eladio, "Resisting Living Death at Marion Federal Penitentiary, 1972," *Radical History Review* 2006, no. 96 (2006): 58–86.

Gordon, Avery. "The Prisoner's Curse." In *Toward a Sociology of the Trace*, edited by Herman Gray and Macarena Gómez-Barris. Minneapolis: University of Minnesota Press, forthcoming.

Grant, Walter Matthews, et al., "The Collateral Consequences of a Criminal Conviction." *Vanderbilt Law Review* 23, no. 5 (1970): 929–1242.

Granucci, Anthony F. "'Nor Cruel and Unusual Punishments Inflicted': The Original Meaning." *California Law Review* 57, no. 4 (1969): 839–65.

Grassian, Stuart. "Psychiatric Effects of Solitary Confinement." *Washington University Journal of Law and Policy* 22 (2006): 325–84.

Haney, Craig. "Mental Health Issues in Long-Term Solitary and 'Supermax' Confinement." *Crime and Delinquency* 49, no. 1 (2003): 124–56.

Harris, Cheryl I. "Whiteness as Property." *Harvard Law Review* 106, no. 8 (1993): 1709–91.

Higginbotham, A. Leon, Jr., and Barbara K. Kopytoff. "Property First, Humanity Second: The Recognition of the Slave's Human Nature in Virginia Civil Law." *Ohio State Law Journal* 50, no. 3 (1989): 511–40.

Horowitz, Elliott. "Circumcised Dogs from Matthew to Marlowe." *Prooftexts* 27, no. 3 (2007): 531–45.

Hoult Verkerke, J. "Notice Liability in Employment Discrimination Law." *Virginia Law Review* 81, no. 21 (1995): 273–85.

Hussain, Nasser. "Beyond Norm and Exception: Guantánamo." *Critical Inquiry* 33, no. 4 (2007): 734–53.

Hyams, Paul. "Does It Matter When the English Began to Distinguish between Crime and Tort?" In *Violence in Medieval Society*, edited by Richard W. Kaeuper. Woodbridge, Suffolk: Boydell Press, 2000, 107–29.

Isaacs, Nathan. "Fault and Liability: Two Views of Legal Development." *Harvard Law Review* 31, no. 7 (1918): 954–79.

Jamieson, Philip. "The Legal Status of Animals Under Animal Welfare Law." *Environmental and Planning Law Journal* 9 (1992): 20–30.

Katz, Marilyn. "Ox-Slaughter and Goring Oxen: Homicide, Animal Sacrifice, and Judicial Process." *Yale Journal of Law and the Humanities* 4, no. 2 (1992): 249–78.

Kohn, Eduardo. "How Dogs Dream: Amazonian Natures and the Politics of Transspecies Engagement." *American Ethnologist* 34, no. 1 (2007): 3–24.

Kosmetatou, Elizabeth. "Lycophron's 'Alexandra' Reconsidered: The Attalid Connection." *Hermes* 128, no. 1 (2000): 32–53.

Lee, Blewett. "Psychic Phenomena and the Law." *Harvard Law Review* 34, no. 6 (1921): 625–38.

Lévitt, Albert. "The Origin of the Doctrine of Mens Rea." *Illinois Law Review* 17, no. 2 (1922–23): 117–37.

Manza, Jeff, and Christopher Uggen. "Punishment and Democracy: Disenfranchisement of Nonincarcerated Felons in the United States." *Perspectives on Politics* 2, no. 3 (2004): 491–505.

Marmer, Lynn. "The New Breed of Municipal Dog Control Laws: Are They Constitutional?" *University of Cincinnati Law Review* 53, no. 4 (1984): 1067–82.

Matthews, Paul. "Whose Body? People as Property." In *Current Legal Problems*, edited by Lord Lloyd of Hampstead and Roger W. Rideout with Jacqueline Dyson, 36:193–239. London: Stevens and Sons, 1983.

Midgley, Mary. "Is a Dolphin a Person?" In *The Animal Ethics Reader*, edited by Susan Jean Armstrong and Richard George Botzler, 166–72. London: Routledge, 2003.

Momigliano, Arnaldo. "The Locrian Maidens and the Date of Lycophron's *Alexandra*." *Classical Quarterly* 39, no. 1–2 (1945): 49–53.

Morris, Thomas D. "'Villeinage … as it existed in England, reflects but little light on our subject': The Problem of the 'Sources' of Southern Slave Law." *American Journal of Legal History* 32, no. 2 (1988): 95–137.

Morton, J. "Weld v. Walker et al." *American Law Review* 14, no. 1 (1880): 57–66.

Nash, A. E. Keir. "Reason of Slavery: Understanding the Judicial Role in the Peculiar Institution." *Vanderbilt Law Review* 32, no. 1 (1979): 7–218.

Neilsen, Eric W. "Is the Law of Acquisition of Property by Find Going to the Dogs?" *Thomas M. Cooley Law Review* 15 (1998): 479–516.

Nunn, Robin L. "Lock Them Up and Throw Away the Vote." *Chicago Journal of International Law* 5, no. 2 (2005): 763–84.

Palmié, Stephan. "Thinking with *Ngangas*: Reflections on Embodiment and the Limits of 'Objectively Necessary Appearances.'" *Comparative Studies in Society and History* 48, no. 4 (2006): 852–86.

Peters, Edward. "Wounded Names: The Medieval Doctrine of Infamy." In *Law in Mediaeval Life and Thought*, ed. Edward B. King and Susan J. Ridyard, 43–89. Sewanee: The Press of the University of the South, 1990.

Phillips, E. D. "Odysseus in Italy." *Journal of Hellenic Studies* 73 (1953): 56–67.

Puech, Henri-Charles. "A propos de Lycophron, de Rab et de Philon d'Alexandrie." *Revue des Études Grecques* 46, no. 217 (1933): 311–33.

Radin, Margaret Jane. "Property and Personhood." *Stanford Law Review* 34, no. 5 (1982): 957–1015.

Rawick, George P., ed. "Elisha Doc Garey, Ex-Slave in Georgia, Age 76." In *The American Slave: A Composite Autobiography*. Vol. 12. 1941. Reprint, Westport, CT: Greenwood, 1972.

Robertson, James. "Houses of the Dead: Warehouse Prisons, Paradigm Change, and the Supreme Court." *Houston Law Review* 34, no. 4 (1997): 1003–63.

Russell, John H. "The Free Negro in Virginia: 1619–1865." *Johns Hopkins University Studies in Historical and Political Science*, ser. 31, no. 3 (1913): 42–87.

Sayre, F. B. "*Mens Rea*." *Harvard Law Review* 45, no. 6 (1932): 974–1021.

Scheppele, Kim Lane. "Facing Facts in Legal Interpretation." *Representations* 30, no. 1 (1990): 42–77.

Schiff Berman, Paul. "An Anthropological Approach to Modern Forfeiture Law: The Symbolic Function of Legal Actions Against Objects." *Yale Journal of Law and the Humanities* 11, no. 1 (1999): 1–45.

———. "Rats, Pigs, and Statues on Trial: The Creation of Cultural Narratives in the Prosecution of Animals and Inanimate Objects." *New York University Law Review* 69, no. 2 (1994): 288–326.

Scott, Rebecca J. "Public Rights, Social Equality, and the Conceptual Roots of the *Plessy* Challenge." *Michigan Law Review* 106, no. 5 (2008): 777–804.

———. "The Atlantic World and the Road to *Plessy v. Ferguson*." *Journal of American History* 94, no. 3 (2007): 726–33.

Senese, Donald. "Building the Pyramid: The Growth and Development of the State Court System in Antebellum South Carolina, 1800–1860." *South Carolina Law Review* 24, no. 3 (1972): 357–79.

Smith, Douglas G. "Citizenship and the Fourteenth Amendment." *San Diego Law Review* 34, no. 2 (1997): 681–807.

Tachiki, Scott N. "Indeterminate Sentences in Supermax Prisons Based upon Alleged Gang Affiliations: A Reexamination of Procedural Protection and a Proposal for Greater Procedural Requirements." *California Law Review* 83, no. 4 (1995): 1117–48.

Tannenbaum, Jerrold. "Animals and the Law: Property, Cruelty, Rights." *Social Research* 62, no. 3 (1995): 539–607.

Tushnet, Mark V. "The American Law of Slavery, 1810–1860: A Study in the Persistence of Legal Autonomy." *Law and Society Review* 10, no. 1 (1975): 119–84.

Vaughan, Alden T. "Blacks in Virginia: A Note on the First Decade." *William and Mary Quarterly*, 3rd ser., 29, no. 3 (1972): 469–78.

Wacquant, Loïc. "Deadly Symbiosis: When Ghetto and Prison Meet and Mesh." *Punishment and Society* 3, no. 1 (2001): 95–133.

Waldron, Jeremy. "Torture and Positive Law: Jurisprudence for the White House." *Columbia Law Review* 105, no. 6 (2005): 1681–750.

West Virginia Bar Association, Executive Council. "The Legal Disabilities of Dogs." *West Virginia Bar Association* 4, no. 7 (1897): 131.

White, Lynn. "The Legacy of the Middle Ages in the American Wild West." *Speculum* 40, no. 2 (1965): 191–202.

Wigmore, John. "Responsibility for Tortious Acts." *Harvard Law Review* 7, nos. 6–8 (1893–94): 315–37.

Wilkins, Pamela A. "The Mark of Cain: Disenfranchised Felons and the Constitutional No Man's Land." *Syracuse Law Review* 56, no. 2 (2005): 85–144.

NEWSPAPER, NEWS SERVICE, MAGAZINE, AND WEB ARTICLES

American Civil Liberties Union. "Enduring Abuse: Torture and Cruel Treatment by the United States at Home and Abroad." http://www.aclu.org/national-security/enduring-abuse-torture-and-cruel-treatment-united-states-home-and-abroad.

Amnesty International. "USA: Ill-Treatment of Inmates in Maricopa County Jails, Arizona." http://web.amnesty.org/library/index/engAMR510511997?open&of=eng-2am.

Animal Legal and Historical Center (Michigan State University College of Law). "Quick Overview of Dog Bite Strict Liability Statutes." http://www.animallaw.info/articles/qvusdogbiteslstatutes.htm.

Barnes, Julian E. "Military Says Special Chair Stops Gitmo Hunger Strikes." *US News.com.* February 22, 2006. http://www.usnews.com/usnews/news/articles/060222/22gitmo.htm.

Barron, James. "Phones Ringing (Eerily?) for Nyack Spook Home." *New York Times*, March 20, 1990.

BBC News. "Abu Ghraib Dog Use 'Lacked Rules.'" March 16, 2006. http://news.bbc.co.uk/2/hi/americas/4812366.stm.

———. "Guantanamo Suicides a 'PR move.'" June 11, 2006. http://news.bbc.co.uk/2/hi/americas/5069230.stm.

Boston University School of Law. "Legal History: The Year Books; Report #1520.003ss." http://www.bu.edu/phpbin/lawyearbooks/display.php?id=22103. (*Filow's* case)

The Bowery Boys: New York City History. "Know Your Mayors: William Jay Gaynor." March 4, 2008. http://theboweryboys.blogspot.com/2008/03/know-your-mayors-william-jay-gaynor.html.

CBS Channel 5, San Francisco. "SF Honors Officers in Zoo Tiger Escape Shooting." February 4, 2009. http://cbs5.com/pets/tiger.mauling.officers.2.926929.html.

Center for Constitutional Rights. "Current Conditions of Confinement at Guantánamo: Still in Violation of the Law." February 23, 2009. http://ccrjustice.org/files/CCR_Report_Conditions_At_Guantanamo.pdf.

———. "Solitary Confinement at Guantánamo Bay." http://ccrjustice.org/learn-more/faqs/solitary-confinement-guantanamo-bay.

Dakwar, Jamil. "Pentagon Report Whitewashes Gitmo Abuses." Human Rights Program, American Civil Liberties Union. February 24, 2009. http://www.aclu.org/2009/02/24/pentagon-report-whitewashes-abuses-at-gitmo.

Danner, Mark. "Tales from Torture's Dark World." *New York Times*, March 15, 2009. http://www.nytimes.com/2009/03/15/opinion/15danner.html?_r=1 &pagewanted=print.

——. "US Torture: Voices from the Black Sites." *New York Review of Books*, April 9, 2009.

Dickerson, John. "Inhumanity Has a Price." *Phoenix New Times*, December 20, 2007. http://www.phoenixnewtimes.com/2007-12-20/news/inhumanity -has-a-price/1.

DogsBite.org. "Arkansas Group (ROADS) Files in Federal Court to Stop Pit Bull Ban." January 5, 2008. http://www.dogsbite.org/blog/2008/01/arkansas -group-appeals-to-federal-court.html.

Fellner, Jamie, and Joanne Mariner, "Cold Storage: Super-Maximum Security Confinement in Indiana." New York: Human Rights Watch, 1997. http:// www.hrw.org/reports/1997/usind/.

Fellner, Jamie, and Marc Mauer. "Losing the Vote: The Impact of Felony Dis-enfranchisement Laws in the United States." The Sentencing Project and Human Rights Watch, 1998. http://www.sentencingproject.org/doc/File/ FVR/fd_losingthevote.pdf.

Ferrara, Joseph. "A New York Ghost Story." Sellsius° Real Estate Blog, October 29, 2006. http://blog.sellsiusrealestate.com/2006/10/29/a-new-york-ghost -story.

Finnegan, William. "Sheriff Joe." *New Yorker*, July 20, 2009.

Glaberson, William. "President's Detention Plan Poses Fundamental Test: Ab-sence of Trials Challenges a Principle." *New York Times*, May 23, 2009.

——. "U.S. May Permit 9/11 Guilty Pleas in Capital Cases." *New York Times*, June 5, 2009.

Hall, E. Vine. "Wills and Ghosts." *Case and Comment* 21, no. 6 (1914): 464–67.

Heinselman, Robert E. "Effect of Superstitious Beliefs or Insane Delusions upon Competency." *Case and Comment* 21, no. 6 (1914): 459–63.

Herdman Ackley, Helen. "Our Haunted House on the Hudson." *Reader's Di-gest*, May 1977.

Higham, Scott, and Joe Stephens. "Punishment and Amusement: Documents Indicate 3 Photos Were Not Staged for Interrogation." *Washington Post*, May 22, 2004.

Holmes, George Frederick. "Uncle Tom's Cabin." *Southern Literary Messenger* 18 (December 1852): 721–31.

Human Rights Watch. "Cruel and Degrading: The Use of Dogs for Cell Extrac-tions in U.S. Prisons" and "How Dogs Are Used in Cell Extractions." Octo-ber 2006. http://www.hrw.org/reports/2006/us1006/3.htm (also /4.htm, /5.htm, and /6.htm).

——. "Supplemental Submission to the Committee Against Torture." June 2006. http://www.hrw.org/en/news/2006/05/03/human-rights-watch -supplemental-submission-committee-against-torture.

Isaacs, Lindsay. "Q&A: Unorthodox Management Defines Maricopa Jail." *American City and County*, October 1, 2001.

Lang, Andrew. "Ghosts Before the Law." *Blackwood's Magazine* 155, February 1894.

Lee, Henry. "2nd Brother Attacked by Tiger Is Sentenced." *San Francisco Chronicle*, December 11, 2008. http://articles.sfgate.com/2008-12-11/bay-area/17129909_1_kulbir-dhaliwal-christmas-day-tiger-attack-police-officer.

Liptak, Adam, Michael Moss, and Kate Zernike. "Accused G.I.'s Try to Shift Blame in Prison Abuse." *New York Times*, May 16, 2004.

Los Angeles Times. "N.M. Repeals Death Penalty." March 19, 2009.

Madigan, Tim. "Caveat Spector." *Skeptical Briefs*, June 1995.

Mann, Henry. "William Jay Gaynor as an Intimate Knew Him: The Lawyer, the Judge, the Mayor, and the Man, Described by a Noted Editor-Author Whose Friendship with Him Covered a Long Period." *New York Times*, September 21, 1913.

Marshall, Carolyn. "Wall Isolating Tiger Habitat Is Shorter than Zoos Advise." *New York Times*, December 28, 2007.

Miller, Peter G. "What Is Stigmatized Property?" *Realty Times*. http://realtytimes.com/rtguide/rtcpages/What_Is_Stigmatized_property (accessed March 26, 2010).

Moore, Solomon. "Number of Life Terms Hits Record." *New York Times*, July 23, 2009.

New York Times. "A Guide to the Memos on Torture." http://www.nytimes.com/ref/international/24MEMO-GUIDE.html.

———. "Dogs Must Be Respected: Justice Gaynor Rules That They Are Property." September 2, 1894.

———. "Immigrants Criminalized." November 27, 2009.

———. "Let Buyer Beware? Indeed!" July 19, 1991.

———. "Rushing Off a Cliff." September 28, 2006.

North Country Gazette. "Case Challenges Verizon/MCI Monopoly on Inmate Phone Calls." September 21, 2006. http://www.northcountrygazette.org/articles/092106PhoneMonopoly.html.

Phillips, Kenneth. "Criminal Penalties for a Dog Bite." Dog Bite Law. http://www.dogbitelaw.com/PAGES/crim.html.

———. "Dangerous and Vicious Dogs." Dog Bite Law. http://www.dogbitelaw.com/PAGES/danger.htm.

Rosenbloom, Stephanie. "Some Buyers Regret Not Asking: Anyone Die Here?" *New York Times*, April 30, 2006.

Schmitt, Eric. "Army Dog Handler Is Convicted in Detainee Abuse at Abu Ghraib." *New York Times*, March 22, 2006.

Seelye, Katharine Q. "Threats and Responses: The Detainees; Some Guantánamo Prisoners Will Be Freed, Rumsfeld Says." *New York Times*, October 23, 2002.

The Sentencing Project. "Felony Disenfranchisement." http://www.sentencing project.org/template/page.cfm?id=133.

Shane, Scott, and David Johnston. "U.S. Lawyers Agreed on the Legality of Brutal Tactic." *New York Times*, June 7, 2009.

Shanker, Thom. "General in Abu Ghraib Case Retires after Forced Delay." *New York Times*, August 1, 2006.

Spiegel, Peter. "General Testifies at Abu Ghraib Trial." *Latimes.com*, May 25, 2006. http://articles.latimes.com/2006/ma/25/nation/na-abuse25.

Stafford Smith, Clive. "Guantánamo Suicides Report." *Reprieve.* http://www .reprieve.org.uk/memosuicidesatguantanamo.

Stolberg, Sheryl Gay. "Obama Would Move Some Terror Detainees to U.S.: Backs Detentions Without Trials if Needed." *New York Times*, May 21, 2009.

Sullivan, C. J. "William Jay Gaynor, NYC Mayor 1910 to 1913, Has Been Forgotten, Along with His Statue." *New York Press*, July 24, 2001.

Taylor, Michael, and Patricia Yollin. "San Francisco: Zoo Keeper Hurt in Tiger Attack." SFGate.com. December 23, 2006. http://www.sfgate.com/cgi-bin/article.cgi?f=/c/a/2006/12/23/TIGER.TMP

Urbina, Ian. "Citing Cost, States Consider End to Death Penalty." *New York Times*, February 24, 2009.

Vlahos, James. "Pill-Popping Pets." *New York Times Magazine*, July 13, 2008.

White Ackerly, William. "Law and Apparitions." *Case and Comment: The Lawyer's Magazine* 21 (November 1914).

Wood, Sara. "Three Guantánamo Bay Detainees Die of Apparent Suicide." U.S. Department of Defense, American Forces Press Service, June 10, 2006. http://www.defense.gov/news/newsarticle.aspx?id=16080.

MISCELLANEOUS WORKS

Brief of the American Civil Liberties Union, ACLU of Pennsylvania, The Legal Aid Society, People for the American Way Foundation, American Friends Service Committee, and California Prison Focus as Amicus Curiae in Support of Respondents, *Beard v. Banks*, 548 U.S. 521 (2006). February 16, 2006, WL 448206.

Cullen, C. T. "St. George Tucker and Law in Virginia, 1772–1804." Ph.D. diss., University of Virginia, 1971.

DuBois, W.E.B. "The Black Code of Georgia, U.S.A." An exhibition at the Exposition Universelle, Paris, April 15–November 12, 1900.

Grassian, Stewart. "California's High Tech Maximum Security Prison Accused of Torture and Mental Abuse." Interview by Mike Wallace. *60 Minutes*, CBS, September 12, 1993.

———. Interview by Mike Wallace. *60 Minutes*, CBS, January 15, 1995.

Obama, Barack. "Remarks by the President on National Security." Speech from the National Archives, Washington, DC, May 21, 2009.

Rutherglen, George A. "The Badges and Incidents of Slavery." Working Paper 68, University of Virginia Law School Public Law and Legal Theory Working Paper Series, 2007, http://law.bepress.com/cgi/viewcontent.cgi?article=1108&context=uvalwps.

United Kingdom. House of Commons. "Report on the Penitentiaries of the United States, Addressed to His Majesty's Principal Secretary of State for the Home Department." Prepared by William Crawford, August 11, 1834.

U.S. Congress. House Committee on Foreign Affairs. Subcommittee on International Organizations, Human Rights and Oversight. *City on the Hill or Prison on the Bay? The Mistakes of Guantanamo and the Decline of America's Image, Part II*, 110th Cong., 2nd sess., May 20, 2008, 33–35. Testimony of P. Sabin Willett.

U.S. Department of Defense. "Review of Department Compliance with President's Executive Order on Detainee Conditions of Confinement." Arlington, VA, February 23, 2009.

———. "Working Group Report on Detainee Interrogations in the Global War on Terrorism: Assessment of Legal, Historical, Policy, and Operational Considerations." Arlington, VA, March 6, 2003.

U.S. Department of Justice. Office of Legal Counsel. "Memorandum for Alberto R. Gonzales, Counsel to the President, *Re: Standards of Conduct for Interrogation under 18 U.S.C. §§2340–2340A*." Memorandum from Jay S. Bybee, Washington, DC, August 1, 2002.

Vaux, Roberts. "Letter on the Penitentiary System of Pennsylvania, addressed to William Roscoe, Esquire." Philadelphia: Printed by Jesper Harding, 1827.

Waldron, Jeremy. "Inhuman and Degrading Treatment: A Non-Realist View." Lecture, New York University Public Law Colloquium, NYU Law School, New York, April 23, 2008.

INDEX